THE

COMPLETE BOOK

OF

VITAMINS

BY J. I. RODALE AND STAFF

RODALE BOOKS, INC.

Emmaus, Pennsylvania

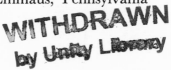

CONTENTS

BOOK I

BOOK II

THE INDIVIDUAL VITAMINS

SECTION I

Vitamin A

SECTION II

The B Complex

SECTION III

Vitamin C

SECTION IV

Vitamin D

SECTION V

Vitamin E

BOOK III

VITAMINS AND DISEASE

SECTION IX

Arthritis

SECTION X

Birth Deformities

SECTION XI

Backache

BOOK I

VITAMINS IN GENERAL

CHAPTER 1

A Brief History

ALL OF US talk a lot about vitamins these days without actually knowing a great deal about what they are and why they are so important. Vitamin research goes on constantly, new discoveries are being reported from time to time and eventually perhaps our scientists will know all of the facts about all of the vitamins. Today 15 vitamins have been recognized and analyzed. Scientists believe that another 15 probably exist and are essential for our health.

Vitamins are organic food substances—that is, substances existing only in living things, plant or animal. They exist in foods in minute quantities; they are absolutely necessary for proper growth and the maintenance of health. Plants manufacture their own vitamins. Animals obtain theirs from plants or from other animals that eat plants. Some animals—but not human beings—manufacture in their own bodies some of the vitamins they need.

Only about 55 years ago someone suspected there might be more in foodstuffs than fats, proteins, carbohydrates and minerals. Then in laboratory experiments it was shown that all these elements might be in the diet and still laboratory animals died of malnutrition. Before the beginning of our century, people ate fruits, vegetables and cereals just about the way nature provided them, with all the food value intact, so it was only when men were subjected to some special condition (such as a long sea voyage) that they developed diseases of diet deficiency.

But when first we began to mill flour for white bread, when we began to refine other cereals and sugar, a lot of diseases cropped up which could only be explained by something that was missing from the food people were eating. Scientists began to search for this important missing link. They discovered vitamins. The name comes from *vita* (life) plus *amine* (the chemical compounds that were originally thought to be vitamins).

Vitamins are not foods in the sense that carbohydrates, fats and proteins are foods. They are not needed in bulk to build muscle or tissue. Carbohydrates, fats and proteins are broken down into other substances which the body uses in the process of metabolism. Not so with vitamins. They retain their original form in the body and are built into body structure, where they are important parts of the machinery of all cells. Just by their presence in the cells, they bring about certain changes and processes. For instance, vitamin B does not cause an increase in weight, as large amounts of fatty foods do. But a very thin individual suffering from some digestive complaint by taking vitamin B might bring about an increase in weight because the presence of vitamin B in the digestive tract would cause food to be completely digested and utilized. Like hor-

[12]

mones, vitamins regulate body processes. As in the case of trace minerals (iodine, for instance) the presence or absence of vitamins in very small amounts means the difference between good and bad health.

The green leaves of plants are the laboratories in which plant vitamins are manufactured. So the green leaves and stalks of plants are full of vitamins. Foods that are seeds (beans, peas, kernels of wheat and corn, etc.) also contain vitamins which the plant has provided to nourish the next generation of plants. The lean meat of animals contains vitamins; the organs (heart, liver, etc.) contain even more, which the animal's digestive system has stored there. The yolks of eggs contain vitamins which the mother animal provides for the use of her young. Fish store vitamins chiefly in their livers.

Basically there are two different kinds—those that can be dissolved in fats and those that dissolve in water. The vitamins found in liver and eggs are fat-soluble. Those in fruits and vegetables are water-soluble.

The vitamins we know most about are called by a letter and also a chemical name. These are: vitamin A (carotene), vitamin B_1 (thiamin), B_2 (riboflavin), B_6 (pyridoxine), the other members of the vitamin B group (such as biotin, choline, folic acid, inositol, niacin, pantothenic acid, para-amino-benzoic acid), vitamin C, the several vitamin D's: D_2 (calciferol) and D_3 (7-dehydrocholesterol), vitamin E (tocopherol), vitamin F, vitamins K, L_1, L_2, M and P.

Researchers have established approximate estimates of the daily requirements of most of the vitamins for perfect health. These amounts are usually spoken of in terms of milligrams. (A milligram is 1/1000 of a gram. A gram is 1/28 of an ounce.) You may also find daily requirements of vitamin A expressed in terms

[13]

of International Units, which are each 1/6000 of a milligram. Although there have been cases of over-doses of a vitamin, it seems that the established daily minimum is really a minimum. Actually from two to four times that much of any vitamin will produce the most abundant growth and health.

Most of the known vitamins are now manufactured synthetically and may be purchased at the drugstore. However, it is generally agreed that these synthetics are not as acceptable as natural vitamins, because the whole action and beneficial effect of vitamins is so complex and so closely related to many other things. Perhaps the manufactured vitamin D, for instance, contains all the substances in just the right proportions that fish liver oil contains. But perhaps—we do not know—the natural vitamin has other substances still unknown to scientists.

For this reason we advise taking brewer's yeast (a natural food product) rather than synthetic vitamin B. We advise fish liver oil capsules and plenty of sunlight rather than a synthetic vitamin D preparation, and so on. In cases of extreme vitamin deficiency, physicians must sometimes prescribe massive doses of a vitamin to be taken orally or injected. But just for the maintenance of good health, let's stick to vitamins in their natural state, in foods.

CHAPTER 2

Must We Take Vitamins?

by J. I. RODALE

WE ARE LIVING in a world that is constantly becoming more artificial, and our bodies are taking on some of this artificial quality. We show it in the status of our health. America has more hospitals, is served by more physicians per capita, has the highest medical bills, uses more synthetic drugs, has the finest medical scientists working in the most elaborately equipped laboratories endowed by great wealth, in the most magnificent educational and research centers found anywhere, and yet—why did draft boards find more ill health in World War II than was discovered during the first World War? Why the pathetic state of undernourishment found among our school children? More than 40 per cent of the nation's potential military manpower has been rejected for physical unfitness — 9,000,000 men of military age unfit to serve!

There is more heart disease, more cancer and more of the other degenerative diseases. But in spite of the mass of evidence which corroborates this fact, many in the medical profession are not in favor of taking vitamins other than those contained in a so-called balanced diet. A certain doctor advised his patient to get his vitamins with his knife and fork. And I would like to show how dangerously wrong this advice is. If you know something about nutrition, then stand and observe people checking out of supermarkets with their purchases. You will see how wrong it is, for how many people today are educated enough to know what a balanced diet is? How many are strong enough to resist such sugary and refined things as ice cream, cakes, sodas and other emasculated sweets and starches that lack any semblance of nutritional intelligence?

First let us see what researchers have found regarding the general nutritional status of the public. In a survey of 6,000 U.S. households conducted by the United States Department of Agriculture it was found that 29 per cent of the diets did not furnish enough calcium, 10 per cent not enough iron, 16 per cent not enough vitamin A, 17 per cent not enough vitamin B and 25 per cent not enough vitamin C. But Dr. Robert Harris, of the Massachusetts Institute of Technology, says that in surveys of this kind the percentages of deficiency are actually much greater, due to the factors that I shall discuss later. In other words, undernutrition is not a disease of the chronically ill and the aged, but actually occurs quite often in the normal, so-called healthy, population.

Dr. Inez Eckblad, Washington State University's extension specialist, made a survey which indicated that teenagers' diets are only slightly better in terms of food value than those in any of the world's starvation areas. She said that six out of ten girls do not get a sufficient amount of one or more of the follow-

[16]

ing: protein, thiamin, riboflavin, calcium, iron, vitamin A and vitamin C. She said teenage diets especially lack calcium, iron and vitamin C. "And the closer the girls get to maturity, the poorer their diets and the fewer nutrients they get in the day's meals and snacks."

Take the Canadian situation. The second issue of *The Land* for 1944 comments: "Dr. Albrecht's paper on calcium, in the previous issue of *The Land* was of amazing interest to Canadians. A recent survey by the Canadian Council of Nutrition shows that 60 per cent of Canadians suffered an 80 per cent calcium deficiency. In this list the deficiency of calcium came second; vitamin B being 90 per cent. Proteins showed a deficiency of 72 per cent. From the content of Dr. Albrecht's discussion the high deficiencies of both calcium and the proteins suggests a more than ordinary significance."

Take the matter of tooth decay. A past-president of the American Dental Association, Dr. Arthur Hastings Merritt, recently stated that tooth decay today, even though a wonderful system of dental care has been worked out, is as bad as it was 100 years ago. This in spite of so-called correct diets, with their generous inclusion of orange juice and other so-called vitamin-rich foods. Nearly every American (95 per cent) needs some dental care; 30 per cent need it badly.

Impossible to Get Nutrients from Diet

Generally speaking, it is quite impossible for the average person to get enough vitamins and minerals from his diet, for many reasons. First we have the controversial matter of the organic versus the chemical fertilizer method of raising our food. There is evidence that the lower the soil fertility, the poorer the nutritional quality of our food. This is shown by the fact

[17]

that in the Midwest in a recent ten-year period, the protein content of the grains was down by 11 per cent. It is shown in the sugar beets in Utah, where chemical fertilizer practices have reduced the sugar content of the beets to such an extent that it has become uneconomic for many farmers to raise them. It is shown in the state of Delaware where it has become almost impossible to raise tomatoes on account of disease in them, due to soil that lacks full fertility elements. The use of nitrogenous fertilizers is causing copper deficiencies, and the overuse of potash fertilizers is creating magnesium deficiencies. These minerals are badly needed in our nutrition and we must correct their deficiency by taking mineral supplements, for our knives and forks will be quite ineffective to accomplish this. A serious situation has recently developed in regard to cattle feed. Due to the overuse of chemical fertilizer nitrogen, it has been found that cattle are not able to absorb much vitamin A from the feed. The same holds true for people. A great vitamin A deficiency is developing in the public due to the greater artificialization of the method of growing our food. The public is consuming food products of marginal quality and if they do not get extra vitamins and minerals, they are bound to become weakened physically. Whole books of evidence can be produced to show the nutritional superiority of organically raised foods, but the Government men, the agricultural scientists and the *Reader's Digest* say: "There is no evidence."

Evidence for Vitamin E

Typically, with regard to vitamin E, there is a "no evidence" chorus and a cynical, jeering attitude of the "experts," to such an extent that a proposal was made

[18]

by the FDA to make it illegal to state on a label that a food or supplement contains vitamin E.

Is there truly "no evidence" that vitamin E is valuable for the health of the heart? Dr. Evan Shute, a highly regarded heart specialist, has published *several hundred* scientific papers on the values and uses of this vitamin, and particularly its alpha tocopherol fraction. Is this "no evidence"?

It is inconclusive, say many doctors, who have been unable to duplicate Dr. Shute's results. When it has been suggested that their failures were due to the use of laboratory-synthesized vitamin E, instead of its natural forms, they have scoffed and insisted that both are chemically identical and there can be no difference in effects on the human physiology.

As this is being written, however, the *New York Herald Tribune* (September 10, 1962) reports from the 142nd meeting of the American Chemical Society that a team of researchers has found synthetic vitamin E to have only 21 per cent of the biological activity of the natural vitamin. These researchers, Ames and Ludwig, experimented two years at the Distillation Products Industries division of Eastman Kodak Company. They have established the reason why those who insist on experimenting with synthetic vitamins can establish "no evidence."

Perhaps now the FDA will give a proper evaluation to this vitamin and the research of the Shute Clinic.

It is also a fact that the over-refinement of food makes it lose much of its nutritive value. This includes the removal of living germ from the wheat in making bread, the consumption of white polished rice. The whole brown rice contains about 300 to 400 per cent more of the B vitamins than the polished variety. Eggs for the market are produced without benefit of roosters and are infertile, lacking important hormones and other living elements. Instead of sugar being consumed in the wholeness of raw sugar cane, it is refined into a chemical compound with all its vitamins removed.

Refining Our Foods

We consume only part of the animal, neglecting the vitamin-rich organs such as the brain, heart, liver, kidney, etc. Primitive people have learned to consume wholeness. We fragmentize our diet, and because we throw away the valuable parts, serious nutritional deficiencies result.

Children these days have ready access to sweets and all kinds of refined foods. In a study of 3,000 juvenile delinquents in the United States, it was found that on an average they ate only three meals a week at home. The rest of the time they consumed over-refined sugars and carbohydrates in cheap luncheonettes and candy stores. Is this one of the causes of their delinquency? Is their brain action defective due to being fed by an unbalanced blood stream? Is the efficiency and character of nondelinquent children being impaired by such a refined diet?

Ezra T. Benson, former Secretary of the United States Department of Agriculture, told a Lincoln Day dinner audience at the National Youth Power Congress that there are great deficiencies in the diet of teenagers. Regarding this talk the *New York Times* (February 18, 1960) quoted him as saying, "Lack of knowledge about proper eating was a factor in the weakening of American family life, and the rise of juvenile delinquency."

In this respect a survey in Manhattan showed that

four out of five persons are mentally disturbed in some way. In my book, *Food for Greater Mental Power,* published by Prentice Hall, I have proven that this condition stems basically from poor diets.

It is a known fact that "only one person in a thousand escapes malnutrition" (Howard Blakeslee, *Wide World* science editor, in the *New York Times*). This was the conclusion of a six-year survey published by the Ellen H. Richards Institute at Penn State University. All this stems from the ignorance of the public of facts about nutrition, and its laziness.

For example, back in 1947-1949 we bought greater quantities of foods that required peeling, washing, trimming and home cooking. Now we leave the store with packages of instant mashed potatoes, dehydrated soups and frozen TV dinners. These items of food weigh less per calorie supplied. The most important effect of these convenience foods is on our food preparation habits. Women no longer want to take the time necessary to prepare fresh foods in the home. The number of hours that the average woman spends in preparing meals has dropped greatly in the past 15 years. What effect has this trend had on our intake of vitamins?

There also seems to be a drop in the consumption of leafy green vegetables. Our consumption in this category for the years 1947-1949 was 98 pounds, and by 1960 it had dropped all the way to 80 pounds. When you realize the average portion of spinach, for example, contains 10,680 units of vitamin A, you can see how a decline of almost 20 per cent in our consumption of green and yellow vegetables can have a drastic effect on the amount of vitamin A we get.

Cabbage consumption has gone from 10.4 pounds in 1956 to 9.4 pounds per person in 1960. In the same

[21]

period, carrots went from 6.8 pounds down to 5.3 pounds. While we used 16.5 pounds of lettuce and escarole in 1956, the amount dropped to 15 pounds in 1960. The fact that even the salad craze has not been able to stem the decline in the use of lettuce, carrots and cabbage is significant indeed.

Celery is down from 7.3 pounds per capita in 1956 to 6.7 pounds in 1960. Sweet potatoes—extremely rich in vitamin A—have taken an alarming drop in favor from 7.6 pounds in 1956 to 6.2 pounds in 1960. Dry edible beans and peas have gone from 8.7 pounds in 1956 to 7.8 pounds in 1960. And bear in mind that I am not comparing one good year with one bad year. In almost every case there has been a steady and distinct decline in consumption of these foods.

It is not surprising, therefore, that a nation-wide study made by the Household Economics Research Division of the Department of Agriculture, in 1955, showed that "nearly half of the nation's families used food that provided less than current allowances of the National Research Council in one or more nutrients."

We need extra vitamins and minerals because of the way we destroy vitamins and minerals in our kitchens. Let's take the case of what we do to the carrot before we eat it. The first thing we do is throw away the top greens. This part has far greater nutritional value than the pulpy lower part. It contains vitamin K, for example. Before it came to us it was stored for some time, which caused it to lose vitamins. The housewife scrapes off the skin, where resides a large portion of the minerals. In many cases the carrots are soaked for a long time, causing some loss of the natural sugar, all the B vitamins, vitamins C and P and much of the minerals except calcium.

If the carrots are shredded there is a loss of 20 per

[22]

cent of the vitamin C, and an additional 20 per cent if used on a salad and allowed to stand for an hour before eating. This loss is due to oxidation; that is, the air penetrating the carrot.

Cooking destroys vitamins, and if salt is placed in the water, there is a greater loss in vitamin C. If carrots are frozen and thawed slowly, vitamin C is lost. So how much of the vitamin and mineral content of the carrot is preserved for one who gets his vitamins with his knife and fork?

And so it goes not only with the carrot but with many other items in our diet. Toast, for example, starts with the devitalized white flour, which is baked and much of its remaining vitamins destroyed. But when this baked bread is again subjected to heat in toasting, the last vestige of nutrition is all but eliminated. We make casseroles in which food is cooked two or three times. We recook leftovers that have hung around for weeks in the refrigerator—losing vitamins every day. In some foods a single cooking destroys more than 50 per cent of the vitamins. We should eat more raw food, but we don't.

The average person rarely eats raw foods. He even prefers his nuts roasted. His attitude on eating raw peas is that it is something done by food faddists. The same applies to carrots and turnips. Such so-called normal people should protect themselves by taking vitamins and minerals.

If food were handled naturally and not tampered with so much in the factories, it would be a different matter. In the factories food is bleached, colored, dehydrated, hydrolized, homogenized, emulsified, pasteurized, gassed, preserved chemically and canned. Not only is there danger from the toxic qualities of these processes, but such toxicities are known to destroy vita-

[23]

mins, fragile substances that easily combine with other substances to form emasculated compounds. We also take in many elements harmful to vitamins in our drinking water—chlorine, aluminum, sulphates, carbon, hydrated lime, fluoride and several others, which the waterworks manager is permitted to use in an emergency.

An additional important reason why we must take vitamins is because of the sedentary life we lead. Primitive man didn't need extra vitamins because he ate a lot of raw, fresh, wild, unprocessed food that was full of vitamins. Also, he was on the move most of the time. From morning to night he was out of doors, moving, working and sweating, which gave him such a well-working digestive apparatus that it enabled him to absorb the maximum of vitamins from his food.

But modern man, with his ulcers, colitis and other intestinal diseases, and his imperfect digestion, does not get the maximum out of his food. Sir Robert McCarrison, a great English nutrition researcher, has spoken of the "colonic lamentations of our civilization." He was comparing us with the Hunzas of India, among whom he lived for ten years. They are a primitive type of civilization, working all day and eating simple unprocessed food. They need no vitamin supplements. They are one of the healthiest peoples on earth.

We must not overlook the fact that some of the vitamin B is made by bacteria in the intestine, but a reduced amount will be manufactured in an intestine weakened by the way of living of a modern sedentary person. This reduces the amount of the intestinal flora. Such a person must take extra vitamin B or he will not be able to face up to the rigors of our way of life. Vitamin B is required for the health of the nerves. These vitamin B-deficient people are perhaps the ones who are always ranting against the stresses and strains of our times. If a person is well-nourished, he can withstand these stresses and strains without breaking down.

Vitamin Thieves

We must take vitamins to restore the vitamins we destroy by our daily practices. Smoking destroys vitamin C, drinking alcoholic beverages uses up some of the body's vitamin B. Coffee also drains some of the B vitamins out of our body. A diet overcharged with artificial sweets cuts in on the B vitamins. Chlorine in our drinking water destroys vitamin E in the body. *Bridges' Dietetics for the Clinician* says so on page 91. Chlorine dioxide used in bread has the same result. Vitamin E is also destroyed by rancid oil or fat in the diet. Inorganic iron compounds likewise destroy vitamin E. This is the kind of iron given in cases of anemia. Sterility, muscular dystrophy and coronary disease may result from vitamin E deficiencies.

Raw fish is a robber of thiamin, one of the B vitamins. So if you eat raw clams and oysters, your body is being depleted of a goodly store of its thiamin. It is interesting to note that the Japanese, who are great eaters of raw fish and polished rice, have a rather low life expectancy.

Various kinds of chemicals are known to destroy vitamins. A widely used chemical sterilizer, ethylene oxide, used extensively in the food industry, destroys the B vitamins, even though all the chemical is removed after treatment.

Chemically fertilized potatoes have a tendency to turn black, so the restaurant people have to use anti-darkening chemicals like sodium bisulphite which destroys the vitamin B—thiamin. The loss is anywhere from 11 to 47 per cent according to test.

[25]

In a recent study in South Carolina (*Charleston Evening Post,* December 1, 1960) it was found that almost half the meat products in the state "contained an injurious addition commonly called dynamite." This is sodium sulphite, which is a basic ingredient of washing and cleaning detergents. State Commissioner of Agriculture William L. Harrelson said, "Pure Food and Drug officials claim that continuous consumption of sodium sulphite destroys some of the body vitamins essential to the good health of human beings." This chemical is found mostly in ground meat such as hamburgers, pork sausages, chili meat and cooked beef rounds.

Drugs are great brigands in robbing the body of vitamins. Estrogen, a hormone administered in certain diseases, cuts down three of the body's B vitamins—thiamin, riboflavin and niacin.

The barbiturates (sleeping pills) block the progress of carbohydrate metabolism and so add to the difficulty of the body's absorption of thiamin.

Medicines given for malaria destroy vitamin B_2, or riboflavin. The sulfa drugs upset the process of manufacturing B vitamins in the intestines. This is why pneumonia patients, who get large doses of sulfa drugs, are left in a state of terrible depression because of vitamin B depletion; this can go for years unless corrected.

Penicillin and chloromycetin destroy niacin, and some people are taking penicillin all the time. Arsenic and sulfa compounds destroy Para-amino-benzoic acid, a B vitamin. Arsenic residues occur widely on fruits and vegetables—residues of insecticides.

Mineral oil, used as a laxative, destroys vitamins A, D, E and K. Fluorides destroy the enzyme phosphatase, upon which many vital processes in the body depend, including its handling of vitamins.

A long list of other vitamin-destroying drugs could be given, but it would make this discussion too technical if we included them all. Suffice it to say that Americans by the millions are using these drugs regularly, and so there is a profound need to restore the vitamins which they remove from their bodies.

Vitamins Fight Poisons

There are many chemicals all about us in our daily environment which destroy or inactivate vitamins. Carbon monoxide from car exhausts, sulphur compounds from chimney smoke, tobacco smoke, miscellaneous poisons in the air, all destroy vitamins when breathed in by human beings. In self-defense, therefore, we must take extra vitamins every day, especially vitamins B and C, as these are known to aid in excreting poisons from the body.

As an example, pantothenic acid, one of the B vitamins, is known to detoxify the poisonous effect of streptomycin (*Science News Letter,* November 19, 1955). This drug given alone can cause deafness, but this condition is prevented if vitamin B is given along with the streptomycin. It has also been shown that vitamin B can help to eliminate some of the DDT which is always accumulating in the body's tissues through what we eat. It also protects against the powerful poison, strychnine. It will neutralize the effects of the sulfa drugs, as well as atabrine and cortisone.

In two successive monthly circulars issued by Hoffman-La Roche, Ltd., a large drug firm (*Courier,* February and March, 1959) the subject covered is "Vitamins in the Treatment of Toxic Manifestations and Side Effects of Drugs." Any doctor who reads the bulletins with their well-documented clinical test data, and then advises his patients to get their vitamins with

[27]

their knives and forks, is not faithful to the best interests of these patients.

Vitamins for Oldsters and Truck Drivers

Older persons absolutely *must* take additional vitamins. As one gets older the little inner fire of the body's metabolism begins to burn with a weaker flame, the organs and glands become less efficient. One hears the expression that the circulation is slowing down. Under such conditions vitamin deficiencies are more apt to develop, because more vitamins are used to speed up the gradually failing metabolism. As we grow older, the process of aging causes us to develop nutritional needs which we did not have when we were younger. By taking extra vitamins we can prevent the senility which is bound to come under ordinary circumstances. It is not necessary to be half dead in our old age. There is medical evidence that the maintenance of the body's reserves of vitamins and minerals can prevent the deterioration of the eyes, ears and hair, and preserve the ability to walk without tottering and think without doddering.

Then, of course, the doctor with his knife-and-fork theory does not consider people who eat all their meals in restaurants where additional chemicalizations are resorted to in the kitchen for various purposes. At least six situations exist there in which sodium chemicals are used.

In recent tests in Germany (*Boston Herald,* June 12, 1957) a group of 152 problem drivers were given 150,000 units of vitamin A daily, "with a striking improvement in their tested driving proficiency." According to the institute of traffic psychology in Karlsruhe, Germany, where the tests were conducted, after dosages of vitamin A were given, more than half the drivers showed improvement in normal alertness lasting an average of six months.

In 1947, 18 drivers of the F. J. Boutell Driveaway Company of Flint, Michigan, were chosen and given a vitamin diet supplement at cost.

What was the result? On the basis of a five-year fleet average, these 18 men had a combined accident frequency of a .28 or 357,143 miles per accident as against .38 or 263,158 miles per accident for the rest of the company's drivers. This was a 35 per cent reduction for the 18 men who had supplemented their diet. In other words, because these truck drivers took vitamins certain people are alive today who might have been killed—people who will be able to use their knives and forks for a long time to come, I hope.

Millions of people in this country are health conscious, and millions more are entering this group every year. Health magazines are showing them the way. These people don't want to be just "ordinary" healthy. They want to be healthy in a "super" way. There seems to be evidence that this can be accomplished. Get your vitamins with your knife and fork, and you will either be sick, or healthy in a minimum or ordinary sort of way. Health is not merely the absence of disease. A real dynamic health may be obtained by going far above the minimum daily requirements of the various vitamins and minerals.

One of the greatest nutritionists of our time, Dr. Henry C. Sherman, who was professor of chemistry at Columbia University, stated that vitamins A and C and calcium were the keys to longer life. He said, "Increases in the quantities of these three substances above levels commonly accepted as adequate have resulted in significant gains among laboratory animals. Clearly it is advantageous to the internal environment that the three nutrients be kept near the physiological saturation point."

Dr. Tom Spies of Birmingham conducted an experiment with 893 people who "had been old from the age of 30." These people, he said, were nutritionally disabled. *Cosmopolitan* (June, 1962) states, "He fed them diets rich in proteins, natural vitamins and minerals, supercharged by doses of synthetic vitamins. To this he added quantities of dried brewer's yeast powder and liver extracts. The effects were almost miraculous. Forty-one of the men in the experiment were accepted for military service. . . . Paul de Kruif, an ardent exponent of Spies' approach, points out that farmers feed their animals supercharged diets to keep them young and vital. Why not do the same for human beings? Dr. Edward J. Stieglitz, the great authority on aging, has noted that an optimum diet contains five times the protein and vitamins of the average minimum diet."

Please note that in Dr. Tom Spies' miraculous experiments he used such natural food supplements as brewer's yeast and liver extract (we use desiccated liver), the kinds of products that the conservative medical men say are used by food faddists.

Medical Attitude

In view of what we have shown, how can doctors ask people to depend on their regular meals for their vitamins? How can doctors depend on the status quo of so-called balanced meals, when such "balanced" meals are leading to more sterility, more cancer, more heart disease and many other degenerative and other diseases? Do doctors reject vitamins because they don't have the facilities to test for them in the human body?

What doctor has ever checked you for a vitamin deficiency?

This is exactly what Dr. Dorothy G. Wieble of the Milbank Memorial Fund said: the reason that nutritional deficiencies are allowed to go unchecked and unnoticed is that doctors don't know how to test for such deficiencies.

But the American Medical Association continues to refer to vitamin-taking by the public as Vitamania and to people who take them as hypochondriacs.

The proof of the pudding is in the eating, and the results obtained by thousands of vitamin-taking people speak more than words. The medical attitude on this subject is a disgraceful scandal.

CHAPTER 3

The Argument for Food Supplements

A RESOUNDING ANSWER to the claim "you don't need food supplements!" including a reasonable scientific argument for natural versus synthetic food supplements appeared in the *American Journal of Digestive Diseases* for March, 1953. Written by Morton S. Biskind, M.D., a careful researcher and a practicing physician, this article makes very clear the great complexity of the problem of supplementing the diet with vitamins.

Dr. Biskind is convinced, from his own observations and the extensive research he has done, that modern diet creates the need for most of us to take food supplements. His list of reasons for taking supplements includes the following: 1. Soil depletion due to modern methods of farming; 2. Increasing use on crops of "incredibly toxic" insecticides; 3. Tendency to pick and ship fruits and vegetables green rather than ripe; 4. Processing and chemicalizing food; 5. Overuse of pure, vitamin-free sugar for as much as ¼ of the average calorie intake; 6. Chemical additives in food, which are worthless nutritionally, but take the place of highly nutritious elements.

Dr. Biskind further states that there are three basic principles of nutritional therapy: it should be complete, intensive and persistent. No halfway measures will succeed. Vitamins, minerals, proteins, phosphates, fats and trace minerals are forever related like links in a chain, when one is considering the way the body uses them. It is useless to strengthen only one or several of these links. All must be equally strong, or the chain will fail. "Yet current practices in nutritional therapy reveal how poorly understood is this simple fact," says Dr. Biskind.

"While the range of permissible dosage for essential nutrients is wide, owing to the numerous safety mechanisms available to the organism, and the therapeutic range is ordinarily at least five or ten times the range for maintenance and often more, this does not mean that (as is often done) massive doses of certain factors should be combined with minimal doses of others," he goes on.

Large doses of vitamin A, prescribed by doctors to alleviate one condition or another, may bring about a deficiency in the B vitamins. Giving all the B vitamins appears to "save" vitamin A, so that one does not need so much. Giving large doses of one or another of the B vitamins may bring on the very symptoms one is trying to cure, since it may cause deficiency in other B vitamins.

Large doses of thiamin alone or in combination with other synthetic B vitamins may do very little for alleviating the symptoms of beriberi, which we know relates to deficiency of thiamin. But giving the entire B complex of vitamins causes prompt amelioration of this disorder.

Says Dr. Biskind, many doctors who scoff at the idea of giving vitamins use some of the vitamins in massive doses like drugs— especially those concerned with the body's use of fat—choline, inositol, etc. They call these "lipotropics" and they give them in large doses like drugs to combat cholesterol deposits. Yet large doses of these B vitamins may actually aggravate the basic nutritional deficiency in the B vitamins, he says.

Considering the evidence presented by Dr. Biskind, who is right in this controversy, do you think, the hired writers of the food industry or the "food faddists" like Dr. Biskind?

Giving all of the B vitamins, along with other substances that accompany them in food such as liver, gets excellent results, according to Dr. Biskind's own experience. "This illustrates further," he says, "that the proper object of nutritional therapy is treatment of the whole organism with reasonably balanced preparations and not simply a pharmacological [drug-like] attack on the liver with massive doses of a single substance. . . . Liver preparations, especially desiccated liver, are in themselves a rich source of the lipotropic substances." He also points out that there is little use giving such supplements unless there is plenty of protein in the diet, for the B vitamins cannot function adequately without lots of protein.

So it seems evident that the average doctor, asking nothing whatever about his patient's diet or way of life except the routine "Do you eat a good diet?" would fail to promote good health, if he prescribed some isolated, synthetic vitamin and mineral preparations to be taken along with the patient's usual diet. This

[34]

diet, of course, was at least partly responsible for putting him out of sorts to begin with—probably a typical American diet of which a large part is refined carbohydrates, products made chiefly of white sugar and white flour.

Factors Which Interfere with Nutritional Therapy

No matter how complete the source of one's diet supplements, the complete repair of a nutritional deficiency may be impossible under certain conditions. "Thus a person continually exposed to a hepatoxin [liver poison] such as one of the industrial solvents or one of the new chlorinated hydrocarbon insecticides, can expect at best only partial relief so long as the inciting agent continues to act. A patient who insists on consuming vast quantities of sugar and other refined carbohydrates to the detriment of protein intake, can similarly expect little benefit from nutritional therapy. Likewise, an individual under the stress of acute anxiety, which impairs absorption and utilization and increases destruction and excretion of the essential nutrients, will not respond even to massive doses of these substances so long as the emotional disturbances continue to act," says Dr. Biskind.

Here are some other circumstances of life and health which may impair one's ability to use the vitamins and minerals in diet to maintain health: poor appetite, diarrhea, insomnia, muscular tension, spasm of the digestive tract, etc. In addition, says Dr. Biskind, "the list of chemicals and drugs which impair cellular enzyme systems and produce tissue anoxia is very long indeed. An incredible number of them are in such indiscriminate use that daily exposure to them is almost unavoidable for many persons. These range from a variety of chemicals used in industry to carbon monoxide, lead and other products of combustion in automobile exhaust, the . . . insecticides . . . paint solvents and drugs such as sulfonamides, antibiotics and estrogens."

Continued exposure to any of these substances causes loss of B vitamins. So, no matter how devotedly one might engage in a program of good nutrition, continual exposure to the above poisons would render it ineffective. In research with animals the same thing is true, says Dr. Biskind. It is well known that even the faintest trace of DDT is stored in the body fat. This poisonous insecticide interferes with the oxidation of foods in every cell of the body. Yet no account is taken of this in planning experiments dealing with nutrition, and no effort is made to secure feed that does not contain DDT. Since practically all of the commercially available feeds contain DDT, it is easy to see that nutrition experiments are distorted.

DDT in extremely low amounts affects a certain enzyme in the heart muscle, says Dr. Biskind. But almost everyone is exposed to DDT and it is stored tenaciously in the body fat, so how can one repair such damage? Sulfa drugs and antibiotics also destroy B vitamins. The hormones given to food animals for rapid fattening remain in the meat and we consume them. These, too, interfere with the regular and proper use of vitamins in the body.

It is essential, says Dr. Biskind, to question any patient very closely about his exposure to all these various chemicals when outlining a nutritional program for him. (Did your doctor ever even mention such items?)

The next time you read in a newspaper or magazine that Americans are well fed and there is no need to eat any special diet or to take food supplements, ask yourself "What American is well fed? Doesn't it depend on what his individual body needs are, how well-planned his diet is, where his food comes from and what kind of soil it grew in, what drugs he is taking and what poisonous chemicals he is exposed to?" All of these things are important and all of these things must be considered in regard to every person as an individual different from anyone else. Now you can see how meaningless are the articles sponsored by the processed food and chemical companies, which attack as faddists anyone who protests against chemicalization and overprocessing of food and name as a "crank" anyone who recommends the daily taking of natural food supplements as the best addition to the best possible diet.

CHAPTER 4

Doctor's Rebuttal Says More Vitamins Needed

THE OTHER SIDE of the coin: Recently this department reported the views of a Yale professor of pediatrics, Martin Riesman, on vitamins.

He thinks Americans feed their children too many. Writing in the *Journal of Pediatrics,* he said, "A healthy, well fed child no more needs a daily vitamin supplement than he does a quart of milk a day."

A Harvard man, N. Ethan Edgington, gives a stern rebuttal. Dr. Edgington says it is sheer bubble-headedness to say, as Dr. Riesman did, that "the potential for hypervitaminosis syndromes [sickness from too many vitamins] is frighteningly real." Dr. Edgington says there are not more than a dozen authenticated cases in the United States.

"It is as likely that your readers are taking too many vitamins as it is that they're making too much money," he writes.

Dr. Edgington says the only potentially toxic vitamins are A, D and K. The safe upper limit daily adult dosage of A is 300,000 U.S.P. units, of D is 80,000 U.S.P. units, and of K is 12 milligrams. By law K supplements sold to the public may not contain more than 1 milligram in the daily dosage.

No nonprescription multiple-vitamin product contains more than 2,500 U.S.P. units of D, Dr. Edgington says, and he has never seen a nonprescription A supplement containing more than 50,000 U.S.P. units in the daily dosage.

Moreover, he says, the products containing these potent ("though by no means toxic") dosages account for a small part of the supplements sold in the United States. They are rare and very expensive.

As for the "healthy, well fed" child, exactly what, he asks, is "well-fed"?

"I know 50 nutritionists," he writes, "and I can tell you that the most debated topic among them is precisely what constitutes an optimum diet. Second, where are all these well-fed children? To the best of my knowledge, there has never been a survey of the American diet, from any source, that indicates that the population as a whole is eating a well-balanced (let alone optimum) diet. There are several surveys which show that inadequate diets are found in poor families only. Tens of millions of Americans therefore most definitely will benefit from vitamin supplements.

"Unfortunately the 'well-fed' child does not 'need' a vitamin supplement. If he did nature would have long ago provided vitamin-pill bushes; we don't really 'need' anything not found in nature. But can science today say that our hypothetically healthy, well-fed child would derive no benefit from a properly balanced vitamin supplement? Emphatically, science cannot and

[39]

I don't care how many Yale professors tell you otherwise.

"For my part, I like to see parents make room in their food budget for vitamin supplements for their children. Any number of foodless foods could well be cut out—candy, pastry, sugar, corn flakes (approximately as nutritious as the box they come in), jelly, crackers, soda pop. But then the best infant supplement I've seen costs about 25 cents a week. Surely a quarter's worth of weekly nutritional insurance is not going to break anybody up in these sunny days."

Reprinted from the *Kansas City Star,* June 13, 1961.

CHAPTER 5

The "Natural vs. Synthetic" Controversy

by J. I. RODALE

FROM INFORMED opinions we have read, it seems that an attempt is being made to make it more difficult to get food supplements and vitamins that come from natural food sources, to the advantage of the artificial synthetic preparations. This paper is being written to show the superiority of the natural versus the synthetic products. It is time that the trend towards artificialization should be reversed, and the public educated to its dangers.

The status of current thinking is illustrated in the remark of Clarence B. Kelland in one of his stories: "Leave our chemists alone and they'll be able to give you synthetic strawberries . . ." We must re-educate this type of mentality.

The main difference between the synthetic and the natural is that the former is not a whole product. It is merely a fragment. The synthetic formula leaves out a part which may be tiny, percentage-wise, but significant just the same. It considers .9999 of the whole, but the ignored one-ten thousandth of one per cent may boomerang in some unexpected manner. This one-ten thousandth of one per cent may be something that our present-day equipment is powerless to identify.

Some Examples

As an example, a few years ago some sea-water fish were brought into a London aquarium, but there was only a small amount of sea water available, insufficient for the needs of the fish. One of the curators, however, said he could make sea water, as its formula was well-known. He assembled the ingredients and made a batch of it. But when a fish was placed in this water it soon died. Three or four times the curator made sea water, being more careful each time, but it did not fail that each time a fish was placed into the water it died.

But then someone suggested that in the next batch of water they made they include the tiniest bit of real water. This they did, and the fish could live in it! Evidently in real sea water there is a gleam of some substance which is too tiny to measure, and which is not in the published formula for sea water, but which is needed by fish in order to live. As tiny as it is, the fish must have it. It would seem, therefore, that science's conception of what sea water is is defective. It seems that man does not know everything yet about how matter is constituted.

Similarly we might artificially produce water by bringing the gases hydrogen and oxygen together, but I would not want to drink it! There still may be something lacking that real water has.

[42]

That science does not know everything that is in matter was shown in a research with rats done at the Agricultural Research Center, Beltsville, Maryland. In the *Journal of Nutrition* (Vol. 70, No. 4, April, 1960) the authors said, "When rats fed a purified ration containing all known nutrients were rendered hyperthyroid, their growth rate was considerably decreased because of a deficiency in the ration of certain *unidentified* nutrients. Evidence was presented suggesting that crude food materials contain at least two different unidentified nutrients. . . ."

Edward L. Pratt, M.D., Chairman of the Department of Pediatrics of the University of Texas Medical School, in an article in the *American Journal of Chemical Nutrition* (September, 1957) said, "The danger in considering specific nutrients is that by so doing we may displace our emphasis which must always be upon foods with their unknown as well as known contributions."

In manufacturing food for plants in the form of commercial fertilizers, the agronomist makes the same error. He fixes up a mixture of nitrogen, phosphorus and potash and thinks he is doing a good job. But he leaves out two dozen "gleams" which the plant must have or disease ensues. When a plant is given composted animal manure or a decayed leaf, it is given a full-bodied food. The manure and leaf, just like the real sea water, enable the plant to live in health. It is the same with vitamin and drug products. The artificial, the synthetic, is never the same as the natural. Something is lacking!

An example: Man needs the adrenal hormone cortisone, of which his system does not generally get enough for lack of exercise and challenge in the average life. This was expressed a little differently by Dr. M.

[43]

Haydon-Baillie (*Medical Press,* April 26, 1961), who said, "The adrenals, too, are now rarely required to respond to fierce and urgent situations, and so fail to make their former contribution of cortical and other hormones, sufficient lack of which is thought to be responsible for several modern diseases."

So many people today do not exercise. As a result their adrenals don't make cortisone, and for lack of it many come down with arthritis. Then they are given artificially made cortisone in which there are many gaps. No pharmaceutical chemist can make cortisone like the adrenals can. The result is that deadly side effects result from the taking of this man-made cortisone—side effects such as the weakening of the spine and brain.

The same is true of lactic acid, the natural form of which can be extracted from milk, to be used as a milk modifier for babies. But according to an article in the *Journal of the American Medical Association* (125: 1179-81, 1944), by mistake the synthetic form of lactic acid was given to some babies, resulting in a few deaths.

Quoting from booklet No. 6, 1948, of the Lee Foundation of Nutritional Research, Milwaukee, Wisconsin: "Adrenalin is an outstanding example of a synthetic product that is being commercialized in disregard of the difference in physiological action. The natural adrenalin is 15 times as active as the synthetic dextro form in its effect on blood vessels, while the dextro adrenalin [synthetic] is 18 times as effective in promoting glycosuria [the presence of a large amount of sugar in the urine].

"Now, since the commonest use of adrenalin is to promote the vascular changes that relieve the asthmatic patient, the glycosuria [diabetes promoting] effect is definitely not wanted. But to get the same vascular effect, 270 times as much of the synthetic stuff must be used, in terms of its unwanted effect of putting sugar into the urine.

"The cost of calling a doctor and of getting a shot of adrenalin by the asthmatic patient when he is struggling for a breath of air is far too much to offset the two-cent saving made by the pharmaceutical manufacturer who puts synthetic adrenalin in the ampule used by that doctor. But, if neither the doctor nor the patient knows the difference, the synthetic stuff will be the one he gets. Although natural adrenalin can be made as a by-product in the processing of glands in making adreno-cortin, makers of this material tell us there is no market for natural adrenalin because of the low price of the synthetic product."

Dangers of Synthetic Vitamins

In the same booklet appears the following: "Pantothenic acid [part of the B complex] is a vitamin now commercially available only in the synthetic form. Probably this is the reason for its effect of causing a loss of sex function, particularly in females . . . this castrating action has been found both in test animals and in human patients receiving the 'vitamins,' according to unpublished reports to us.

"Pure natural vitamin E was found to be three times as potent as pure synthetic vitamin E (*Nutrition Reviews,* 5: 251-253, 1947).

"Of course, the poisonous nature of the synthetic vitamin D sold as 'Viosterol' and 'Vigantol' is well established. It causes blood in the urine very quickly in children, by its destructive action to the kidneys. Deaths have been reported from the ordinary dosages used to 'protect' from rickets (*Journal of the American Medical Association* 130: 1208-1215, 1946)."

[45]

Niacin is another of the B complex vitamins that can be made only in the synthetic form. It is often used in ground meat, to "assure retention of its color," says *Consumer's Bulletin* (March, 1962). "In Philadelphia, Pennsylvania, two cases of niacin poisoning involving five persons were reported in 1961 that involved the same symptoms, intense flushing of the skin, a feeling of warmth, itching, and some abdominal discomfort." In the natural method, a person gets his niacin and pantothenic acid from brewer's yeast, wheat germ and desiccated liver, with no harmful effects.

Similarly, when nicotinic acid was added to ground meat to prevent darkening of the meat, outbreaks of food poisoning occurred. This happened to 88 persons out of 145 as described in the *Nebraska Medical Journal* (42: 243-245, May, 1957). Nicotinic acid is another fraction of the B complex which is obtainable in a natural form from brewer's yeast, etc. In the case just mentioned it was produced synthetically.

The *Journal of the American Medical Association* (May 3, 1952) describes a severe shock with collapse in a 57-year-old physician who received thiamin injections. Several other cases of thiamin intolerances are described in *Annals of Allergy* (May, 1952, pp. 291-307). This never happens to people getting thiamin from whole natural products such as brewer's yeast, wheat germ or desiccated liver.

An illustration of what can occur appeared in the *Journal of the American Medical Association* (August 22, 1959) as reported by Arthur U. Rivin, M.D. Dr. Rivin found that niacin, a B vitamin, is effective in reducing cholesterol levels in the blood stream, as has been reported by the Mayo Clinic. However, Dr. Rivin, using 3 to 6 grams of synthetic niacin per day in treating a 23-year-old man to reduce cholesterol

[46]

levels, found that jaundice resulted, presumably from a toxicity presented by the synthetic vitamin, actually a drug. The cholesterol level was considerably reduced, but treatment had to be discontinued after 14 months due to liver complications.

In humans, attempts to treat various disorders with synthetic vitamin B have often proven unsuccessful, while responses to vitamin B from natural sources have been gratifying in the very same cases. One such clinical experience was related in the *Canadian Medical Association Journal* (Vol. 44, p. 20, 1941). Fifteen cases of skin disease were treated with injections of synthetic vitamin B. There was no improvement noted from these treatments until yeast or liver extract was given. Observing physicians noted that a general beneficial effect was obtained.

The *American Journal of Digestive Diseases* (January, 1940) remarks that B complex therapy offers more help to many cases of digestive disturbances than careful dieting, or drugs. In an experiment, patients with digestive disorders were treated with brewer's yeast extract and had an excellent response in the loss of distressing symptoms. The patients were then taken off the yeast extract and given synthetic thiamin and riboflavin (both B vitamins). The symptoms returned. The test was tried in reverse by giving thiamin and riboflavin to patients as the first treatment, and the results were not beneficial. The yeast was then tried, and the symptoms simply disappeared.

Advantages of Natural Vitamin C

Take the case of vitamin C. The natural product can be taken in the form of products made from rose hips, bell peppers or the acerola cherry, and it can be made synthetically in the form of pure ascorbic acid. The difference is that the natural product is not "pure." However, its so-called impurities are in the form of other vitamins and minerals. This is highly desirable from a curative viewpoint. A balanced package is superior to a narrow, purified fragment. This has been proven many times. For example, many medical experiments on the dangers of caffeine in coffee were done where pure caffeine was given instead of the whole coffee bean which contains vitamin B and many minerals. The results would be different.

Let me cite an experiment which was performed behind the Iron Curtain and which was reported in the Russian medical journal called *Vitamin Research News* (No. 1, 40, 1946). Mice were fed a deficient diet which is known to produce scurvy, and when it was apparent that they were all suffering from this disease, they were divided into two groups and treated with vitamin C, which is known to cure this condition. But one group was given the vitamin produced synthetically, while the other had the benefit of vitamin C obtained from a plant. The group that was fed on the natural vitamin C was completely cured within a short time, but not the other.

Let us take another case which is described in the British publication *Nature* (January 1, 1952). The authors, St. Rusznyak and A. Szent-Gyorgyi studied a disease involving fragility of the walls of the blood vessels. They treated one group of laboratory animals with peppers, a natural food known to contain large amounts of vitamin C. The second group received synthetic vitamin C. The disease was cured only in the first group of animals. There must be an unknown factor in peppers—the "gleam"—that is closely asso-

[48]

ciated with its vitamin C and which cannot be separated from it.

Synthetic D

Another example came to my attention in a book by E. W. H. Cruikshank (Williams and Wilkins, 1951). Three groups of chicks were fed on the same diet. The first group received no vitamin D at all. The second group was given synthetic vitamin D. The third group received a natural vitamin D preparation made from cod liver oil.

The chickens receiving no vitamins gained 259 grams of weight, the synthetic D group gained 346 grams, but those that had the benefit of the natural vitamin D gained 399 grams. But here is the most important part of the experiment. In the "no vitamin" chicks 60 per cent died. In the synthetic group 50 per cent died. However, in the natural vitamin D group there was not a single death.

A book was published in 1936 by the U. S. Vitamin Company, called *Vitamin and Mineral Therapy*. It was written by E. H. Dubin and Casimir Funk, the latter the man who discovered vitamin B, and it contains the following statement, "Synthetic vitamins: These are highly inferior to vitamins from natural sources, also, the synthetic product is well known to be far more toxic."

The *Journal of the Indian Medical Association* (August, 1951), in discussing folic acid, states that giving whole liver or the whole vitamin B complex has advantages over giving folic acid by itself, because "deficiency diseases are multiple in character and the imbalance of vitamins is thus avoided."

Dr. C. W. Jungblut, writing in the *Journal of the*

[49]

American Medical Association (November 20, 1937), reported that, in his extensive experiments with monkeys, he found that administration of a factor from citrus fruit, identified as vitamin C, prevented the graver effects caused by polio. Synthetic vitamin C proved approximately half as effective as the natural substance.

The *Journal of Immunology* (August, 1942), reveals that guinea pigs, given a diet deficient in vitamin C, could not be entirely cured of the resulting scurvy by synthetic vitamin C. But the feeding of fresh cabbage (rich in vitamin C and the things which accompany it in nature) brought them back to normal.

The Finnish journal *Annales Paediatrae Fenniae* (Vol. 2, part 2, 1956) tells of two children dying from overdoses of calciferol—synthetic vitamin D—over a period of several years. Calciferol (not taken from fish liver oil, mind you, but manufactured according to chemical formula in a laboratory) is said to be 400,000 times as active as cod liver oil. It is inconceivable that such a thing could happen if you are getting vitamin D from fish liver oils, unless of course you disregard all instructions for dosage.

The *American Review of Tuberculosis* (Vol. 72, p. 218, 1955), describes a study of failures of vitamin A metabolism in TB patients. Synthetic vitamin A and cod liver oil were given. "The response was much better with the cod liver oil concentrate than with synthetic vitamin A," say the authors.

The story of vitamin P is the best example we know illustrating the superior value of natural vitamins over synthetic ones. Vitamin P is a substance that occurs along with vitamin C in foods. So when you take synthetic vitamin C made in a laboratory, you don't get any vitamin P of course. But when you eat foods rich in vitamin C or take vitamin supplements made from natural foods such as rose hips or green peppers, the vitamin P comes right along with the vitamin C. And we have discovered that in countless situations where vitamin C alone is not effective, the combination of the two will work wonders.

A disease producing blindness in babies is called retrolental fibroplasia. Medical authorities were baffled until they discovered that such babies in the birth process had been given pure oxygen to keep them alive. But man is not adapted to pure oxygen. In the air he gets it as a package along with many other elements.

Boris Sokoloff, an outstanding cancer researcher, warns in his book, *Cancer, New Approaches, New Hope,* that animals kept on "purified" diets are more susceptible to cancer than those kept on natural diets. Again, that word "purified" indicates that the substances omitted from synthetic diets and vitamins are vitally important and can be obtained only from food. Yet we go on "purifying" flour by milling away the wheat germ, the very life of the wheat, then adding a few synthetic vitamins to the assassinated but "pure" wheat. Can there be a connection with the fact that the cancer rate is increasing among our bread-eating people?

Optical Activity

There is a startling difference which can be determined by scientific test between a synthetic and a natural compound. It was Pasteur who discovered that the reaction of a substance to polarized light shows a remarkable variation which can be measured on a certain optical instrument. It never fails in such tests that if an artificially produced compound throws the light on this machine in one direction, a similar naturally extracted compound will throw it in the other

[51]

direction. This is known as the optical activity of the compound.

Dr. William Held, writing in the *Chicago Daily News* (October 23, 1950), speaking about the case of the deaths of babies fed on synthetic lactic acid, which I have discussed, said, "Dextrolactic acid (the right rotary sugar of milk) is a food, while levolactic acid (the kind that polarizes light to the left) is a poison." He says, "The moral for mothers is to use only natural dextrolactic acid for milk modification."

Talking about right- and left-handed optical action of molecules, the Lee booklet already referred to says, "Where a food product must be composed of, say right-handed molecules, the left-handed may be as useless as in the case of left- and right-hand bolts and nuts in machinery. If you needed right-handed cap screws to put the head of your auto engine back on, left-hand screws would only serve to cause confusion and probably a failure to get the machine back into operation, unless you can find among them enough of the right screws to finish the job."

In spite of this difference between the natural and the synthetic, the *Journal of the American Medical Association* says, as quoted in *Cosmopolitan* (December 21, 1940), "There is no detectable difference between the synthetic chemical vitamin and the natural ones. Ascorbic acid is just as good vitamin C as one gets from an orange." This was in 1940. In 1958 (December 13) the *Journal of the American Medical Association* said the same thing: "Whether the body obtains its vitamin C from synthetic ascorbic acid or from orange juice, the manner in which this substance is utilized by the body is exactly the same."

But many physicians do not think that way. Dr. Julian M. Ruffin, in the *Journal of the American*

[52]

Medical Association (November 1, 1941) said, "The fact that single deficiencies are rarely, if ever, encountered is an excellent argument against the treatment of deficiency states with chemically pure substances. There are probably other vitamins as yet unknown which are essential to health." He went on to illustrate with a case history of a man, 26, admitted to Duke Hospital complaining of loss of weight, diarrhea, weakness, sore tongue and numbness of the extremities of six months duration. Examination showed deficiencies of at least three vitamins: pyridoxine, riboflavin and ascorbic acid. He was given pyridoxine (50 milligrams) intravenously for ten days, with no improvement. Then large intravenous doses of riboflavin, niacin and ascorbic acid failed also to produce any effect. Finally a 3-cubic-centimeter daily dosage of liver extract (a natural source of all the B vitamins) was followed by rapid improvement, then complete recovery. The natural source provided the necessary combination, or the unknown nutrients that were needed.

Dr. Alexander Berglas, a physician connected with the Pasteur Institute, said, "In spite of the therapeutic value of synthetic vitamins in the treatment of certain diseases, one should not believe that the mere ingestion of the pure synthetic vitamins, even if identical in chemical structure to the natural vitamins, necessarily has the same effect on our body as the consumption of vitamins in combination with their natural concomitants. The latter are not to be dismissed as 'excess baggage,' but must be thought of as the result of millions of years of evolution of optimal combinations."

In a successful experiment with mental cases performed at the University of Southern California and the University of California by Drs. Watson and Comrey (*Journal of Psychology,* 1954, 38:pp. 251-264),

[53]

certain natural vitamins and minerals were successfully used, namely, "vitamin A and vitamin D (halibut liver oil), vitamin E, soya lecithin, wheat germ, kelp, bone meal, red bone marrow, desiccated liver, alfalfa, parsley, escarole, watercress, etc."

Henry M. Turkel, M.D., of Detroit, whose paper on the nutritional treatment of mongoloids was read before the American Association for the Advancement of Science in 1959, used the following natural substances in his successful treatments—bone meal, desiccated liver, organic iodine, rutin, vitamins A, B, C, D and E from food sources and an abundance of mineral products.

Norman Jolliffe, M.D., former health officer of New York City, writes an article in the *Journal of the American Medical Association* (November 1, 1941) on "Treatment of Neuropsychiatric Disorders with Vitamins." He obtained some success when patients were given by mouth "a fish liver oil in an amount containing 10,000 units of vitamin A and a source of the entire vitamin B complex. Such products as 30 grams of brewer's yeast, 20 grams of vegex, 45 cubic centimeters of aqueous liver extract or 60 grams of wheat germ cereal are preferred to synthetic products in capsule form from which some factors as yet impossible to encapsulate are likely to be missing."

In connection with the administration of the entire vitamin B complex in a natural form, he remarks, "This practice is based on the empirical observation that these patients seem to do better when at least a quantity of the entire B complex is given."

A very important observation by Dr. Jolliffe pertains to the fact that some of the synthetic vitamins contain added preservatives. He says, "Cutaneous tests performed on these patients demonstrated sensitivity to the preservatives and not to the thiamin. Subsequent administration of crystalline thiamin dissolved in saline solution was in no instance followed by either local or general sensitivity in the same patients."

The Associated Press ran a startling item in the newspapers across the country June 13, 1956. It said, "A 23-year-old girl, made almost helpless by a muscle-wasting disease [muscular dystrophy], has been restored to almost normal activity after treatment with wheat germ oil, Dr. Ira Manville of the University of Oregon Medical School reported Tuesday to the Society for Experimental Biology and Medicine." The news release says further, "There is no known cure for the ailment."

Dr. Manville had read somewhere that wheat germ oil was able to cure muscular dystrophy experimentally produced in rabbits. His first attempt to cure human muscular dystrophy with wheat germ oil resulted in failure. Later he discovered that the purified wheat germ extract, which was successful on the rabbits, for some reason did not work on humans.

A particular brand of wheat germ oil which supposedly retains natural vitamins and minerals in its makeup was given to the girl. This did the trick!

Yet the AMA time and time again warns that people are wasting their money by taking wheat germ, in spite of the record of its use by physicians, in articles in its own journal, including Drs. Manville, Ruffin, Watson, Comrey and Jolliffe which we referred to here.

CHAPTER 6

Should You Beware of Synthetic Vitamins?

Is THERE ANY difference between a natural vitamin
and a synthetic one? No, says the pharmaceutical industry, which derives a large portion of its business
from manufacturing synthetic vitamins that drugstores
can sell at bargain-basement prices and that doctors
can use as drugs. Synthetic vitamins are superior, says
the pseudo-scientific Medical Profession, preferring
chemicals that can be administered by injection to the
complicated and difficult-to-understand ingredients of
health-building foods.

Standing against the combined weight of the medical
establishments, there have been only a few spokesmen
for the wisdom of nature, such as J. I. Rodale, who
maintain that the only true vitamins are the vitamins
contained in natural foods or derived from them. What
is manufactured in a laboratory is a drug, which may
be useful as a therapeutic chemical administered by

a doctor, but is a substance too dangerous for people to risk dosing themselves with it.

Unfortunately, both the food nutrients and the laboratory chemicals are called "vitamins." This leads to a great deal of confusion—as much as there might be in the world of commerce if nylon and rayon, both developed as synthetic substitutes for silk, were indiscriminately to be labeled "silk" along with the natural product, and the producers tried to tell us there was no difference between the three fabrics. Yet even the doctors who have long maintained that there is "no difference" are beginning to recognize that there are definite dangers in the laboratory-produced chemicals they insist on calling "vitamins," as *Prevention* has long warned its readers. Enough evidence is piling up so that the day may yet come when your doctor will advise you to get your vitamins only from food sources, just as we do.

Synthetic Vitamin (?) D

The most recent example that has come to our attention was contained in a speech made to the Ontario Medical Association on May 30, 1964, by Dr. Helen Taussig, Professor Emeritus of Pediatrics at Johns Hopkins Hospital and Medical College. Dr. Taussig, a scientist of international reputation, warned that some infants recently had been born with deformed hearts, mental retardation, and accompanying inborn defects that she believed were caused by doctors administering excessive doses of vitamin D during pregnancy.

Although Dr. Taussig did not specify that the vitamin D administered had been synthetic, there is nothing else it could have been. It is only as a laboratory synthetic that a doctor can obtain vitamin D in

[57]

an isolated form. In nature, this vitamin is always accompanied by vitamin A. These two vitamins interact so closely, and are so necessary to one another, that it is only in profound ignorance of nutrition that a doctor could even contemplate administering one without the other.

It has been known for many years, for instance, that large amounts of vitamin D in the system, if not balanced by proportional amounts of vitamin A, will lead to hypercalcemia. This is an excess of calcium in the blood serum, caused by its being drained from the bones. It leads to emotional disturbances, mental confusion, and weakness of bones and muscle. It does not occur even when very large amounts of vitamin D are taken in fish liver oils, in which this natural vitamin is accompanied naturally by vitamin A. What makes hypercalcemia occur is the doctor's injection or prescription of vitamin D alone.

This synthetic vitamin D that the doctor uses is manufactured by dissolving ergosterol in a commercial solvent, propylene glycol, and then bombarding the resulting mixture with ultraviolet light. This is what they claim is the same vitamin as the crystalline material found in egg yolk and fish liver oils. But nobody ever got hypercalcemia from eating eggs, or even eating whole cod livers as they do in Scandinavia. This disease comes from the type of "vitamin D" that you get from a doctor, or perhaps buy for yourself if you are so ill-advised as to buy bargain vitamins in the drugstore.

Vitamin A

When it comes to vitamin A, the situation is even more absurd. This vitamin occurs plentifully in nature. In the average diet, it occurs in large quantities in butterfat. Since *Prevention* does not recommend the eating of any milk product, thus excluding both butter and cream from the diets of those who follow our advice, we do recommend the taking of supplements of fish liver oil. But for doctors who see no objection to eating butterfat, the use of a synthetic vitamin A is an obvious absurdity.

What is this synthetic vitamin A? It is prisms of a yellow material obtained by distilling petroleum ether at a temperature of 120 to 125 degrees. Petroleum and its products are useful as fuels, but otherwise are among the most toxic and dangerous known to man. Time after time, petroleum dyes, chlorinated hydrocarbon chemicals, and even the paraffin wax that used to be used to coat milk cartons, have been implicated as causes of cancer and of severe and frequently fatal toxic reactions.

Yet the pharmaceutical industry would rather make "purified" vitamin A from petroleum than package and sell halibut liver oil, which contains quantities of vitamin A large enough for any purpose whatsoever. Why? Because the fish liver oil must be handled very carefully, and even then might turn rancid unless it is sold reasonably fresh, while the petroleum derivatives will keep for years. Doctors also prefer the synthetic because it isn't "contaminated" by accompanying vitamin D and vitamin E. It says in the book that vitamin A is good for certain eye and skin disorders, so they just want to administer vitamin A without ever dreaming that a substantial portion of the effect that vitamin A has may be due to its interrelations with other nutrients.

As a consequence, we get reports such as a recent one in the *New Scientist* (October 3, 1963) that vita-

[59]

min A in excess will cause cells to dissolve and damage cell membranes. A very careful reading of the article reveals that vitamin A alcohol, a synthetic, was used in the experiments at Cambridge University. We do not doubt for a minute that this synthetic substance will do precisely what is stated. But is there any relationship between this laboratory-manufactured material and natural vitamin A as it occurs naturally in food?

Natural A Builds Health

While the dangers of synthetic vitamin A are being increasingly brought to light, here are some of the recent discoveries about the role of natural vitamin A in building and preserving health.

Experiments at the University of Liverpool by J. N. Thompson and others have demonstrated that this vitamin in the diet is essential, in rats, not only for normal vision but also for reproduction (*Proceedings of the Royal Society,* series B, volume 159). Both male and female rats were rendered blind and sterilized by feeding with diets deficient in vitamin A. When foods containing substantial amounts of vitamin A were added to their diets, these effects were reversed. The conclusion of the experiment was there was a strong possibility the vitamin relates to fertility as well as eye health in man.

Vitamin A in the diet is vital to proper absorption and use of protein, it was reported in the *New York State Journal of Medicine* (January 15, 1964) by Oswald A. Roels, Ph.D., Associate Professor of Nutrition at Columbia University. Basing his study on experiments and studies made among children suffering from the protein deficiency disease kwashiorkor in Indonesia, Roels found an intimate interdependence between

[60]

dietary vitamin A and protein. Among 500 Indonesian children suffering from the deficiency disease, he determined that the same amounts of protein in the diet gave far more increase in height and weight when the diet also included palm oil, a rich source of natural vitamin A. He also found that a deficiency of protein made it much more difficult to absorb and utilize vitamin A, so that the two nutrients were shown to work far better together for the promotion and maintenance of health than either could do separately.

John R. Campbell, Assistant Professor of Dairy Husbandry at the University of Missouri, reported in *Hoard's Dairyman* (June 25, 1963) that lack of vitamin A because feed is dried and bleached left dairy cattle susceptible to ringworm infection, while changing the feed to fresh green leafy hays, thus providing ample vitamin A, will clear up the infections and promote resistance to any future infections.

It will be noted, however, that all these beneficial results were obtained with natural vitamin A ingested by eating natural foods. Such regimens frequently involve the consumption of very large quantities of this natural vitamin every day over a period of months. Not a single toxic reaction of any kind was reported. The natural vitamin served only to build and protect health. Yet the chemicals the druggist sells and the doctor dispenses, taken in the same quantities over the same period of time, might well have produced serious metabolic disturbances.

We could go on and on. Despite all claims that there is "no difference" between natural and synthetic vitamins, every single one of the synthetic vitamins has been found, when dispensed in large amounts and in purified form, to be capable of inducing reactions that are toxic at the least and sometimes both serious and

[61]

dangerous. Yet as vitamins occur in food, with their natural interrelationships preserved, we know of no cases where they have done anything but wondrous good. We believe in vitamin supplements and we recommend them highly to our readers. But be sure you get the right kind—the kind that are either natural high vitamin foods, or are warranted and labeled to be derived entirely from natural food.

CHAPTER 7

Can Vitamins "Overstimulate" You?

VITAMINS ARE NOT "stimulants" in the sense in which we generally use the word. They are not medicines, even though synthetic preparations of them appear generally on the counters of drug stores. They are chemical substances which act as catalysts in various processes that go on inside the body.

What do we mean by "catalysts"? We mean that tiny amounts of each vitamin combine chemically with oxygen and with enzymes, minerals and hormones to form other chemical compounds. If the vitamin is not present, or if the oxygen, enzyme, mineral or hormone is not present, the chemical reaction cannot take place. If too little of these substances is present, the reaction may take place, but imperfectly. If there is too much of any vitamin, it is either stored (in the case of the fat-soluble ones) or eliminated (in the case of those that are soluble in water).

You can easily see, therefore, that there is no question of vitamins rushing hither and yon in the body, prodding nerves and cells into violent activity like military men bullying their men into superhuman effort. Drugs have this effect on the body. But not vitamins or minerals which are completely natural components of foods and also of every cell of the body. On the other hand, there are circumstances under which the body has far greater need for certain vitamins because, in these cases, certain conditions of the body have altered the chemical requirements.

An article in the British journal, *Medical Press* (August 6, 1958) called "Vitamins in Health and Disease" tells us more about such conditions. The article is by Audrey Z. Baker and Isabel Winckler.

Hardening of the arteries narrows the space through which blood may flow, so it may be a cause of an impairment of the vitamin supply to the tissues. If the blood vessels most affected are those that supply the brain, the symptoms of deficiency would naturally be of one kind. If vessels leading to the heart were involved, symptoms would be different.

Fevers seem to increase the body's need for vitamins. Vitamin A is very low in diseases in which the patient is feverish. The same lowering of vitamin A levels has been found in tuberculosis patients. Low vitamin C levels have been found not only in tuberculosis, but in chronic rheumatic or arthritic disorders as well. Some researchers report that there is increased need for the B vitamins during infections of any kind. The requirement of rats for vitamin B_1 and possibly two other B vitamins is twice as high at outside temperatures of 91°F. as at 65°. This certainly indicates that we may need far more vitamins during summer heat.

The need for several vitamins is related to changes in the activity of the thyroid gland. People whose thyroid glands are overactive may need massive doses of vitamin A. It has also been found that there is increased need for vitamin C and all the B vitamins. The concentration of vitamin C in tissues is lowered. Here again, massive doses of these vitamins may be necessary to bring the levels up to normal.

In pregnancy the increased intake of food necessitates an increase in vitamins. There is a great increase in the need for vitamin B during periods of violent exercise. We are told that the calorie requirements for an active physical worker may be increased above that of a sedentary man by 80 per cent and the protein requirements by 70 per cent. In vigorous exercise, certain B vitamins are lost in perspiration, too.

Some news about aspirin. We know that when patients who have a virus infection take aspirin, or other pain killers containing the salicylates, the excretion of vitamin C is greatly increased. We know, too, that the duration of aftereffects of influenza have been reduced when massive doses of the B vitamins and vitamin C were given. The illness was shortened and psychological disturbances connected with it were rapidly eliminated.

These psychological disturbances included such things as long convalescence, depression and persistent loss of zest and energy. The general range of dosage meant here by "massive" was 300 to 500 milligrams of vitamin C daily, 50 to 200 milligrams of thiamin, 50 to 100 of pyridoxine, 50 to 100 milligrams of niacin, up to 10 milligrams of riboflavin and up to 25 milligrams of pantothenic acid. Naturally we recommend getting all these vitamins in natural foods that are rich in them, like brewer's yeast and desiccated liver (for B vitamins) and rose hip preparations for natural vitamin C.

[65]

In cases of trouble with the adrenal glands, vitamin C is apparently important. The adrenals help protect the body from shock. It is customary in some hospitals to give as much as 1000 to 2000 milligrams of vitamin C before and after surgery to prevent or treat shock.

Vitamin C and the B vitamins have been used as therapy in cases of barbiturate overdosage, drug-induced delirium, acute alcoholic psychosis and delirium tremors. High dosages were used in all these treatments—many times greater than would be necessary to satisfy normal human requirements. Vitamin C and the B vitamins have also been used to treat mental states that followed pneumonia and influenza.

It can be stated, say our authors, that with our present knowledge there is evidence that many diseases, not primarily due to nutritional vitamin deficiency, can be related to a defective supply of vitamins and that some such conditions respond to massive doses of vitamins, especially the B complex and vitamin C.

Here are some other conditions and the dosages of vitamins which have been used to treat them: tuberculosis—10,000 to 40,000 International Units of vitamin A daily. Cirrhosis of the liver—50,000 to 100,000 units of vitamin A. Overactive thyroid—200,000 to 400,000 units of vitamin A daily.

Vitamin K has been used in doses of 2 to 5 milligrams daily to prevent hemorrhage before and after operations, in doses of 20 milligrams daily to treat bad effects of taking aspirin.

Thiamin (vitamin B_1) has been used in doses of 9 to 10 milligrams daily for cardiac conditions, 100 to 200 milligrams daily for Bell's palsy and 200 to 300 milligrams daily for herpes zoster or shingles.

Riboflavin has been used for migraine headaches in doses of 10 to 30 milligrams daily.

[66]

Other B vitamins have been used to treat the mental confusion of old age, radiation sickness, pink disease, cirrhosis of the liver, pernicious anemia. Vitamin B_{12} has been used in extremely large doses (5000 micrograms daily) for treatment of trigeminal neuralgia (otherwise known as *tic douloureux*).

Vitamin C in large doses has been used for heat exhaustion, peptic ulcer, burns, virus infections, hepatitis, hardening of the arteries and, combined with vitamin A, ulcerative colitis.

Our authors tell us that there has been a tendency for tables of minimum requirements to be given official sanction and then to be repeatedly quoted as though they were final and absolute. However, they say, the official minimum requirements of some of the vitamins have been worked out from observations on as few as 3 people. There is no basis for the assumption that vitamin requirements are uniform even in good health, they say. In disease there is even more likelihood that the need will vary.

From the *Medical Press* article we learn again the lesson that there can be no hard and fast rules where vitamins are concerned. You must decide for yourself, on the basis of your own knowledge of yourself, what amounts you should take. You can, of course, guide yourself to some extent by the daily recommended minimum which will appear on the label of any vitamin preparations you buy.

CHAPTER 8

How Much Do You Need
of Each Vitamin?

How CAN YOU tell what doses of vitamins and minerals you should be taking?

First of all, read the recommended daily minimum which will be listed on the label of any food supplements you buy. What do we mean by the daily minimum or MDR?

This is the very least amount of that particular vitamin that will keep the average person from suffering from a deficiency disease caused by lack of that vitamin. The officials who lay down these requirements tell us that 30 milligrams of vitamin C daily will keep the average healthy person from getting scurvy. One milligram of thiamin will keep him from getting beriberi. And so forth.

Everyone admits that what will protect you from a deficiency disease is not the amount that will keep you at your best. So there is a second set of official figures—the recommended daily allowance. Getting this amount of the various vitamins and minerals is supposed to keep one in "good nutritional status." Most nutritionists believe that you will be in a lot better health if you use these figures only as the basis for your nutritional planning and actually get much more of all the vitamins and minerals than these allowances.

Note the official tables included here for all those vitamins and minerals for which such figures have been worked out.

Now let's take the individual vitamins and see how the tables help us to plan meals and doses of supplements.

Vitamin A

The recommended daily allowance of vitamin A is 5000 units. Capable nutritionists estimate that, for perfect health and protection from disease, you may need as much as four times the recommended allowance. This would mean, for an adult, about 20,000 units of vitamin A.

Can you get too much? Our richest source of vitamin A is fish liver oil, and there have been records of people getting too much. Polar bear liver is richer in vitamin A than any other substance. Foolhardy explorers in arctic regions who have ignored warnings and eaten polar bear liver have suffered from vitamin A poisoning.

Bicknell and Prescott in their book *Vitamins in Medicine* tell us that three-quarters of a pound of this liver may contain as much as 7 to 8 million units of vitamin A. Symptoms of poisoning are nausea, vomiting, diarrhea, drowsiness, sluggishness, desire to sleep. It is, of course, inconceivable that one would get that much vitamin A from food supplements without downing bottles and bottles of the stuff all at once.

[69]

Minimum Daily Requirements

	Infants	Children (1–5)	Children (6–11)	Children (12–over)	Adults	Pregnancy Lactation
Vitamin A	1500 I.U.	3000 I.U.	3000 I.U.	4000 I.U.	4000 I.U.	.....
Thiamin (B₁)	.25 mg.	.50 mg.	.75 mg.	1 mg.	1 mg.	.....
Riboflavin (B₂)	.6 mg.	.9 mg.	.9 mg.	.9 mg.	1.2 mg.	.....
Niacin (B₃)	.....	5 mg.	5 mg.	5 mg.	10 mg.	.....
Vitamin C	10 mg.	20 mg.	20 mg.	30 mg.	30 mg.	.....
Vitamin D	400 I.U.	400 I.U.	400 I.U.	400 I.U.	*	.....
Calcium	.....	.75 mg.	.75 grams	.75 grams	.75 grams	1.50 gr.
Phosphorus	.....	.75 gr.	.75 gr.	.75 gr.	.75 gr.	1.50 gr.
Iron	.....	7.5 mg.	10 mg.	10 mg.	10 mg.	15 mg.
Iodine	.....	.1 mg.	.1 mg.	.1 mg.	.1 mg.	.1 mg.

Recommended Daily Allowances

	Infants	Children (1–5)	Children (6–11)	Children (12–over)	Adults	Pregnancy Lactation
Vitamin A	1500 I.U.	1500–2000 I.U.	2500–3500 I.U.	4500–6000 I.U.	5000 I.U.	6000–8000 I.U.
Thiamin (B₁)	.4 mg.	.6 mg.	.8–1.2 mg.	1.2–1.7 mg.	1.2–1.8 mg.	1.8–2.3 mg.
Riboflavin (B₂)	.6 mg.	.9–1.2 mg.	1.2–1.8 mg.	1.8–2.5 mg.	1.8–2.7 mg.	2.5–3 mg.
Niacin (B₃)	4 mg.	6–8 mg.	8–12 mg.	12–20 mg.	12–18 mg.	18–23 mg.
Vitamin C	30 mg.	35–50 mg.	60–75 mg.	80–100 mg.	70–75 mg.	100–150 mg.
Vitamin D	400 mg.	400 mg.	400 mg.	400 mg.	*	400 mg.
Iron	6 mg.	7–8 mg.	8–10 mg.	15 mg.	12 mg.	15 mg.
Calcium	1 gr.	1 gr.	1–1.2 gr.	1–1.4 gr.	1 gr.	1.5–2 gr.

* Officially it is not considered necessary to set a minimum of vitamin D for adults since there is little chance of their getting rickets as children do.

Other case histories of vitamin A poisoning have usually involved children whose mothers have given them spoonfuls rather than drops of concentrated vitamin A, thinking that it is the same as fish liver oil. Of course, fish liver oil contains other things than vitamin A and vitamin D, so a teaspoonful of fish liver oil would contain far less vitamin A than a concentrated preparation containing nothing but vitamin A.

Then there are cases of patients whose doctors prescribed massive doses of vitamin A for some condition of ill health. The patient who goes on taking such medication for months or years is likely to run into serious trouble. Twelve cases of chronic vitamin A poisoning were reported in this country in 1950— surely not a very large number considering the number of people who regularly take vitamin supplements. So it is rather obvious that taking the usual vitamin supplement, especially when it is a natural supplement like fish liver oil, can become hazardous only if one pays no attention at all to the amount of the supplement he is taking.

One further note about vitamin A. As you know, the vitamin itself occurs only in food of animal origin —fish livers, butter, eggs, liver and so forth. Carotene, which appears in green and yellow fruits and vegetables, is made into vitamin A inside the body. In counting up the amount of vitamin A you get each day, however, it is wise to keep in mind that vegetable juice, carrot juice for instance, being highly concentrated, yields a very high amount of carotene.

Vitamin B

In a famous laboratory test with rats, it was found

that cancer could be prevented with a diet consisting of 15 per cent brewer's yeast. Of course, brewer's yeast contains other things than the B vitamins—protein, carbohydrate, minerals—but the concentration of B vitamins in brewer's yeast is high. So it doesn't sound as though there is such a thing as getting too much of the B vitamins, does it?

Quite the contrary. The B vitamins are soluble in water, so any excess that your body does not use is harmlessly excreted. It is not stored to cause possible trouble later on. If you get yourself a list of common foods and their vitamin content (a good one is available from the Superintendent of Documents, Washington, D.C., entitled *Agriculture Handbook No. 8, Composition of Foods,* price 65¢), you can easily check on the approximate amount of the three major B vitamins you are getting in your diet. You will probably be shocked to find that on most days you don't come anywhere near even the minimum requirement, especially in riboflavin, which is the one B vitamin so scant in foods that it is very difficult to get enough of it.

We would certainly suggest that you get as much as four times the recommended amount of the B vitamins. There is one important caution, however. So far as the B vitamins are concerned, we know definitely that one or several of these does no good unless you have the others that should go along with it. Furthermore, taking one by itself or several without the rest may do you serious harm. This is the reason why we protest so sharply against the use of synthetic B vitamins. Scientists have not as yet identified all the B vitamins. So, since we do not know what they are, we obviously cannot include them in synthetic vitamin B tablets. But we do know that they all come together in foods like liver, brewer's yeast, wheat germ, etc.

[72]

Eddy and Dahldorf in their book, *The Avitaminoses* (published by Williams and Wilkins, Baltimore, Maryland), tell us that the interrelationships among B vitamins are complicated and numerous. Riboflavin is poorly absorbed unless thiamin is present. Giving large amounts of niacin by itself produces sudden and unexpected symptoms in laboratory animals. This shows us that the so-called "enrichment" of cereals is bound to have a devastating effect eventually, for *all* of the B vitamins are removed when flour is refined and only two or three are replaced synthetically.

Scientists who specialize in this field know that those of us who regularly eat "enriched" cereals are building up an imbalance of these B vitamins which may be responsible for harmful results later on. Those of us who take synthetic B vitamins are courting trouble. So, the rule is a simple one—if you get your B vitamins from a natural source, you can't possibly get too much. Taking them from a synthetic source, you are almost certain to get the wrong amounts.

Vitamin C

What about vitamin C? We are inclined to think of vitamin C as the miracle vitamin because of the wonders we have witnessed this vitamin working. Since so many things to which we are exposed day after day (cigarette smoke, industrial fumes, air pollution, drugs, etc.) use up vitamin C rapidly, we say you simply can't get enough vitamin C. If you must skimp on some vitamins, don't skimp on C. It helps in the work of the other food elements, thus making all of them more effective. Be especially sure you get plenty of vitamin C in winter when colds are going round and when you probably get less of it in food. If you feel a cold coming on, don't be afraid to take "massive doses"

[73]

—as much as several thousand milligrams a day, spaced carefully at intervals. You can almost certainly head off the cold this way.

The minimum amount of vitamin C that will keep a guinea pig from getting scurvy is two milligrams a day. Yet, if allowed all the vitamin-C-rich food it can eat, such an animal will consume 20 times this much. Is it a mistake to believe that human beings could profit by doing likewise? The recommended daily allowance for an adult is about 70 milligrams. Twenty times this is 1400 milligrams a day. We don't think that's a bit too much. Of course, you should get as much of it as you can in food and that means eating a lot of fresh raw food—fruits and vegetables. Then, too, you should take completely natural vitamin C food supplements.

Vitamin D

How much vitamin D should you get? This is a hard one to answer. As you can see from the chart, 400 milligrams daily are recommended for children. No amount is specified for adults. The experts seem to feel that adults cannot get rickets since their bones are already formed. But can't adults get other diseases associated with the wrong use of calcium, with which vitamin D is intimately associated, and don't they get them all the time? And isn't this an indication that anything which will guard the individual's store of calcium and help in its assimilation is valuable?

It is possible to get too much vitamin D, especially if you are taking the synthetic form of it—that is, something which is not fish liver oil. For a long time there has been considerable controversy as to whether the harmful effects of enormous doses of vitamin D came from the vitamin itself or from impurities in the

[74]

solution in which it was given. Some of the vitamin D preparations seem to be more toxic than others.

However, Dr. Eddy in *The Avitaminoses* states, "It is apparent that the danger of overdosage is remote when the usual preparations of vitamin D are used." The early symptoms of vitamin D "poisoning," as it is called, are: nausea, loss of appetite, vomiting, cramps, diarrhea, tingling in the fingers and toes, dizziness and so forth. Of course, these are symptoms of many other disorders, too. When you get too much vitamin D, your body does not use calcium properly any longer and this is what causes the complaints. In some way not understood by physiologists, vitamin D controls calcium and phosphorus in your body. If there is not enough vitamin D, this machinery will go awry. If there is too much, it will go wrong in a different way.

How much is too much vitamin D? Practically all of the cases of overdoses related in medical journals are concerned with children who have been taking several times the prescribed dose of cod liver oil, or adults whose doctors were giving them vitamin D in massive doses to see what the effect on their state of ill health would be. For laboratory animals, 100 times the "protective" dose is harmful. Four thousand times the protective dose is definitely injurious and 40,000 times the protective dose is strongly toxic. Applying this to human beings, damage might follow 1000 times a curative dose of 3000 units—which would involve taking 30,000 grams or about 1000 ounces of cod liver oil —a near impossibility.

Doctors have given 5,000,000 units a day over a period of two weeks. They have gotten unpleasant symtoms on doses as low as 200,000 units a day.

The recommended daily minimum of vitamin D for children is 400 units. Officially, adults are not supposed

[75]

to need vitamin D at all unless their habits of life shut them off entirely from sunlight, for the sun manufactures vitamin D in our skin, you know. And 400 units a day is a far cry from 200,000 units a day! So we think there is very little chance of any of us getting too much vitamin D if we are taking natural products —fish liver oil, in this case, and paying attention to how much we take.

Vitamin E

Vitamin E is being used to prevent heart and circulatory disorders. Doctors who prescribe vitamin E for heart patients sometimes use massive doses of this vitamin. The two specialists who have done the most work on this treatment, Drs. Wilfrid and Evan Shute of the Shute Clinic, London, Ontario, Canada, warn against using large amounts of vitamin E if you suffer from high blood pressure. The vitamin has a tendency to raise blood pressure when it is given in large doses to someone not used to it. This seems to be the only situation in which vitamin E could prove to do harm —and this would be brief, but disquieting.

If your blood pressure is high, therefore, take vitamin E with great caution, starting with a small amount and increasing it very gradually to make certain that all goes well.

If you have no high blood pressure, how much vitamin E should you take? In days before we ate refined foods, it is believed that we might have gotten as much as 50 to 100 milligrams of vitamin E in our diet. So it seems to us that one should get at least that much in food and in supplements. Experts recommend that heart patients begin with small doses and gradually increase the dose until they feel their best, then continue it there.

CHAPTER 9

Have You a Vitamin Deficiency?

How CAN YOU tell if you have a vitamin deficiency? Are there any easy-to-recognize signs or symptoms? Is there any reason why one should suspect that skin disorders, dry hair, poor eyesight, bruises or sore mouths signify more than just a temporary or chronic condition that "runs in the family"?

There are many easily recognizable signs of vitamin deficiency — either slight or very, very serious. You yourself can tell whether or not you need more of one vitamin or another by simply observing yourself and your own health. We want to make one correction on that last sentence. It is doubtful that anyone was ever deficient in one or two vitamins. If you have even one symptom of deficiency in one vitamin, then it is almost certain that you are deficient in all others as well.

Why is this? Because, generally speaking, all the vitamins occur in the same foods. If you eat a diet that consists largely of these good foods, then you will be much less likely to be very deficient in vitamins. But if you consistently eat foods that are short in vitamin A, for instance, then you will almost surely be short on B vitamins, too, and vitamin C, perhaps vitamin E and vitamin K as well. So when you are reading the facts below, don't decide that you need just one vitamin. No one does. You need them all.

Vitamin A deficiency results in one unmistakable symptom which, if you have not noticed it in yourself, you undoubtedly have seen in your family or friends— night blindness. This is chiefly an inability to adapt to bright lights or to darkness. If you can't see for quite a while when you come into a bright room from darkness, or when you are exposed to a sudden glare (such as headlights from an oncoming car at night), then you certainly have a deficiency in vitamin A.

If you find it uncomfortable to go outside in bright sunshine without dark glasses, then you are short on vitamin A. Notice how many of your friends squint when they are outside on a sunny day. Do you know anyone who doesn't? Folks who are getting plenty of vitamin A have no difficulty keeping their eyes wide open in bright sunlight.

Part of the job of vitamin A is to protect what the doctors call the "specialized epithelial surfaces" of the body—the mouth tissues, and those of the respiratory system, the salivary glands and those of the digestive tract and the organs of the reproductive system and the skin. So lack of vitamin A can cause disorders of any of these or, perhaps more important, a slight deficiency in vitamin A can weaken one or all of these parts of you so seriously that they are likely candidates for any infection that comes along.

We know definitely, for instance, that the throat and lungs of a person deficient in vitamin A invite cold

[78]

germs, for the cells there, lacking this all-important vitamin, simply don't have the stamina to withstand the germs which are, of course, ever-present. Skin that is rough with the appearance of "goose pimples" especially on the elbows, above the knees, on buttocks and upper arms; hair that is dry, brittle and often full of dandruff—these are sure signs of vitamin A deficiency. Perhaps you are taking vitamin supplements. Did you know that if there is anything wrong with your liver, your body may not be able to use vitamin A? This suggests that you take larger doses and make certain that all the other vitamins necessary for liver health are abundant in your diet.

B Vitamin Deficiencies

We would like to consider each of the B vitamins separately and give you the list of symptoms produced by the deficiency of each. But every time we talk about separate B vitamins, we get letters from people who have decided to take the one B vitamin we have talked about. Where can they get it, they ask. Sorry, folks, but you cannot get B vitamins separately unless you take them in a synthetic form which is likely to do you more harm than good.

So we will talk about symptoms of B vitamin deficiency—all the B vitamins—thiamin, riboflavin, niacin, pyridoxine, pantothenic acid, folic acid, biotin, choline, para-amino-benzoic acid, inositol, etc. Have you ever had a sore tongue, sore lips, with perhaps cracks that don't heal at the corners of your mouth, a burning sensation on the inside of your mouth? Is your tongue ever bright red and glossy, or slightly purple, with, perhaps, deep crevices in it? Does your tongue ever feel swollen? All these are symptoms of vitamin B deficiency—so definite and certain that they can be

[79]

cured almost overnight by massive amounts of B vitamins.

Here are other more general symptoms of vitamin B deficiency, in animals and in man: seborrhea (a greasy scaling about the ears, nose and eyes), breathlessness, nervousness, neuritis, serious defects in memory, spots before the eyes, diarrhea, colitis, insomnia, dizziness, headache, lack of appetite, weakness in legs, lassitude, burning sensations in the feet. This does not mean that every headache or every case of colitis is due to vitamin B deficiency alone. Other causes may be present. But in cases of severe depletion, where patients have been hospitalized because of vitamin lack, all these symptoms were present. So how are you going to know whether or not your symptoms are caused partly by vitamin B deficiency unless you get enough of it in your diet for once in your life and see how you feel then?

Remember, please, you cannot get vitamin B in natural form unless it is in the form of food—brewer's yeast, desiccated liver and so forth.

Most of Us Lack Vitamin C

As we mentioned earlier, one reason for the widespread deficiency in vitamin C these days is the fact that all of us are exposed to hundreds of various poisons, every day of our lives—carbon monoxide gas, insecticides in our food, tobacco smoke, drugs and so forth. It is the job of vitamin C to neutralize poisons in the body *and the vitamin is destroyed in this process.* So the more poisonous our environment becomes year by year, the more vitamin C we need. And the more canned and processed foods we eat year by year, the less vitamin C we are getting.

The one surest sign of vitamin C deficiency is bruising. We mean by this that if you are getting enough vitamin C you will never bruise, unless, of course, you are subjected to some violent accident. However, the average healthy person getting the average number of bumps and knocks day by day should never have a bruise. A bruise means that certain small blood vessels have been destroyed and the blood has rushed out of them into the surrounding tissue. If you are getting enough vitamin C, your blood vessels are strong enough that they do not break at the slightest bump. When you take your bath tomorrow, look yourself over and note how many bruises you have. Even if you've been gardening, carpentering, sawing wood, moving furniture, you should not have bruises.

As you know, scurvy is the disease people get who have not had nearly enough vitamin C. Here are the symptoms of scurvy: weakness, easy fatigue, listlessness, shortness of breath, aching bones and muscles, rough, dry skin, bruises on legs, gradually spreading to the upper part of the body, swollen, bleeding gums that are spongy to the touch, loose teeth, old ulcers and scars that open again, new wounds that fail to heal.

We are told that few people in our country today get scurvy. But we are also told that many of us have a deficiency in vitamin C that is not enough to put us to bed, but is certainly enough to cause many different kinds of symptoms like those above.

Other Vitamins Less Likely to be Lacking

Vitamin D is, as we all know, especially necessary for children, for it must be present for their bones to grow straight. But it is also necessary for adults, for you must have vitamin D for your body to use calcium and phosphorus—two important minerals. Osteoporosis and osteomalacia are diseases of folks past middle age whose bones become soft and brittle. Part of the reason is undoubtedly too little calcium in the diet at mealtime. Could not part of it be that there is too little vitamin D for the body to use in connection with whatever calcium is available?

Vitamin E is essential for the proper working of the muscles and the reproductive tract. In animals such disorders as miscarriages, infertility, menstrual disorders and so forth are common when the animals' diet does not contain enough vitamin E. In animals, too, muscular dystrophy can be produced by depriving the animals of vitamin E. The vitamin E which we and our children should be getting has been removed from foods during the refining process.

Vitamin K is, as the nutrition books say, "widely distributed" in foods. It is necessary for the blood to coagulate properly, so any tendency toward hemorrhaging or excessive bleeding may indicate too little vitamin K in the diet.

Vitamin P (sometimes called bioflavonoids) occurs with vitamin C in fresh foods and works in conjunction with vitamin C.

CHAPTER 10

Unsuspected Vitamin Destroyers

IF YOU WERE marooned on a desert island and had to live entirely on raw clams, oysters and other shell fish, that might not seem such a terrible hardship. These fish are high protein foods with a high mineral content and to many people they are delicious. But you would very soon find yourself losing your appetite, growing weak and failing in eyesight. If this limited diet continued for many weeks, you would experience spastic paralysis of the limbs and would eventually die.

All of this would happen because, as we are informed in the chapter on "Antimetabolites" of the new third edition of *Modern Nutrition in Health and Disease* (Lea & Febiger, 1964, edited by Wohl and Goodhart) raw shell fish contain an enzyme that destroys vitamin B_1, more commonly referred to as thiamin.

The book has for many years been a standard manual of nutrition for the medical profession. Brought up to date in its new edition, it is an authoritative and

[83]

comprehensive survey of the increasingly complex field of nutrition. And much of the information it contains makes it clear that anyone would be a fool to think he can get all the vitamins he needs with his knife and fork, and quit worrying about nutrition. Not only are our vitamin requirements difficult to obtain from food alone, but it also seems that wherever you look these days, there are more and more antimetabolites being unveiled that can afflict us with serious vitamin deficiencies if we are not careful.

B_1 Deficiency Deadly

Thiamin, which we have seen can be destroyed by an enzyme from raw clams and oysters, is intimately concerned with the process of digesting and using carbohydrate. It is the carbohydrate in our diets on which we largely depend for the supply of glucose in the blood that is the prime nutrient of the brain and source of energy to all our cells. As soon as we set up an interference with the carbohydrate metabolism, we can expect trouble to strike almost anywhere. Inability of the brain to function properly is one of the obvious results. Less well known, a thiamin deficiency has a definite effect on the heart and will weaken that vital organ considerably. If the deficiency is allowed to go on long enough, the heart will fail.

Yet while thiamin is so indispensable to our most vital organs, to a greater and greater extent it keeps on being refined out of our foodstuffs. This vitamin is a component of the outer husks of rice, the germ and bran of wheat and, in fact, that portion of all grains that is invariably milled away to give the grains a lighter color and finer texture. Since the need for thiamin is so obvious, it is replaced in so-called "enriched" flours and cereals by a cheap synthetic chemical.

[84]

This, being divorced from the other numerous discovered and undiscovered B vitamins with which it needs to be associated, is just about useless within our systems. It does nothing to help with the problem of supplying us daily with adequate thiamin in combination with all the other B complex vitamins. In fact, we know of no way that you can reliably get an adequate supply of these infinitely precious vitamins except by taking a good food supplement that contains them. Brewer's yeast and desiccated liver are the best we know, closely followed by wheat germ.

Remember that while laboratory scientists like to examine the effect of an antagonist on one particular vitamin substance, so far as the B vitamins are concerned anything that destroys one of them is also destroying or at the very least weakening the entire B complex. It is only in terms of enormous therapeutic doses, that a doctor will administer by injection, that a single one of the B vitamins can be said to act independently like a drug. In terms of nutrition, we might just as well consider the B complex as a single big vitamin of many parts that becomes ineffective when any one of those parts is missing.

Drugs Destroy B and C

From our point of view then, destruction of thiamin by the eating of oysters amounts to very much the same thing as the destruction of riboflavin (vitamin B_2) by sulfanilamide and in fact all the sulfa drugs. And they both equal the effect of penicillin and chloromycetin which will destroy the nicotinic acid in our systems and in that way create within us a deficiency in all the necessary functions of the B complex vitamins. In fact, almost any drug you can take will have a destructive effect on one or more of the B vitamins. And even more dangerous, any drug you can take without exception will use up the precious store of vitamin C in your system.

Drugs Are Poisons

This is because all drugs are poisons. They are poisons that for the most part can be very useful in medical emergencies, but that does not alter the fact that any drug taken into the body has toxic effects. This has been proven over and over again, even of substances that for many years were considered harmless. Consider aspirin, and the fact that 15 years ago J. I. Rodale's was a voice crying out in the wilderness that aspirin is a drug and must do damage to the human system. Such warnings were a joke at that time, but now it is known that aspirin is a potent cause of ulcers and that to take so much as a single aspirin tablet will cause a certain amount of internal bleeding and do definite damage to the system. And since one of the chief functions of vitamin C is to combine with toxic materials, neutralize their toxicity and carry them safely out of the system, every time we introduce a drug, whether it be aspirin, the nicotine of cigarettes or a barbiturate sleeping pill, we are unwittingly using up most or all of our store of vitamin C. This vitamin has other work to do for us, like strengthening the walls of the capillaries and building the cartilaginous and connective tissues that are vital to health. But this work cannot be done unless we have enough vitamin C to do it and it is extremely difficult for our bodies to contain that much vitamin C if we use any kind of drugs.

The answer, of course, is that the only way to play safe is to take substantial amounts of rose hips supplements daily.

[86]

Fat-Soluble Vitamins

All of the fat-soluble vitamins (A, D, E and K) are destroyed by mineral oil. Vitamin E is destroyed by bleaching agents such as are used to bleach white flour. Dicoumarol, a drug, and the sulfa drugs destroy vitamin K.

In a more general sense, many other substances are destroyers of vitamins because they act to interrupt the chemical reactions of vitamins within the enzyme systems in which they function. Drugs that contain toxic metals such as arsenic, lead, mercury and bismuth destroy vitamins. Astringents, laxatives and solvents may cause destruction of vitamins. Narcotics and pain killers such as alcohol, morphine and aspirin destroy them, too. Bleaching agents are destructive of the fat- and water-soluble vitamins alike. The extent to which common foods are bleached is just beginning to be appreciated. The sulfuring of foods and the addition of sulfites to foods such as meats brings destruction of vitamins. The nitrates and nitrites deposited in vegetables by chemical fertilizers destroy vitamin A.

An interesting angle to the problem of insecticide residues in food is this: a considerable proportion of this residue reacts chemically with the food when it is cooked. The nature of the product that results is quite unknown. We do not know whether it is less or more toxic than the residue itself.

When foods are fumigated (dates, for example) we are told that all of the fumigant is not recovered, suggesting that it has combined with the food and hence cannot be removed.

Chemical treatment of water uses chlorine, a powerful oxidizing and bleaching agent. When there is enough of this chemical in the water to add taste and smell to it, undoubtedly enough must enter the body to react on the vitamins in the digestive tract. Vitamin E is the substance hardest hit. Fluoridation destroys the enzyme phosphatase, upon which many vital processes depend. Chemical vapors in the air around factories readily destroy vitamins A, B, C and K.

Charcoal is an absorbent material for all vitamins, so in the intestines it may render ineffective about half the usual vitamin content. Tranquilizers are fairly new drugs, widely taken by hundreds of thousands of people in this country. Although research is not completed, we are told that under certain circumstances, there is a loss of nutrients when these drugs are used.

Enzyme systems are harmed, too, when the proteins they contain are harmed. We are told that nitrogen trichloride, used to bleach flour, changes the protein of the flour into a slightly different substance, chemically speaking. The spray-drying of eggs causes a loss of thiamin in them. Rancid fat in the diet results in serious losses of vitamin A and E. Among other anti-vitamin E agents are carbon tetrachloride, pyridine, sulfathiazole and sodium sulfite.

What Can You Do About It?

Had enough? Undoubtedly as research proceeds we will uncover many more enemies of vitamins and of enzymes than these. The science of nutrition is in its infancy. And we must not forget, too, that new and more powerful chemicals are being produced every day. These undoubtedly add to the menacing picture, and it may be many years before we discover exactly the kind and the amount of harm they can do.

What's the answer? Should you throw up your hands in disgust and declare that there's no use trying to live healthfully and, henceforth, ignore all this informa-

[88]

tion? We don't think so, or obviously we wouldn't use up space telling about it. We think that the above information is the biggest part of the answer to the eternal question—"Why should we take vitamins? Grandpa never did."

Most grandpas of present-generation Americans lived on farms. Just look over the items listed above and see how many of them Grandpa was exposed to. He may have eaten raw eggs, though we rather doubt it, and chances are he never saw a raw oyster unless he lived near the coast. Alcohol is the only other substance he could have known. So in addition to eating foods rich in vitamins, since they had not been refined and otherwise processed, Grandpa did not lose his precious vitamins to the chemical and drug industry as his grandchildren have had to do.

There is, of course, only one answer—replace these lost vitamins. And replace them in direct proportion to the amount you think you have lost. How can you tell? Are you exposed daily and hourly to deadly substances like arsenic, lead (painters are), insecticides? Is your doctor giving you hormones? Do you take drugs —antibiotics, sleeping pills, aspirin? If you have taken sulfa drugs in quantity during the past several years, you're almost bound to be short on B vitamins. Do you drink or smoke? Do you eat white bread and other bleached foods or can you say honestly that your meals consist largely of natural foods? Do you drink chlorinated and/or fluoridated water daily?

No one can tell you how much of the various vitamins to take to make up for what you lose to vitamin robbers. You must figure this out for yourself and you can, without too much trouble, by studying the information above carefully.

And the next time someone tells you you're a foolish

food faddist to waste time and money taking vitamins, ask him if he ever heard of all the facts given above. Ask him if he thinks this information alone is a valid enough reason for taking vitamin food supplements.

CHAPTER 11

Do We All Need More Vitamins?

VITAMINS BY DEFINITION are food elements indispensable to health. Yet in the past few years there has grown up in medical and government circles a new fad of pretending that people don't need vitamins unless they are suffering from deficiency diseases. Doctors go on prescribing vitamins, of course, for all the hundreds of uses, including simple maintenance of good health, for which doctors know vitamins are valuable. Yet their public spokesmen try to give the impression that if you spend a few dollars for a vitamin supplement on your own, you are somehow being hoaxed; while if you first spend five or ten dollars for a visit to your doctor and then get your vitamins on his advice, this, by some distorted logic, is a saving of money.

It is to the everlasting credit of the medical profession, however, that its politicians have never been able to steamroller its true scientists. This has never been more apparent than in today's vitamin controversy, with doctors all over the country refusing to be silenced and continuing to publish, at the rate of more than 100 a month, articles extolling the need for vitamins and the value of taking vitamin supplements on one's own. Among those we admire most in this large group of independent, health-minded scientists, are two from the Department of Oral Medicine of the University of Alabama Medical Center in Birmingham. Their names are E. Cheraskin and W. M. Ringsdorf, Jr., and they have jointly published a true wealth of papers reporting their well-controlled investigations into the effect of vitamins on health. One of the most exciting of these was a paper they presented in May, 1964, to the 18th annual meeting of the American Academy of Dental Medicine in New York, published in the *Journal of Dental Medicine* in October of the same year. "Vitamins in Health and Disease," the title of this report, is a comprehensive investigation of the vitamin status of our country today and how much actual need there is for people to take vitamin supplements.

Their conclusion, which is not mere opinion but very well validated scientifically, is that the use of these indispensable adjuncts to health ought to be far more widespread than it actually is. Where today only one person in five is actually taking daily vitamin supplements, doctors Cheraskin and Ringsdorf show clearly that if every man, woman and child in the country were to take such supplements, the general level of health would be vastly benefited.

Vitamin Levels Decline

Why should this be? Does nobody eat well enough to get all the vitamins he needs directly from his diet?

The answer, as Cheraskin and Ringsdorf show, is that year by year the vitamin content of our food supply keeps declining. Quoting a study made by the Department of Health, Education and Welfare and published in 1960, they point out that in the 14 years from 1944 to 1958 there was a uniform decline in the vitamins available from food. In ascorbic acid (vitamin C) this amounted to a 23 per cent difference. There was 22 per cent less vitamin A available, 16 per cent less vitamin B_1, 6 per cent less riboflavin and 8 per cent less niacin available through food. This is attributed to the obvious fact that today's farmers are interested in producing only greater yields per acre, even if this means sacrifice of the nutritional quality. Compound this with new techniques of harvesting food plants before they have reached maturity, when their vitamin content is lower, so that they may be stored for a longer period of time, and it would be strange indeed if our present-day food could be found as nutritious as that of our unsophisticated forebears. Add further losses from cooking, and it becomes obvious that Cheraskin and Ringsdorf are perfectly right when they state that from soil to consumption, any particular product might lose as much as 90 per cent or more of its nutrient value.

At a time when most people can afford all the food they need for hunger satisfaction, the above figures do not mean that there are many suffering from frank deficiency disease. But Cheraskin and Ringsdorf point out that between optimum health, a condition enjoyed by practically nobody, and definite, specific illness, there is a large area which they call "suboptimum health or incipient illness." "This area," they say, "deserves special attention for two reasons. Firstly, it is the point at which one can interrupt the chain which produces overt and serious illness. Secondly, there is

[93]

reason to believe that a large fraction of the population falls in this category."

Rose Hips for Healthy Mouths

The health of the mouth—ability to resist tooth cavities and gingivitis—is apparently the first to suffer from marginal deficiency in nutrition that keeps the general health from being as good as it otherwise might. This is the reason for the interest and studies of Cheraskin and Ringsdorf, who specialize in oral health. And this is the reason that they are more aware than most other doctors of the remarkable effect that vitamin supplements can have in increasing the ability to resist and overcome disease. They have found that by adding substantial amounts of vitamin B_6 (pyridoxine) to the supposedly adequate diet, they can secure a 55 per cent reduction in the number of new cavities occurring. They have found that by adding vitamin C to the supposedly adequate diet, they can secure an equivalent decrease in gingivitis.

Thy have also found that by using natural vitamin C accompanied by bioflavonoids, as we find it in rose hips, and by using natural vitamin B complex as it occurs in brewer's yeast, they have been able to secure far greater resistance to oral disease than is possible with the isolated and purified vitamins.

Having shown this much clearly, these remarkable investigators then go on to point out that while experiments with a single vitamin are easier to control clinically and easier to report, in actual life outside the laboratory a vitamin deficiency almost invariably will turn out to be a multiple deficiency. "The usual clinical case is that of multiple vitamin deficiency," they state. "Only under very isolated circumstances and particularly under experimental conditions is it possible to demonstrate a single deficiency state. Accordingly, it is appropriate that we turn our attention to multivitamin therapy . . ."

What they are getting at here is simply that it is impossible for the layman and in most cases for the doctor to diagnose that a particular difficulty is due to deficiency in one single vitamin and that alone.

Vitamins Boost "Perfect" Health

As a demonstration of the correctness of this approach, they cite a number of experiments made with military cadets—the carefully screened and selected flower of our young manhood, at the peak of health by every medical standard. Without going into all the complex details, we can point to the extremely convincing results.

Among these cadets without vitamin supplementation, there were 14.9 days per year, on the average for each, of complaints of minor respiratory difficulty (colds, etc.) and gastrointestinal trouble (indigestion). When they were given a multivitamin supplement, the mean number of days of complaint per cadet decreased from 14.9 to 9.7. This represents approximately a 35 per cent improvement in health among young men defined as being already in the prime of health. Among a similar group, in England, it was found that six days of multiple vitamin supplementation was able to cut almost four seconds off the time it took to run a course that originally took less than two minutes. Football players at Louisiana State University demonstrated that while vitamin supplementation had no effect on the number of bruises and injuries they received in the game, those who had the vitamin supplement recovered 23 per cent faster.

From all of the evidence cited in this remarkable paper, there is only one reasonable conclusion: there is hardly a person in the entire country, no matter how healthy he may be at the present time, whose health would not be substantially benefited by supplements of all the known vitamins, particularly in the natural interrelationships in which they are found in such high-vitamin foods as rose hips, brewer's yeast, fish liver oil and wheat germ oil. And what is true of athletes and military cadets is even more true of us. We need vitamins. We need more vitamins than we can possibly get by eating the kind of food that is available in our markets. We aren't going to let anyone tell us that we have to wait until we are sick enough to need a doctor and get his prescription before we can take the vitamins we need.

CHAPTER 12

Vitamins for Aging Patients

A MEDICAL DOCTOR who believes that some of the symptoms of aging can be reversed with large doses of vitamins wrote an article about his theory in the *Journal of the American Geriatrics Association* for November, 1955.

"Perhaps the saddest fact that every human being must face is that, if he lives long enough, he will eventually undergo progressively increasing deteriorative changes in the structure and function of the body until these become so severe that he can no longer survive," says Dr. William Kaufman. "The so-called 'normal' aging process makes his joints less flexible, decreases his muscular working capacity and strength, impairs his co-ordination and sense of balance, brings about mental changes, and increases capillary fragility—in addition to causing many other obvious or subtle changes in the bodily structure and function."

How right he is! And how cheering the news that,

in an actual controlled test, he showed that certain of these disagreeable traits of old age can be reversed. For his test, Dr. Kaufman concentrated first on mobility of joints. He has developed a method for measuring how supple one's joints are—wrists, fingers, shoulders, thigh and knee can be manipulated in such a way that one's physician can get an exact estimate of just how much movement is hindered and how much freedom of movement is left. So Dr. Kaufman used this method with his patients—663 of them—to test the effectiveness of vitamins in decreasing stiffness and increasing flexibility.

B Vitamin Used

He concentrated on one of the B vitamins, niacin (in the form of niacinamide), and gave enormous doses of this vitamin to his patient every couple of hours for several doses, then measured the joint function again. He found, without any exception, that the joint mobility in every patient taking large amounts of this one B vitamin alone or in combination with other vitamins improved to a clinically significant degree. He tells us that in individual cases, taking this one B vitamin raises the measurement of mobility from 6 to 12 units during the first month, and from 1/2 to 1 unit each month that therapy is continued thereafter. He points out that not all joints improve equally well. Some almost immovable joints improve not at all, but others recover full or partial range of movement. In all cases, however, the improvement generally is quite considerably above that to be found in untreated patients.

In addition to the huge doses of niacinamide, he also gave large doses of vitamin C and several other B vitamins and fairly high doses of vitamins A and D. He also used injections of vitamin B_{12} in some instances.

[98]

He did not notice, he said, that any or all of these added to the improvement, although he is quite sure that they did not hinder it in any way.

Along with increased movability of joints, Dr. Kaufman found that patients' muscles functioned better after they had been taking vitamins for some months. He discovered this by measuring the strength of their handgrips, using a machine for this purpose, and another test in which the patient makes strokes on a tally. In every case the proficiency of the patients improved. Dr. Kaufman did not create any supermen or super women, he tells us. But the patients, by taking vitamins, improved to such an extent that they could go about their daily work without undue fatigue whereas before they had not been able to.

They also found, almost without exception, that their sense of balance improved. "Many patients with subjective and objective evidence of impaired balance sense recover their ability to balance themselves normally during the first three months of niacinamide therapy and this benefit continues for as long as they take this vitamin." Those who did not notice any benefit from taking just the one B vitamin sometimes found that there was improvement when they took, as well, other B vitamins, including vitamin B_{12}.

Checking on the mental state of his aging patients, Dr. Kaufman found that a considerable number of them noticed an improved state of mind. Depression and nervousness, over-reacting to noise and other stimuli—these were symptoms that seemed to be improved while patients were taking the B vitamin. Some did not have this experience, and Dr. Kaufman says there is no way of knowing who will and who will not. In many cases adding the other B vitamins helped in alleviating mental symptoms.

Vitamin C in Massive Doses Used

Dr. Kaufman used vitamin C to improve the condition of blood vessels (especially the small vessels, or capillaries) of his patients. He tells us, "After the age of 50, with increasing age there was a significant trend toward increased capillary fragility, *even in those patients who had from 50 to 75 milligrams of ascorbic acid [vitamin C] in their average daily diet.* Decreased blood levels of vitamin C have been reported in older people."

He gave them large doses of vitamin C (1500 to 2000 milligrams a day, divided into doses of 250 milligrams each) and found that, after three to six months of treatment, the capillaries became much less fragile. What would this mean to the patients? Capillary fragility seems to be one certain forerunner of "strokes" because the fragile blood vessel wall can easily collapse, causing hemorrhage. When such a hemorrhage occurs in the brain, the heart or an important artery, the result can be permanent crippling or death.

Why do you suppose, with evidence like this available, all doctors do not advise their older patients to take large doses of vitamin C daily? Think of the suffering and heartache that could be avoided!

In addition to helping the tone of the blood vessel walls, the large doses of vitamin C improved the condition of the patients' teeth and gums. Those who still had their own teeth reported that loose ones were tightening. Dentists reported that there was an improvement in gum structure. One dentist who followed carefully eight of these older patients who took both the B vitamins and vitamin C for more than six years noticed that he did not find the anticipated resorption of alveolar tissue so often seen as part of aging. This

[100]

refs to the shrinking of gums and the bone structure beneath them which results in loose teeth, bleeding and eventual drying up of the gum tissue.

Vitamin B₁₂ for Mental Symptoms

Dr. Kaufman's work with vitamin B_{12} is exciting. He describes the following symptoms for which this vitamin provided constant relief: fatigue, increased nervous irritability, mild impairment in memory and ability to concentrate, mental depression, insomnia and lack of balance. Sometimes the following symptoms were present as well: dyspepsia, sensations of numbness, difficulty in bladder control, breathlessness associated with impaired heart muscle sounds. None of these patients had anemia or the brilliantly red tongue which is associated with pernicious anemia.

None of the vitamins helped at all, *except vitamin B_{12}*. Dr. Kaufman gave it in injections—100 micrograms once a week. Less than this did not seem to bring improvement. Omitting the vitamin B_{12} injections caused all the symptoms to recur slowly.

Dr. Kaufman's conclusions are as follows: "Vitamins used in doses which are far in excess of quantities available from food as it is ordinarily prepared and eaten may be considered to act as pharmacologic agents [that is, drugs]. The prolonged continuous oral administration of niacinamide (alone or in combination with other vitamins) can effect remarkable changes in bodily function and structure of an aging population which subsists on a diet adequate in calories and protein."

It seems to us that Dr. Kaufman's experience with his 663 patients is living proof that aging is a stress situation necessitating far more of all the food elements than are needed for a non-stressful situation. The older

[101]

person should be taking much larger doses of vitamins and minerals than the younger person. In addition to his much greater need, the older person tends to eat less healthfully, thus depriving himself of even more desperately needed food elements. It's so much easier to live on toast and tea or cereal or pleasant-tasting cakes; the tendency is always to avoid healthful foods rich in protein, and fresh fruits and vegetables rich in vitamins and minerals. But Dr. Kaufman tells us that even when one is getting enough protein and calories, he can still benefit, as he becomes older, by taking extremely large doses of vitamins. We would, of course, add mineral supplements as a most important part of the treatment, since minerals and vitamins work together for the body's welfare.

CHAPTER 13

Recent Comments on Vitamins

THE FOLLOWING IS a compilation from the Rodale *Health Bulletin,* on the subject of vitamins in general: April 20, 1963. *Gerontology.* A new "old age remedy" based on vitamins was recently discussed at the Hungarian Congress on Gerontology, says a French paper. It is claimed that a daily dose of four pills composed of vitamins A, D, E, K, B_1, B_{12} and C associated with nicotinic acid and methylandrostenediol (a chemical body-builder) produced a clear improvement in body fluids and a weight gain of several pounds.

June 6, 1963. *Vitamins Relieve Fatigue.* For nonspecific fatigue or general debility, a treatment that yielded definite improvement among an experimental group of patients is reported by Dr. C. H. Leslie, of St. Louis, Mo., in the May issue of *General Practice.*

Medication used consisted of a central nervous system stimulant combined with vitamins C and B complex. Of 28 patients in the group, 15 showed marked

[103]

improvement, and 12 showed moderate results. No side effects were reported. Nine patients reported a slight flush (due to niacin, a B vitamin in the medication), which Dr. Leslie describes as not objectionable.

The combination of a central nervous system stimulant and niacin was reported by another researcher, quoted by Dr. Leslie, to produce both physical and mental improvement in elderly patients. Recently, in a group of 91 patients (ranging in age from 32 to 73) with mild confusion, memory defects, inertia or mild depression, 80 per cent were reported to have improved after similar treatment, Dr. Leslie said. In both of these investigations, it was noted that improvement in appetite was one important effect of the medication. This effect would be particularly valuable in treating a patient convalescing from illness or surgery, and in treating the patient whose fatigue is due to inadequate nutrition, Dr. Leslie stated.

July 20, 1963. *Deficiencies.* Teenage girls commonly suffer from vitamin deficiencies, according to Dr. Robert S. Goodhart, director of the National Vitamin Foundation. "They all seem inclined either to stuff themselves or starve themselves, with little thought as to the nutritive value of food," he adds.

September 21, 1963. *Hospital Gives Vitamins to Its Workers.* Free vitamins are the latest thing in employee fringe benefits. Employees at Wesley Medical Center, Wichita, Kansas, collect a free multi-vitamin-mineral capsule every day as they pass through the cafeteria lunch line.

About one month ago the hospital personnel office decided to test the capsules as an added fringe benefit. So far, about 50 per cent of the workers are taking advantage of it, and the number is increasing. A hospital pharmacy official told *Health Bulletin* he noticed that employees were buying more vitamins for their families since free vitamin dispensers were installed.

November 2, 1963. *National Vitamin Foundation Disagrees with FDA.* While the Food and Drug Administration was reporting in Washington on its prosecution of firms which claim that Americans are undernourished, the National Vitamin Foundation was saying that studies "provide incontrovertible proof that a great many Americans of all ages and socio-economic brackets are subsisting on diets which fall substantially short of the recommended dietary allowances in respect to one or more essential nutrients."

That information is contained in an advance copy of the foundation's annual report, "How Well-Nourished Are Americans?" The report says, "We believe that under-nutrition in this country, in regard at least to the vitamins on which pertinent studies have been made, is of sufficient prevalence to meet one of the criteria previously mentioned for adopting the approach of routine prophylaxis." In other words, everyone ought to take vitamins regularly.

November 2, 1963. *Birth Defects.* Extra vitamins during pregnancy may reduce the chances of bearing a deformed child, Dr. Lyndon A. Peer of Newark, New Jersey, reports. Dr. Peer says that supplemental vitamins cut in half the number of babies born with cleft palate. He suggests that some women may need supplements to make up for vitamins lost in poorly prepared food.

November 16, 1963. *Breath-Holding.* Dr. V. S. Shuttleworth of Monmouthshire, England, treats babies who have severe breath-holding spells with large doses of Vitamin D_2. He believes that the frustration and rage which lead to breath-holding may be caused by rickets resulting from vitamin D_2 deficiency. In the

[105]

November issue of *The Practitioner* he reports a high degree of success in treating such children with vitamins.

November 23, 1963. *Youth.* The 23-year-old wife of Supreme Court Justice William O. Douglas said this week in a *Washington Post* interview that her husband will stay in his job despite the fact that he reached 65 a month ago. "Some people wondered how my husband would keep up with me," she said, "but I'm taking vitamin pills to keep up with his pace."

January 25, 1964. *Vitamins.* The *Journal of the American Dental Association* reports that a multivitamin trace mineral supplement reduces the depth of depressions in the surface of diseased gums. Twenty-two dental students with gingivitis who were given the supplement showed inprovement. Twenty-one given a fake pill showed no change. "These changes appeared in dental students that had no apparent multivitamin deficiency, trace mineral deficiency or both," write Drs. W. M. Ringsdorf and E. Cheraskin, both of Birmingham, Alabama.

March 21, 1964. *Milkshake.* The Chicago Cubs will bolster their baseball prowess this season with a nutritional drink containing vitamins, niacin, riboflavin, iron and other nutrients. It's the same milkshake-type supplement that was approved by the National Aeronautics and Space Administration for use by astronauts on a moon jaunt. Bob Whitlow, the Cubs athletic director, hopes to convince the boys that they should replace their usual hot dog and coke snacks with the supplement. "This stuff gives the player quick energy with minimum bulk," he explains.

March 28, 1964. *Cancer.* Vitamin B_{12} has been shown to slow the growth rate of cancer of the nervous system in children, two doctors from London, England, report. Their studies at The Hospital for Sick Children involved over 100 children. Among 82 who were treated with vitamin B₁₂, 32 survived up to 12 years (39 per cent). With conventional treatment, eight out of 25 survived (32 per cent). The findings are reported in the December, 1963, issue of *Archives of Disease in Childhood*.

May 9, 1964. *Vitamin Abnormality*. Women who have frequent stillbirths or give birth to babies that die soon after delivery may be helped by large doses of vitamin B₆ during late pregnancy, a Boston pediatrician believes. Dr. Clara Waldinger, writing in *Postgraduate Medicine*, states that some infant deaths may be due to an inherited biochemical defect which prevents the baby from obtaining enough vitamin B₆. (When they survive, such children develop severe convulsions and become mentally retarded if they are not treated soon after birth with large doses of the vitamin.)

June 27, 1964. *Heart*. Eliminating fats from the diet also eliminates a big source of vitamins A and D, which help ward off disease, a French biochemist told the Inter-American Congress of Cardiology in Montreal. Dr. Pierre Mandel of Strasbourg Medical School thinks that aging—measured in physiological terms as well as in chronological terms—is related to the prevention of heart trouble. Many people who think of themselves as 40 years old are really 70 physiologically, he said, urging people over 50 to take vitamin supplements to assure themselves of full nutrition.

July 11, 1964. *Senility*. Several high-potency vitamins plus a mental stimulant reduced many of the symptoms of senility in a dozen patients, two doctors report in the *Journal of the American Geriatrics Society*. Loss of memory, untidiness, irritability and apathy were some of the common problems which im-

[107]

proved under treatment. It is believed that many of these symptoms result from poor blood supply to the brain, the doctors state, and at least one of the B vitamins in the preparation, nicotinic acid, is known to improve circulation.

July 18, 1964. *Some People Need More Vitamins Than Others.* Nutritionists make a fundamental error when they try to set up uniform requirements for vitamins and minerals for everyone, charged Frederick B. Hutt, Ph.D., at a New York State Nutrition Institute held at Cornell University July 9-10. Dr. Hutt's specialty is poultry husbandry. He has found in his research that genetic differences make Rhode Island Red chickens far less efficient at metabolizing thiamin and riboflavin than other types of chickens. That means that they need three to four times as much of these vitamins in their feed as other chickens do to maintain health and egg production.

People are hybridized just like chickens, said Dr. Hutt, and chances are that our genetic differences create the same kind of variations in vitamin and mineral requirements. His research shows that inborn differences in chickens—and probably people also—result in differences in the amount of enzymes synthesized in the body. If an animal or person is less efficient at synthesizing enzymes, more vitamins will be needed in the diet to achieve full health.

BOOK II

THE INDIVIDUAL
VITAMINS

SECTION I

Vitamin A

CHAPTER 14

Some Basic Information

ONE OF THE EASIEST vitamins to obtain in a well-rounded diet, not lost to any great extent in cooking or storing, vitamin A is generally present in the average American diet in sufficient quantity to prevent serious deficiency diseases. But, on the other hand, nutritionists suspect that a borderline deficiency of vitamin A is quite common in America. That is, most people seem to get enough to protect them from serious consequences but never enough to be free from complaints of "not being up to par." A survey done in the schools of New York City showed that a slight vitamin A deficiency was the most common diet deficiency found among the children.

Vitamin A can be secured from both animal and plant sources. The animal sources are better in general, for there the vitamin appears as a substance in itself, whereas in plants we eat "carotene" which is then changed into vitamin A in the body. However,

[111]

considering all angles of a well-rounded diet, many of the plant sources of vitamin A are excellent food, because they also provide other vitamins as well.

Symptoms of Vitamin A Deficiency

Vitamin A can be stored in the body (in the liver, chiefly) so there may be considerable depletion of it before symptoms of deficiency occur. The first obvious symptom is called night blindness. Since we have already discussed this in an earlier chapter, we will not go into any details here. Not being able to read or work in a medium-dim light is another symptom. Or there may be itching and burning or slight redness of the eyelids.

A skin disease, especially in children, is another symptom of vitamin A deficiency. In adults a serious deficiency in vitamin A leads to a horny condition of the mucous membrane of the mouth, the respiratory system and the genitourinary system. Bladder stones are produced in rats by vitamin A deficiency, also diseases of the nerves somewhat akin to sclerosis in human beings. It has been found in many cases that abundant vitamin A in the diet helps greatly the condition of people with hyperthyroidism or goiter. Inability to store fat is a symptom of not enough vitamin A.

Vitamin A helps to fight infection not by killing off the disease germs, but by providing for the health of the mucous membranes which the germs attack. Because of this property, it is powerful against colds, sinus trouble and pneumonia. Scientists have observed that, especially in children, symptoms of very serious vitamin A deficiency are always preceded by colds and other respiratory troubles.

Perhaps most important of all its functions, vitamin A contributes enormously to growth and dental health in growing children. It is essential for the child to have vitamin A while his teeth are being formed and he is growing to his full stature. Way back when our grandmothers were raising their children, they knew how beneficial was a daily dose of cod liver oil, even though they may not have known why.

Daily Requirements of Vitamin A

Taking vitamin A in sufficient quantity relieves all symptoms of deficiency very quickly. However, there are several conditions that prohibit the body from absorbing this vitamin. Gastrointestinal or liver diseases or infections of any kind limit our capacity to use vitamin A. The continued taking of mineral oil dissolves the store of vitamin A in the body and carries it away before it can be absorbed. (One of the many good reasons for not taking mineral oil!)

Since vitamin A is stored in your body, it is not absolutely necessary to eat some of it every day. However, since there is no way of checking how much reserve store you have left, you may find that all your vitamin A has been exhausted and you are suddenly showing symptoms of deficiency, unless you're pretty faithful about getting enough of the vitamin over a period of time. The daily recommended allowances of vitamin A have been set as follows:

Moderately active adults ... 5000 International Units per day
Children up to 12 years old . 1500-3500 International Units per day
Children over 12 .... 4500-6000 International Units per day
Pregnant women .... 6000 International Units per day
Nursing mothers .... 8000 International Units per day

Many nutritionists believe that these amounts are too low and that actually everyone should have more vitamin A than these figures indicate. The easiest way

[113]

to obtain it without much attention to diet is to take fish liver oil. Halibut liver oil contains about a hundred times as much as cod liver oil. These oils are sold with the number of units of vitamins A and D that they contain specified on the label, standardized so that you cannot make a mistake in dosage. Buy the oil in the most economical form, for the amount you want to take. (Do not take more than the recommended dose, as overdoses of vitamin A may be toxic.)

Of course, it is best if you also include in your diet regularly other foods that contain vitamin A. These are listed below along with an estimate of the amount of vitamin A in each. Here are some suggestions on cooking and storing foods that contain the vitamin: the food value is lost if the fat in which it is contained becomes rancid. Always keep your fish liver oil in the refrigerator. Vegetables containing vitamin A do not lose it when they are cooked, for it is not soluble in water.

Foods Containing the Largest Amounts of Vitamin A

Foods	International Units of Vitamin A
Alfalfa leaf meal, dry	8,000 in 100 grams
Apricots, fresh	2,790 in 3 medium apricots
Apricots, dried	2,230 in 4-6 halves
Apricot nectar	1,086 in ½ cup
Asparagus, fresh	1,000 in 12 stalks
Beans, snap	630 to 2,000 in 1 cup, cooked
Beet greens	6,700 in ½ cup, cooked
Broccoli	3,500 in 1 cup, cooked
Butter	3,300 in about 8 tablespoons
Cantaloupe	3,420 in ½ cup of cantaloupe balls
Carrots, fresh	12,000 in 1 cup, cooked
Carrots, dehydrated	117,000 in 1 cup, cooked
Celery cabbage	9,000 in 1 cup
Chard	2,800 in ½ cup, cooked
Cheese, cheddar	2,000 in a 5-inch cube

[114]

Foods	International Units of Vitamin A
Cheese, cream	2,000 to 2,210 in 6 tablespoons
Cheese, roquefort	2,500 to 4,000 in 2 sectors
Cheese, Swiss	1,970 to 2,700 in 4 slices
Cod liver oil	85,000 in 100 grams
Collards	6,870 in 1 cup, cooked
Cream	1,640 in 6 tablespoons
Dandelion greens	13,650 in 1 cup, cooked
Eel	660 to 13,650 in 1 serving
Eggs, whole, fresh	1,140 in 2 eggs
Eggs, whole, dried	3,632 in 1 pound
Endive (escarole)	10,000 to 15,000 in 1 head
Kale	7,540 in ½ cup, cooked
Kidney, beef	1,150 in ½ cup cooked, cubed kidney
Lettuce, green	4,000 to 5,000 in 6 large leaves
Liver, fresh beef	19,200 in 1 piece, cooked
Liver, fresh calf	20,500 in 2 slices, cooked
Liver sausage	5,750 in 3 slices
Mango	1,000 to 1,500 in 1 mango
Margarine (A added) ...	1,980 in about 8 tablespoons
Milk, dry, whole	1,400 in 1 cup
Mustard greens	6,460 in 1 cup, cooked
Nectarines	2,800 in 2 nectarines
Olives, green	1,500 per pound
Papaya	2,500 to 3,000 in 1 papaya
Parsley	5,000 to 30,000 in 100 sprigs of parsley
Peaches, yellow	880 to 2,000 in every medium peach
Peaches, yellow, dried ...	3,000 to 3,250 in every medium peach
Peas, split	1,680 to 1 pound
Peppers, green	3,000 in 2 peppers
Peppers, red	2,000 in 2 peppers
Persimmons	2,600 in 1 persimmon
Prunes, dried	1,600 to 2,500 in 12 medium prunes
Pumpkin	1,200 to 3,400 in 1 cup, cooked
Sardines, canned in oil ..	1,080 per can
Spinach, fresh	9,420 in ½ cup, cooked

[115]

Foods	International Units of Vitamin A
Spinach, canned	5,500 to ½ cup
Squash, winter	4,950 in ½ cup, cooked
Sweet potatoes	7,700 in 1 medium potato, baked
Sweet potatoes, dehydrated	21,900 in 1 small potato
Sword fish	1,595 in 1 serving
Tomatoes, fresh	1,100 in 1 medium tomato
Tomato juice	4,770 in 1 pound
Tomato puree	8,540 in 1 pound
Turnip greens	9,540 in ½ cup, cooked
Watercress	4,000 in 1 bunch cress

CHAPTER 15

Vitamin A and Longevity

THE FOUNTAIN OF YOUTH! Since time immemorial man has been seeking it. And today the birthday of anyone over 80 rates a newspaper notice with the inevitable question "To what do you owe your long life?" How varied are the answers! For every ten people who declare, "I lived this long because I never touched liquor or tobacco" there are bound to be ten more who attribute their longevity to "a daily glass of beer and pipeful of tobacco." For every 90-year-old farmer who states he lived so long by keeping busy, there seems to be a 95-year-old watchman who knows that the only way to live to a ripe old age is to "take it easy."

And no doubt all of the answers are partly right. For surely each of us has his own peculiar make-up and, up to a certain point, what is one man's meat may be another man's poison.

But it seems to us that by now we should know more

than we do about growing old healthfully and happily, especially since our population is showing a steady increase in individuals over the age of 65.

It should not be too difficult, it seems to us, to determine by experiments with rats which elements in food lead to longevity and which do not seem to be related to long life. We are fairly certain of one thing—longevity appears to have some relation to heredity. In a volume entitled *Vitamins and Hormones* (Academic Press) appears an article by Dr. Clive M. McCay of the Laboratory of Animal Nutrition at Cornell University.

Dr. McCay tells us he believes that heredity influences longevity. He tells of one experiment at Cornell in which the careful records kept of each litter of rats indicated that a small number of the mother rats were responsible for a large per cent of the long-lived rats, and a small group of mother rats was responsible for the short-lived ones. In human experience it appears, too, that children and grandchildren may expect to live long if their ancestors did. Since there is absolutely nothing we can do about heredity, it would seem best for those of us who descend from short-lived parents to take special care with diet and other aspects of living so that we may bequeath to our children a longer expectation of life.

Dr. Henry Sherman of Columbia University has done a most intensive study on diet and longevity. His experiments were originally reported in the *Proceedings of the National Academy of Science* (Vol. 31, p. 107; Vol. 35, p. 90) and the *Journal of Nutrition* (Vol. 37, p. 467). Of course, the experiments have also been discussed as the classical experiments in this field by almost every writer on nutrition since that time. As you know, the life span of a laboratory rat is only a few

[118]

years, so that many generations of them can be studied in one man's lifetime. The rats used for these experiments were a community of the Osborne-Mendel strain. Their history showed that they were very normal, happy rats. There was nothing unusual at all about them. They had been living and thriving on diet A (whole wheat and milk) for 67 generations. So there can't be any question in anybody's mind about whether or not this diet was adequate. Hadn't it kept hundreds of rats healthful and fertile over 67 generations? (Remember, please, that rats make their own vitamin C, so they do not need the assortment of fresh fruits and vegetables we human beings need.)

Increasing the Amount of Vitamin A

Now suppose, said Dr. Sherman and his associates in this experiment, we should increase this adequate diet with considerably more of one of the vitamins, then we might get some idea of how longevity might be increased. So they took one group of the rat family and doubled their allowance of vitamin A. The gentleman rats survived for a 5 per cent longer time and their wives lived 10 per cent longer than any of their relatives on the "adequate" diet they had been eating over the years.

Then for one group of rats the amount of vitamin A in the diet was once again doubled without making any other change in the diet. Rats getting this quadruple quantity of viatmin A every day lived (for the males) 10 per cent longer and (for the females) 12 per cent longer than the other rats.

But, you may ask, of what use would these extra years be if you lived them in a state of senility, being a burden to those around you and not able to enjoy yourself? *The added years were not senile years.* It's

[119]

difficult with rats to decide on a criterion of "useful life." With these rats it was observed that the reproductive life of the females was increased in even larger proportion than the length of life.

In terms of human beings this means that double or quadruple amounts of vitamin A might bring about a 15 to 20 per cent increase in years of life, and an even greater increase than that in active and useful life. Roughly estimated it seems that we might expect to live to the age of 110 or 120 without any difficulty, and to be "in the prime of life" up to the age of 70 or even older. Incidentally when Dr. Sherman and his associates doubled the vitamin A ration once again, they found there was no further improvement. So it seems that you cannot go on and on adding vitamin A to the diet and increasing the benefit. There is, it appears, a level beyond which your body cannot use extra amounts of vitamin A. But it seems certain that this level is far, far higher than we have been led to believe up to now.

Many researchers feel that the daily recommended requirements have been set far too low. But here we have definite proof of how much too low they are— at any rate in the case of laboratory rats. And there is no reason to believe that the same would not be true of human beings. The recommended allowance of vitamin A is 5,000 International Units daily for an adult man or woman. Is it possible that 20,000 units daily would result in much better health and much greater length of useful lives? Until experiments with human beings have demonstrated this, we cannot say for sure. And this means we will never be able to know, for certainly human beings cannot be as rigidly controlled in their diet as rats and we doubt if there is any human being who would consent to be the subject of a nutritional experiment all his life. However, there seems to be no reason for not taking 20,000 units of vitamin A per day if you want to, and perhaps your own lengthened life will give you the answer.

Why Vitamin A Food Supplements Are So Essential

We must point out several other angles involved in the vitamin A story. If you are depending on your meals alone for vitamin A, keep in mind that vitamin A itself does not occur in foods. Carotene, which does occur in foods (yellow and green foods chiefly), is made into vitamin A by the body. If, through any disorder, you are not able to convert carotene into vitamin A and you are not taking any food supplement that contains vitamin A itself, then you will surely suffer from a deficiency.

Two New York physicians discovered and reported that diabetics are unable to transform carotene into vitamin A. This experiment, too, was performed with laboratory rats. All the rats were fed carotene rather than vitamin A. Then studies were done which showed that the diabetic rats had only one-fourth as much true vitamin A in their bodies as the nondiabetic ones. But when true vitamin A, as in fish liver oil, was fed, both the diabetic rats and their healthy controls showed an equal amount of vitamin A. Dr. Albert E. Sobel and Abraham Rosenberg of the Polytechnic Institute of Brooklyn, who made the announcement of these experiments, said, "these studies carry the clear indication that the diabetic rat must receive some source of preformed vitamin A, such as fish liver oils, rather than the usual carotene source, such as vegetables. The discovery that the conversion of carotene to vitamin A is impaired in experimental diabetes can be regarded as the first step toward the discovery of an agent to

[121]

control the premature aging of the arteries found in individuals suffering from diabetes mellitus."

Once again we have a link between vitamin A deficiency and aging! Now surely anyone who suffers from diabetes should be taking a fish liver oil supplement to prevent night blindness, skin disorders and the other symptoms of vitamin A deficiency, and those of us who suspect there is anything wrong with the function of our livers should also be taking fish liver oils, because liver disorders, too, interfere with conversion of carotene (in food) into vitamin A in the body.

Note please that the rats in Dr. Sherman's experiment were not kept on the just-adequate vitamin A diet until they began to approach middle age, and were then given the double and quadruple doses. No, they were fed from birth on the bigger doses. And the lesson here is plain for us to see. Most of us are not even conscious of our health, or of how we are taking care of it, until middle age or perhaps a little earlier when we contract some annoying disease, or begin to notice lines in our faces, or gray hairs, or bad teeth, and all of a sudden we scramble desperately around trying to make up for all the years we have ignored our health. Dr. Sherman's experiment does not show what will happen to rats whose diet is enriched with vitamin A late in life. But it does show that those growing up with it reap worth-while benefits. So our suggestion would be: if you have children, give those youngsters the best possible start toward a long and happy life by increasing their vitamin A, either in meals or supplements or both. And for those of us who are middle-aged or older, who knows? Perhaps increased vitamin A will postpone those wrinkles, gray hairs and other signs of aging for another 10, 15 or even 20 years! At least there's no reason not to give it a try!

[122]

CHAPTER 16

The Uncommon Services Vitamin A Performs

VITAMIN E is the specific nutrient most often mentioned in connection with the heart and the rest of the circulatory system. We do not mean to imply by this attention to vitamin E that other nutrients are not important to circulation. *All* nutrients are vital to good health, and each contributes directly or indirectly to the health of every organ of the body. We were pleased, therefore, to see an article in the *Medical Journal of Australia* (August 19, 1961) in which other nutrients, vitamins A and D, were discussed in connection with their value to the circulatory system.

F. C. H. Ross and A. H. Campbell became aware of the incomplete and inclusive information on the effects of vitamins A and D on the heart. For 10 years previous, Dr. Ross had used vitamins A and D in the treatment of certain patients. On studying the records of these patients, it became apparent that the group of patients treated with these nutrients had shown reduced incidence of heart disease. In trying to understand the reason for this effect, various explanations were suggested. One of the most obvious was the possibility that the vitamins influenced the body's use of cholesterol.

In order to check this, the effect of vitamin A and D capsules upon the incidence of coronary heart disease was observed over 5½ years in 136 patients, with 271 patients serving as controls. (That is, they received ordinary medication with no vitamins A and D added.) The capsules used each contained 6,000 units of vitamin A and 1,000 units of vitamin D suspended in 0.1 milliliter of peanut oil. They were given 3 times a day for a period of at least 6 months, from 2 to 5 years in most cases. Tests were set up to determine whether, in fact, the patients could objectively be considered as victims of heart disease.

Of the 407 patients observed, those in the treated group of 136 who developed coronary heart disease were only 8 (5.8 per cent), while the number in the untreated group of 271 who became afflicted was 43 (15.8 per cent).

Cholesterol Level Reduced

It was seen that the vitamin preparation had a definite effect on the serum cholesterol level when the level was above 250 milligrams per 100 milliliters. In 13 subjects the serum cholesterol level was reduced an average of 30 milligrams per milliliter after two to four weeks, a figure considered statistically significant. In contrast the untreated controls showed no significant alteration in their average cholesterol levels after a similar length of time.

As the data came in and the authors consulted other researchers, they became convinced that the vitamin A

[124]

was really the active ingredient in the capsules, with the vitamin D contribution uncertain. The authors then voiced some misgivings as to the amount of vitamin A being consumed by the average person. They noted that it is likely to be 15 per cent below the amount actually available in common foods, and that this is dangerously close to the recommended allowance of vitamin A. ". . . the minimal requirements of vitamin A are not know with certainty and the recommended figure may be too low to prevent a disordered cholesterol metabolism in older persons on a diet of high fat . . . it can be presumed that many individuals consume less than the estimated requirements."

Good Income No Guarantee of Good Nutrition

The writers further concerned themselves with the fact that high economic status does not guarantee an optimum intake of the proper nutrients. Furthermore, the authors write, "In Australia and America, owing to changing food habits, there has been a definite fall in vitamin A consumption per head in the last 20 or 30 years. . . . It is of interest also that in under-developed countries such as New Guinea with a low incidence of coronary heart disease, the vitamin A intake is high. . . . Of course, the fat-poor diet may be equally important in such groups. But the Eskimos, who are reputed to have a fat-rich diet with a low incidence of coronary heart disease, have a high vitamin A intake from fish and marine animal livers."

There are other areas of health in which vitamin A figures importantly and which are no more publicized than the coronary heart disease relationship. For example, *Nutrition Reviews* (August, 1959) tells of vitamin A in relation to oral cancer, the cancer that constitutes 8 or 10 per cent of all cancer observed in the

[125]

United States. N. H. Rowe and R. J. Corlin constructed a study to explore the possible relationship between a shortage of vitamin A and precancerous sores. Five groups of hamsters were set up with cancer-causing agents and vitamin A supplementation figured. The incidence of clinically observable tumors was so much greater in the unsupplemented group that "These data suggest that vitamin A deficiency increased the susceptibility of hamsters to carcinogen-induced benign and malignant tumors."

The removal of the stomach due to cancer or some very serious ulcer condition is likely to result in a strong vitamin A deficiency. The *Lancet* (February 20, 1960) carried a report on four men and a woman who had undergone such surgery and all showed vitamin A deficiency afterward. The authors decided that "vitamin A should be administered prophylactically [as a preventive measure] to patients who have undergone gastrectomy. A course of 100,000 International Units of vitamin A given daily for two weeks every six months, seems advisable." Patients who have undergone such serious surgery can ill afford to miss the valuable aid vitamin A can give in bringing the body back to good health.

There are of course many references in the literature to vitamin A as a treatment for acne and other skin diseases, as well as its happy effect on poor vision and its value as an infection-fighter. This chapter intends to cover the lesser known aspects of this vitamin's value in preserving health. In this connection it might be of interest to mention that drinking alcohol causes a rise in the vitamin A content of the blood stream, provided there is a normal store of it in the liver to draw from. So reliable is this reaction in animal experiments, that it can be used by a blood specialist

[126]

to tell if the liver does have a good vitamin A supply. (So says an ad in *Food Technology* [August, 1954] placed by Distillation Products Industries.) If the vitamin is present a drink of liquor will bring it into the blood, and if it does not show up in the blood, it can be assumed that the body is suffering from a basic shortage of vitamin A. If it is true that vitamin A shortage is related to heart disease, is it not possible that alcoholism and heart diseases have a connection through the vitamin A factor? If each drink demands more vitamin A from the liver's reserve, then a habitual drinker whose vitamin A intake is not what it should be could easily fall prey to heart disease brought on by a vitamin A shortage.

CHAPTER 17

Do You Need an A Supplement?

VITAMIN A has a strange power of creating controversy. It gets more publicity than most vitamins, and the public is torn between knowing the need for vitamin A and the fear of getting too much. Recent reports in the medical journals should improve vitamin A's reputation.

The white, frequently raised skin changes that sometimes occur on the mucous membranes inside the mouth, the nose or the genital organs, are known as leukoplakia, and are recognized by many researchers as a mark of vitamin A deficiency. This is cause for concern. Leukoplakia is a frequent forerunner of skin cancer. In the *Archives of Dermatology* (November, 1963) Johnson, Ringsdorf, and Cheraskin reported on the results of using vitamin A as an experimental treatment for leukoplakia. The doctors were working on the established fact that vitamin A is necessary for maintaining the outer skin as well as the internal lining of the body cavities. Significant degenerative changes inside the mouth were observed in animals suffering from vitamin A deficiency. In monkeys 10,000 units of vitamin A a day for thirty days returned affected gums to normal.

Enormous Doses Prescribed

In this study 40 patients received either synthetic vitamin A in 50,000-unit capsules or placebos of corn oil that closely resembled the vitamin A capsules. The patients were instructed to take a total of eight capsules a day (400,000 units), preferably two after each meal and two at bedtime. There were about 21 days between the initial and the final appointments. "It will be noted that the majority of the patients (95%) provided with the placebo remained unchanged. In contrast, one-half of those given vitamin A demonstrated qualitative improvement. . . . It will be noted . . . that no histopathologic change was noted in any of the individuals given placebo therapy. In contrast, 56% of the vitamin A subjects improved. . . . On a percentage frequency distribution basis, the majority of the vitamin A supplemented group improved in one or more of the methods utilized to measure change. In contrast the group given placebo medication remained essentially unchanged."

The enormous amounts of vitamin A used in this experiment did not cause a single unfortunate reaction in any of the patients. If there is a danger in the reasonable use of vitamin A supplements, it is hard to find evidence of it.

Dr. R. F. Krause, writing in the *American Journal of Clinical Nutrition* (June, 1965), describes a man who took 50,000 international units of vitamin A daily for

17 years as a supplement, with well balanced diet. He died of a stroke at 79. An autopsy showed that this large intake of vitamin A did not produce a single harmful effect. Examination of the patient's liver showed that storage of excessive amounts of vitamin A did not influence the composition of liver fatty acids at all.

In the *American Journal of Clinical Nutrition* (February, 1965) we are told that only eight cases of hypervitaminosis have ever been described in adults. The article describes a ninth case and warns against a possible overdose of vitamin A. At the same time the authors report that excessive intake of vitamin A must persist from eight to twelve months before any kind of disease symptom can be expected to show up. Another researcher says it takes at least 50,000 international units of vitamin A a day as a supplement for 18 months to produce any symptoms at all. Another reports that two million international units in a single dose is the only way to create acute hypervitamin A symptoms.

If It's Natural It's Safe

The type of vitamin A used as a supplement is important in its effect. In a letter to the *Journal of the American Medical Association* (December, 1962), Robert A. Peterman, M.D., reminded the physician readers that "conversion of pro-vitamin A carotenoids to vitamin A [the body's change of carotene vegetable substances to vitamin A] in vivo is very inefficient and is influenced by many factors. Extensive testing for toxicity done on pure beta-carotene, the most potent and important of the pro-vitamin A carotenoids, has provided compelling proof of the lack of toxicity of this compound and of its inability to cause a hypervitaminosis.

"Fifteen human subjects received daily oral dosages of beta-carotene equivalent to 100,000 international units of vitamin A for three months. Serum carotene values rose from an initial 128 to 308 after one month, but did not rise above this level during the remainder of the observation period. Serum vitamin A levels of these subjects *were not elevated* (his emphasis). There were no clinical signs of vitamin A toxicity, indicating that excessive amounts of beta-carotene are not absorbed after oral administration and that conversion to vitamin A does not automatically follow absorption." Dr. Peterman went on to remark that he knew of no diet anywhere in the world too high in carotenoids, but if there were, "our experience would not indicate that this would raise any question of hypervitaminosis A. The most that could happen would be widespread, but harmless, carotenemia [yellowing of the skin]."

Dr. Peterman seems convinced that vitamin A, as it occurs naturally in foods, can present no problem no matter how much we get. Vitamin A in a synthetic form may be something else. There is a productive marriage between vitamin A and other nutrients that occur together in foods. We never recommend that anyone take a supplement that is simply a single isolated vitamin. Every vitamin works best and is safest in its natural combination. For this reason, we recommend the fish liver oils supplements, which contain vitamins A and D, as well as other important nutritive elements which can work together for best effect. A single vitamin is a drug when it occurs in synthetic form and is best used under the supervision of a physician.

Even doctors who are most conscious of a possible overdose of vitamin A are aware of its necessity, and would urge that any patient be certain of a sufficient supply. Vitamin A's protection against night blindness, infection, skin irritations and blemishes is well known. Without sufficient vitamin A, genitourinary troubles are likely to sprout up. Stones in the bladder and other malfunctions are common consequences of vitamin A shortage. Goiter and vitamin A have also been linked by researchers.

Fertility Experiment

A report carried in the *Journal of Dairy Science* (June, 1963) gave strong evidence that vitamin A plays an important part in the quality of male semen. An experiment involving eight mature dairy bulls divided the bulls into two groups without regard to age or breed. All received the same balanced diet except that group two received a supplement of 45,000 units of vitamin A daily.

The trial lasted 29 weeks and semen samples were collected from each bull weekly. The results showed that "volume and concentration of spermatozoa were increased significantly in favor of the vitamin A supplemented group. . . . And a decrease in the percentage of abnormal spermatozoa was also observed in favor of the vitamin A supplemented group."

Supplementation of livestock feeds with vitamin A has become increasingly common. Beef cattle show vitamin A deficiency symptoms even though rations apparently contain adequate quantities of carotene. The problem is nitrates, commonly used in chemical fertilizers. Their presence in the feed reduces carotene conversion to vitamin A, and interrupts its absorption. In an article titled "Effect of Nitrates on Animal Metabolism" by W. M. Beeson of the Department of Animal Sciences at Purdue we read, "Man and animal have been poisoned by eating or drinking food and

[132]

water containing nitrates and/or nitrites . . . for many years. This is not a new problem; it has been recognized as a potential hazard to livestock production and human life by the medical and veterinary professions for more than 100 years. Since the end of World War II, the nitrate problem has become even more prevalent due to greater use of nitrogen fertilizer to increase crop yields and thus a higher level of nitrates in the soil, seeds and water. . . ."

If the nitrate problem is a hazard to livestock, it is a hazard to humans as well. Not only do we get the nitrates that cling to chemically fertilized foods grown everywhere, we get these compounds as additives to our processed foods. You are almost sure to get a dose of these chemicals when you buy a packaged meat. Not only do plant foods we eat contain less vitamin A (carotene) than they should, but nitrate-loaded foods destroy much of the vitamin A we do get into our systems.

Obviously we cannot presume that our regular diets give us all of the vitamin A we can use. We must plan to eat vitamin-A-rich foods to bolster a sagging supply. The especially rich ones include apricots, asparagus, carrots, cantaloupe, eggs, liver and kidneys, olives, parsley, peaches, peas, green peppers, pumpkin and sweet potatoes. But to be sure that our losses of vitamin A—due to modern methods of food raising and processing—are not going to affect our health, we should include a good fish liver oil supplement.

How much of a supplement should you take? How much can you take safely? Even the most conservative papers agree that 25,000 units of vitamin A a day is perfectly safe. We think that even the most timid vitamin A user should take that much. Many experts have stated that anything below 50,000 units a day is harm-

[133]

less and cannot cause hypervitaminosis A under any circumstances. This should suit persons who have some doubts about the amount of vitamin A they get from their diets. Those who wish to take even more of the vitamin regularly would do well to consult a physician, asking him to check for early signs of too much vitamin A.

Whatever you do, do not let yourself be discouraged from using supplementary vitamin A. Your body can't do without the proper amount of this nutrient, and a regular supplement is the only sure way to protect yourself against a deficiency.

CHAPTER 18

Unavoidable Nitrates Destroy Vitamin A

Look at the labeling on a package of hot dogs the next time you are in the market. You will find that they are loaded with sodium nitrate and sodium nitrite both. The same is true of any type of sausage or preserved meat you can find on your store shelves these days. As we have long warned, these artificial nitrates and nitrites are poisons. That is what makes them good preservatives. They kill the bacteria of decay, and while they will not kill you outright, in the long run their effect on you is just as deadly.

Sausages, however, at least are required to be labeled with the identities of the toxic preservatives they contain. We who know better can read the labels and avoid eating such foods. But what about a head of lettuce, an ear of corn or a cut of steak? These bear no labels at all, yet their burden of the poisonous nitrates keeps increasing year by year and for all we know may already be as great as that required to be specified on sausage labels so that those who wish to can avoid poisoning themselves.

An enlightening article on this subject has been published by the Purdue University Agricultural Experiment Station at Lafayette, Indiana. Dated April, 1964, it is titled "Effect of Nitrates on Animal Metabolism" and is by W. M. Beeson of the Department of Animal Sciences of Purdue. "Man and animal have been poisoned by eating or drinking food and water containing nitrates and/or nitrites . . . for many years," is the way this study begins. "This is not a new problem; it has been recognized as a potential hazard to livestock production and human life by the medical and veterinary professions for more than 100 years. Since the end of World War II, the nitrate problem has become even more prevalent due to greater use of nitrogen fertilizer to increase crop yields and thus a higher level of nitrates in the soil, seeds and water. As a result the livestock industry has two problems to consider: (1) nitrate toxicity and equally important (2) effect of sub-toxic levels of nitrates on animal performance, especially carotene and vitamin A metabolism."

Food Pollution Increasing

It is the so-called subtoxic levels with which we are concerned here, since obviously a food containing enough nitrate to kill us outright would not be permitted on the market. We are told by Mr. Beeson that the amount of nitrates to be found in plants increases with the increasing application of nitrogen fertilizer. It is also increased when anything interferes with normal plant growth, such as an unusually dry growing season, cool weather and the use of weed killers. "Immature plants (and what food is ever allowed to ripen

[136]

to maturity these days?) tend to be higher in nitrates than more mature plants . . ."

The most significant metabolic meaning of this, it is pointed out by Mr. Beeson, is that in the first place the plant foods being eaten contain far less vitamin A (carotene) than they should. And in the second place, these nitrate-loaded foods are destroying the vitamin A in our systems. Numerous researches are cited to show that nitrates and/or nitrites make it more difficult and sometimes impossible for the liver to store vitamin A. Also "the nitrate ion has been shown to depress thyroid function. . . . recently Sell and Roberts (1963) have clearly shown that feeding .4% dietary nitrite to chicks (one) depressed growth, (two) lowered vitamin A liver levels and (three) caused hypertrophy of the thyroid gland."

It is one more evidence of how wrong narrowly oriented scientific authorities can be when they measure the amount of vitamin A needed to prevent a frank deficiency and declare, with no consideration of this omnipresent vitamin A antagonist that we can hardly avoid if we want to go on eating, that we can get enough vitamin A in our foodstuffs. Have you noticed how many more children and teenagers these days need eyeglasses than used to even ten or twenty years ago? Have you noticed what large numbers of young people are afflicted with acne? Have you, perhaps, followed the vital statistics from year to year and observed that there has been a steady decline in the fertility rate in recent years?

These are all signs of vitamin A deficiency and one of the obvious big reasons that such a deficiency should be so prevalent is the increasing amount of nitrates to be found in our food supply.

It is a development that J. I. Rodale warned against

[137]

nine years ago, in a remarkable editorial that he wrote for the February, 1956, issue of *Organic Gardening* magazine. At that time Mr. Rodale said:

"Basically, the difference between using nitrogen in pure chemical form or in the form of animal manure or in that of a leaf is the same as the difference between feeding pure nitrogen to people in pill form as compared to giving it to them in scrambled eggs or peas. I see no other difference. What would happen to the race if our diet were to consist of pure inorganic chemicals? I know that it would become completely sterile in about four or five generations. Thus would the race die out.

"In agriculture we have the phrase, 'Dying out of the variety,' with respect to seed. The seed of a plant raised with chemical nitrogen gradually loses its reproductive potency over the years. Soon its production declines to an uneconomic level and the agricultural scientists have to build new vigor into it. What they do then is to hybridize, or cross the tired seed with some primitive variety which has grown in places where little chemical fertilizer has been used—places like Nicaragua, or, in the old days, in the interior of Russia—places where the nitrogen was not applied to the soil in the form of straight nitrogen but as part of leaves, weeds and manure. What would be the status of United States agriculture if we had continued to farm with the old seed can just about be imagined!

"In the leaf, the nitrogen is in a combination that nature made. For millions of years nitrogen in this form has fed plants and trees. When an earthworm dies, its body with its nitrogen in the form of protein, decomposes and furnishes food for growing things. That is how nature decreed it. But in a chemical fertilizer, nitrogen is not in the protein combination. It used to be in the form of straight nitrates, that is, nitrogen combined with only oxygen. Today they are using anhydrous ammonia a great deal (nitrogen and hydrogen). But these are pure chemicals without the benefits of the other things found in living protein, and which nature has a use for; otherwise she would not have put them there."

Soil Chemistry

Mr. Rodale continues, "Let us see what takes place in the soil with regard to nitrogen. It usually starts with ammonia. The bacteria in the soil, working on the organic matter, produce ammonia from it, and this cannot be done in any way except by means of the soil bacteria. The ammonia is then turned into a nitrite, then into a nitrate, also through soil bacteria, and is now ready for the plant. What I mean to bring out is that whether the ammonia is furnished in chemical fertilizer form or comes from the organic matter, it is the bacteria that must work upon it to produce the nitrite.

"The ammonia compound consists of nitrogen, hydrogen and oxygen. In the first step, the bacteria remove the hydrogen and make the nitrite, which is NO_2, that is, two atoms of oxygen and one of nitrogen. At this stage the nitrogen compound is a toxic and dangerous substance. By adding another atom of oxygen the nitrite is then transformed into a nitrate (NO_3) which loses the toxicity of its previous form. But nitrates can be unstable and revert to the poisonous nitrite form.

"In the *Agronomy Journal* for January, 1949, there was an article, 'Nitrate in Foods and its Relation to Health,' written by the late Dr. J. K. Wilson of the Cornell Department of Agronomy, in which he said, 'In 1943, the author pointed out that nitrates in the food of animals may be reduced by bacteria to nitrites

[139]

and that these are likely to cause poisoning through combination with the hemoglobin of the blood.' What Wilson means is that after the nitrite becomes a nitrate, it can revert to the nitrite form. Wilson then goes on: 'The nitrate content of any food is a direct measure of the potential amount of nitrite that may appear, and the toxicity that follows will depend on the rapidity of the reduction . . . The present practice of applying large applications of nitrate of soda to crops in order to produce succulent material with a bright green color and to obtain heavier yields may be responsible in most cases for the high content of nitrate in these foods.'

"Then Wilson sums up as follows: 'Leafy vegetables, frozen foods, and prepared baby foods were analyzed for their content of nitrate. From the findings it is suggested that the nitrate in such foods may contribute to hemoglobinemia found in infants and may produce certain toxic, if not lethal, conditions in adults. The high content of nitrate in the foods may be attributed in many instances to the application of nitrogenous fertilizers, especially nitrate of soda, to the growing crops.'

"The nitrate does not stand alone as such. It is part of a protein compound—and as we have mentioned before there can be trillions of variations in the formula for protein. Thus there can be variations in the quality of the protein, and in some of them the nitrate can be more stable than in others. From observation it has been seen that organically grown food makes healthier people and animals. The protein content is higher and of better quality. So it is not merely a question of, is nitrogen nitrogen, or is ammonia ammonia? Bacteria for millions of years have been breaking down organic matter to secure its nitrogen. Suddenly, the scientist appears on the scene and gives the bacteria an entirely different kind of synthetic raw material with which to work. There is some kind of difference, and the scientist should have been more thorough about finding it. He should have first tested its effect on human beings who eat such chemically produced food. This was never done.

"In the old days chemical fertilizers contained many 'impurities,' representing valuable trace mineral elements and organic matter. But as technology improved it led to the manufacture of purer forms of nitrogen, which led to more fragmentation and more danger— and higher prices, incidentally.

"In closing may I quote from an article by Sir Albert Howard, entitled 'Natural v. Artificial Nitrates,' which appeared in the August, 1945, issue of *Organic Gardening*. He said, 'Is it not reasonable to suppose that man, by his very nature, is incapable of producing with exactitude the natural elements of the earth? . . .*The New English Weekly* of March 29, 1945, supports this view, quoting the case of natural as compared with artificial nitrates:

" ' "It is always good to see the difference between natural and laboratory products emphasized, in recognition of the imponderable elements with which Nature endows substances, which can by no scientific skill be added to the synthetic product. The case in point is that of nitrates, and the Report emanates from one of the U.S.A. universities. It states:—'natural nitrates have something that the artificial lacks, and there is no completely adequate substitute for it in the field of agricultural fertilizers. Chilean nitrate contains small amounts of vital impurities such as magnesium, iodine, boron, calcium, potassium, lithium, and strontium, which are to plants what the vitamins in fresh foods are to human beings. It has been found that natural nitrate does something that makes apples stay on trees; that it does something to corn that results in better live stock fattened on it; that chickens raised on nitrated feed lay better eggs of greater fertility. It is just as impossible to make artificial nitrates that duplicate natural nitrates as it is to make synthetic sea water that contains all the elements of natural sea water."

" 'It is just here that the danger of scientific research lies. No scientist has ever produced, or is ever likely to produce, life, and the natural universe holds mysteries that will never be reduced to a formula or manufactured in the laboratory. The crucial test of real scientific achievement is whether it recognizes and respects the supremacy of Mother Earth, or ignorantly attempts to substitute the false for the true.' "

The words of Mr. Rodale and Sir Albert Howard are even truer today than when they were written. If it is at all possible, we urge our readers to limit their food consumption to foods that have been organically produced without pesticides or herbicides and with only natural fertilizer. We don't suppose that is entirely possible for anybody, though the higher percentage you can reach of restricting your diet to organic foods, the better off you're obviously going to be.

CHAPTER 19

The Glow of Vitamin A

COSMETICS FIRMS make millions selling potions to women who want to avoid dry, old-looking skin. Yet it's no secret among dermatologists that a woman can do her skin more good with a vitamin A supplement than she can by slathering expensive blends of sheep oil and hormones on her face. The vitamin can bring fullness and tone to her skin and even soften blemishes. Equally important to a lady who cares about her appearance, vitamin A helps to prevent colds and the puffy, weepy unattractiveness that comes with them.

Every medical or nutritional book treating vitamins in any detail mentions vitamin A's vital effect on the complexion. When the vitamin is short, the cells on the surface shrivel up and die, with several layers beneath doing exactly the same thing. The result is a wrinkly, dry, coarse appearance which is anything but attractive.

While researchers have long been aware of vitamin

A's ability to maintain the integrity of the skin, it remained for Hermann Pinkus, M.D., and Rosie Hunter, reporting in the *Journal of Investigative Dermatology* (January, 1964), to perform a direct experiment in which the accumulated hard, dry, dead cells were measured with and without a vitamin A supplement. The investigators used ten healthy adults and repeatedly stripped the dead cells from small areas on their arms by pulling away a piece of cellophane tape which took dead cells with it. The tape was scraped and the horny cells were counted.

Daily Vitamin A

With 150,000 units of vitamin A daily for a month, the number of horny cells that could be stripped off a single area decreased in all subjects. The number of healthy cells was increased in nine of the subjects. Vitamin A appeared to have a retarding effect on the development of the hardened (keratinated) cell. The researchers concluded that "vitamin A has an 'anti-keratinizing' effect and . . . this is achieved by cells remaining immature (young) longer."

What vitamin A does for the outer tissues of the body it does, more importantly, for the tissues inside. The mucous membranes are kept moist with vitamin A; without it the mucous secretions fall off. These changes may occur in the mouth, the respiratory tract, the urinary tract, the female genital tract, the prostate and seminal vesicles, and in the eyes and paraocular glands. When the cells in these membranes dry up, they slough off and clog organs, interfering with important systemic functions. Another function of the sticky, mucous-coated areas is to intercept infectious organisms before they can penetrate the body. This is disrupted when vitamin A is missing. For this reason a

[144]

lack of vitamin A is often a prelude to colds and more serious infections.

The normal retina of the eye carries vitamin A in combination with a specific protein (opsin), in the form of a pigment known as visual purple. When this visual purple is exposed to light, it must be converted to visual white. This reaction reverses with varying exposures to light and dark. However visual purple is only partially restored with each exposure, so a fresh supply of vitamin A must always be on tap to keep up the amount of visual purple necessary for good eyesight.

Bright Eyes Too

The imperfect fulfillment of this change back and forth causes impaired vision in dim light when it abruptly follows exposure to a bright light. This "night blindness," or lack of dark adaptation, is quickly normalized with supplementary vitamin A.

Speaking of vitamin A and the eyes, it is worth noting that the brightness and the clarity of the whites of the eye depend on vitamin A. The texture of the eyelids and the corners of the eyes is also maintained best when plenty of vitamin A is available.

Liver, eggs and fish liver oils give you straight vitamin A, but you get most of your supply in the form of carotene. Carotene, which occurs in abundance in dark green and deep yellow vegetables and yellow fruits, is converted by the body into vitamin A. For this conversion you need bile in the intestinal tract and conditions favorable to the absorption of fat in general. Chronic diarrhea, pancreas dysfunction, celiac disease, or sprue seriously interfere with the proper absorption of fats. An absence of bile or the surgical removal of major portions of the bowel can make you miss the

[145]

vitamin A you need. There can be a failure to convert the dietary carotene into biologically active vitamin A when liver disease, diabetes or hypothyroidism are present. Mineral oil taken as a laxative increases the danger that carotene and vitamin A absorption will be impeded because both dissolve in the mineral oil and can be carried right out through the intestinal tract. The liver stores about 95% of the body's vitamin A reserve and normally this amount increases with advancing age. Of course a pregnant or nursing mother requires more vitamin A at this time than any other.

Health-conscious people realize the pitfalls that threaten all vitamins before they can work for you, so they turn to supplementary vitamins for insurance.

Natural "A" Works Best

Which shall it be—natural or a synthetic vitamin A? Pick synthetic A and you get a version of distilled petroleum ether. We know that petroleum in almost any of its chemical forms can be a danger to humans, and has caused cancer in experimental animals. The alternative is a natural vitamin A supplement made from halibut or cod liver oil, also rich in vitamins D and E. Because fish liver oil must be handled carefully and used fresh, lest it turn rancid, many doctors lean on the more stable synthetic forms. It may not work as well, but it keeps.

The *New Scientist* (October, 1963) created a stir with a report that vitamin A in excess will cause cells to dissolve and damage cell membranes. Many readers glossed over the very significant information, that, in the experiment, vitamin A alcohol, a synthetic, was used. A synthetic substance might have the stated damaging effect on the cells, but there is a significant

[146]

difference between the laboratory manufactured vitamin A and the natural substance that occurs in food.

Observe what added natural vitamin A can do for the diet. In the *New York State Journal of Medicine* (January 15, 1964) Oswald A. Roels, Ph.D., Associate Professor of Nutrition at Columbia University, proves that vitamin A in the diet is necessary for the proper absorption and use of protein. In a study of 500 Indonesian children suffering from kwashiorkor, he found an intimate relationship between dietary vitamin A and protein. The same amounts of protein in the diet produced a much greater increase in height and weight when the diet also included vitamin A-rich palm oil. Also, a deficiency of protein cut down the absorption and utilization of the vitamin A. Obviously the two nutrients work much better together for the promotion and maintenance of good health than either of them could do separately.

Blind and Sterile

J. N. Thompson and others at the University of Liverpool, whose experiments were recorded in *Proceedings of the Royal Society* (series D, volume 159), found that male and female rats were rendered blind and sterile merely by being fed diets deficient in vitamin A. When foods containing substantial amounts of vitamin A were once more added to the diets, these effects were all reversed. The researchers concluded that vitamin A likely has an effect on fertility as well as on eye function in man.

These beneficial effects were obtained with natural vitamin A, ingested by eating natural foods. There was not a single toxic reaction of any kind reported. The natural vitamin only served to build and protect health. Yet we all know that this is not always true of the synthetic chemicalized version of vitamin A that the druggist sells and the doctor dispenses.

This very situation was described in scientific detail in *Nature* (October 10, 1964). Dr. J. A. Lucy and J. T. Dingle treated rabbits with vitamin A alcohol and this substance caused large indentations in the surfaces of certain cells. These cells became spherical and lost hemoglobin as breaks appeared in the membranes. It was noted that an instability of red cell membranes was produced by an excess of vitamin A alcohol, and that it took a vitamin E preparation to prevent this unwanted result.

In short it was concluded that vitamin A alcohol does penetrate the cell membrane and only the stabilizing action of vitamin E prevents the subsequent rapid rupturing of the cell membrane that occurs with excess vitamin A alcohol alone.

Obviously a natural source of vitamin A is the only sensible one to use. If for some reason, one should be forced to use synthetic vitamin A preparations, the inclusion of a vitamin E supplement somewhere in the diet is essential. Fish liver oil perles or fish liver oil in liquid form are the most reliable natural forms of vitamin A.

CHAPTER 20

Why Are They Slandering Vitamin A?

IT WILL HARDLY come as a surprise to anyone that there is a concerted campaign underway, in which the agencies of the Department of Health, Education and Welfare are cooperating, to discredit the value of vitamin supplements. One can only guess at the reasons. One guess is that as the nutritive quality of our food supply keeps deteriorating, because of chemical fertilizers, chemical additives to animal feeds, and the modern processing methods that try to replace old-fashioned quality, the food industries are getting increasingly sensitive to criticism that becomes more valid and widespread.

The best defense is a good offense, and it might have been expected that the food industries would respond to criticism by attacking the critics—those who point out that the way to protect yourself against less nutrition in foods is to take vitamin and mineral supplements. We have no way of knowing whether such a counter-

[149]

attack was actually decided upon in conference and planned. We do know, though, that the food industries have put enormous pressure on the periodicals in which they advertise to induce the publication of articles telling the public it doesn't need food supplements. We doubt very much that the food industry cares whether people buy supplements or not. But if they can discredit the advocates of supplements, they will be silencing their most dangerous critics.

Paid "Research"

Nor does the campaign stop there. After all, the food processing companies make large grants to colleges and can expect those colleges to pitch in with some scientific verification when they have a propaganda point to make. And lo and behold, in the past two years we have seen dozens of scientific articles —frequently articles on the great value of particular vitamins—interlarded with completely unnecessary and out-of-place remarks about there being no need for extra vitamins in the average diet.

Yet no matter how much power several billion dollars' worth of advertising and endowments may wield, it remains a tough job to find anything wrong with vitamins. Here are substances that are absolutely essential to human life and have been proven so. They do no harm, and they work miracles in hundreds of different ways. You could go over the country with a fine-tooth comb and not find a single user of vitamin supplements—at least the natural ones—who does not know that he feels better and is in better health for his habit of gaining full nutrition daily. It is possible to get too much of anything, of course. You can breathe too much oxygen, or eat too much liver, or drink too much water from a mountain spring. It isn't very likely, but it can be done. And in the same way, it is at least theoretically possible to get too much of a vitamin—especially one of the oil-soluble vitamins which are stored in the liver instead of being eliminated in the urine like those that are water-soluble.

We believe it is out of this propagandistic need to attack vitamins, and the fact that scientifically most vitamins are invulnerable to such attack, that we have lately been finding in the scientific literature a spate of rather pathetic attempts to discredit vitamin A.

Typical of them is an article that appeared in the April, 1964, issue of *Nutrition Reviews,* entitled "Toxic Reactions of Vitamin A." *Nutrition Reviews,* it should be pointed out, is published by the Nutrition Foundation of Park Avenue, New York, a "research" organization that is entirely supported by the food industry, executives of which make up its entire board of directors. The above-mentioned unsigned article makes a valiant effort to please the sponsors.

Toxic?

The first example it drags in of toxic reactions to vitamin A is one that was recorded back in 1943 when the *Biochemical Journal* published an account of a single person who had become ill after eating polar bear liver. Now polar bear liver is an uncommon food, to say the least, and one of the points of its uncommonness is that it contains fantastic amounts of vitamin A—20,000 international units per gram—which is 2,000 times as much as you will find in a vitamin A-rich food like beef liver. It might also be added that in the 21 years since 1943 there has not been recorded another single case of intoxication from eating polar bear liver. We'd say this is really scraping hard at the very bottom of the barrel, but what else can you do

[151]

if you have drawn the assignment of attacking vitamin A and have to find a way to do it?

"Actually, hypervitaminosis A seems to be relatively infrequent, judging from the paucity of published accounts," the anonymous author has to admit rather shamefacedly. But he is not so easily to be defeated. He has also managed to dredge up a more recent isolated case, one reported in the *Archives of Internal Medicine* in 1963, of a woman who got toxic reactions after dosing herself with 325,000 international units of vitamin A daily over a period of months. And this, we might add, was not in a natural form but was a vitamin A tablet she had bought in a drugstore.

The article we have quoted is perhaps a poor specimen. We think we could do a better job ourselves, if we felt that our readers needed any special warning about the obvious fact that we have pointed out hundreds of times in this magazine—that vitamins are potent and highly effective substances, which always involve certain dangers when they are taken singly and in isolation. Vitamins are not found singly in foods, and vitamin preparations should never be taken singly by any person concerned with his health. In the case of vitamin A, there is a definite interaction with vitamin D. Neither is as effective without the other. Either can be toxic without the other. And that is why we recommend the fish liver oils which contain vitamins A and D together as a source, and we never recommend that any reader take a supplement that is exclusively vitamin A or exclusively vitamin D.

An isolated vitamin taken in large quantity is a drug, and is dangerous even when administered by a doctor. To drug yourself this way, without the supervision of a doctor, is the height of folly.

But even when we have granted and proclaimed

[152]

this, the fact remains that any cases of actual adverse reaction to vitamin A are so few and far between, and depend on the ingestion of such ridiculously enormous quantities of the vitamin, that they are nearly meaningless for anyone of average intelligence. The benefits of the vitamin, on the other hand, are so common and widespread that you would really have to be an idiot to let yourself be frightened into depriving yourself of this absolute necessity in human diet.

Deficiency Dangerous

If your child is deficient in vitamin A he will probably develop rickets because without this vitamin, calcium and vitamin D cannot interact properly for bone formation. He will not grow properly. A person lacking vitamin A cannot see well at night and may be totally blind in a dim light. He will find it impossible to adjust to sudden changes of light. He will have a rough dry skin. He will get frequent colds. His hair will turn gray faster and his skin will wrinkle easier. All his mucous membranes, including those of the mouth and the genitourinary system, will tend to become hard and scaly. He may get stones in his bladder and he may also develop a goiter. And this is only the beginning of the many protective and health-building functions that vitamin A exercises—always in conjunction with the other vitamins and minerals, of course. Nutritional science today has not yet even discovered how vitamin A does its work, so you can imagine how far off we are from anything like a thorough catalog of all the work that vitamin A performs.

There are many foods that synthesize vitamin A. If they were organically fertilized and kept free of pesticides; if they were allowed to grow until mature; if they were distributed fresh and eaten fresh by you; you could in all probability get as much vitamin A as you need from your regular diet. You should still eat the vitamin A-rich foods, which are generally delicious and certainly good for you even if their nutritive store has been depleted. They include apricots, asparagus, carrots, cantaloupe, eggs, liver and kidneys, olives, parsley, peaches, peas, green and red peppers, pumpkin and sweet potatoes. Eat them by all means. And then, just to be sure that modern food processing is not robbing you of the full vitamin A nutrition you require, get yourself a good cod liver oil or halibut liver oil A and D supplement to take as well.

Don't let yourself be frightened by stories that are planted in newspapers about toxic reactions to vitamin A. They are scarce as hen's teeth, and then only to vitamin A taken as a drug, which is by no means what you are doing when you take an A and D supplement. You need the nutrition that vitamin A provides. Unless you develop a sudden taste for polar bear liver, we'll bet our bottom dollar it will never harm you.

CHAPTER 21

Don't Ignore These Lesser-Known Vitamins

ANYONE WHO CAN READ, and who is the least bit aware of nutritional elements in the diet, knows about the more common vitamins and minerals. He sees lists of added synthetic-nutrients on cereal boxes, white bread wrappers and patent medicine bottles—thiamin, vitamin C, iron, B_{12}, riboflavin, vitamin A, vitamin D are all familiar names. There are other vitamins, just as important to good health, which have not had the public relations job they deserve. This creates a danger because people tend to ignore them in their daily diets and in the supplements they use. We would like to sketch a few of the less prominent B vitamins here to make our readers aware of their value.

Inositol's modern claim to fame is its action against cholesterol. *Newsweek* magazine (September 11, 1950) reported a paper read to the 118th National Meeting of the American Chemical Society which offered evidence of inositol's power in lowering cholesterol levels.

The experiment was simple. Two groups of rabbits received one gram of cholesterol daily, while one of the groups got, in addition, half a gram of inositol. The animals were kept on a controlled diet. At the end of the experiment, the rabbits who were fed cholesterol alone showed a cholesterol increase of 337 per cent, while those fed inositol with their cholesterol dosage showed a much smaller increase, 181 per cent. The results were considered to be indicative—though not directly comparable to the effect inositol has on cholesterol readings in man.

Because inositol's status as a full-fledged B vitamin has been established only recently, there is much that is still to be learned of its activity in the human body. *Science News Letter* (May 19, 1956) reported that human blood serum can be replaced by inositol. It is needed for the growth and survival of cells in bone marrow, eye membranes, embryo, intestines, etc. The fact that inositol occurs in large amounts in tissues of the human brain, stomach, kidney, spleen, liver and the heart muscle, gives some clue to its value in the diet. Inositol also appears in desiccated thyroid gland and in human hair—a fact which has led to much speculation as to its value in restoring color to gray hair, or even restoring hair to bald heads!

Pre-operative Measure

In a booklet, *Inositol,* published by Corn Products Sales Company (Chemical Division), the observed physiological values of inositol are listed. For example, inositol given to those about to be operated on for stomach cancer is considered to be a valuable pre-operative procedure because it cuts down on total liver fats. It also seems to have a mild inhibitory action on certain types of cancer cells. In *Science* (97, 515, 1943) it was reported that intravenous injection of inositol into mice with transplanted cancers retards the growth of the tumors to a degree directly proportional to the dosage of the inositol.

Herbst and Bagley (*Journal of Urology,* 59, 505, 1948) administered inositol to six patients with cancer of the bladder, and concluded that it had a favorable effect. The original tumors were found to have lessened in size as a result of the treatment.

In the *American Journal of Digestive Diseases* (8, 290, 1941), inositol was pointed out as an agent against constipation. It was found by Martin, *et al.,* to have a marked effect on peristaltic action of the stomach and small intestine (that is, the muscular action which moves fecal waste through the alimentary canal).

Principal dietary sources for inositol are dried lima beans, beef brains, beef heart, desiccated liver, cantaloupe, grapefruit, peaches, peanuts, oranges, peas, raisins, wheat germ, cabbage, brewer's yeast and many other vegetables, meats and fruits in lesser amounts.

Choline

The value of choline in human existence is exemplified by the fact that it is richly contained in colostrum, the name given to the extra-rich milk mothers give in the first days of nursing—the milk nature provides to give the infant a good start in his weakest days. This has been enough to prod scientists on to finding what other services toward maintaining or regaining good health in later years choline could perform. The list is impressive.

Choline has been identified by University of Toronto researchers to be essential to the health of the heart and blood vessel system of young rats (*Science,* June 11, 1954). Young rats after short periods on a diet

[157]

low in choline and high in fat, as well as older rats on choline-deficient diets for longer periods, develop damaged heart arteries and aorta (the main artery of the heart). The walls of these important blood vessels get fat deposits and show hardening. The doctors also stated that choline is needed for healthy livers and kidneys. These findings were intended for further testing on higher species until their relationship to man could be established.

Favorable Action on Heart Disease

Choline's ability to act favorably in cases of heart disease was demonstrated by L. M. Morrison and W. F. Gonzales and recorded in the *Proceedings of the Society of Experimental Biology and Medicine* (January 1950). A group of 230 acute heart disease patients were studied. One hundred and fifteen of these served as controls. They were discharged from the hospital on recovery after about six weeks. They were then observed for a three-year period. The other 115 patients, when they were released from the hospital on the same basis as the first group, were also observed for three years. But during this time they were given a choline supplement for varying lengths of time—one, two or three years.

Of the 115 patients who did not receive choline, 35 patients, or 30 per cent, had died after three years. Only six of these died of a cause other than heart disease. In the choline-treated group of 115 patients, 14 patients, or 12 per cent, had died after three years. Five of these deaths were due to some cause other than heart disease.

In a German journal, *Deutsche Medizinische Wochenschrift* (February 16, 1951), choline was named as a successful agent in the treatment of hepatitis.

[158]

Thirty-seven patients were involved in this experiment. Ten of the 37 served as controls; other patients were treated only with choline and choline compounds. It was found that treatment with choline reduced the duration of virus hepatitis to about half.

An experiment described in an Italian journal was excerpted by the *Journal of the American Medical Association* (September 16, 1950). In this case the action of choline against hyperthyroid conditions was examined. Choline hydrochloride was administered to 14 women and one adolescent girl for two weeks—one gram by mouth daily. Eight patients took the medication, half strength, for another two weeks. By the 4th day to the 12th day the patients experienced a feeling of well-being. The circumference of the neck diminished by one centimeter. When the medication was stopped, the subjective symptoms reappeared in the majority of the patients. They were again controlled by reintroduction of the treatment. In three patients with acute hyperthyroidism, combined treatment with choline hydrochloride and 150,000 units of vitamin A every five days for two or three weeks gave good results.

Foods especially rich in choline are snap beans, soybeans, egg yolk, lamb kidney, beef liver, calves' liver, pork liver, peas, pork kidney, spinach, brewer's yeast and wheat germ.

Biotin

The B vitamin biotin, according to an article in *Scientific American* (June, 1961), is so potent that no human cell contains more than a trace of it. Liver, one of the richest sources, contains less than one part biotin per billion. Still it is an essential constituent. Earl Ubell, science editor of the *New York Herald Tribune*, explained the valuable function of biotin this

[159]

way in his column of April 16, 1959: "The biotin molecule . . . grabs a big protein molecule composed of thousands of atoms. . . . This new protein is capable of sweeping an atom of carbon dioxide and hooking it onto a number of other molecules which are important in the production of fat and other body substances. But here's the important step: the protein that does this cannot function without biotin. So, without biotin the body's fat production is impaired."

Avidin and Biotin

Researchers have found a poisonous substance, avidin, in raw egg white. If fed large doses of egg white, humans and animals develop skin rashes, loss of hair and muscular incoordination. Biotin acts as an antidote for this reaction, but the avidin removes biotin from whatever other important chemical work biotin performs. So, when biotin is busy counteracting avidin in egg white, it can't do its regular job, and this accounts for the rashes, hair loss, etc.

A severe rash, seborrheic dermatitis, and Leiner's disease, a condition which manifests itself in a burned-lobster appearance of the skin, are described in the *Journal of Pediatrics* (November, 1957) as due to a biotin deficiency. Nine cases of seborrheic dermatitis and two cases of Leiner's disease in infants are described as showing marked improvement when treated with biotin. The doses given were 5 milligrams of biotin injected intramuscularly daily for 7 to 14 days. Milder cases are affected well by 2 to 4 milligrams orally for two to three weeks.

Such a lack of biotin is a rarity. Biotin, as was seen above, is needed by the body in only minute amounts, but it *must be there.* You can be sure your quota is being met if these foods are frequently in your diet:

beef liver, lamb liver, unpolished rice, soybeans, soy flour, salmon, sardines, cauliflower, cow peas, brewer's yeast.

Natural Occurrence Important

It should be remembered that, as with all vitamins, we approve only of those which occur naturally. This is especially true of the B complex. They are safest and most effective when taken with their natural components. It is true that synthetic vitamins are used therapeutically or experimentally by doctors, but when this is done, it is done under controlled conditions, and the doctors are presumed to be on the lookout for nutritional imbalances which can create real problems.

We are impressed once more, as we go through the information on the more obscure B vitamins, that they are all contained in abundance in natural foods and natural food supplements—brewer's yeast, wheat germ, desiccated liver, all of the organ meats. If you are eating the natural way, if you are supplementing your diet to make up for the stresses caused by poisons you can't avoid in our modern environment, your B vitamin problems are solved. You are getting what you need to keep nerves, metabolism, digestion, etc., healthy.

CHAPTER 22

More on Mongolism

Dr. Ionel Rapaport, the University of Wisconsin psychologist who furnished statistical proof that fluoride in the drinking water at the level advocated by fluoridationists is associated with an increase in mongoloid births, is a very quiet man in the United States. His discoveries and conclusions have generally been ignored by American science. The Public Health Service, so far as its publications would indicate, has never checked into the brilliant Rapaport studies and apparently would rather not know their validity.

If you ask fluoridationists about the Rapaport investigations, they will dismiss them with the completely false statement that the mongolism link was discredited by the Berry report. We have previously examined the statistically weak and badly organized Berry report, and shown that far from discrediting the Rapaport conclusions, it actually lends them some confirmation when subjected to careful scrutiny.

Dr. Rapaport himself made a thorough and scathing reply to the Berry report, but not in the United States. It was published in the French scientific periodical, *La Nature*. We do not pretend to know why it is that Dr. Rapaport is so quiet on this side of the ocean. Is it because the American scientific journals refuse to publish his work? Is it because he has been bullied in some way and is afraid to take a public stand in defense of what he knows to be the truth? All we can do is guess what particular technique of suppression is being used against this brilliant scientist.

However it is done, Dr. Rapaport has apparently managed to pursue his researches, even though he has not managed to publicize them in the country most affected by them.

To learn what new information Dr. Rapaport is bringing to life about the relationships between fluorides and mongolism, you have to keep careful watch over the French medical literature. It was in the French *Bulletin of the National Academy of Medicine* (Volume 145, pp. 450-453) that we found a singularly significant contribution. It is an experiment that was conducted on drosophila flies to illuminate the mechanism by which fluoride intake can cause mongoloid births.

The drosophila is widely used for such experiments because its hereditary structure is a simple one, involving only four pairs of chromosomes, and those easily examined. In the human being there are 23 pairs and it is the existence of an extra chromosome (making three) of the number 21 type that most frequently characterizes the complex of physical and mental defects known as mongolism.

What Dr. Rapaport wished to investigate was the discovery by three French scientists, Jerome, Lejeune and Turpin, that in mongolism the system does not properly use tryptophane. This substance is one of the essential amino acids, the constituents of protein that the body cannot manufacture itself but must secure in the diet in order to maintain its normal metabolic process. If the tryptophane metabolism is abnormal in mongoloids, this raises the question of whether the abnormality might occur not as a result of the mongoloid condition, but rather as a cause of it. And since Dr. Rapaport had already discovered that there is an association between fluoride intake and the occurrence of mongolism, it raised in his mind the further question of whether fluoride can cause abnormalities of the tryptophane metabolism.

This is a question that was possible to investigate on the drosophila because this fly, with its extremely simple hereditary structure, also possesses a tryptophane metabolism.

For his experiment, Dr. Rapaport bred laboratory varieties of drosophila in a medium containing substantial amounts of sodium fluoride. His first important observation was that "a great number of males, reared in the fluorised medium, presented a reddish coloration of the eyes, instead of the apricot white of the controls." This is a strong indication of change in the tryptophane metabolism, since it is tryptophane that is responsible for the brownish red segment of the pigment in the eye of this fly. The change in color indicated that the metabolic transformations of tryptophane had been accelerated in some respects and retarded in others.

Another known effect of this kind of change in the drosophila is the development of melanic (dark pigmented) tumors. This occurred in 40.64% of the females and in 15.97% of the males.

It was also established experimentally that these

[164]

changes occurred more frequently as the age of the parent increased. This is consistent with the knowledge that the rate of mongoloid births in human beings increases with the age of the mothers.

Dr. Rapaport's conclusion is that the study is significant, in that it reveals the mechanism by which dietary fluoride may alter heredity and cause the mutation-like mongoloid, by disturbing and altering the metabolism of the essential amino acid tryptophane in the mother, and subsequently in the child.

One caution: Do not make the mistake of supposing that the finding that fluoride can cause a type of cancer in drosophila flies also means that fluoridated water will cause the same cancer in humans. The amounts of fluoride used for these experimental purposes were far larger than the one part per million in fluoridated water. And this particular experiment was framed as it was because it is known that irregularities in tryptophane metabolism will cause melanotic cancer in the drosophila. Although it might conceivably do the same in human beings, it has never been shown that this is so and there is no particular reason to suspect it.

CHAPTER 23

Diarrhea Can Be Dangerous

THE DISCOMFORT of diarrhea is the least important thing about it. What really counts is that diarrhea, continued long enough, can deplete your nutritional reserves so that you are ripe for infection and serious illness. Diet can do more to prevent and treat diarrhea than any drug known. What you eat determines how well your body will hold up under the strain, and how quickly you will get back to normal.

Most of us have suffered the type of diarrhea which occurs with stomach cramps that come and go after a day or two. For an adult this is not serious, and if left alone, the body will soon return to normal. However, there are types of diarrhea that continue for weeks and even years. These can be a serious threat to the body and steps must be taken to make up for the great nutritional losses that occur with such a chronic problem. Intestinal surgery can result in chronic diarrhea. So can malformed intestines or poor function of the muscles involved in normal elimination. Aside from these mechanical problems there are allergenic and infectious diseases which cause serious diarrhea. Chief among these is celiac disease or sprue. Trouble with the pancreas or the liver can also result in prolonged diarrhea.

Replace Potassium

Patients who have chronic diarrhea have large, frequent stools with excessive loss of water volume, and with it much of the potassium necessary for other body functions. These losses must be replaced through careful diet. Until they are, the victims of chronic diarrhea appear listless, fatigued and show a distended abdomen. Inside, tissues are depleted and nutritional values in circulating plasma are thrown off. Foods rich in potassium, such as fresh fruit and vegetables, and fish and meats (particularly organ meats) can be used to restore the losses and promote weight gain.

A shortage of potassium also means a disturbance in the muscle tone of the bowels, and this disrupts the peristalsis reflex (the wave-like motions of the intestines which push waste into the colon). Normal peristalsis is vital for the proper use of fats from foods. Further, the bowel, stretched because there is a loss of muscle tone, causes pain and vomiting along with a loss of appetite.

The important nutrients frequently lost in diarrhea were discussed in the *Journal of the American Medical Association* (April 14, 1962). Among the first to go is iron. Chronic diarrhea is associated with the inability to absorb enough iron, and over a period of years the body stores are depleted. Sometimes iron takes folic acid and vitamin B_{12} along with it. Dr. Frank H. Gardner suggested in the article that generous supple-

[167]

ments of ascorbic acid be included when one replaces the iron. He wrote, "We believe that patients with this depletion absorb medicinal iron better when it is administered with ascorbic acid."

The *JAMA* article noted that vitamin B_{12} absorption depends on its combination with calcium for full benefit to the body. When certain types of diarrhea are present, calcium forms insoluble compounds and passes right through. Therefore calcium supplements can be valuable to insure vitamin B_{12} absorption. This is especially true in patients with celiac disease who lose extremely large amounts of calcium.

Low levels of vitamin C in patients with diarrhea are easily understood: many patients simply don't have the appetite to eat enough foods rich in vitamin C; the vitamin C is poorly absorbed because the lining of the bowel is damaged; in diarrhea the demand for vitamin C increases because a sick body uses it more rapidly than a healthy one; and finally, disease-causing bacteria frequently present with diarrhea absorb vitamin C before it can be used by the body. No wonder Dr. Gardner suggests massive amounts of ascorbic acid when diarrhea occurs.

Gluten Allergy

Of course, the best known cause of celiac disease and sprue with their frightening diarrhea symptoms is allergy to gluten-containing grains—barley, wheat and rye cereals are particularly named. When they are excluded from the diet, patients can absorb fats, proteins and vitamins again and the problem of diarrhea usually corrects itself. It is *Prevention's* feeling that diarrhea is just one of the problems involved with most cereal foods, and an individual is much better off to avoid them altogether, whether he is allergic or not.

Obviously a well-rounded selection of vitamin-rich foods along with regular intake of natural food supplements—to assure a steady supply of the nutrients mentioned above—is the best way to prevent diarrhea and the best way to handle it if it should occur. There are certain foods, however, which seem to have a particular power in the treatment of diarrhea. Many doctors have found them safer and more effective than antibiotics and other drugs which can have serious side effects that only complicate the diarrhea problem. Bananas and carob (St. John's bread) are two foods which have a good record as treatments for diarrhea.

In the *South African Practitioner* (January, 1959) Thomas R. Plowright, M.D., of Fresno, California, told of his experience in using carob to treat an outbreak of diarrhea among a group of migrant workers during the harvest season. All of the children were under four and some of them were as young as one year of age. An average of 50 cases of diarrhea a month at the local hospital was usual. Dr. Plowright concluded that poor eating habits, inadequate diet, excessive exposure to heat and bad sanitary conditions at the camps were causing the diarrhea. The children brought to the hospital were having as many as 15 to 20 stools a day and all of the usual anti-diarrhea medications failed.

Desperation Measure

Desperation led Dr. Plowright to try a preparation of carob flour on half of the 40 babies in the hospital. All the usual treatments began with a period of no feeding at all, followed by a highly mineralized preparation given with diluted boiled milk. As the child improved, the strength of the milk was increased until he was discharged. The 20 babies participating in the

[169]

experiment received the same treatment, except that they were given a 5 per cent solution of carob flour preparation—as much as could be tolerated every four hours. As soon as a true-formed stool was passed, the carob preparation was diluted half and half with the infant's "going home" formula. The babies on the carob preparation went home within a little more than seven days, while the usual stay on the regular treatment was a little over 14 days.

We like to recommend carob flour as a food rather than a medicine. It can be sprinkled on fruit or used as a flavor in fruit drinks. It has a rather sweet "chocolate" flavor that children seem to enjoy. Above all it is a very worthwhile food containing vitamins and minerals in ample quantity. Whether or not you make carob a regular part of your menu, why not have some on hand for use in case of sudden attacks of diarrhea? It is not readily available at the supermarkets and usually has to be gotten through a health food store or a mail order supplement house, so keep a supply.

Try Bananas

Many mothers depend on the anti-diarrheal action of bananas for both prevention and treatment and they include them in their children's diets frequently. According to Dr. J. H. Fries in the *Journal of Pediatrics* (37:367, 1950) bananas are more valuable than apples and other raw fruits in their antidiarrheal action. This supports the findings of E. W. Bruebaker in the *Journal of the Michigan Medical Society* (36: 40, 1937), who described the treatment of 56 cases of diarrhea in infant children. Those who were treated with bananas recovered faster than controls who were given other therapy.

According to Dr. Fries the pectin contained in

[170]

bananas swells and causes voluminous soft, bland stools that clear out the intestines; the number and kind of intestinal organisms are changed favorably because bacteria are absorbed by the pectin and the growth of beneficial bacteria species is promoted; bananas also help to maintain nourishment and weight.

The measures one must take against diarrhea are plain enough. First be sure that your diet is high in nutrition-rich foods, and that you are taking a complement of natural vitamins and minerals which can compensate for any diarrhea losses. Meanwhile add extra carob, or pectin-rich food such as bananas or applesauce to your usual menu. This should be effective for adults as well as infants.

Do not ignore persistent diarrhea. It can be a very serious, sometimes fatal, disease.

CHAPTER 24

Thiamin

VITAMIN B₁ IS also called thiamin. It has been known as an important factor in human nutrition for almost 50 years. New discoveries about its effect on body processes are still being made from time to time. Vitamin B₁ deficiency is being studied with great attention as a possible cause of polio; cancer researchers are studying its effect on the incidence of cancer; vitamin B₁ is a preventive of sea and air sickness.

Severe vitamin B₁ deficiency results in the disease called beriberi, rather unusual in this country, but formerly a common ailment of Oriental people who lived chiefly on polished rice. The seriousness of this disease in the Japanese navy near the beginning of this century interested a medical officer in experimenting with the diet of the sailors. He found that a diet including barley, vegetables, fish, meat and milk eliminated the disease. Now vitamin B₁ has been chemically analyzed, named thiamin, and made synthetically.

Symptoms of beriberi are numbness and tingling in the toes and feet, stiffness in ankles, pains in legs and finally paralysis of leg muscles. As the disease becomes worse, disturbances of heart function may occur. Similar symptoms of less severity may indicate a milder deficiency of vitamin B_1—not enough to cause beriberi, but enough to do serious damage to the body.

Why We Need Vitamin B_1

Thiamin is also necessary for growth. Laboratory animals deprived of thiamin develop more slowly and do not attain to the growth of their brothers and sisters who are on a diet containing an ample amount of this vitamin. Thiamin promotes good appetite and better functioning of the digestive tract. It improves the muscles of the stomach and intestines and has often been effective in curing stubborn cases of constipation.

Thiamin also plays an important part in the oxidation process that goes on constantly in each individual body cell. It is an active part of a co-enzyme which is necessary for the oxidation of pyruvic acid, one of the products of carbohydrate oxidation. In other words, the enzyme which carries on this process requires a collaborator (in this case, thiamin) to do its work properly. Nervous tissue is especially dependent on carbohydrate oxidation for its functioning, so nervous tissue is one of the first to show the effect of vitamin B_1 deficiency. This is the reason why thiamin has been called the "morale vitamin," for a lack of it results in depression, irritability, fatigue and inability to concentrate.

Since carbohydrate oxidation goes on at a rapid rate when hard physical work is done, a larger amount of thiamin is needed by someone who works hard physically. Although small amounts of it are stored in certain body tissues, any amount more than the body needs is excreted in the urine each day. Therefore it becomes necessary to include thiamin in each day's diet in ample quantities. The eating of sugar, as well as excessive smoking and drinking, depletes the body's store of thiamin, so more of the vitamin is needed by persons who can't control their sweet tooth, and by those who use tobacco and alcohol.

Authorities do not agree completely on the daily human requirement of thiamin, for their figures depend on whether you wish to take only the minimum amount (which will barely protect you from signs of deficiency) or the optimal amount which some authorities feel is the best guarantee of robust health. The daily allowances recommended by the Committee on Foods and Nutrition of the National Research Council are:

Men—moderately active	1.8 milligrams
very active	2.3 milligrams
sedentary	1.5 milligrams
Women—moderately active	1.5 milligrams
very active	1.8 milligrams
sedentary	1.2 milligrams
Pregnant women	1.8 milligrams
Nursing mothers	2.3 milligrams
Children under 1 year	0.4 milligrams
1-3 years old	0.6 milligrams
4-6 years old	0.8 milligrams
7-9 years old	1.0 milligrams
10-12 years old	1.2 milligrams
Girls 13-15 years old	1.4 milligrams
16-20 years old	1.2 milligrams
Boys 13-15 years old	1.6 milligrams
16-20 years old	2.0 milligrams

Loss of Thiamin in Storage and Cooking

In mature, dry, unbroken seeds (grains of wheat, for instance) loss of thiamin in storage is apparently very slight. When foods are heated with dry heat, they lose less thiamin than if they are cooked in water. There is also less loss in an acid than an alkaline solution. For instance, adding soda to beans that are cooking doubles the destruction of the thiamin. Losses of thiamin in roasted meat are high because of the high temperature. Take this into account when you are figuring the thiamin content of your beef roasts. Toasting bread at a high temperature destroys some thiamin, too. It is hardly necessary to point out that all foods retain more vitamin content when they are stored (covered from the air) in the refrigerator or in a cool place. When you cook vegetables, the cooking water should be saved. It contains valuable amounts of vitamin B_1 as well as other vitamins. Use it in soups or broths.

Vitamin B_1 Deficiency and Bread

The main reason why vitamin B_1 deficiency is quite general in America is that one of the richest sources of this vitamin is wheat germ which is, by present milling methods, removed from the flour we use. In the average diet where bread forms a large item (toast for breakfast, sandwiches for lunch) we are consuming a food that is sadly lacking in vitamin B_1. Unless we make up for it with quantities of other vitamin B_1 foods we're bound to have deficiencies. At present most bread and flour in this country is "enriched," meaning that a specific amount of thiamin and other B vitamins have been added synthetically to the flour.

However, many medical researchers have shown that once a natural substance is removed from a food, it cannot be replaced by chemists in exactly the right proportions and combinations to produce the same nutritional effect as natural foods. By the same token,

[175]

experiments have shown that synthetic vitamin preparations cannot correct vitamin deficiencies as well as natural preparations do. Take your vitamins in natural preparations.

When books on nutrition call our modern white bread "enriched," the quotation marks indicate, as often as not, the author's doubt as to whether the bread has been enriched after all, in a form that the body can use. Well, then, what about bakers' whole wheat bread? In most cases a preservative has been added (a) to keep insects from consuming the flour before it reached the baker and (b) to keep the bread from molding before it reaches the consumer. These preservatives are strong chemicals—so toxic that insects know better than to eat them, powerful enough to prevent mold from growing. This is why bakers' whole wheat bread is worse for you than bakers' white bread.

Foods that contain vitamin B_1 in significant amounts are listed here. Be sure you include enough of them in every day's menu. By "enough" we mean simply that each member of your family should receive from his everyday meals enough thiamin to make up the recommended daily requirement for his age and occupation. If he is not getting enough at meals (and most of us are not), he should supplement his food with brewer's yeast and wheat germ, both of which are rich in vitamin B_1.

Foods Containing the Largest Amounts of Vitamin B_1 (Thiamin)

Foods	Milligrams in Vitamin B_1
Almonds	.25 in 100 almonds
Asparagus, fresh	.16 in 12 stalks
Avocado	.12 in ½ avocado
Bacon, medium fat	.42 in 12 slices broiled
Barley, whole	.40 in 6 tablespoons

Foods	Milligrams in Vitamin B_1
Beans, fresh limas	.25 in ½ cup cooked
Beans, dried limas	.60 in ½ cup cooked
Beef brains	.25 in 2 slices
Beef heart	.54 in 2 slices
Beef, lean	.10 to .13 in average serving
Bran, wheat	.52 in 4 cups
Bread, bakers' light rye	.16 in 4 slices
Bread, bakers' whole wheat ..	.28 in 4 slices
Brussels sprouts	.11 in 7 sprouts cooked
Cashew nuts	.66 in about 60 nuts
Cauliflower	.09 in ¼ of a small head
Collards	.19 in ½ cup, cooked
Cornmeal, white, whole grain	.41 in 100 grams
Cornmeal, yellow, whole grain	.45 in 100 grams
Crackers, graham	.30 in 10 crackers
Dandelion greens	.19 in 1 cup steamed
Egg yolk, fresh	.32 in 6 yolks
Farina, enriched	.37 in ½ cup
Figs, dried	.13 in 6 medium figs
Flour, buckwheat	.31 in 100 grams
Flour, rye, whole	.47 in 100 grams
Flour, soy	.82 in 100 grams
Flour, whole wheat	.56 in 100 grams
Ham, lean, fresh	.96 in 1 slice
Ham, lean, smoked	.78 in 1 slice
Ham, picnic	.94 in 1 slice
Hominy	.15 in ½ cup cooked
Kidney, beef	.45 in ½ cup diced
Lamb, leg, roast	.21 in 2 slices
Lentils, dried, split	.73 in 1½ cups
Liver, beef, fresh	.27 in 1 slice
Liver, calf, fresh	.52 in 2 slices
Milk, dried skim	.35 in 10 tablespoons
Milk, dried whole	.30 in 10 tablespoons
Oatmeal, rolled oats	.55 in ¼ cup uncooked
Peanut butter	.20 in 6 tablespoons
Peanuts, roasted	.30 in 100 peanuts
Peas, chick	.35 in 1½ cup cooked
Peas, fresh green	.36 in 1 cup cooked
Peas, split	.87 in 1½ cup cooked
Pecans	.72 in 100 pecans
Plums, fresh	.15 in 2 plums
Pork, lean loin	1.04 in 1 slice

Foods	*Milligrams in Vitamin B₁*
Pork, salt	.18 in 1 piece broiled
Pork, sausage	.22 in 6 links cooked
Pork, spareribs	.92 in 5 pieces cooked
Raisins, seeded	.15 in 1 cup
Rice, brown, unpolished	.29 in ¾ cup steamed
Soybeans	1.14 in ½ cup dried
Turnip greens	.10 in ½ cup steamed
Veal, chops	.18 in 2 medium chops
Veal, cutlet	.18 in 1 slice
Veal, leg roast	.17 in 2 slices
Veal, stew meat	.17 in 4 slices
Walnuts, black	.33 in about 100 nuts
Walnuts, English	.48 in about 100 nuts
Wheat bran	.52 in 5 cups
Wheat, entire	.56 in 10 tablespoons
Wheat germ	.68 plus in about 3 tablespoons
Yeast, brewer's	3.23 plus in about 3 tablespoons

CHAPTER 25

Thiamin and the Ability to Learn

All of us know by now that good nutrition results in better health, fewer infections, more endurance and stamina. We know that we improve physically when our diet is adequate in vitamins, minerals and enzymes. Does diet have any effect on *mental* health and *mental* processes? Why not? Are not the nerves and the brain cells affected by that same good diet that assures us of healthy skin, teeth and eyes? Recently we came across a book which fascinated us, for it dealt with this very subject—nutrition and its relation to one aspect of mentality.

Written by Ruth Flinn Harrell, Ph.D., *Effect of Added Thiamin on Learning* tells the story of an experiment which really began years ago when Dr. Harrell observed a curious phenomenon in a patient at Johns Hopkins Hospital. This young man had been in an accident and was suffering from aphasia—the loss of the power of expression by speech or writing. He was being re-educated so that he might speak and write once more. While this lengthy process was going on, the patient suddenly began to learn at a much more rapid rate than before. So decided was his improvement that he was very soon cured and back in his old job.

Dr. Harrell became intensely interested in the reason for this sudden spurt in learning capacity. She carefully went over every minute detail of this patient's environment in the hospital and could find nothing unusual except that, five or six days before this sudden acceleration in learning took place, a B-vitamin product had been added to the patient's diet. Investigating further, Dr. Harrell observed experiments on white rats which learned to follow the intricacies of mazes much more rapidly when their diet contained this product. Experimenting further, she worked with several children who had never learned to speak and were considered so mentally handicapped that language was beyond their capacity. These children learned much more rapidly when vitamin B complex was added to their diet and, in two instances, developed speech and were able to live as normal children.

The processes of learning are complex indeed. In spite of hundreds of years of devoted and learned study, we still do not understand fully what biological, chemical, nervous, mental or electrical processes go on in the human body when we are learning something. But something in the vitamin B complex appeared to make this process easier and faster. Dr. Harrell believes that ". . . learning is, at least in part, conditioned by the presence or absence of a particular food constituent. If that be the case, it would appear further that there is a certain nutritional state of the nervous system which must be realized for the effective utilization by the learner of the teaching he receives."

[180]

Importance of Thiamin to Nerves

She quotes two other authorities. Bruno Minz, working at the Laboratory of the Sorbonne University in Paris, announced in 1938 that a cut nerve exuded a liquid which was found on analysis to contain thiamin and that an electrically stimulated nerve gave off 80 times more thiamin per unit of volume than a resting nerve. R. R. Williams, in a lecture reprinted by *Yale University Press* in 1939, summarizes the facts known up to that time: "It is now known that the passage of a train of impulses over a nerve fiber results in a chemical alteration of the fiber itself which must constantly be repaired by active metabolic processes within the fiber if it is to continue to respond to repetitions of the stimulus. The nature of the mechanism involved has long been surmised in a general way to be catalytic, for it would not be possible to account reasonably for the very large physiological effects which are produced by minute quantities of the substance except on the assumption that the vitamin is used over and over again."

The word "catalytic" used by Dr. Williams indicates a process that takes place in the presence of some substance that is not itself involved or used up in the process. For example, carbohydrate foods can be turned into energy by oxidation in the body. But for this process to take place, certain vitamins must be present. They are present in very small amounts and they do not actually became energy themselves—they just act as the spark to bring about this desired reaction. Protein foods are used by the body as building materials for cells, but they can be used only when certain vitamins (or catalysts) are present.

Dr. Harrell planned, organized and executed a scien-

[181]

tific experiment involving human beings, to discover exactly what is the effect of thiamin on the process of learning. This six-week experiment took place at the Presbyterian Orphans Home at Lynchburg, Virginia. One hundred and four children ranging in age from 9 to 19 were involved. At the beginning of the experiment the children were divided into two groups, as nearly alike as possible, according to age, health, intelligence, background and so forth. This was to guarantee as nearly as possible that the two groups would begin the experiment evenly matched.

Throughout the six-week experiment, every child in the orphanage took a pill before going to bed. Half of the children received in this pill two milligrams of thiamin. The other half swallowed a pill which looked, smelled and tasted exactly like the thiamin pill, but which contained nothing of any food value. No one involved in the experiment—including Dr. Harrell, the personnel of the orphanage or the children—had any idea at any time which children got the thiamin and which did not. The one person who had this information was hundreds of miles away keeping records of the experiment which were mailed to her each day. All this caution was for the purpose of making certain that no psychological factors could possibly influence the results. No teacher could, perhaps unconsciously, favor the children taking thiamin—she had no idea who they were.

All the children devoted some time each week to the taking of certain tests in learning. The mental tests included mathematics, completing designs, encircling numbers whose sum is 10, underlining all 4's on a page full of numbers, etc.—all of the tests frequently used in studying children's mentality. The physical tests included such things as throwing baseballs and darts and testing the strength of grip in the right and left hand. In addition, tests for the accuracy of hearing were given to all children before and after the experiment.

In the initial test of hearing, Group A, the one which was not getting the vitamin, scored higher than Group B, indicating keener hearing in both right and left ears in this group generally. On repetition of the tests six weeks later, it was found that Group B was superior to A in acuteness of hearing in both right and left ears. In taking the first learning test, Group A scored higher than Group B, showing that there was just a little more mental and physical skill among the Group A children to begin with. However, over six weeks, Group B made measurably greater gains than Group A in every single one of the 18 activities to test learning ability.

Checking over daily events after the experiment was over, it was found that there had been eight accidents or illnesses, such as cuts, burns, etc., among the children of Group B and only one such example is Group A. Yet, in spite of this, Group B gained about one-fourth more in learning ability than Group A over the six weeks of the experiment! The vitamin had done the job.

The public school system in our country is among the most progressive in the world. It has money to provide magnificent buildings with study, athletic and recreational facilities that are unmatched. Modern school systems are not concerned only with instilling facts into the brain of a young person. They also aim to turn out a complete, mature, self-sufficient personality.

Considering all this, how does it happen that Dr. Harrell's book has, so far as we know, gone completely unnoticed in school board and faculty circles? Here is absolute proof that an infinitely small amount of *one vitamin* given over the ridiculously short period of six weeks can produce children who are superior both mentally and physically. What astonishing results could be obtained over a period of years, feeding ample amounts of all the vitamins!

Probably our national apathy about diet problems is responsible. Also a great deal of blame must be laid to the food manufacturing companies, whose advertising has convinced, or almost convinced, Mr. and Mrs. America that their food is everything it should be. Yet over 50 per cent of the average American diet consists of white sugar and refined cereals and their products —worthless as food and potentially dangerous, for their assimilation by the body uses up precious stores of vitamins and minerals which are not replaced by our daily diet.

What can we do about it? First of all, we can make certain that our own children get plenty of vitamins and minerals in their everyday diet and in food supplements. Then, as civic-minded individuals, we are naturally concerned about our neighbors' children. Why not make good nutrition a year's project for the Parent-Teacher Association? You'll have to watch carefully that the program doesn't degenerate into a dull recital of the facts everybody already knows about nutrition—that we must have proteins, carbohydrates and fats, that we should eat fruits and vegetables, that children should drink milk—everyone will get bored with a program like this. *You* have the responsibility of keeping before the group the facts that are not well-known about nutrition.

CHAPTER 26

You Can't Afford to Have a B₁ Deficiency

AFTER ABOUT 20 to 35 days the normal patient develops the first symptoms: easy fatigue, loss of appetite, irritability and emotional instability. This describes the first days of a deficiency of vitamin B_1 (thiamin), according to the *Pennsylvania Medical Journal* (June, 1943). Sounds familiar, doesn't it? Probably everyone reading these pages can think of several acquaintances who have exhibited these very traits and wondered what was wrong.

As the deficiency progresses, confusion and loss of memory appear, followed closely by gastric distress, abdominal pains and constipation. Heart irregularities crop up, and finally, prickling sensations in the lower extremities, impaired vibratory sense and tenderness over the calf muscles.

The article goes on to say that to secure a beneficial therapeutic result, a constant intake of B_1 must be maintained. This vitamin cannot be stored in the body in significant amounts, for most of it is excreted. An individual who was receiving 100 milligrams of B_1 a day, by mouth, was found to excrete 86 milligrams in the feces and 11 milligrams in the urine. It is obvious from this that close watch must be maintained on one's thiamin intake, for a single day without it could wipe out even a healthy person's supply. Where illness or stress of any kind is involved, and the vitamins are called upon to help in repairing damage, the vigil against shortages becomes even more necessary.

The value of thiamin in treating certain physical and mental disorders has been illustrated through articles in the medical journals of the world. Here are some of the reports filed by scientists on their experience with this nutrient.

B_1 Essential To Pregnant Women

In the *Journal of Pediatrics* (September, 1944) D. W. Van Gelder and F. U. Darby told of beriberi occurring in infants and even being present at birth. The authors blame this condition on the diet of the mother, either in pregnancy or during lactation. An adequate intake of all the B vitamins is essential at these times. For infants with large heart (a symptom of beriberi), in whom no other reason for this condition is apparent, large doses of thiamin hydrochloride are recommended. Also, in the case of a nursing mother whose diet is nutritionally lacking, the child should receive additional B_1 until foods containing this vitamin are added to his diet.

In the *Texas State Medical Journal* (May, 1943) L. P. Hightower advocates the administration of vitamin B_1 to all patients with indefinite heart symptoms, particularly if there is a history of dietary deficiency.

He recommends injections of 100 milligrams of thiamin per day, accompanied by a diet high in vitamin-B-rich foods. We are told that this is usually followed by prompt improvement. The size of the heart is reduced and encouraging alterations appear in the electrocardiogram.

An article in the *British Heart Journal* (January, 1944), by A. Schott, describes three cases of circulatory disturbances due to vitamin B_1 deficiency. Two of the patients had taken excessive amounts of alcohol (known to take a toll of the B vitamins in the body), and the third patient's condition was caused by deficient diet only. Each of the three responded favorably to treatment with thiamin.

In reviewing the possible causes of vitamin B_1 deficiency, C. J. O'Sullivan, in the *Journal of the Irish Medical Association* (April, 1952), lists insufficient dietary intake, defective utilization, inadequate absorption, interference from antibiotics in the intestines and increased demand in illness, fever and pregnancy.

Heart Failure a Common Symptom

Dr. O'Sullivan tells of a 72-year-old man who seemed to be suffering from bronchitis and failure of the right side of the heart. Antibiotics and cardiac therapy were begun, but response was poor. The patient worsened slightly during six days of this treatment.

Attending doctors decided to review his nutritional history, and found him suffering from an inadequate B vitamin intake. The diagnosis was changed to right heart failure on a thiamin deficiency basis. Dramatic and early response followed treatment with 100-milligram injections of thiamin, plus thiamin tablets. The heart disease symptoms ceased and the patient was soon walking.

[187]

The doctor commented that the unusual feature of this case was the complete absence, apart from heart failure, of the usual classical signs of B₁ deficiency. It may be, he goes on, that the fatal right heart failure of some illnesses is due to this thiamin deficiency developed during such an illness, due to poor storage capacity in the body for vitamin B₁ and partly to the inadequate diet of such individuals. Any increased demand then, coupled with lack of appetite, usual in such cases, could conspire to such a consequence.

We wonder how many heart patients are told to include a good intake of B-vitamin-rich foods, such as brewer's yeast and the organ meats in their diet? Even well persons need this fortification. Certainly a heart patient needs everything in the way of good nutrition that he can get. Desiccated liver is a good source of B vitamins and is especially valuable for low-fat diets because the fat has been removed.

Alcohol Can Cause Thiamin Deficiency

Alcoholism and the deficiency of B vitamins are often mentioned together, and rightfully so. A letter to the *British Medical Journal* (December 4, 1945), stated the situation exactly. It explained that alcohol does not inhibit the action of vitamin B₁ but that the high caloric value of alcohol increases the patient's requirement for all the B vitamins. At the same time, the alcoholic, from lack of appetite, reduces his dietary intake. Alcoholic psychoses probably are due, says the correspondent, to a lack of vitamin B₁ and niacin, both of which are needed to process carbohydrates such as alcohol. These vitamins are being used much faster than they are replaced, if they are replaced at all. The signs of vitamin B₁ deficiency are usually the first to appear, though an alcoholic suffers from many nutritional deficiencies.

It has been suggested that a shortage of B_1 is what makes an alcoholic turn to drink in the first place. He feels a hunger for some lack, and tries to satisfy this craving with alcohol. Of course, this only aggravates the craving and increases the lack, and a vicious cycle is soon operating.

Sciatica and Herpes Zoster

Victims of sciatica, the painful inflammation of the sciatic nerve which runs down the back of the thigh and leg, can take some hope from a letter by E. Braner, which appeared in the *British Medical Journal* (April 15, 1944). He told of obtaining good results from the use of vitamin B_1 injections in treating this disease. For quick results Dr. Braner used ampules containing 25 milligrams of thiamin per cubic centimeter. Three to six injections on consecutive, or alternate, days were given.

Herpes zoster, that stubborn and painful clustering of small blisters near the ear (sometimes called shingles), was effectively treated with thiamin by A. L. Oriz (*Medical World,* November, 1958) in 25 cases. The patients were given intramuscular injections of 200 milligrams of thiamin hydrochloride daily, but the doctor expressed the opinion that even a lesser dosage would have been equally effective.

S. Waldman and L. Pelner told of similar results (*New York State Medical Journal,* September 15, 1947). Twenty-three cases of herpes zoster were treated with a combination injection consisting of 1 cubic centimeter of thiamin (100 milligrams per cubic centimeter) and 1 cubic centimeter neostigmine methylsulphate (1 : 2000). The injection was repeated every other day until the severe pain was relieved. In seven cases, two injections were enough to bring results; and in 13 others six injections or less were required. Of the remaining three patients, two did not continue the treatment, and one got relief from vertebral injections.

These results strike us as remarkable, considering that many physicians tell their patients they have no cure for this ailment.

Impairment of the field of vision, as well as the ability to focus, known as amblyopia, is usually connected with the consumption of alcohol and tobacco. F. D. Carroll, in the *American Journal of Ophthalmology* (June, 1945), tells of a case in which about half of the patient's calories came from alcohol, with his consumption of B vitamins considered inadequate. Without decreasing tobacco or alcohol consumption, or improving diet, normal vision was restored by administration of 40 milligrams of thiamin per day by mouth, and 20 by vein. Improvement was maintained after the hospital stay as long as the patient took two 10-milligram tablets of thiamin a day; without them vision became impaired.

Taking Some of the Pain Out of Dentistry

In dentistry the use of vitamin B₁ has shown itself to be beneficial in a number of ways, as witness the article by J. L. E. Bock (*U.S. Armed Forces Medical Journal*, March, 1953). Dr. Bock says that dental postoperative pain is promptly and completely relieved in most patients by the administration of thiamin, and much pain can be prevented by using thiamin before the operation. The healing time of drying tooth sockets is greatly reduced by thiamin therapy.

The low pain threshold which is peculiar to many dental patients may be indicative of thiamin deficiency.

[190]

In most cases dental pain is relieved promptly by the oral infiltration of 10 milligrams of thiamin hydrochloride, the results being equal to 100 milligrams injected intramuscularly.

It is quite possible, says Bock, that the loss of thiamin from the nerves is one of the major chemical factors in the production of pain. There is ample evidence that replacement of free thiamin to injured and diseased nerves not only restores proper functioning, but relieves pain. Perhaps thiamin is not the sole factor in producing pain, but, says Bock, it is of prime importance in nerve physiology and should be given whenever a problem concerning the nerves arises, or is suspected.

Morning Sickness Responds to B₁

As we have seen earlier, in pregnancy a thiamin deficiency in the mother can result in the same condition in the child, when he is born, or can show itself in a nursing baby as the result of thiamin-poor milk from the mother. In tests of 50 patients, 16 of whom were pregnant women, Lockhart, Kirkwood and Harris (*American Journal of Obstetrics and Gynecology,* September, 1943) found that, in late pregnancy and early post-delivery, the thiamin requirement is three times that of a nonpregnant woman.

Many expectant mothers suffer from almost constant nausea and vomiting. In the *American Journal of Obstetrics and Gynecology* (August, 1942), an article tells of complete relief from this condition by the administration of vitamins B₁ and B₆ intramuscularly or intravenously. The dosage of B₁ was 25 to 100 milligrams and the B₆ was usually 50 milligrams. The number of injections and the intervals between them varied with individual patients. Of 44 patients treated with thiamin, 6 showed excellent results, 33 improved in varying degrees and 5 showed no improvement. Vitamin B_6 gave even better results, completely relieving nausea in 12 of 36 cases, and varying improvement in the rest. Two of the patients were relieved of accompanying migraine. None had any undesirable side reactions.

Even better results for vitamin B_1 were recorded in the correspondence section of the *Journal of the American Medical Association* (July 22, 1944). M. M. Marbel tells of an English study of constant vomiting among pregnant women. Each patient was given an intramuscular injection of 100 milligrams of thiamin hydrochloride every other day. Fifty per cent improvement was noted after the first injection, and the vomiting ceased after the fourth and fifth injection in every case. All the patients gained weight within a week, and went on a general diet, after a week, without any recurrence of vomiting.

These are but a few of the findings on the therapeutic effectiveness of vitamin B_1 as contained in a compilation published by Merck and Company, Inc. Why doctors don't make more use of this information we do not know. Perhaps they haven't the time to read the necessary literature. If this is the case, any doctor should be grateful to have these facts brought to his attention. We can think of no other legitimate reason a doctor would have for ignoring these authoritative findings, when they might be effective in treating a patient. In every case researchers pointed out that there were no dangerous side-effects from the theraputic use of thiamin. How many of the popularly used drugs can claim as much?

CHAPTER 27

Riboflavin

RIBOFLAVIN IS ONE of the B-complex vitamins, which means that it occurs mostly in foods in which the other B vitamins occur and that it will probably be lacking in a diet in which the other B vitamins are also deficient. Riboflavin is soluble in water rather than in fat. Although cooking does not destroy much of the riboflavin in food, cooking in an alkaline solution causes serious loss of the vitamin. This is one reason why we caution never to use baking soda when cooking vegetables.

Exposure to light also causes considerable loss of riboflavin. For instance, a bottle of milk standing on the porch in daylight loses from 50 to 70 per cent of its riboflavin within two hours. Five to 15 per cent of the riboflavin in milk is lost in pasteurization or irradiation with ultraviolet rays.

Nutritionists, in general, believe that riboflavin deficiency is the most common vitamin deficiency in

America. It occurs in individuals for one or several of these reasons: 1. long established faulty dietary habits; 2. food idiosyncrasies ("I don't like salads, I won't eat liver!"); 3. chronic addiction to alcohol; 4. arbitrarily selected diets for relief of symptoms of digestive trouble; 5. prolonged following of a restricted diet in the treatment of a disease such as peptic ulcer, chronic colitis, diabetes and so forth. There are cases, too, of individuals who are unable to assimilate riboflavin because of a faulty secretion of hydrochloric acid in the stomach or a lack of phosphorus in their diets. (Bone meal is rich in phosphorus.)

Symptoms of Riboflavin Deficiency

Serious riboflavin deficiency causes disease symptoms in the skin, mouth, lips and eyes. They are: reddened, bald-looking patches on the lips, with cracks at the corners of the mouth; a purple or magenta-colored tongue; scaly outbreaks around the nose, forehead and ears; burning and dryness of the eyes; photophobia (great distress in very bright light); disorders of the cornea of the eye; in some cases a burning sensation in the feet; trembling, dizziness, mental sluggishness and lack of normal sensations in the legs. There also may be a "twilight blindness" somewhat like the "night blindness" caused by lack of vitamin A. Then, too, lack of riboflavin seems to make one more susceptible to infectious diseases.

How or why the lack of riboflavin causes these particular symptoms is not known. What we do know is that riboflavin is an active part of several enzymes (complex substances that are necessary to the oxidation process in the body). Riboflavin is carried to various cells where it helps in the complicated process of metabolism.

[194]

There is disagreement among the experts as to how much riboflavin we need every day. In general this boils down to whether you want to take only that amount that will protect you from signs of deficiency or whether you want to take much more than that, for flourishing, robust health. Incidentally, when a great deal of fat is taken in the diet, the need for riboflavin increases. The standard daily requirements of riboflavin as determined by the Food and Nutrition Board of the National Research Council are:

Men, moderately active	2.7 milligrams per day
very active	3.3 milligrams per day
sedentary	2.2 milligrams per day
Women, moderately active	2.2 milligrams per day
very active	2.7 milligrams per day
sedentary	1.8 milligrams per day
Infants under one year	.6 milligrams per day
1-3 years old	.9 milligrams per day
4-6 years old	1.2 milligrams per day
7-9 years old	1.5 milligrams per day
10-12 years old	1.8 milligrams per day
Girls 13-15 years old	2.0 milligrams per day
16-20 years old	1.8 milligrams per day
Boys 13-15 years old	2.4 milligrams per day
16-20 years old	3.0 milligrams per day
Pregnant women	2.5 milligrams per day
Nursing mothers	3.0 milligrams per day

Foods Containing the Largest Amounts of Riboflavin (Vitamin B₂)

Foods	Milligrams of Riboflavin
Beans, dried soy	.31 in ½ cup
Beans, kidney or navy, dried	.24 to .32 in ½ cup
Beans, lima, dried	.24 to .75 in ½ cup
Beet tops	.17 to .30 in ½ cup steamed
Bluefish	.07 to .20 in 1 piece
Cheese, Cheddar	.50 to .55 in 5 one-inch cubes
Cheese, cottage	.29 in 5 tablespoons
Cheese, Roquefort	.45 in 2 sectors
Cheese, Swiss	.37 to .52 in 4 slices

Foods	Milligrams of Riboflavin
Collard greens	.22 in ½ cup steamed
Crabmeat	.23 to .35 in ½ cup
Eggs, fresh, whole	.34 in 2 eggs
Endive (escarole)	.20 in 1 head
Flour, soy	.34 in 4 ounces
Flour, stone-ground whole wheat .	.48 in 4 ounces
Hazelnuts	.40 in 4 ounces
Heart, beef	.60 to .90 in 2 slices
Heart, lamb	.60 in 2 slices
Heart, pork	.54 in 2 slices
Hickory nuts	.60 in 4 ounces
Kidney, beef, lamb or pork ..	1.95 to 2.1 in ½ cup cubed
Lamb, leg, roast	.26 in 2 slices
Liver, fresh beef	2.80 in 1 slice
Liver, fresh calf	3.30 in 2 slices
Mackerel	.20 in 1 piece
Milk, whole fresh	.17 in ½ cup
Milk, dried whole	1.50 in ¾ cup
Milk, dried skim	1.96 in 10 tablespoons
Mustard greens	.20 to .37 in 1 cup steamed
Oysters, solids and liquids ...	.23 to .46 in 5 oysters
Peanut butter	.16 to .32 in 6 tablespoons
Peanuts, roasted	.16 to .50 in about 100
Peas, fresh green	.18 to .21 in 1 cup steamed
Pork, loin	.20 in 1 slice
Spinach	.24 to .30 in ½ cup steamed
Turkey	.19 to .24 in 2 slices
Turnip greens	.35 to .56 in ½ cup
Veal, chops	.27 in 2 small chops
Veal, cutlet	.28 in 1 small slice
Veal, roast	.27 in 2 slices
Veal, stew meat	.26 in 3 slices
Watercress	.22 in 1 bunch
Wheat, bran	.35 to .60 in 4 ounces
Wheat, germ	.48 to 1.50 in 4 ounces
Whey	5.9 in 4 ounces
Yeast, brewer's	5.45 in 4 ounces

CHAPTER 28

Niacin

THE WORD "pellagra" probably has little significance for most of us who are eating even a reasonably good diet. But not so long ago this disease was widespread, especially in the southern part of our country. It was suspected for a long time that pellagra was a deficiency disease, for it appeared chiefly among families who lived mostly on corn and corn products. The reason for this one-sided diet was that sharecroppers and poor farmers did not raise their own vegetables and fruits, did not have their own cows and, because of their poverty, could not buy meat, milk or fresh produce from the store.

As it turned out, after many years of research, corn does not produce pellagra, but a dependence on corn products to the exclusion of other vitamin-rich foods results in pellagra. Pellagra causes a painful skin disorder, inflammation of the tongue and lining of the mouth, and serious digestive disorders, as well as mental depression. The three *D*'s of pellagra, in doctors' terminology, are "depression, dermatitis and diarrhea."

The long-sought cure for pellagra was niacin, the third of the B vitamins. Niacin (or nicotinic acid as it used to be called) was familiar to chemists 75 years ago, but it was not known until more recently that it is a member of the B complex of vitamins. While pellagra has been improved by the giving of niacin, it has been found that this is a disease involving many different deficiencies, so that all the vitamins of the B complex are probably involved along with niacin in effecting a cure. It is also interesting to note that the intake of other foods complicates the requirement for niacin. "The idea is still prevalent," says one famous nutritionist, "that dietary inadequacy implies semi-starvation." It is hard for most people to understand that all the food eaten affects the whole picture of nutrition or malnutrition. Someone may be eating a diet high in the calories of sugar and starch which will provide a lot of energy, but will also result in a deficiency of niacin. The quantity of it you need is directly related to the amount of sugar and starches you eat and the amount of energy you use up during the course of the day.

Symptoms of Niacin Deficiency

Assuming that none of us is suffering from pellagra, why should we be interested in getting enough niacin? The symptoms of niacin deficiency, less than that involved in pellagra, are everywhere. Look around you and you will probably find many friends and members of your family suffering from one or another of these physical symptoms: tender gums, diarrhea, nausea, insomnia, indigestion, abdominal pain, irritability, loss

[198]

of appetite. Mental symptoms include: neurasthenia, anxiety, dizziness, fatigue, numbness in various parts of the body, backache, headache, melancholy, depression. When the body's need for niacin is not satisfied, a brave and hearty person may become tired, apprehensive and pessimistic. He will constantly expect accidents and disasters; his entire personality may change. His friends may tell him with long faces that he is having a "nervous breakdown," when all that may be the matter is a deficiency of niacin, which usually accompanies a thiamin deficiency, as these two B vitamins occur in many of the same foods.

Niacin Forms Enzymes

One of the functions of niacin in the body is to form enzymes (body chemicals) which are part of the chemical chain that assimilates sugars and starches. When the amount of niacin in the diet is insufficient, none of the enzyme systems that deal with the digestion of carbohydrates can function, so various disorders of the digestive tract and the nervous system result. Because of the complexity of the way our bodies function, a breakdown in the niacin-containing enzymes brings about a breakdown in the bodily functions of riboflavin and thiamin, two other B vitamins. So, even if you are getting enough of these two vitamins, they will do you no good so long as you do not get enough niacin as well.

Finally, niacin is the vitamin B a derivative of which has just been announced as the cure for tuberculosis. So you see that this vitamin B is very powerful and necessary.

How Much Niacin Do We Need?

The recommended daily requirements for niacin have been set as follows:

[199]

	Milligrams
Men, moderately active	18
very active	23
sedentary	15
Women, moderately active	15
very active	18
sedentary	12
Pregnant women	18
Nursing mothers	23
Children under one year—up to	4
1-3 years	6
4-6 years	8
7-9 years	10
10-12 years	12
Girls 13-15 years	14
16-20 years	12
Boys 13-15 years	16
16-20 years	20

Foods Containing the Largest Amounts of Niacin

This vitamin is produced synthetically and you will find synthetic niacin in various vitamin products for sale at your drugstore. The niacin used to "enrich" breakfast foods and bread is synthetic. We advocate taking only natural vitamins, in the foods in which they appear in nature, so we urge you not to waste your money buying synthetic niacin. It has been shown again and again in experiments that synthetic vitamins do not produce the results that natural vitamins do, especially in the case of the B vitamins, where nutritionists agree that foods containing all of the B complex are superior in every way to any one of the B vitamins taken separately. Brewer's yeast and desiccated liver are two of the richest sources of niacin and all the other vitamins of the B complex.

Food	Milligrams of Niacin
Almonds	5 in 80 almonds
Beef, fresh chuck	5 in 2 slices
Beef, hamburger	4.3 in 1 hamburger cake

Food	Milligrams of Niacin
Beef, loin steaks	4.6 in 1 steak
Beef, rib steaks	4.7 in 2 slices
Beef, round steak	5.2 in 1 piece
Beef, rump	4.2 in 2 slices
Beef, soup meat	5.5 in 2-3 pieces
Beef, stew meat	4.3 in 3 pieces
Beef, tongue	5 in 12 slices
Buckwheat	4 in 100 grams
Chicken	8.6 in 3 slices
Fish, medium fat	4.2 in 1 piece
Flour, whole wheat	5.6 in 100 grams
Ham, fresh	4.1 in 1 slice
Heart, beef	6.8 in 2 slices
Heart, pork	8 in 2 slices
Kidney, beef	10 in ½ cup cubed
Lamb, leg roast	5.9 in 2 slices
Lamb, shoulder roast	5.2 in 4 slices
Lamb, sirloin chops	5.9 in 2 chops
Lentils, dried	3 in 1½ cup cooked
Liver, fresh	16.1 in 1 piece
Mackerel, Atlantic	5.8 in ½ cup
Mackerel, Pacific	8.7 in ½ cup
Mushrooms	6 in 7 mushrooms
Peanut butter	16.2 in 5 tablespoons
Peanuts, roasted	16.2 in 100 peanuts
Pork, Boston butt	4.5 in 1 slice
Pork, loin	4.4 in 1 slice
Pork, spareribs	3.9 in 4 pieces
Rice, brown	4.6 in ¾ cup
Salmon	7.4 in 1 piece
Swordfish	9.1 in 1 piece
Turkey	7.9 in 2 slices
Veal, chops	6.3 in 2 medium chops
Veal, cutlet	6.4 in 1 slice
Veal, roast	6.3 in 2 slices
Veal, stew meat	6 in 4 slices
Wheat bran	32 in 4 cups
Wheat germ	4.6-7 in 12 tablespoons
Yeast, brewer's	36.2 in 12 tablespoons

CHAPTER 29

Pyridoxine

THE B COMPLEX is still a great mystery to nutritionists. There are probably many more B vitamins as yet undiscovered, and in future years we may find that many conditions classified today as "diseases" may be simply deficiency states of one or another of the unknown B vitamins. To those of us who are not scientists, it may seem strange that chemists can know with absolute certainty that other chemical compounds are present in a substance like yeast, for instance, aside from the known vitamins, yet they cannot identify these compounds, synthesize them or even guess at what their function may be. The science of nutrition has made such great strides in recent years that we may be sure many of these mysteries will be solved in the near future.

Meanwhile—and we cannot stress this point too strongly—it is wisest to take any B vitamin not by itself in a synthetic form, but in some natural food substance, such as brewer's yeast or desiccated liver, which contains all the B vitamins, known and unknown. They interact with one another in many complex ways and taking only one or two may throw out of balance the function of all the rest, with serious consequences.

Pyridoxine, one of these fractions of the B vitamins, formerly called vitamin B_6, was isolated by scientists in 1938 and made synthetically the following year. There is still considerable controversy among nutritionists as to its importance in human nutrition, but it is generally agreed that pyridoxine is a necessary element in a healthy diet. Different animals on a diet deficient in pyridoxine react differently. Rats develop a severe skin condition in which their paws, ears and noses become sore and swollen. Their muscle tone deteriorates, resulting in drooping shoulders, weakness and a peculiar gait. Further deficiency brings on insomnia, nervousness and damaged heart muscles. In dogs, lack of pyridoxine brings on anemia; in pigs it produces convulsions, like epilepsy; in other animals it results in nervousness, tenseness, irritability and sometimes paralysis.

Pyridoxine in Human Nutrition

In human nutrition, pyridoxine has been used in curing some symptoms of the disease pellagra which were not improved by other B vitamins. It has been given in treatment of muscular rigidity and the stiffness and tremor which often afflict the hands of elderly people. However, not nearly enough experiments have been conducted. Some researchers have reported results with pyridoxine that seem almost miraculous. Others have had little or no success in using it. So it seems that the activity of pyridoxine in human nutrition is very complex and must be given considerably more study before nutritionists agree on recommending how much pyridoxine a person needs each day.

From what research has been done, it seems that pyridoxine is needed by the body to break down into usable substances certain of the amino acids, or proteins, in much the same way that thiamin (vitamin B_1) acts to break down carbohydrates so that the body can use them. The amount of pyridoxine one needs, then, may depend partly on how much one eats of these certain proteins.

The Council on Pharmacy and Chemistry of the American Medical Association, reporting on the status of pyridoxine research in 1951, reviews a number of cases of "morning sickness" in pregnancy which were relieved by the administration of pyridoxine. They also tell us that in the mouse, the amount of pyridoxine needed depends to some extent on the amount of protein in the diet. With the rat, dog, mouse and chick, the amount of pyridoxine necessary for good health seems to be about the same as the amount of thiamin necessary.

Significance in Cancer Research

Science News Letter for February 16, 1952, reported the synthesis of the phosphate form of pyridoxine, which is the form in which the body uses this vitamin. This discovery, said the report, "is expected to give science a new, useful tool for cancer research," since cancer tissue has a very low level of vitamin B_6 and uses amino acids differently from the way they are used by normal tissues.

If for no other reason than this one report (cancer tissue shows a low level of pyridoxine), we would recommend an ample supply of pyridoxine in your diet. Tests are also being conducted on treatment for

[204]

leukemia, using pyridoxine, but much more research must be done before final results are established. Keep in mind that it is important to take pyridoxine in its natural form, in combination with the other B vitamins. Remember, too, that pyridoxine does not exist in natural form apart from the other B vitamins. Any preparation that is sold just as pyridoxine would have to be synthetic. Get your pyridoxine from foods and natural food supplements such as desiccated liver and brewer's yeast.

It seems that you need about the same amount of pyridoxine as you need of thiamin, which is:

	Milligrams
For a moderately active man	1.8
For a moderately active woman	1.5
For children up to ten	0.4 to 1.2
For young people over ten	1.2 to 2.0

In other words, you can obtain your daily quota of pyridoxine in three tablespoons of brewer's yeast or several pieces of liver.

Pyridoxine is not lost in quick cooking to any great extent, although much of it may dissolve and be thrown away in the water in which foods are slowly cooked. Roasting or stewing of meat can also result in great losses of pyridoxine.

Foods Containing the Largest Amounts of Pyridoxine

Food	*Milligrams of Pyridoxine*
Bananas	.30 in 1 medium banana
Beans, dried lima	.55 in ½ cup
Beef, heart	.12 in 2 slices
Beef, liver	.80 in 1 piece
Beef, round steak	.77 in 1 piece
Beets	.11 in ½ cup
Cabbage	.29 in 1 cup
Chicken	.13 in 2 pieces
Halibut	.11 in 1 piece

Food	Milligrams of Pyridoxine
Molasses	.27 in 3 tablespoons
Peas, fresh	.19 in 1 cup
Peas, dried	.30 in 1 cup
Peanuts, roasted	.30 in about 100 peanuts
Pork loin	.27 in 1 piece
Potatoes, Irish	.16 in 1 medium potato
Potatoes, sweet	.32 in 1 medium potato
Turnips	.10 in ½ cup
Veal	.13 in 2 slices
Wheat germ	.58 in about 3 tablespoons
Yeast, brewer's	1.30 in about 3 tablespoons

CHAPTER 30

Pantothenic Acid

THE NAME of pantothenic acid comes from the Greek word, "panthos" meaning "universal." This member of the B complex of vitamins occurs apparently in all living cells—in yeasts, molds, bacteria and individual cells of all plants and animals.

Although the exact place of pantothenic acid in human nutrition is still being debated, many animal experiments have shown that it is a very necessary part of the diet of rats, dogs, chicks, pigs and so forth. For instance, a number of black rats were fed on a diet containing ample quantities of all the vitamins except pantothenic acid. Within six weeks, their growth was retarded, skin eruptions began to appear and their black hair began to turn gray. Presently they took on the appearance of old age: they became wrinkled, bald, thin and emaciated; some of them contracted skin ulcers. As soon as pantothenic acid was added to

[207]

their diet, their hair turned black and they became healthy once again.

In dogs a lack of pantothenic acid causes ulcers of the intestinal tract. Pigs deprived of this vitamin develop a peculiar goose-stepping gait and are finally unable to walk at all. In several species of animals severe damage to the adrenal glands results from lack of pantothenic acid.

Pantothenic Acid in Human Nutrition

It has been claimed that pantothenic acid, administered to human beings, relieves peripheral neuritis (inflammation of nerve endings) and alcoholic psychoses which did not respond to other B vitamins. Pantothenic acid is present in human blood and urine, and a deficiency of it has been found in the blood of patients who are deficient in other B vitamins. Reported cases of fatigue, breathlessness, fainting spells and disturbed pulse rate seem to indicate a failure of the adrenal glands, which might be due indirectly to a deficiency of pantothenic acid in the diet.

The symptom of "burning feet" which was noticed among prisoners of war in Japanese camps was spectacularly improved with the administration of calcium pantothenate. Researchers have not decided, however, whether the burning feet were caused by a deficiency of pantothenic acid, or whether the vitamin simply acted as a medicine to cure this particular symptom.

Apparently pantothenic acid works in conjunction with riboflavin, another B vitamin, for an injection of pantothenic acid into the blood increases the level of riboflavin in the blood. Perhaps too little pantothenic acid in the diet also disrupts the function of inositol, another B vitamin. It seems too that this lack may interfere with certain intestinal bacteria which are

[208]

thought to manufacture other B vitamins in the intestine. You will see that all of this information is more or less theoretical. Pantothenic acid was discovered only recently and, since its action in the body is very complex, nutritionists cannot say as yet how much of this B vitamin human beings need daily, or what specific conditions of ill health indicate a deficiency of pantothenic acid.

Importance of Pantothenic Acid

But undoubtedly it is important for all of us to get ample amounts of this vitamin, not by itself, but in foods or food supplements that contain the other members of the B complex, with which this vitamin cooperates in performing certain functions in the body. No one has yet proved satisfactorily that pantothenic acid deficiency results in graying hair in human beings. Undoubtedly, much more investigation is now being done on this aspect of nutrition. The *British Medical Journal* for March 22, 1952, tells us that two scientists who have studied poorly nourished children in the tropics report that many of these children have gray hair, which is restored to normal color when pantothenic acid is given. So it seems to us that, with further investigation, the problem of gray hair may be solved one of these days.

Pantothenic acid is present in many of the same foods which contain other B vitamins—liver, yeast, egg yolk, peanuts, wheat germ and so forth. Like other B vitamins, it dissolves in water and is lost when you drain off the water in which foods have been cooked. It is destroyed immediately when baking soda is added to food. So use care when cooking foods that contain the B vitamins. Cook them at low heat for as little time as possible; don't add baking soda during the cooking process, and do save and use the liquid in which they were cooked.

For optimum health it has been estimated that you should get between 5 and 10 milligrams of pantothenic acid daily. Liver contains an average of more than 5 milligrams of pantothenic acid per 100 grams. In cooking liver, some of this vitamin is lost. And raw liver is, of course, most unappetizing. Desiccated liver, dried at low heat, preserves all the vitamins and enzymes. In addition, the valuable food elements of whole liver are concentrated in this highly nutritious form. Take desiccated liver as a food supplement to be sure of an ample daily supply of all the B vitamins, including pantothenic acid.

Foods Containing the Largest Amounts of Pantothenic Acid

Foods	Milligrams of Pantothenic Acid
Artichokes, Jerusalem	.40 in 4 artichokes
Barley	1.0 in 7 tablespoons
Beans, dried navy or lima	.83 in ½ cup
Beef, brain	1.8 in 2 pieces
Beef, heart	2.0 in 2 pieces
Beef, lean	1.0 in 1 piece
Beef liver	5.2 in 1 piece
Broccoli	1.4 in 1 cup
Carrots	.2 in ½ cup
Cauliflower	.92 in ¼ head
Cheese	.96 in five 1-inch cubes
Chicken	.90 in 3 slices
Corn	.31 in ½ cup
Cowpeas	2.1 in 1½ cups
Egg, whole fresh	2.7 in 2 eggs
Egg, yolk	6.3 in 8 yolks
Kale	.30 in 1 cup
Lamb, leg	.81 in 2 slices
Milk, fresh whole	.29 in ½ cup
Milk, skim	.36 in ½ cup
Mushrooms	1.7 in 7 mushrooms

Foods	*Milligrams of Pantothenic Acid*
Oats, rolled	1.3 in ¾ cup
Oranges	.49 in 1 medium orange
Oysters	.49 in 5 medium oysters
Peas, fresh	.60 in 1 cup
Peas, dried	2.8 in 1½ cups
Peanuts, roasted	2.5 in 100 peanuts
Potatoes, Irish	.65 in 1 medium potato
Potatoes, sweet	.95 in 1 medium potato
Pork, bacon	.98 in 25 slices
Pork, ham	.66 in 1 slice
Pork, muscle	1.5 in 1 piece
Rice, bran	2.20 in ¾ cup
Rice, polished	.40 in ¾ cup
Salmon	1.1 in ½ cup
Soybeans	1.8 in ½ cup
Strawberries	.26 in ½ cup
Walnuts, English	.80 in 100 walnuts
Wheat, bran	3.0 in 5 cups
Wheat germ	1.0 in 6 tablespoons
Wheat, whole	1.3 in ½ cup
Yeast, brewer's	10.0 in 3 tablespoons
Zucchini	.30 in ½ cup

CHAPTER 31

Para-Amino-Benzoic Acid

ONE OF THE LATEST of the B vitamins to be studied and one that has achieved importance because of a peculiar characteristic is Para-amino-benzoic acid which, for convenience, is known as Paba.

What we know about Paba we know mostly because it is, in chemists' terms, "antagonistic" to the sulfa drugs. No one is exactly sure just how or why. But the general way in which Paba acts seems to be this: In the chemistry of the body, many substances are linked together in chains of molecules. The substances that make up the sulfa drugs are almost the same as those that make up Paba. When the sulfa drugs are taken into the body they combine with other protein substances in the digestive tract. Because they are so much like Paba chemically, they will naturally combine with the same substances Paba should combine with. If the sulfa drugs get there first, and if they are there in greater quantity than Paba, they will do the combining and Paba will be crowded out. On the other hand, if Paba gets there first in greater quantity than the sulfa, it will win the competition for a place in this chemical combination and the sulfa will be ineffective.

What actually happens to one's health as a result of this peculiarity of Paba is not so good. As you know, the American diet is sadly deficient in B vitamins. So unless an individual is very health-conscious and is deliberately taking extra B vitamins in his diet, chances are that there will be precious little Paba or any other B vitamin in his digestive tract at any given time. Now, if he contracts some infection for which his doctor prescribes sulfa, the drug will, of course, elbow out the Paba and his deficiency will be even more acute than it was before.

In addition, it seems that Paba influences the intestinal bacteria so that they can produce folic acid, another B vitamin. Folic acid in turn helps the body to assimilate pantothenic acid. So here is a chain of events that leads almost certainly to a lot of disagreeable symptoms when one has been taking sulfa drugs: the Paba is unable to function chemically, which results in a lack of folic acid which results in a lack of pantothenic acid. So at least three of the known B vitamins are drained out of our systems entirely.

You have probably heard of, or perhaps experienced, the possible bad effects of sulfa drugs: digestive disorders, great nervousness, extreme depression—all these are symptoms of the lack of B vitamins which the sulfa drugs produce. Chemists have been so interested in this special aspect of Paba that they have done most of the experimenting trying to find out the how and why of this relationship of Paba and the sulfa drugs. As a result, they have had little time to investigate the more positive aspects of Paba. Why does the body

[213]

need it? What exactly does it contribute in the way of health? In what foods does it occur? We have very sketchy knowledge of any of these subjects.

In his book, *Vitamins and Hormones* (Vol. II, Academic Press), S. Ansbacher gives this definition of a B vitamin: 1. It is a natural constituent of yeast, liver and/or (whole grain) cereals. 2. It is water-soluble. That is, it dissolves in water rather than fat. Water-soluble vitamins cannot be stored in any great quantity in the body as the fat-soluble ones can. 3. It is a growth substance for bacteria, yeasts, fungi and/or molds. This means that the cells of these organisms must have the vitamin or they cannot grow or live. 4. It is physiologically active in small amounts. You do not need it in the amounts in which you need protein or carbohydrate foods. Microscopically small amounts of the vitamin are enough, because it does not actually become a part of your body structure—it aids in the process by which proteins, carbohydrates and fats become part of the body. 5. It causes a deficiency disease when it is lacking in the diet.

On the basis of this definition, Paba is a B vitamin. You can see from what we have said above about Paba how closely it works with the other B vitamins, especially pantothenic acid and folic acid. In the article in this book on how and why hair turns gray, we find that the vitamins mentioned most frequently as those which protect the natural color of the hair are pantothenic acid and Paba.

Those foods in which Paba is plentiful are: liver, brewer's yeast, milk, eggs, rice bran, whole wheat, wheat germ, molasses and, to a certain extent, beef and pork muscle meats.

CHAPTER 32

Folic Acid

ONE OF THE MOST recently discovered of the B complex of vitamins is folic acid, or pteroylglutamic acid as it is sometimes called. Its discovery reveals more interest-ing things about the way nutrition research is carried on, especially when it is dealing with any food factor as complex as the B vitamins. As we have pointed out many times, the B vitamins represent one of the most complicated of all the food elements and one about which we really know little as yet. Researchers work-ing at widely separated places on entirely different projects turned up significant facts about a certain food substance. One group, working with chickens, discover-ed a curative property of substance X. Another group found that certain conditions of ill health could be brought about by including all the known parts of the vitamin B complex in a diet, but omitting a certain substance Y. Still another group located a substance Z which had nutritional advantages to recommend it.

[215]

When all this research was published and studied, it was discovered that all these workers had been dealing with the same substance—which we now call folic acid. In 1941 it was isolated from spinach leaves and was named "folic" because it appears so abundantly in green leaves or foliage.

Symptoms of Folic Acid Deficiency

The chief place of folic acid in nutrition seems to be the prevention of several different kinds of anemia. That is, folic acid brings about the proper growth and reproduction of the red blood cells in the bone marrow of the body. Vitamin B_{12} has been heralded as the preventive of anemia. B_{12} is undoubtedly powerful, but there are certain forms of anemia which B_{12} has no effect on, which are cured or prevented by folic acid.

Besides anemia, other symptoms of folic acid deficiency, in men and animals, are diarrhea, glossitis (inflammation of the tongue), gastrointestinal disorders, leukopenia (a decrease in the normal number of white corpuscles). Lactation is improved in rats by the administration of folic acid. Hatchability of hen's eggs is improved. Folic acid has also inhibited the effect of certain kinds of cancer in mice. In lambs a serious deficiency in folic acid leads to the symptoms described above and generally results in pneumonia and death. Folic acid has been used successfully, it is reported, in the treatment of anemia associated with rheumatoid arthritis, in agranulocytosis (a lack of a certain kind of corpuscle), in celiac disease (a chronic indigestion in infants and children) and in disorders resulting from doses of the sulfa drugs.

The very beneficial action of folic acid in relation to the harm done by sulfa drugs is not clearly understood, but it is believed that the sulfa drug interferes with the

[216]

bacteria in the intestine that manufactures folic acid. So if these drugs are given without vitamin B as a food supplement, a folic acid deficiency may very possibly result. This would explain many of the symptoms of depression, fatigue and general ill health that frequently follow when one has been taking sulfa drugs.

With folic acid, there arise the questions that concern us with many different food elements—is a folic acid deficiency caused by a lack of this vitamin in the diet, or may it be caused by an inability to absorb the vitamin? If so, what conditions must be present for a proper assimilation of folic acid? And, on the other hand, is it possible that other essential food elements are not absorbed because there is not sufficient folic acid present to aid in this absorption? These questions have not been fully answered as yet. But we do know, without a doubt, that folic acid is a very necessary part of our diet. The fact that, individually, we may have difficulty absorbing it is a good reason for making certain that we have an overabundance of this vitamin every day. We also know that its function in the body depends on the other B vitamins, so we must get our folic acid in foods or food supplements that contain the rest of the B vitamins.

Folic acid is one of the B vitamins most easily destroyed by high heat and exposure to light. So eat raw as many foods as possible that are rich in folic acid. Don't leave your salad greens, spinach, beet greens or parsley lying on the kitchen sink while you're preparing the rest of the meal. Get them fresh from the garden and have them on the table within five minutes. If you must buy them at the market, wash them rapidly and put them into the refrigerator until just before you serve them. With foods such as dried lima beans or meat, which must be cooked, never throw away the

[217]

cooking water—the most valuable part of all your B vitamins has passed into this liquid during the cooking. Keep the liquid to use in soups or sauces.

Foods Containing the Largest Amounts of Folic Acid

It is believed that the quantity of folic acid in greens may be indicated by the amount of green coloring matter or chlorophyll. So you will find folic acid in vegetables of a deep green color, whether or not they are listed below. The minimum daily requirement for folic acid has not been determined, so we cannot advise you on any definite amount of the following foods to eat every day.

Food	Micrograms of Folic Acid
Asparagus	118-124 in 12 stalks, 5 inches long
Bananas	95 in 1 medium banana
Beans, dried limas	330 in ½ cup
Beans, green	71 in 1 cup
Beans, wax	23-27 in 1 cup
Beef, round steak	100 in 1 piece
Beets	42 in ½ cup diced
Beet greens	25 in ½ cup
Bread, whole wheat	69 in 4 slices
Broccoli	90-110 in 1 cup
Cantaloupe	130 in ½ cup cantaloupe balls
Carrots	97 in 1 cup
Cauliflower	44 in ¼ small head
Cheese	30 in 5 one-inch cubes
Chicken	120-250 in 3 slices of chicken
Eggs	86 in two whole eggs
Endive	62-75 in 1 head endive
Ham	58-130 in 1 slice of ham
Kale	100 in 1 cup
Lettuce, leaf	69-84 in six large leaves
Liver	380 in 2 slices
Mushrooms	98 in ½ cup cooked mushrooms
Oranges	83 in 1 small orange
Oysters	240 in 4 medium oysters
Parsley	17 in ten sprigs
Peanuts, roasted	28 in 10 peanuts

Food	Micrograms of Folic Acid
Peas, green	22-23 in 1 cup
Pork loin	65-140 in 1 piece
Potatoes, Irish	140 in 1 small potato, baked
Radishes	11-13 in 10 red radishes
Salmon	870 in ½ cup salmon
Spinach	225-280 in ½ cup
Swiss chard	62-70 in ½ cup
Tomatoes	12-14 in 1 small tomato
Veal chops	92-170 in 2 medium chops
Watermelon	150 in 1/3 slice
Wheat germ	140-160 in 6 tablespoons
Wheat, whole	95 in 5 tablespoons
Yeast, brewer's	1040 in 3 tablespoons

CHAPTER 33

Biotin and Raw Eggs

IT SEEMS THAT during the research that went on around the discovery of the vitamin biotin there was renewed interest in the fact that laboratory animals do not do well on diets that include a lot of raw egg white. Now egg white is a protein and proteins are essential for life and health. Other proteins seem to be far more valuable as food when they are eaten raw. So what could be the cause of this peculiar reaction to egg white? Was it some poison in the egg white that disappeared when it was cooked? Or was it something else in the diet that did not get along with egg white?

Actually in the laboratory experiments, animals on very good, nutritious diets invariably showed symptoms of great distress if the diet contained a high amount of raw egg white. The animals lost their hair, became sluggish and nervous and contracted a dermatitis chiefly around their eyes, noses and paws.

[220]

Foods rich in the B vitamins prevented these symptoms. But which of the B vitamins was involved? By feeding carefully controlled diets in which trials were made with each of the known B vitamins, it was finally revealed that the newly discovered vitamin biotin was the victim. Further research showed that there is a substance in egg white, called avidin (the hungry protein), which binds the biotin in our digestive tract so that it cannot be utilized by our bodies. The laboratory animals were consuming an amount of egg white which used up every vestige of biotin, so that they suffered from a severe biotin deficiency.

Experiments Show Harm Done by Raw Egg White

As word got around in the scientific journals, researchers looked further into this strange phenomenon. A group of workers at the University of Wisconsin tried nutritious diets plus egg white on five different kinds of animals—chicks, rats, rabbits, monkeys and guinea pigs. Their results are reported by J. G. Lease, H. T. Parsons and E. Kelly in the *Journal of Biochemistry,* March, 1937. They found that the first four animals showed similar symptoms of baldness, skin eruptions, swelling, scaliness and redness about the eyes, ears, paws and mouth. In the rat only, there were nervous symptoms as well. The guinea pig showed the least reaction to the egg white. The diets fed were healthful, nutritious diets, containing plenty of all the necessary vitamins. However, about 40 to 50 per cent of the daily ration was dried, uncooked egg white.

In 1939 E. Uroma published an account of the reaction of children to raw egg white. In *Acta Societatis Medicorum Fennicae Duodecim,* Vol. 21, 1939, he described feeding one raw egg daily for from one to three weeks to 48 children between the ages of one

[221]

week and seven months. It was found that the blood of three of the children developed antibodies against the egg white—seeming to indicate that some poisonous substance was present and the antibodies were mobilized to fight it. Two of these children also developed a slight eczema on the face and neck. This breaking out disappeared when the eggs were omitted from the diet. It began to appear that raw egg white had indeed a very serious effect on the health of human beings.

Then came the famous experiment that provided final proof of the harmfulness of raw egg white. V. P. Sydenstricker, S. A. Singal, A. P. Briggs and N. M. DeVaughn of the University of Georgia School of Medicine set out to produce the so-called "egg white injury" in human beings and, if possible, cure it by administering biotin. Their experiment is reported in *Science* for February 13, 1942. Seven human volunteers agreed to the test. This is the diet they were placed on: polished rice, white flour, farina, cane sugar, lard, butter and lean beef. This diet contains practically no biotin. Then the volunteers were given vitamin and mineral supplements to make up for the vitamins and minerals that were missing from their food, so that whatever symptoms they showed could not possibly be the result of some other vitamin deficiency. Then they were given each day enough raw egg white to make up 30 per cent of the total caloric intake.

Only four of the volunteers followed through to a satisfactory termination of the experiment. This is what happened: during the third and fourth week all four developed scaliness of the skin, without any accompanying itching. In the seventh week one man developed a dermatitis over his neck, hands, arms and legs. During the seventh and eighth weeks all the volunteers developed a gray pallor of their skin and mucous membrane and later extreme dryness of the skin, with additional scaliness.

After the fifth week they all developed other kinds of symptoms as well — depression which progressed to extreme lassitude, sleepiness and, in one instance, a mild case of panic. All experienced muscle pains, excessive sensitivity to touch and localized sensations such as numbness, tingling and "pins-and-needles." After the tenth week they began to lose their appetites and feel nauseated. Two of the volunteers complained of distress around their hearts and an electrocardiogram revealed that their hearts were not normal. The blood of all showed a decrease in hemoglobin (the red pigment that carries oxygen to the cells) and in red blood corpuscles, even though their diet was planned to prevent anemia. The cholesterol content of their blood was also very high. When biotin was given to them, the symptoms disappeared within several days.

Now the conditions of this experiment are exaggerated, of course, as this kind of test necessitates. In real life, it is hardly possible that anyone eating such a diet as these volunteers were eating would at the same time be taking raw eggs and vitamin supplements. Since the symptoms of the human subjects were so similar to those of animals deprived of biotin, it seems we are safe in assuming that a biotin deficiency can indeed be induced in human beings who eat a great deal of raw egg white.

Possible Relationship Between Biotin and Cancer

Somewhat later, interest was aroused in the possibility of biotin having something to do with cancer formation. It was found that certain kinds of cancer contained more biotin than normal tissue. Biologists reasoned that if an excess of biotin caused the cancer, they

[223]

might prevent it by feeding raw egg white whose avidin content would neutralize the biotin. Three researchers at the University of Wisconsin experimented with rats, feeding them a diet that included butter-yellow, a cancer-causing substance. Then they fed one group of the rats raw egg white, another group raw egg white plus biotin and a third group cooked egg white, in which the avidin had been destroyed by the heat. Of the rats which ate the cancer-producing diet to which nothing had been added, 77 per cent developed liver tumors. The rats on any or all of the other diets developed from 10 to 18 per cent of liver tumors, which indicated that something in the white of egg protected them against tumor growth. The authors comment on the fact that the egg white exerted this protective effect equally well whether it was fed raw, or with biotin, or cooked to overcome the effect of the avidin. It would seem from this experiment that the peculiar relationship of biotin and avidin has nothing to do with cancer formation, even though signs of severe biotin deficiency appeared in those rats who received raw egg white in their diets, without any extra biotin.

Our study turned up numerous other experiments on biotin-avidin, but nothing that gave us any more of a clue as to just where we should stand on the raw egg white controversy. Our favorite book on animal nutrition, *Nutrition of the Dog,* by C. M. McCay of Cornell University (published by Comstock) tells us that as early as 1898 it was discovered that the feeding of raw eggs was often followed by vomiting and diarrhea in dogs. It was also found that from 30 to 50 per cent of the raw egg white could be recovered from the dog's feces, indicating that he had digested only 50 to 70 per cent of it. On the other hand, tests showed that the same dog digested 90 per cent of cooked egg white. One researcher thought that this might be due to the rapid rate at which raw egg white leaves the stomach—the digestive juices simply do not have time to digest it. Raw egg starts to leave the stomach almost as soon as it reaches it. An hour and a half after it is eaten the egg white is well on its way through the small intestine. Boiled egg white, on the other hand, remains in the stomach two or three hours, until well digested. Knowledge of this fact about boiled egg white is valuable for someone on a reducing diet. If you eat your eggs hard-boiled, they will stay in your stomach longer and ward off those uncomfortable hunger pangs.

Helen T. Parsons and a group of fellow workers showed in an article in *Proceedings of the Society of Biological Chemistry* (Volume 31, p. 77) that in rats the effects of raw egg white could be prevented by including certain amounts of brewer's yeast or dried liver in the diet.

Dr. McCay is one of the country's outstanding animal nutritionists. In his recommendations for feeding dogs, he advises *that you should not feed raw eggs,* but feed whole, hard-boiled eggs, shell and all. He admits that no one knows why the raw egg white is not digested properly by dogs. He also mentions that it is better digested if it is thoroughly beaten or thoroughly mixed with milk before it is eaten.

Why Should Raw Egg White Be Harmful?

We have only one possible solution for the egg-white question. Wild animals do not, of course, cook their food. Many wild animals eat bird's eggs. Nature provides ingenious and extremely successful ways of protecting new young life in various species. Could it be that avidin has been placed in egg white so that animals which prey on eggs will discover that the egg white eventually makes them ill and will be forced to find other kinds of food? Can avidin in egg white be just one of mother nature's ways of maintaining the proper balance among all the different kinds of life? Perhaps, who knows, if there were no such substance as avidin, birds would long ago have become extinct and the valuable functions they perform— scattering seed, pollinating flowers and destroying insects—would have suffered.

However, if it is possible for any animal to perceive the potential harm in raw egg white, you would think that dogs would refuse to eat it; whereas there is nothing they enjoy more than a fresh raw egg, even if they must steal it from the chicken house and break the shell themselves. So far as we know, however, no one has ever done any research on how many whole raw eggs any one dog will eat during a given time, if he is left to his own devices. Maybe he is able to sense just when to stop in order not to do himself harm. But, if this is so, why did the laboratory animals in the experiments above not refuse to eat the raw egg white after it had begun to produce unpleasant symptoms in them?

There is one other possible explanation, too. You will notice that in all of the experiments in which raw egg white produced unhealthy symptoms, *only the egg white was fed*. No one tried to induce "egg white injury" by feeding whole eggs. So perhaps we were intended to eat raw eggs, and "egg white injury" is another example of what happens when we eat part of a food and throw away or change another part. We were meant to eat foods whole, undivided, unrefined and untampered with—of this we are certain. We know that egg yolk contains large amounts of biotin. Perhaps egg yolk contains other substances, too, aside from biotin which protects against the hungry protein, avidin.

CHAPTER 34

B_6—First Line of Defense

THE REMARKABLE revelations that came out of the First International Symposium on Vitamin B_6 (pyridoxine) in July, 1964, set scientists wondering, "why don't we do this more often?" The meeting focused the attention of the whole scientific community on the accomplishments of a single nutrient that many of them barely noticed before. Now that more doctors know pyridoxine is essential to the health of the blood, the brain, and the body's defenses against infection, it is bound to be used more and more as a tool of progressive physicians.

To explore the full potential of B_6, researchers must discover just why it does what it does. Though the mystery is far from solved, announcements were made of experiments that show pyridoxine is contained in phosphorylase, an enzyme essential to metabolizing glycogen, a sugar. In fact Krebs, at the University of Washington, has found that one-half of the vitamin B_6

content of the body is stored in the phosphorylase of the muscles. The relationship between sugars and B₆ was further sealed by evidence from other delegates showing that without vitamin B₆ the body can barely tolerate glucose and becomes sensitive to insulin.

Essential Body Regulators

Pyridoxine is essential to our production of three important body regulators: the histamines (they act to regulate the width of the arteries, the heart rate and the blood pressure; they stimulate smooth muscle reaction and control the secretion of saliva and gastric juices); noradrenaline (a hormone produced with adrenalin in the brain; mainly a vasoconstrictor, it maintains blood pressure in shock, hemorrhage, low blood pressure); and serotonin (a substance released from the blood when antibodies are formed to fight infection).

Doctors who puzzle over the cause of kidney and bladder stones heard Gershoff, of the Harvard School of Public Health, point up the relationship between vitamin B₆ deficiency and the body's production of oxalic acid, a factor in stones. A recent survey in Thailand strongly suggests that bladder stones and kidney stones may be related to inadequate intake of vitamin B₆. The Burmese also showed a tendency toward stones in the urinary tract coupled with low levels of vitamin B₆.

A representative of the University of Pittsburgh (Axelrod, *et al.*) declared that pyridoxine plays such a basic role in the metabolism of protein that the production of defending antibodies is impaired and a lack of immunological response is emphasized when there is a poor supply of pyridoxine. Experiments demonstrated the fact with skin grafts which took easily in

[229]

rats made deficient in pyridoxine; those with sufficient pyridoxine mustered the antibodies necessary to reject the invasive skin grafts. This means of course that these pyridoxine-deficient rats would also be unable to reject truly harmful invasions to the system.

Monkeys and Man

The University of California representative (Greenberg) reported on a series of experiments with rhesus monkeys made deficient in vitamin B_6, which shed new light on hardening of the arteries, dental caries and liver disease. The arterial lesions which developed in vitamin B_6-deficient animals were widespread and the arterial damage resembled that encountered in man. Cholesterol metabolism in vitamin B_6-deficient monkeys was also affected.

Monkeys short on pyridoxine developed four times as much dental caries as control animals. Furthermore, tooth development was affected and degenerative changes in the gums, tongue and jaws were of "considerable magnitude."

Greenberg also discovered that animals deficient in vitamin B_6 for even a short period develop liver damage. The liver becomes enlarged and smooth, pale with fatty alterations. If the deficiency is prolonged, scarring often associated with nodules occurs.

Pyridoxine deficiency related to tooth decay was also investigated by Hillman (State University of New York). He conducted a clinical trial of vitamin B_6 supplementation involving 540 new mothers at a community hospital with a nonfluoridated water supply. Clinical and x-ray examinations of the patients both immediately after birth and six weeks after birth revealed "significantly less incidence of caries in the

[230]

patients. A pyridoxine lozenge program included an intake of 20 milligrams of pyridoxine per day. These favorable results highlight the need for further intensive exploration of the possible protective effect of vitamin B₆ against dental caries."

Anemia Transfusions Eliminated

A team from the Metropolitan Hospital of Cleveland, Ohio, reported on the "typical" pyridoxine-responsive anemia in an adult male patient who has been under observation for nine years. His condition was described as "a combination of severe anemias which was unresponsive to various therapeutic agents and could only be managed by transfusion." After many experiments with various dosages of pyridoxine both orally and by injection, a dosage level of 50 milligrams of pyridoxine hydrochloride given orally every day stabilized the patient's blood level without injections. The analysis of 72 other cases of pyridoxine-responsive anemia in human beings was presented. "The authors suggest that it would seem reasonable to try a trial of pyridoxine therapy in instances where etiologic [source] mechanisms for anemia cannot be defined."

Science (October 30, 1964), reporting on the symposium, remarked that accounts of vitamin B₆ in textbooks on animal nutrition invariably state that a deficiency of this vitamin is not likely to occur because of its abundance in natural feedstuffs. The up-to-date view of the status of vitamin B in farm animals as presented by Fuller of the University of Georgia does not agree. Fuller concluded that "In order to insure the well-being of animals and to permit maximum expectation of economical production in farm animals, nutritionists should provide supplemental pyridoxine in feeds for non-ruminants [grass eaters] of all species during the period of active growth and reproduction."

How Much Is Enough?

The U. S. Army Medical Research and Nutritional Laboratory at Denver, Colorado, told of some recent studies on humans aimed at estimating the vitamin B_6 requirement of man. These studies were conducted with young, healthy adult male subjects aged 18 to 22. They were given liquid pyridoxine-free diets with high and low protein intakes. The most marked symptoms observed during deficiency periods in these subjects were abnormal brain functions. In fact one subject (remember these were perfectly healthy young men) on a low protein intake had a grand mal (epileptic) convulsion during the seventh week of deficiency. As a result of these studies, the optimum daily vitamin B_6 diet for subjects on a high protein diet was set at about 1.75 to 2.0 milligrams per day and for subjects on a low protein diet 1.25 to 1.5 milligrams per day. The researchers concluded that other factors such as stresses, sex, and age all have an important bearing on vitamin B_6 requirements.

According to Borsook of the California Institute of Technology, individual requirements for B_6 vary more than that of other vitamins, and complicate the definition of requirements. One test involving the tryptophan (an amino acid that requires B_6 for processing) load on young men indicates that while 2.76 milligrams of vitamin B_6 is adequate for 90 per cent of the population, ten per cent cannot get along on it. Furthermore, it is difficult to fulfill the recommended dietary allowance of 1.5 to 2.0 milligrams per day of vitamin

[232]

B_6 for women and older men if the calorie intake is restricted to what is recommended for their height, weight and age. So, if the object of a recommended daily allowance is to prevent a vitamin B_6 deficiency, then the data indicate that 1.5 to 2.0 milligrams are not enough for everyone. To cover all possibilities, the requirement would be in the range of 2.5 to 7.0 milligrams of vitamin B_6. "Borsook concluded that the case is strong for increasing the vitamin B_6 in the food supply. He suggests adding B_6 to the present flour enrichment formula."

We too are in favor of a supplemental increase of pyridoxine in the diet, but we prefer to use the supplement in a natural form, rather than a synthetic additive. We believe health-conscious people should attempt to eat foods rich in all of the B vitamins, which automatically include pyridoxine, so that they receive these vitamins in their proper relative strength.

The following foods are so rich in vitamin B_6 that they would quickly bring your daily intake of this vitamin up to the recommended daily allowance: brewer's yeast, wheat germ, soybeans, blackstrap molasses, beef liver, corn, barley and unpolished rice. Have at least one of these every day, either in regular meals or as a natural food supplement. With an element so vital to the overall health of the human body, one cannot afford to chance a deficiency.

The International Meeting did plenty to promote pyridoxine's powers to some medical men who might have gone on forever treating kidney stones only with sulfas and surgery, bad teeth only with fluorides and fillings and recurrent infections only with questionable antibiotics. The same could be done with meetings on the other B vitamins, vitamin C and vitamin E.

CHAPTER 35

Vitamin B$_{12}$

ONE OF THE MOST dramatic discoveries in recent scientific history was the discovery of vitamin B_{12} in April, 1948. Researchers had known for a long time that liver as a food contained some substance that would combat pernicious anemia—a disease whose outcome was always fatal before this discovery was made. However, many anemic patients could not eat liver in the quantities they had to consume to cure their disease. Some of them had unpleasant reactions to liver extract and physicians believed that there were many different substances in liver and liver extract, too, that were not necessary for the anemia cure and that simply added to the bulk of the dose these patients received.

A group of workers at the Merck Laboratories began an intensive search during which they isolated one substance after another from liver trying to find the anti-pernicious-anemia factor, as this element was called. Each of these substances was then tested to see whether or not it would cure this disease. Finally, out of many tons of liver, a few tiny grains of a red crystalline substance were obtained. Dr. Randolph West of the Presbyterian Hospital in New York City, one of the country's leading authorities on anemia, who had been working in collaboration with the Merck Laboratories, injected five-millionths of an ounce of the new substance into the muscle of a victim of pernicious anemia. Bedfast, tormented with upset stomach, pallor, sore mouth, shortness of breath and the indescribable fatigue of pernicious anemia, this patient had a blood count of only 1,500,000 red blood corpuscles per cubic milliliter, rather than the normal 4,500,000. Six weeks after the injection, her blood count had risen to normal and she was in good health.

Pernicious anemia is a failure in the body to manufacture enough red blood cells in the bone marrow to supply what the body needs daily. In some individuals this failure is believed to be caused by the lack of a certain secretion in the stomach, called "the intrinsic factor" whose job it is to extract the B_{12} from food. For such people injections of B_{12} mean the difference between good health and death from the wasting starvation that is pernicious anemia.

Other Diseases Respond to B_{12}

Since that day in 1948, medical journals have been full of reports on vitamin B_{12} therapy. Parisian doctors tried vitamin B_{12} for multiple sclerosis and reported great improvement in those patients who took the vitamin. South African physicians used B_{12} in treating the neuritis of chronic alcoholism and diabetes mellitus, with a "dramatic response" in 9 out of 11 cases. A

Pennsylvania doctor gave vitamin B_{12} to patients with osteoarthritis and osteoporosis. Of the 33 cases of osteoarthritis, 20 patients had obtained results within a week, 7 of whom had complete relief from symptoms. By the end of the third week all but 3 patients showed some benefit. The two cases of osteoporosis were without symptoms by the end of the third week.

An issue of the *Journal of the American Medical Association* reports on the use of vitamin B_{12} in France for multiple sclerosis, spastic paraplegia, cerebellar atrophy, polyneuritis, Korsakoff psychosis (a disorder frequently caused by alcoholism resulting in hallucinations, falsification of memory, etc.) and spinocerebellar disorders. A group of Ohio scientists, working with a number of undernourished children at a Fresh Air Camp and Hospital gave 11 of the children vitamin B_{12}. Five of them "responded dramatically" and, within a few weeks, had surpassed in growth and physical efficiency well-nourished children of their own age, showing that, in some instances, normal growth and development in children may depend on their supply of vitamin B_{12}. A report by Barnett Sure of the University of Arkansas indicates that, in laboratory animals, the success of reproduction and lactation is assured by a diet containing ample B_{12} and folic acid, whereas control animals on the same diet, minus these two B vitamins, could not bear litters successfully or nurse their young.

This brings us to perhaps the most important of all the aspects of vitamin B_{12}—the way in which it works along with other B vitamins. As you know, the B complex of vitamins is called a "complex" because, instead of being one vitamin, it has turned out to be a large number of related vitamins, which appear generally in the same foods.

Meaning of the B Complex of Vitamins

These B vitamins, so important for all aspects of health, have not been put into foods by nature just as a hit-and-miss proposition. They are closely related to one another in chemical structure and activity. Several of them cannot function at all—and so cannot benefit our bodies in the slightest—unless their fellow-vitamins of the B complex are with them, in just the proportions and combinations in which they exist in natural foods. So, we repeat again what we are continually stressing in these pages: *get your vitamins from natural food sources;* get them at your daily meals. And, since all of us need food supplements because of the serious lack of vitamins and minerals in the refined and processed foods we eat, we should take as supplements natural food products.

Of course, liver is the answer if you're especially concerned about preventing anemia. Vitamin B_{12} was discovered so recently that information about the different kinds of food that may contain it is scarce. We do know that it exists in powdered whole milk, cheese, egg yolk and, to a certain extent, in meats. But it is most plentiful in liver.

Researchers have also discovered that vitamin B_{12} is made by bacteria which exist in decaying waste products. But they have not had the amazing success in administering this form of vitamin B_{12} that they have had with B_{12} from liver. So, put liver on the family menu at least once a week—oftener, if you like it. And put desiccated liver at the top of your list of food supplements. Regardless of what other foods contain the miraculous B_{12}, liver will probably remain its best and most abundant source.

[237]

CHAPTER 36

Absorption of Vitamin B₁₂ by the Body

WHY IS IT that doctors report such near-miracle results when they inject vitamin B₁₂ and yet we do not hear nearly so often about dramatic improvements from taking vitamin B₁₂ by mouth, either in a vitamin preparation or in food?

The answer seems to have something to do with the way in which vitamin B₁₂ is absorbed and used by the body. A number of years ago a researcher named Castle showed that the stomachs of people who have pernicious anemia do not contain a certain substance which he called "the intrinsic factor." This factor seemed to be necessary for the body to absorb vitamin B₁₂. If it was not present, the vitamin was excreted unchanged and the patient's anemia did not improve.

Under these circumstances it didn't matter very much whether or not a person got vitamin B₁₂ in his diet. If he didn't he might easily develop a lot of conditions due to lack of vitamin B₁₂. But even if he did, he could still develop these same conditions if his stomach was lacking in the "intrinsic factor." He just wasted all the vitamin B$_{12}$ he was getting in food. Said Dr. Castle in the *Annals of Internal Medicine* for May, 1951, "Presumably because of the lack of the so-called gastric (intrinsic) factor, in most patients with pernicious anemia the daily oral administration of as much as 50 micrograms of vitamin B$_{12}$ is relatively ineffectual."

As soon as this theory became widely known, researchers working with vitamins began to develop preparations which would include the intrinsic factor along with the vitamin B$_{12}$. This was difficult because nobody knew what the intrinsic factor actually was— they just knew that it was something existing in the stomach juices. So someone decided to give vitamin B$_{12}$ along with part of the stomach from an animal, assuming that such an addition would contain enough of the intrinsic factor (whatever this is) from the animal's stomach to help in assimilating the vitamin.

And such experiments appeared to work. Increasing the amount of the stomach concentrate given with the vitamin B$_{12}$ appeared to increase the amount of the vitamin that was assimilated. And decreasing the amount of stomach preparation seemed to decrease the amount of the vitamin that was assimilated and used.

Then it was discovered that use of gastric juice made an even better record. Giving a certain amount of gastric juice from the stomach of a normal human being along with the vitamin B$_{12}$ brought about much greater absorption of the vitamin than giving part of an animal's stomach. This seemed to suggest that the intrinsic factor prepared from one kind of animal stomach may have such an affinity for vitamin B$_{12}$ that

[239]

it does not release all of the vitamin when it is taken in by an animal of another species. Sounds complicated, doesn't it? It is—very complicated.

A New Form of B₁₂ Possibly Effective?

At this point in the story, in the spring of 1958 to be exact, several English researchers came along to challenge the whole idea of the existence of the intrinsic factor. Dr. J. G. Heathcote and Dr. F. E. Mooney of St. Helena's Hospital, London, stated that, in spite of an enormous amount of work, there is very little agreement among researchers even on limited properties of the supposed intrinsic factor. They say that it has never been isolated or identified. And this, of course, is true.

They go on to say that vitamin B_{12} is relatively ineffective in treating pernicious anemia by mouth, so they claim that the vitamin alone is not what brings relief to anemia patients. But, they say, a particular thing happens to vitamin B_{12} in the stomach. The protein which is "bound" to the vitamin B_{12} is changed into a substance called a "peptide" and in this form it can be absorbed into and through the stomach wall. To prove this they tried to show that a peptide taken not from an animal's stomach but from a mold or bacteria source can bring about the assimilation of vitamin B_{12} from the stomach of the sufferer from pernicious anemia. They called this preparation vitamin B_{12} peptide.

Treating anemia patients with this preparation— giving it by mouth, that is—they got excellent results. They gave 780 micrograms of their preparation (containing 100 micrograms of vitamin B_{12}) daily for 8 days. Then they gave half that amount for 14 days.

[240]

"We believe, therefore, that intrinsic factor as currently understood, has no real existence per se, and that the fundamental process preceding absorption of vitamin B_{12} is simply one of normal degradation or digestion of animal protein."

This news about the new vitamin B_{12} product comes from *Drug Trade News,* for June 2, 1958. In fairness to researchers who disagree with this point of view entirely, the *News* admitted that this is only a theory and that in spite of success with various patients a great deal more work needs to be done.

Within a matter of months there was another development in vitamin B_{12} research. This time, 3 doctors from Finland discovered that calcium should be present in the digestive tract at the same time as the vitamin B_{12} and the intrinsic factor. Under these circumstances, they say, patients who had other disorders in which vitamin B_{12} cannot be absorbed did very well with the vitamin. But pernicious anemia victims did not. They then listed in the *Lancet* (January, 1959) the other conditions under which vitamin B_{12} is poorly assimilated or not assimilated at all: lack of hydrochloric acid in the stomach, rapid passage of the half-digested food through the intestine (we suppose this might be caused by taking laxatives as well as by other things), decrease in the absorptive area (in the case of someone, part of whose digestive tract has been removed by operation), envelopment of the vitamin by fat droplets or abnormal intestinal bacteria.

The Value of an All-Round Good Diet

An article in the *New York Times* for February 17, 1958, throws more light on the possible relation of calcium to the absorption of vitamin B_{12}. Two doctors

[241]

at Mt. Sinai Hospital in New York have worked out the theory that vitamin B_{12} and the intrinsic factor act somewhat like two clasped hands. One hand touches the intrinsic factor, the other hand touches the vitamin B_{12}. And calcium, they say, appears to act like a handcuff for the linkage of these two hands.

Such an idea is not unusual in the field of nutrition, of course. We know that calcium cannot be properly absorbed without vitamin D and phosphorus. We know that other vitamins and minerals depend upon one another very heavily for proper absorption. So it is not surprising to find that calcium apparently has a lot to do with the absorption of vitamin B_{12}.

A diet so poor as to result in pernicious anemia would undoubtedly be short on calcium as well as short on vitamin B_{12}. We know that pernicious anemia is common among older people, many of whom eat very little of foods that contain either vitamin B_{12} or calcium. It is true, too, that people who have suffered from kidney stones, or hardening of the arteries are often advised by their doctors to get as little calcium as possible because the doctors believe that such deposits are caused by too much calcium in the diet.

It is too bad that such ideas persist. True, kidney stones contain lots of calcium and the plaques that line the hardened artery are made up partly of calcium. But this does not mean that the patient is getting too much calcium. It means, rather, that his body is not using calcium properly and so the calcium is deposited where it should not be. All of us need calcium in large amounts. It is particularly essential for older people whose bones tend to become brittle and whose hearts may be disabled. Calcium is essential for many, many body functions.

[242]

This is why we recommend taking bone meal as the surest and most natural source of calcium, along with phosphorus and other valuable minerals. And surely the story above is ample evidence of the value of completely natural vitamins and minerals. Vitamin B_{12} depends on a natural substance (the intrinsic factor) to be absorbed. In addition, calcium may be necessary, too, for the body to use it properly. And certainly the story above shows that it is the best kind of wisdom to get plenty of vitamin B_{12} in your food every day.

What should you do if your doctor has found that you have something wrong and cannot absorb vitamin B_{12} by mouth? Certainly if the occasion is an emergency, we suggest taking vitamin B_{12} injections at least until you can build up the right conditions of health for absorbing the vitamin by mouth. You see, an injection of B_{12} does not go to the stomach to be absorbed. It goes directly into the tissues. This is why it is quickly effective given in dosages by injection.

Incidentally, it is encouraging to know that the two doctors quoted in the *New York Times* also believe that lack of vitamin B_{12} may lead to mental illness, psychosis or a form of anemic heart trouble. Dr. Herbert, one of the physicians, said that "perhaps 15 out of 1000 hospitalized psychotics could benefit from B_{12} injections and that a 'significant percentage' of aged persons were ill as a result of pernicious anemia from too little of the intrinsic factor."

CHAPTER 37

The Many Things They Can Do With B₁₂

A SEARCH THROUGH the medical literature of the past decade discloses a surprising number of diseases which respond to injections and oral application of vitamin B_{12}. Most of the experiments using this vitamin to treat disease administer it by injection. There are two main reasons for this: first, this method permits the use of a large dosage which will reach the blood stream quickly; second, it bypasses the problem of the "intrinsic factor," the substance necessary in the stomach to process B_{12}. In many patients a sufficient supply of this intrinsic factor is not present, for one reason or another, and in such case the B_{12} does not have the chance to take effect if it is taken orally.

The most famous use for vitamin B_{12}, as we have mentioned earlier, is as an effective treatment for pernicious anemia. A typical report of the success doctors experience when treating anemia in this way is found in the *Lancet* (December 13, 1952). The vitamin was injected intramuscularly into 54 patients, and a response was obtained with as little as 12.5 micrograms, though best results followed dosage of 100 micrograms. After the initial response had been obtained, the authors put the patients on maintenance doses of from 45 micrograms to 150 micrograms every four or five weeks, depending upon the individual. This dosage was kept up for about a year. There were no relapses and no symptoms recurring.

The *Journal of the American Medical Association* (October 24, 1953) carried a report from *Paris Hospital Week* in which 15 pernicious anemia cases were treated with massive doses of vitamin B_{12}. Single injections of 1000 micrograms were found to be effective in maintaining normal blood and marrow over a period of time, from 128 to 358 days. This indicated to the researchers that the vitamin could be stored in the body.

These Paris doctors were emphatic about the fact that vitamin B_{12} was well tolerated and entirely nontoxic, no matter how or in what form it was given. In some pernicious anemia cases as much as 1000 micrograms of vitamin B_{12} daily were administered with no ill effects and with an apparent cure as the result.

Painful Bursitis Gone

Those who have suffered from the effects of bursitis would be hard put to describe the pain they experience. Every movement of the affected joint brings new torture, and even at rest the pain never really leaves the area. Bursitis gets its name from the bursa, or pocket, into which the round end of the bone fits to form a movable point. There is a buffer surface of fluid and tissue to give these bones an easy, frictionless movement. If this fluid thickens, or the tissue becomes

[245]

inflamed, or calcium deposits form, bursitis is the result. Though it might occur in any one of the 140 bursae in the body, the shoulders are the most common sites.

In the June, 1957, issue of *Industrial Medicine and Surgery,* Dr. I. S. Klemes, Medical Director of the Ideal Mutual Insurance Company and J. C. Penney Company in New York City since 1953, told of his great success in treating bursitis with vitamin B_{12}. Dr. Klemes's treatment has been effective in all types of bursitis cases and, in five years of using it, he reports that only three patients have not responded favorably. The injections of 1000 micrograms of B_{12} are given daily for 7 to 10 days, then 3 times per week for 2 or 3 weeks, then 1 or 2 per week for 2 or 3 weeks, depending on clinical indications. To bursitis sufferers, who have tried the orthodox treatments, this news should be a godsend.

Liver Infection and B_{12}

The treatment of hepatitis, a liver infection, has been greatly enhanced by vitamin B_{12} therapy. The *Journal of the American Medical Association* (December 20, 1952) tells of three groups with acute hepatitis, 100 patients in each. Group 1 was given a good diet plus brewer's yeast and a multivitamin preparation, group 2 got the good diet without any food supplements, and group 3 got the same as group two, plus 30 micrograms of B_{12} per day orally, for the first 5 days in the hospital. The group which received the B_{12} showed the most rapid return to normal appetite, and in this group the enlarged liver returned to its proper size in from 8 to 14 weeks sooner than the other two groups. A similar experiment was carried on at the United States Army Hepatitis Center in Japan, and reported in the *American Journal of Medical Science*

[246]

(January, 1955). Two separate groups of 44 hepatitis patients with approximately the same degree of illness, were given identical treatment and diet, except that one group received 30 micrograms of B₁₂ every other day for the first 10 days in the hospital. The overall length of illness for each of the B₁₂ patients was 47.5 days, compared with 57.2 days for the control group who received no B₁₂.

Dr. M. Caruselli, in *La Riforma Medica* (1952, 66, 840) tells of his results in treating asthma with vitamin B₁₂. He worked with a group of 12 asthma patients, giving them daily subcutaneous injections of 30 micrograms of B₁₂ for 15 to 20 days. Ten of the 12 patients showed a decrease, then disappearance of all symptoms. Two cases had a recurrence after 3 and 8 months respectively, but they responded to renewed treatments and were once again free of asthma. The doctor noted also that the general condition of the patients was improved with the administration of B₁₂—there was a gain in weight and a feeling of well-being.

Is Multiple Sclerosis Beyond Help?

Those facing the problem of multiple sclerosis will be interested in the results obtained by three French doctors (Lereboullet, Pluvinage and Coty) in treating seven MS patients with B₁₂. Their findings were printed in the *Journal of the American Medical Association* (August 5, 1950). Three patients receiving 30 micrograms of vitamin B₁₂ every other day found that they could walk more easily and stand erect without support. Another patient who was given 15 micrograms daily for 6 days and 45 micrograms for 3 weeks, was improved in the first week. Though he had been bedfast, he was then able to walk with a cane. The same dosage in a fifth patient brought increased stability in

[247]

standing and walking, as well as a slight regression of other disorders. The sixth patient noted an improvement in vision, and in the seventh "great improvement" was brought about by giving doses of 135 micrograms of vitamin B₁₂.

In experimental groups of diabetic patients it was found that the body of a diabetic absorbs more vitamin B₁₂ than a nondiabetic. These observations, carried in the *Journal of Clinical Nutrition* (September-October, 1953), indicated that these diabetics were more in need of B₁₂ than the controls who did not have diabetes at all. When the body has a sufficient supply of a water-soluble vitamin, such as B₁₂, it eliminates any excess through the urine, and the amount can be easily measured. The fact that the diabetics who were involved with the above experiment expelled much less vitamin B₁₂ than the normal controls, shows that there was a definite need in their systems for the B₁₂ which they absorbed. It would seem from this that foods high in the B vitamins (organ meats, brewer's yeast, desiccated liver) are even more essential to the diet of a diabetic than of those who are not plagued by this disease.

Dosage for Osteoarthritis and Osteoporosis

Two chronic diseases of the bone, osteoarthritis (a severe and painful swelling of the joints) and osteoporosis (an abnormal increase in the porousness of the bones) have shown themselves responsive to vitamin B₁₂ therapy. In *Medical Press* (March 12, 1952) we read of an experiment involving 33 typical cases of osteoarthritis and two cases of osteoporosis. All other therapy was discontinued for a month before vitamin B₁₂ was given and no other anti-rheumatic or pain killer

[248]

was allowed during the course of treatment with B_{12}. Injections were from 30 micrograms to 900 micrograms of vitamin B_{12}, but optimum dosage was figured to be about 100 micrograms per week.

At the end of the first week, 20 patients reported benefit, and 7 of them had obtained complete relief. At the end of the second week, 4 more showed partial relief. By the final day of the third week, 30 of the original 33 osteoarthritis patients had been either wholly or partially relieved, and both of the osteoporosis patients had shown relief in the first week of the experiment.

A Type of Cancer

It is interesting to report on the effect of B_{12} on a certain type of malignancy, neuroblastoma. This is a tumor of the nervous system and is the commonest form of malignant tumor in childhood. The *British Medical Journal* (September 4, 1954) told of observing remarkable regression in these tumors due to treatment with vitamin B_{12}. Ten cases were studied (but two were disqualified due to the possible effect of previous surgery) and "striking regression" of tumors was noted in 4 of them. Three others had survived, at the time of publication, for periods of 30, 13 and 14 months, even though the usual survival rate in such cases is figured at 5 to 11 months. The remaining patient had begun with little hope, but even he showed a marked regression of a spreading liver cancer. It was agreed that B_{12} deserved further investigation as a cancer therapy in the light of these results. We have seen no other evidence of work in this direction, however.

These reports do not, of course, exhaust the possible

therapeutic uses of vitamin B12. We have seen less detailed evidence of this vitamin's effectiveness in treating such things as the pain remaining after tooth extractions and the nerve pains sometimes experienced by malnourished persons. It has been used to speed healing, since it plays a vital part in the synthesis of body protein, which is so important to the healing of wounds. It works as a supplement to a high-protein diet, healing even faster than the protein alone.

A Good Tonic

The *South African Medical Journal* (November 2, 1957) declared that various degrees of B12 deficiency produce vague symptoms of ill health, such as sore tongue, weakness and psychological disturbances. The report continued by saying that there is some justification for practitioners injecting B12 for its tonic effect, particularly on the elderly. It is also recommended for treating xanthelasma, a formation of yellow plaque-like tumors on the eyelids (*Journal of Investigative Dermatology,* February, 1955), and as a growth factor for children who are undersized due to long sickness or malnutrition. There was even an article in the *Denver* (Colorado) *Post* for November 15, 1956, quoting Dr. A. Lee Lichtman, who treats Madison Square Garden (New York) athletes, on the benefits of vitamin B12 for an athlete. He said that bruises and black eyes can be reduced in severity if the athlete is conditioned in advance with the vitamin.

You say you don't have any of these diseases? We hope not, but if you think you have a guarantee of immunity you haven't been reading the statistics. Just by being born you earn yourself a 50-50 chance to contract a degenerative disease. Good nutrition is the best way of improving your chances for health, and

[250]

vitamin B$_{12}$ is a vital nutritional element. Be sure you get your share of this vitamin, and then some.

Some mental illness is attributed to lack of vitamin B$_{12}$ says a headline in the *New York Herald Tribune* for February 17, 1959. The article goes on to say that as many as 7500 inmates of mental institutions in this country may owe their conditions to a lack of vitamin B$_{12}$.

Dr. Victor Herbert at Mt. Sinai Hospital, New York, and Dr. Zaida Castro have developed a test involving the vitamin. Lack of vitamin B$_{12}$ is known to produce brain damage which in turn may make the victim behave as if he were suffering from schizophrenia or some other psychosis.

The blood of several hundred mental patients was measured for vitamin B$_{12}$ content. In about one per cent it was found to be lacking. If this is generally true, then there are 7500 persons in mental institutions who could perhaps be discharged simply by giving them a shot of the vitamin.

The trick is to discover whether or not the patient is short on vitamin B$_{12}$. And the two researchers at Mt. Sinai believe they have such a test. Actually, what they are testing for is the intrinsic factor. If they find the patient has some of this mysterious substance in his digestive tract, then it is easy to discover whether there is any vitamin B$_{12}$ there along with it.

CHAPTER 38

Vitamin B₁₂ and Vascular Disorders

"This article deals with the problem of a possible causal management of all vascular diseases by systemic administration of high doses of vitamin B₁₂."

How would you feel if you came suddenly upon these words in a medical journal of the highest integrity? Wouldn't you be as surprised and excited as we were? Reading further in the English summary to this German article we found that the author believes that this same therapy with vitamin B₁₂ may be useful in treating such things as diabetes, rheumatic diseases, ulcers, as well as certain disorders in neuropsychiatry, dermatology and others.

"The dramatic success following systemic administration of high and highest doses of vitamin B₁₂, as experienced by the author, necessarily led to the conclusion that vast fields of modern pathology [disease] must be subjected to a completely new way of thought with many consequences for therapy now and in the future," says Dr. H. Grabner in the October 31, 1958, issue of *Munchener Medicinische Wochenschrift* (*Munich Medical Weekly*). The patients he describes are only a few, but, says Dr. Grabner, "in full knowledge of the pitiable terminal conditions of those affiliated with vascular diseases I will not hesitate to make known my results."

Dr. Grabner tells us that no one knows for certain what causes heart and blood vessel diseases. He says that there are more than 100 different varieties of vascular diseases. But still we do not know, he says, "what damage of a chemical, physical and allergic nature is rather the actual result of the chronically progressive vascular diseases that finally lead to terminal stages." Anything that is done for heart and blood vessel diseases "helps," he says, that is, some of the symptoms disappear. But no one has claimed a cure for any of these diseases.

How Does Vitamin B₁₂ Act to Cure?

He believes that such diseases come from an original damage to the blood vessel. Then the body, in a self-healing effort, "solders" the damaged areas with connective tissue, layers of fat and calcium. What kind of damage might cause this process to start? Dr. Grabner believes that it may be a form of anemia and says that it may originate in a lack of tone in nerves. So, the whole disorder—or rather the whole series of disorders classified under this heading—may be due to a disturbed blood supply to the vessels.

He tells us that "in all the cases under treatment by me at the time there must be established as fact prevailing an absolutely improbable improvement in every respect." His successes in treatment show, he says, that a new concept of cause and treatment must be considered—not only of the circulatory diseases, but all the degenerative diseases so common after middle age. The following disorders should be considered in a new light, he believes: diabetes, ulcers, rheumatic diseases and numerous neurological and psychiatric concepts including polio and muscular dystrophy as well as epilepsy and schizophrenia.

Dr. Grabner makes no claims for curing these diseases. He says merely that massive doses of vitamin B_{12} should be tried by physicians treating such patients.

What a wonderful prospect it is—the thought that any or all of these plagues which disable, torment and kill millions of people might be caused basically by a lack of something that is triggered by vitamin B_{12}!

And perhaps the amount of vitamin B_{12} in the diet may not be the main consideration in this particular case, for it is well known that vitamin B_{12} is not absorbed easily by the body. Many people seem to lack the ability to absorb it at all.

Cases of Mental Confusion Improved

We feel that the most encouraging part of Dr. Grabner's article deals with the effects of vitamin B_{12} upon the mental confusion several of his patients were suffering from. This is perhaps the most distressing aspect of growing old. Families and friends are cut off from the mentally confused sufferer because he is unable to communicate normally with them. He imagines wrongs which have not been done; he is unable to conduct his affairs and becomes a burden on those around him. If injections of vitamin B_{12} can alleviate just this one condition which prevails among so many older folks—what a blessing it would be!

[254]

Here are some of the stories of Dr. Grabner's patients: first a retired civil servant, aged 76. This gentleman had been under treatment for many ailments, all related to the wearing out of the system of blood vessels and heart. He suffered from intermittent claudication, which is an inability to walk without extreme pain in the legs. His mind was affected, with alternating states of extreme depression and childish mirthfulness. A siege of pneumonia brought about a state of complete mental confusion necessitating the patient's hiring a housekeeper. When he came down with a siege of sciatica, Dr. Grabner prescribed injections of vitamin B_{12}. He gave 400 micrograms daily at first.

After the fourth injection the patient greeted the doctor at the door, fully dressed, fresh-shaven and wearing a tie. "An unprecedented turn of events," says Dr. Grabner, "when one recalls how helpless and utterly dependent his life had been in the last two years. But not only that—there was no trace of confusion. For the first time now it became clear to the patient that his wife had died of a stroke 5 months earlier. Mentally he appeared completely ordered and oriented and remains so today."

After two weeks of the 400-microgram injections daily, Dr. Grabner cut the amount to 200 micrograms daily, then cut that to every other day and finally was giving twice weekly injections of 200 micrograms. This is how he describes the patient's present condition: "He is in the best of health and completely normal mentally. He is fully able to leave the house daily, attends to his own purchases personally and even occasionally visits taverns. At the present time there is not the slightest trace of the coronary spasms and asthmatic attacks that occurred so frequently before, nor even of the

[255]

ambulatory disorder of the kind described, apart from an occasional and extremely moderate spasm."

The second patient Dr. Grabner describes was 68 years old, in advanced emaciation, too weak to stand up. He was bedfast for weeks. He suffered from difficulty in breathing, slow heartbeat (result of too much digitalis) and confusion to such an extent that his wife had mentioned appointing a guardian for him.

He also suffered from acute vascular disorders of the lower limbs. In the past he had had arthritis with degeneration of the knee and hip joint; he had been given digitalis and antispasmodics until he lost appetite, lost weight, had spells of dizziness and also at times complete disorientation in time and space. He had been discharged from the hospital and sent home "to die in peace."

Dr. Grabner began with injections of 200 micrograms of vitamin B_{12} every second day, much against the wishes of the patient's wife, incidentally, for she had no faith in this treatment. There was an early return to orientation, an increase in appetite. By the end of 4 weeks the patient was able to leave his home for the first time in many months. He can now walk for two hours without the dreaded attacks of cramps in his legs which came upon him after as little as 20 minutes of walking in 1957.

Says Dr. Grabner, "The improvement in every respect has so continued that the patient and his wife were able to take . . . a vacation (this was 4 months after the treatment was started). He is completely and entirely the person he formerly was, able to fulfill all his social commitments in every way and to visit regularly with his cronies at their regular table for his evening half-pint of beer."

[256]

The third patient was a pastry chef, 58 years old. Five years previous to treatment he began to have attacks of dizziness and ringing in the ears. Later he suffered from cramps in the legs and an infected spot on a toe. He had a latent diabetic condition and a number of symptoms of vascular disease. For about two months Dr. Grabner gave him injections of vitamin B_{12} (200 micrograms daily).

The patient remained free of cramps and could work a full day. He said, "I could never in the past work at all the way I can today."

A 56-year-old nurse suffered from rheumatic pains, nightly cramps in the legs, difficulty in breathing, fatigue and diabetic symptoms. After the second injection of vitamin B_{12}, the pains ceased and the patient (about 6 months later) began to work full time again.

The next patient was 63 years old and suffered from the condition called "intermittent claudication"—the inability to walk for any length of time without excruciating pain, and discoloration of the toes. He also had night cramps in the legs. Once again vitamin B_{12} injections resulted in a cessation of pain. The patient is planning to resume full-time work.

The next patient described is a woman, only 38 years old. Under treatment for lumbago, this woman was given every sedative and injection and physical therapy known, according to Dr. Grabner. A partial paralysis was diagnosed as a prolapsed disc. She became almost completely helpless and had to be assisted with even the simplest activities. Dr. Grabner gave her injections of 1000 micrograms of vitamin B_{12} daily. After the second injection her improvement was so striking that she drove her car to the doctor's office!

[257]

Two weeks later she went off with her husband on a vacation to Italy—in perfect health!

There are two more case histories given in this extraordinary article. One of them was 76 years old and the victim of great mental confusion. The second, the same age, suffered from shingles as well as a serious vascular and heart condition. Dr. Grabner gave a combined antibiotic and vitamin B_{12} treatment for the shingles and says that he does not know which effected the complete cure within about two weeks. He feels sure that the vitamin played a large part in the cure. The heart and vascular symptoms greatly improved meanwhile.

Although he does not review the case in detail, Dr. Grabner also tells about another patient who suffered for 18 months with an infectious acute inflammatory skin disease. After all this time in the hospital, the young man had attempted suicide, in complete hopeless desperation. After 8 injections daily of 200 micrograms of vitamin B_{12}, almost all eruptions disappeared, including infections in the throat, bladder and urethra.

How We Can Use This Knowledge

Says Dr. Grabner in conclusion, "Cases of vascular diseases of most diversified nature were treated with massive, parenterally-administered injections of vitamin B_{12}. The dramatic results force us to a radically new concept of the origin and treatment of all vascular disease, and also other problems of the older person." We should, he feels, at least test this therapy on diabetes, ulcers, rheumatism, polio, muscular dystrophy, epilepsy, schizophrenia and other mental health problems.

Can you think of any more important contribution

that could be made to good health in America today than a thorough investigation of Dr. Grabner's methods and further case histories? Do you suppose anyone is going to take up his challenge and use his methods to prove that they will work for other practitioners, too?

CHAPTER 39

Miscellany on Vitamin B12

Vitamin B12 has been found to be effective against the sore, red and denuded tongue that "is seen so often now that antibiotics are so widely used," according to an editorial in the *Lancet* for September 12, 1953. It takes only 6 to 24 hours for the mouth to return to normal after a dose of 100 micrograms of vitamin B12 sprayed around the inside of the mouth.

The vitamin is also potent against the ravages of lead poisoning. And one form of vitamin B12 acts as a swift antidote to cyanide poisoning. Mice apparently dead from cyanide doses have revived and become normal again after injections of vitamin B12.

Vitamin B12 in quantity is found only in foods of animal origin. But a report in *The Vegetarian* for March-April, 1958, indicates that it is present in kelp in such quantity that 2 or 3 ounces of the seaweed daily might be sufficient to provide the daily requirement of a vegetarian.

[260]

Studies show that vitamin B_{12} is closely related in function to all the following nutrients: 4 of the important amino acids or forms of protein, folic acid and pantothenic acid (two B vitamins) and vitamin C. This is another good reason for getting the best possible diet rather than trying to make up for a poor diet with synthetic vitamins, which do not include all the important nutrients.

How Much Vitamin B_{12} Can You Take?

Can large doses of vitamin B_{12} be dangerous? We know that massive doses of the fat-soluble vitamins A and D can prove dangerous if they are continued over a long period of time, because they accumulate in the body. But a report by two researchers from the Merck Institute for Therapeutic Research (*Nutrition Reviews,* February, 1951) states that doses as large as 1600 milligrams per kilogram of body weight proved completely harmless to laboratory animals. This is a massive dose indeed, since doses of vitamin B_{12} are usually reckoned in micrograms. (A microgram is only 1/1000 of a milligram.) And these animals were given 1600 milligrams per kilogram of weight! The vitamin B_{12} was given by injection.

Most of a group of heart patients, given vitamin B_{12} injections (30 micrograms), showed considerable improvement, a decrease in the size of the heart, increased urination and a feeling of well-being. The doctor who reports on these patients, Dr. J. I. Manrique of Argentina, reminds us that all of them had been on diets very low in vitamins. He suggests that vitamin B_{12} be given in all cases of congestive heart failure where any deficiency in vitamins is suspected.

Vitamin B_{12} is being produced from a sterile sewage sludge at the municipal sewage disposal plant in Mil-

[261]

waukee. Apparently the bacteria in the sewage manufacture the vitamin B₁₂ which is then extracted from the sludge. Although this process sounds as if it were as far removed as possible from good health practices, we are assured that the process used to extract the vitamin insures purity. In other words, what remains is the "crystalline" vitamin, with no impurities. *Chemical Week* (August 4, 1956) states that the vitamin produced this way is being used only in animal and poultry feeds, not for human beings.

The method used to produce the vitamin B_{12} that appears in food supplements for human beings is a fermentation process involving a bacteria called *streptomyces*. Such processes are used in industry to produce antibiotics, alcohol, vitamins, citric acid, beer, wine and other products. They are all called "fermentations" regardless of whether alcohol or something else is the product that finally results.

Vitamin B_{12} is the natural product which results from such a controlled fermentation. It happens to be produced by some of the same bacteria that also make antibiotics. So the processor gets two products instead of only one from his "fermentation."

Many microbes produce vitamin B_{12}. But naturally, commercial producers prefer to get it from a bug that also gives them an antibiotic. Eventually, of course, the vitamin is completely separated from the antibiotic, so that one substance does not contain any of the other substance. Usually some species of streptomyces (bacteria) is used to produce vitamin B_{12}, because these organisms also produce antibiotics. The vitamin B_{12} from such a process is, of course, a naturally occurring product.

Adding just a bit of vitamin B_{12} to the diet can turn runts into giants according to some 1955 investigations

[262]

of Dr. Norman Jolliffe of the New York City Health Department. Said Dr. Jolliffe as reported in the New York *Journal-American:* "The problem of undergrowth still remains in countless families in the nation. So we made a study of a selected group of 100 boys and girls. And we found that it is not the lack of enough good foods that accounted for growth failure in these cases.

"What happened was that the children just would not eat the very foods which they particularly needed for normal growth—proteins, vegetables, mineral-rich foods. Their appetites were poor, too, in many cases. Their minds were resistant to being fed properly.

"Mostly it was the influence of the mother's mind upon the child's mind; she was anxious, worried, and the child sensed that." Experiments have shown that vitamin B_{12} can restore growth in cases in which growth had virtually stopped. Other children felt better, happier. Dr. Jolliffe says, "Vitamin B_{12} has the special effect of producing body proteins of which blood and tissues are formed."

Summer is the big season for hives and rashes. They come from food allergies, heat, grass and dozens of other summer things. Those who suffer search avidly, and most times hopelessly, for a cure. Now new hope has risen for these sufferers with the discovery that vitamin B_{12} is probably the answer they're looking for. It brings prompt and complete clearing of these itchy welts, say S. William Simon and Paul Edmonds in the *Journal of the American Geriatrics Society* (January, 1964).

Simon and Edmonds say that a majority of the 100 cases they have recorded to date showed relief or cure on B_{12}. In the current report, eight males suffering from rashes brought on by such ailments as bronchial asthma, hay fever, anxiety neurosis, etc., were relieved or cleared entirely by B₁₂ injections. The amount they use to do the job is minute, just one injection of 1 milligram in 1 milliliter of water per day. Why would anyone plagued with a bothersome rash pass up such an easy chance for relief?

Anti-Cancer Action

The silence that has greeted B₁₂'s proven value as an anticancer agent is one of the true wonders of the cancer crusade. When dangerous drugs manage to slow cancers to prolong life, even for days, the papers are full of it—with concern about the dreadful side effects swept aside in the enthusiasm. B₁₂ has been reliably effective in the treatment of a fairly common childhood malignancy of the nerves, neuroblastoma, for more than a dozen years, yet an occasional mention in a medical journal is all this miracle rates. The most recent was an article in *Archives of Disease in Childhood* (December, 1963) which said, in part, "In view of the many cases recorded in this hospital (The Hospital for Sick Children, London) and elsewhere treated solely with vitamin B₁₂ with great success, it cannot be denied that this substance has a significant influence on the growth rate of neuroblastoma."

CHAPTER 40

The Discovery of Vitamin C

As LONG AGO AS 460 B.C. physicians knew about scurvy.
Hippocrates wrote of it in that year. In the time since
then soldiers in isolated camps, sailors on long voyages
and family groups during time of famine or crop failure
have been victims of scurvy. Until quite recently there
were epidemics of scurvy throughout northern Europe.
There were 30,000 cases of scurvy among the soldiers
in our own Civil War. During the first World War
there were more than 11,000 cases of scurvy and 7,500
fatalities from it among Allied soldiers fighting in the
Near East. More sailors have died of scurvy than have
been killed in all the naval battles ever fought.

At some date in history, someone decided that scurvy
must be caused by something people ate or didn't eat.
For instance, during the early days of colonization a
group of sailors desperately ill from scurvy were put
ashore on the New England coast to die. Indians who
found them gave them a tea made from evergreen

needles and the men recovered almost immediately. Captain Cook, the famous sailor, took his ship on a three-year voyage around the world and not a sailor got sick, for Captain Cook carried a large supply of barley on board, which was sprouted and made into a drink. He cleverly gave the drink only to officers at first, so that the sailors got the idea it must be something very special. Thereafter they insisted on having a daily dose of the barley-sprout liquid.

By the beginning of the nineteenth century it was well known that lemon juice protected against scurvy and it became a mandatory daily drink for all British seamen. By 1932 researchers had discovered in lemon juice a crystalline substance which protected guinea pigs from scurvy. Now we know this substance as vitamin C, or ascorbic acid, as it is called in chemistry. Incidentally, guinea pigs, the ape family and human beings are the only animals that do not make vitamin C in their bodies, and so must have it in their food. This is one reason why guinea pigs rather than other animals are used in laboratory experiments on vitamin C.

Vitamin C Deficiency Widespread

Vitamin C is the one vitamin most people seem to have heard something about. In other words, they have a vague idea that they ought to drink orange juice and from time to time eat some salad. Beyond that, their knowledge is quite incomplete. "But after all," you may say, "we surely don't have scurvy today. Nobody I know has died of scurvy!" True, in the United States the deficiency disease of scurvy has been largely conquered, due to the splendid publicity given to the healthfulness of fruits and vegetables, and also to the fact that most fruits and vegetables are available here year-round.

[266]

But in this country we have a condition that is perhaps almost as distressing as scurvy: a large part of our population gets just enough vitamin C to prevent symptoms of scurvy, but not nearly enough to prevent other harmful results on their body economy. These folks have, as doctors put it, a "sub-clinical" case of scurvy, which is difficult to detect without doing careful laboratory tests to determine the amount of vitamin C in the blood.

So we have millions of Americans who swig down their fruit juice at breakfast, feeling righteous about it, and give not another thought to vitamin C for the rest of the day. As a result, we are a nation that suffers continually from minor ailments such as colds, sinus trouble, bleeding gums, pyorrhea, mineral deficiency, cataract, loose teeth and so forth. Not scurvy, no, but certainly not good health. Tests have shown that people in the West get more vitamin C than Easterners. Two-thirds of the college students tested in a Western college got sufficient vitamin C in their daily diet, while only one-fourth of the students in Massachusetts and Rhode Island colleges got enough. In summer and fall people generally get more vitamin C because they are eating fresh fruits and vegetables in quantity. In winter and spring they do not usually eat so much of these foods and what they do get have been so long in storage or in transport that most of the vitamin C is gone.

Vitamin C Performs Many Functions in the Body

What is the function of vitamin C in the body? As the red blood cells carry oxygen to each individual cell of the body, so vitamin C carries hydrogen, another substance necessary for the proper burning of our foodstuffs. In addition, vitamin C is necessary for the health of our connective tissues, the substance which

[267]

binds all the individual cells together, composes cartilages, veins, ligaments and so forth. If this substance
is not in good repair, many disastrous consequences may
result.

For instance in a child who does not get enough vitamin C, the bones do not grow at the proper rate or
perhaps do not grow at all. The joints may swell.
"Growing pains" may be caused by deficiency of vitamin
C. Suppose there is not enough of the vitamin to keep
the walls of blood vessels in good repair? The tiniest
vessels, the capillaries, break and a slight hemorrhage
follows. This is actually what happens when one suffers
a bruise. Have you noticed that some people, particularly older people, seem to bruise very easily, while
others can get a hard knock and show no bruise at all?
Bruising indicates lack of vitamin C, for the discoloration that follows is nothing but the hemorrhaging of
the tiny capillaries.

Vitamin C is so important for the prevention of
hemorrhaging that it is often given before and after
surgical operations or tooth extractions. Lack of vitamin C also affects the dentine of the teeth, causing it
to wear away, resulting in damage to the enamel and
finally decay. Our "sub-clinical" deficiency of ascorbic
acid is undoubtedly one good reason for the widespread
amount of tooth decay in America. Vitamin C is also
necessary for the proper absorption of iron in the body,
so it becomes extremely necessary in anemia, which
may be caused by lack of the vitamin even though
ample iron is present in the diet.

The precious minerals such as calcium and phosphorus which our body needs for so many functions are
stored in our bones until they are needed. If not enough
vitamin C is present, the tissues of this storage place

[268]

will not retain the minerals and they are lost to us. Finally vitamin C is a powerful agent against the infections that plague us. An individual who gets over and above his daily quota of the vitamin will not be subject to these many infections. Other articles in this book tell almost unbelievable stories of the effectiveness of vitamin C in the treatment of diseases we have come to think of as mysterious and incurable.

How To Preserve Vitamin C In Foods

Storage and preparation of food is more important to the preservation of vitamin C than it is to any other vitamin. This means simply that *vitamin C is the most highly perishable vitamin there is.* It is soluble in water. If you bring home from market a head of cabbage or lettuce and soak it in water to "crisp" it, all its vitamin C content immediately disappears into the water. Since cabbage is one of the foods richest in this vitamin, make certain you do not ever waste it by soaking cabbage. Wash all vegetables as rapidly as possible in cold water and place immediately in your refrigerator, preferably in a "crisper" or airtight container, for contact with air also destroys vitamin C.

To get the most value from vitamin C foods, it is best to eat them raw, just as soon as possible after they are picked. If you must cook them, follow these simple rules. Have the water boiling briskly before you put the vegetables in, for the boiling water destroys an enzyme which helps to cause loss of vitamin C. Boil them for a minute or so, then turn down the heat and let them cook more slowly for the briefest possible time —just until they are tender. Even with this amount of care, perhaps a fourth of the vitamin C will have passed into the cooking water, along with other water-

[269]

soluble vitamins, such as the **B** vitamins. So save all water in which you have cooked vegetables! Keep it in the refrigerator, tightly covered, and use it for soups, gravies or other recipes that call for water.

When you are preparing vegetables to eat either raw or cooked, do the whole job just before they are served or cooked. Let's say you're shredding cabbage for cole slaw, dicing carrots or slicing string beans. Every cut surface of the vegetables means loss of vitamin C, so do not ever let prepared or shelled vegetables stand before using them. Steaming, stewing, baking and frying are all destructive to vitamin C because of the long periods of cooking time or the high temperatures required. If you are making a meat stew or soup which requires long, slow cooking, do not add the vegetables until a few minutes before serving—just long enough to tenderize them. Open-kettle canning of home-canned tomatoes, for instance, destroys practically all vitamin C. From this point of view, commercially canned tomatoes are much richer in this vitamin, as they have been canned by vacuum pack so that no air enters to destroy this vitamin. Frozen vegetables kept at very low temperatures retain vitamin C reasonably well.

We scarcely need to remind you that baking soda added to cooking water destroys not only some of the vitamin C but other nutrients as well in the vegetables you are cooking. So if you drop a pinch of soda into green beans or peas, to give them a nice green color, you might just as well look at them and not bother to eat them at all, for there will be little food value left. One final caution—contact with copper destroys vitamin C. If you have beautiful and expensive copper cooking utensils, hang them on the wall for decoration, but never, never use them to cook in. Beware, too, of chipped enamelware pans, for the base of enamelware is copper.

Recommended Requirements

Here are the minimum daily requirements for vitamin C as determined by the Food and Nutrition Board of the National Research Council:

	Milligrams of vitamin C
Children under 1 year	30
Children 1-3 years	35
Children 4-6 years	50
Children 7-9 years	60
Children 10-12 years	75
Girls 13-20 years	80
Boys 13-15 years	90
Boys 16-20 years	100
Men	75
Women	70

Foods That Contain Most Vitamin C

In the chart below we give you the names of foods high in vitamin C. When you are planning how to include enough vitamin C in the family menus, keep in mind the facts we have told you above about its perishability. And, for safety's sake—because this vitamin is so perishable and because none of us gets enough of it especially in the winter—do add rose hips to your food supplements. They contain, gram for gram, more vitamin C than any of the foods listed below. And they are the outstanding natural food supplement containing this most elusive and necessary vitamin. You can take them as powder or in capsule or tablet form. Or you can gather your own rose hips and make them into puree.

Food	Milligrams of vitamin C
Asparagus, fresh green	20 in 8 stalks
Beans, green lima	42 in ½ cup

[271]

Food	Milligrams of vitamin C
Beet greens, cooked	50 in ½ cup
Broccoli, flower	65 in ¾ cup
Broccoli, leaf	90 in ¾ cup
Brussels sprouts	130 in ¾ cup
Cabbage, Chinese, raw	50 in 1 cup
Cabbage, green, raw	50 in 1 cup
Cabbage, inside leaves, raw ...	50 in 1 cup
Cantaloupe	50 in ½ small cantaloupe
Chard, Swiss, cooked	37 in ½ cup
Collards, cooked	70 in ½ cup
Currants, red	40 in 1 cup
Dandelion greens, cooked	100 in 1 cup
Grapefruit, fresh	45 in ½ grapefruit
Grapefruit juice, fresh	108 in 1 cup
Grapefruit juice, canned	72 in 1 cup
Guavas	125 in 1 guava
Honeydew melon	90 in ¼ medium honeydew
Kale, cooked	96 in ¾ cup
Kohlrabi	50 in ½ cup
Leeks	25 in ½ cup
Lemon juice	25 in 1 tablespoon
Lime juice	18 in ¼ cup
Liver, beef	30 in 1 slice
Liver, calves	25 in 1 slice
Liver, chicken	25 in ½ cup
Liver, lamb	20 in 1 slice
Loganberries	35 in 1 cup
Mandarin orange	46 in 2 small oranges
Mustard greens, cooked	125 in ½ cup
Orange	50 in 1 medium orange
Orange juice, fresh	120 in 1 cup
Orange juice, canned	80 in 1 cup
Parsley	70 in ½ cup
Parsnips	20 in ½ cup
Peas, fresh cooked	40 in 1 cup
Peppers, green	125 in 1 medium pepper
Peppers, pimento	200 in 2 medium peppers
Persimmon, Japanese	40 in 1 large persimmon
Pineapple, fresh	38 in 2/3 cup
Pineapple juice, canned	25 in 1 cup
Potatoes, sweet	25 in 1 medium potato
Potatoes, white, baked	20 in 1 medium potato
Potatoes, white, raw	33 in 1 medium potato

Food	Milligrams of vitamin C
Radishes	25 in 15 large radishes
Raspberries, black	66 in 1 cup
Raspberries, red	23 in 1 cup
Rose hips	500 to 6000 in 100 grams
Rutabagas	26 in ¾ cup
Spinach, cooked	30 in ½ cup
Strawberries, fresh	50 in ½ cup
Tangerines	48 in 2 medium tangerines
Tomatoes, canned	20 in ½ cup
Tomatoes, fresh	25 in 1 medium tomato
Tomato juice, canned	48 in 1 cup
Turnips, cooked	22 in ½ cup
Turnips, raw	30 in 1 medium turnip
Turnip tops, cooked	130 in ½ cup
Watercress	54 in 1 average bunch

CHAPTER 41

You ARE Vitamin C

SINCE THE FIRST sample of vitamin C (or ascorbic acid) was extracted from a laboratory beaker of lemon juice in the days of the mid-twenties, constant experimentation with this vitamin has given us ever-increasing proof of man's dependence upon a good supply of vitamin C. It is almost impossible to keep up with the research in this field, for the powerful influence of vitamin C on the body is always challenging scientists to see what else this magic substance can do to keep us healthy or if it can be used to treat an illness that seems to have no cure.

In a book, *Vitamin C,* published by Merck and Company, Incorporated, Rahway, New Jersey, we came across many interesting facts about vitamin C and its use, both as a preventive medicine and a treatment in the relief of many symptoms.

Though we have always been convinced of the body's need for vitamin C, we were astounded at the many ways in which experimentation has shown it to be effective, and dramatically so.

It is not too great an exaggeration to say that we *are* vitamin C! It is the vital ingredient which welds the cells together and these are, after all, the very stuff of flesh, bones, blood and organs. Without vitamin C these things cannot maintain themselves—and without these things we cannot exist.

We know that the body does not manufacture ascorbic acid, nor can it be stored. It must come to the body in a steady and undiminished supply by way of the foods we eat—fresh vegetables, fresh fruits, rose hips, etc. (Fresh liver is also a rich source of vitamin C.)

Once in the body, ascorbic acid is absorbed by the walls of the small intestine. However, since the food passes through the small intestine quickly, there is a limited amount of time for this absorption to take place. The *American Journal of Physiology* quotes an experiment which indicates that only small amounts of vitamin C can be absorbed at a single time, and the rest is wasted when it has once passed through the small intestine. It is, therefore, obvious that the dosage of ascorbic acid must be spread across the day, allowing for small amounts to be taken which can be quickly assimilated. The body will expel in the urine any surplus or unabsorbed vitamin C.

How Vitamin C Is Depleted

The ease with which vitamin C leaves the body is emphasized by several experiments which have shown:

1. Ascorbic acid is drained by prolonged treatment with ACTH or cortisone, used for arthritis cases. Patients showed symptoms of scurvy which were relieved only by the administration of large doses of vitamin C

[275]

(*American Medical Association Archives of Internal Medicine,* December, 1951).

2. Sulfa drugs stimulate the urinary excretion of vitamin C to 2 or 3 times the normal amount. The author of a piece in *Southern Medicine and Surgery,* September, 1943, suggests the administration of 100 milligrams of ascorbic acid per day to replenish the lost stock during sulfa therapy. We are opposed to the use of sulfa drugs, and we consider 100 milligrams of ascorbic acid a very minute therapeutic dose when the body is subjected to such stress as sulfa treatment.

3. Prolonged administration of antibiotics may result in deficiencies of vitamin C and vitamins of the B complex, too (*Annals of Internal Medicine,* December, 1952). The German journal, *Klinische Wochenschrift,* March 15, 1955, goes further by saying that blood and urine levels of almost all vitamins fell during antibiotic therapy.

4. Deficiencies of vitamin A are sure to lead to depletion of vitamin C resources. Vitamin B and vitamin E work more efficiently in the body when enough vitamin C is present (*Journal of Nutrition,* May 10, 1948).

5. The blood level of ascorbic acid is lowered by smoking. Nicotine added to a sample of whole human blood of known ascorbic acid content decreased the ascorbic acid content of the blood by 24 to 31 per cent (*American Journal of Digestive Diseases,* March, 1953).

Those are just some of the ways vitamin C supplies can be depleted in the body. Now for a few instances of the uses this workhorse vitamin C is put to:

In Formation of Teeth and Bones:

1. Its use as a bone maker is demonstrated by an

[276]

experiment which is detailed in the *Journal of Physiology* (November 30, 1942). It was found by experiments that two milligrams of vitamin C per day are needed to insure adequate regeneration of an injured bone of a small laboratory animal, and less than one milligram would seriously retard regeneration. In humans the same results would be produced by 40 and 20 milligrams of vitamin C.

2. It is presumed that the teeth of infants are affected in a way similar to the way the teeth of experimental guinea pigs were affected in a report carried in the *Journal of Dentistry for Children* (third quarter, 1943).

In vitamin-C-deficient guinea pigs the dentine in the developing teeth ceased to form and the pulp became separated from the dentine by liquid. There was either a cessation of dentine manufacture, or the dentine manufactured was of inferior quality. The pulp itself was shrunken and, free from the dentine, was apparently floating in a liquid. Rapid repair followed the administration of vitamin C in natural form. Obviously infants whose teeth are forming must receive sufficient vitamin C.

Collagen Formation and Wound Repair:

1. Experimental human scurvy was induced by reducing ascorbic acid to zero for 13 weeks. With total vitamin C deficiency, failure of wound healing occurred—the tissues, under microscope showed a lack of intercellular substance. Vitamin C dosage brought about good healing and considerable intercellular substance appeared within 10 days (*New England Journal of Medicine,* September 5, 1940).

2. A 50 per cent diminution of tensile strength in healing incisions was one result of freely induced vita-

[277]

min C deficiency for experimental purposes. Unfavorable conditions such as decreased blood supply or excessive wound tension prevent primary wound healing in the absence of vitamin C (*Surgery, Gynecology and Obstetrics,* January, 1947).

3. The *Journal of the American Medical Association* (May 28, 1955) states that in the evaluation of vitamin needs for surgical patients, ascorbic acid is the only nutrient whose lack has been proved to delay or prevent wound healing in man. Many surgeons prescribe large doses of vitamin C for their postoperative patients.

4. In 62 burn cases the *New York State Journal of Medicine,* October 5, 1951, reports that use of ascorbic acid shortened the interval before skin grafts could be performed, and antibiotic therapy was seldom required. Also, it stated that the use of ascorbic acid hastens the healing period and lessens the need for other therapy.

Vitamin C for Pregnant Women:

1. Latent scurvy may be present in the infant at birth, according to the *Proceedings of the Society for Experimental Biology and Medicine* (November, 1942). It was shown that the umbilical cord carries vitamin C to the infant from the mother. Therefore, a major deficiency in the mother would certainly be reflected in the child, as she is the only source of vitamin C supply for her baby.

2. The *Canadian Medical Association Journal,* January, 1942, reported that the percentage of successful pregnancies among poor women was increased by giving them ample foods containing vitamin C, thiamin and riboflavin (two B vitamins). Infants born to the

women in the test were rated good, fair and poor. The percentages of "good" babies born to the mothers in relation to their diets were: 62.3 per cent to those on poor diets; 72.3 per cent to those on good diets; 92.5 per cent to those on supplemented diets. The course of pregnancy was good on 66 per cent of the women on poor diets, 85 per cent of those on good diets and 94 per cent of those on supplemented diets.

3. Mothers' milk analyses showed a high content of vitamin C, which points to the baby's need for this element since it is included in this most natural of diets (*American Journal of Diseases of Children,* September, 1945).

4. In cases of habitual spontaneous abortion, the *Journal of the American Medical Association* (July 28, 1951) suggests the administration of ascorbic acid and vitamin D to all pregnant patients who have essential hypertension. It is thought that these vitamins in high enough dosage will reduce fragility of the blood vessels and tendency to premature separation of the placenta.

Gastrointestinal Disorders:

1. In the treatment of peptic ulcers by supplementing an antacid with ascorbic acid, the addition of vitamin C was followed by longer remissions and fewer relapses when compared with control groups who received antacid treatment without ascorbic acid. It is recommended that more consideration be given to ascorbic acid supplementation in the therapy of peptic ulcers (*American Practitioner,* February, 1952).

2. The *British Medical Journal* for May 17, 1947, details a case in which the patient was hemorrhaging from the digestive tract. His intake of vitamin C had been low in recent years due to symptoms of peptic

[279]

ulcer. Within half an hour after the intravenous injection of 1000 milligrams of ascorbic acid, the patient who had appeared near death became alert and cheerful. It took three weeks for the urine tests to show a saturation of the body with vitamin C. Vitamin P was also administered. No more blood vomiting occurred. Blood gradually disappeared from the stool.

3. *American Journal of Digestive Disease,* October, 1948, suggests that when a patient continues to bleed uncontrollably in spite of repeated transfusions, the possibility of a vitamin C deficiency must be considered. Two such patients were given injections of 100 milligrams of ascorbic acid every two hours and a cessation of the hemorrhage was brought about. Recovery followed. The article states that the diet of an ulcer patient should be fortified with ascorbic acid because of its favorable effect in case of hemorrhage.

Vitamin C Therapy for Infection:

1. In cases of rheumatic infections, scarlet fever and diphtheria, it was illustrated by a group of patients that fever accompanied by infection may increase vitamin C utilization and thus create a shortage in the body's supply (*American Journal of the Diseases of Children,* September, 1942).

2. *Journal of the American Medical Association* (July 17, 1948), cites several references to support the contention that adequate doses of vitamin C are essential in the diet of patients with rheumatic fever.

3. In cases of whooping cough, an experiment with 90 children proved ascorbic acid to be effective. The children were given ascorbic acid orally or by injection in a daily dosage of 500 milligrams for the first 7 days, gradually reduced until 100 milligrams daily was reach-

ed. This last dose was continued until recovery was complete. The results of the experiment: duration of disease in children receiving ascorbic acid, 15 to 20 days; average duration for children receiving vaccine, 34 days. When ascorbic acid therapy was started during the catarrhal stage, the spasmodic stage was prevented in 75 per cent of the cases (*Journal of the American Medical Association,* November 4, 1950).

Two Problems That Plague Older Folks:

1. Severe ulcers of the cornea of the eye have been treated with good results by intravenous injections of ascorbic acid. Large amounts of ascorbic acid have been suggested to aid the dwindling metabolism of the lens when cataract is present (*American Journal of Ophthalmology,* June, 1951).

2. *Geriatrics,* August, 1954, reports painful arthritis shows response to vitamin C treatment. High vitamin C intake resulted in significant decrease in pain and some improvement in appetite and well-being, though there was no improvement in mobility or swelling of joints.

In multiple sclerosis, objective and subjective improvement was noted in the majority of cases when large doses of ascorbic acid were administered.

These cases do not, by any means, comprise our total evidence for the effectiveness of vitamin C. We could continue indefinitely if space permitted us to do so. However, we feel that with the list you have just read, our aim has been accomplished. The wide range of uses for vitamin C has been demonstrated satisfactorily, we think. No person knowing these things and having an interest in good health would allow himself to risk the danger of sustaining a deficiency of this absolutely essential nutrient.

[281]

CHAPTER 42

How Much Vitamin C Do You Need?

THE ANSWER TO the question, "How much vitamin C do you need?" seems to be "as much as you can get" with no qualifications or apologies. We might almost say the question itself sounds to us like asking "How much air do you need?" You need air constantly every minute of the day and night. You need vitamin C every day. Your body cannot manufacture it any more than it can manufacture air. And, since vitamin C is soluble in water, most of what you take in your meals on any given day is used and then excreted within a short time.

One gets "clinical" scurvy when his intake of vitamin C is 15 to 20 milligrams per day. If capillary fragility is a test for scurvy, then the daily minimum intake should be set between 20 and 30 milligrams, for it takes that much vitamin C to prevent the capillaries from becoming so fragile that they will rupture under slight pressure. Years ago it was thought 50 milligrams, which is enough to elevate the vitamin C content of the blood, was the ideal amount to get in daily fare. Now we consider that 100 milligrams a day is optimum. Caught in the middle of the controversy as to whether the official recommended requirement should be higher or lower than this, the National Research Council finally recommended 75 milligrams as the ideal daily intake for adults. Their full recommendations appear on page 271.

Get More Than the Recommended Amount

Walter H. Eddy and Gilbert Dahldorf, M.D., in *The Avitaminoses* (Williams and Wilkins Company, 1944), say, "in the case of ascorbic acid there is very clear-cut proof that in experimental animals an intake twice or 3 times that required to prevent clinical signs is necessary to prevent anatomical stigmata of certain organs." In other words, we know from animal experiments that if you get two or three times the amount of vitamin C that will protect you from scurvy, you probably will prevent any organs from showing signs of deficiency. Your gums will probably not redden and swell, for instance; you may not bruise easily. But even so, is this a sign of perfect health? We believe that you may need, for perfect health, even more vitamin C than twice or three times the recommended amount!

Here are some of our reasons for this belief. First, we know that early man ate his food right from the trees, bushes and plants. He had no way to preserve it. So he must have gotten enormous amounts of vitaman C. Over the thousands of years, this kind of diet made the freshness of foods important. Cells that are accustomed to a certain chemical procedure cannot adapt themselves to change overnight—by which we mean, in the history of man, several thousand years. Now perhaps the most important thing about fresh

[283]

foods is their vitamin C content. It is not possible, at least for those of us who live in the North, to do all our eating outdoors, picking our food right off the tree or bush year-round. Yet that is undoubtedly the way our early ancestors lived. So we must somehow manage to supply year-round all the vitamin C we might get if we were living an idyllic life in the tropics with fruits and vegetables everywhere available, just for the picking.

Second reason for getting far more vitamin C than the recommended amount: Modern life exposes us to countless substances that use up our slender store of vitamin C at a rapid rate.

Third reason for getting far more vitamin C than the recommended amount: We eat so much worthless food today that we must take extra pains to get enough vitamin-C-rich foods. Every thing we eat in the way of cereal or bread products crowds out the fresh fruits and vegetables we should have had that day. All the fancy desserts, the soda fountain items, the between-meal and midnight snacks of crackers or pie, the hot cakes for breakfast, the cup of coffee at "coffee break" time—all these could and should be replaced in the healthful diet with foods rich in vitamin C—fresh raw fruits and vegetables.

Fourth reason for getting far more vitamin C than the recommended amount: We cook our foods to worthless pottage, from which all vitamin C has fled. Brussels sprouts contain 130 milligrams of vitamin C per serving. But after you have soaked them, cooked them in lots of hot water and then thrown away the cooking water, you will be lucky if they contain one-tenth that much vitamin C.

Finally, listen to the words of our two authorities,

Eddy and Dahldorf, when they say that the problem is different in different individuals. Some excrete more vitamin C than others. Some probably don't use it as efficiently as others. Those of us who have infections of any kind—acute or chronic, even very mild ones—should get more vitamin C.

How You Use Vitamin C Is Important

In an experiment involving 29 cases of mild scurvy, 26 of the patients responded within 10 days to 300 milligrams of vitamin C given by mouth. The other 3 showed no improvement. They were then given vitamin C by injection. Still their scurvy persisted. Then they were given the juice of 10 lemons daily and their symptoms disappeared. Undoubtedly the food element that worked the cure was something else that occurs with vitamin C in natural foods—was it vitamin P? Possibly.

It is also true that the other foods in your diet may have something to do with preventing scurvy. It has been discovered that people who are on generally good diets—that is, with plenty of the other vitamins and minerals—can go without vitamin C much longer without developing scurvy. For this reason some researchers think that man may be able to manufacture his own vitamin C internally if he has supplies of enough other necessary food elements.

Scientists have noted the similarity between the changes that take place in scurvy and in senility. The bones and the teeth especially show lack of vitamin C in patients with scurvy and in many older people. "The decline in vitamin C content of human tissue after the age of 45 indicates an increased rate of destruction or wastage of this vitamin in older people," says Pro-

[285]

fessor Sherman of Columbia, one of our country's greatest nutritionists. Larger amounts of the vitamin are needed to saturate the blood of older people. Possibly the part that vitamin C plays in helping tissues to breathe may eventually be the clue that will aid our understanding of senility.

Meanwhile, we know for certain that the older we grow, the more vitamin C we need. And, of course, this is the very time of life when trouble with dentures or bad teeth causes many of us to stop eating fresh raw foods entirely.

In a study conducted at the Long Island Hospital in Boston, 140 patients—all "elderly"—were tested for the vitamin C content of their blood and the effects of a greatly increased intake of the vitamin. There were 39 arthritics, 25 diabetics and 12 patients with multiple sclerosis in the group.

Reporting in *Geriatrics* (Vol. 9, p. 375, 1954), L. C. Cass and his associates who conducted the test tell us that they observed that elderly institutionalized persons receive very little fresh fruit in their diet and have low blood levels of vitamin C. The chronic arthritis and multiple sclerosis patients who got a high (massive doses) vitamin C intake every day said that their pain was less and they had an improved appetite and sense of well-being.

The massive doses of vitamin C that were given consisted of 4 grams (4,000 milligrams) daily of vitamin C. They received this large amount for three months with no sign of any serious aftereffects. There's no doubt of it—lack of vitamin C must be responsible for many of the ills we fall heir to in the later years of life.

CHAPTER 43

"Getting Old" and Vitamin C Shortage

THE FOLLOWING excerpts are from Dr. McCormick's paper "Have We Forgotten the Lesson of Scurvy?" published in the *Journal of Applied Nutrition,* Vol. 15, nos. 1 and 2, 1962. The numbers appearing in the text refer to the bibliography which can be obtained by writing to the above journal.

After the discovery and isolation of vitamin C in 1928, and the establishment of its causal relationship to scurvy, the declining incidence of this disease has led to complacency, scurvy being thought of as a well-nigh extinct disease. This has resulted in failure to recognize and treat subclinical forms of this disease and its complicating relationship to many other diseases.

Subclinical Scurvy and the Rheumatic Diseases

Here Dr. McCormick cites old writings in which symptoms that suggest arthritic lesions were attributed to scurvy. From this he deduced that lesser but similar

[287]

symptoms of chronic rheumatic disease might also be due to deficiency of vitamin C. A therapeutic trial confirmed the deduction.

Lind cites Sennerti (1624), who, writing on scurvy, states: "In some, though more rarely on each motion of their joints, a noise was heard as from broken bones or like the crackling of nuts (crepitus)." This is suggestive of our modern arthritic lesions. Engaleno, also cited by Lind, states that "gout is known to proceed from scurvy, by not being fixed but shifting from one joint to another and its being quickly cured by antiscorbutics." Harvey, also cited by Lind, divides scurvy into three kinds—mouth scurvy, leg scurvy and joint scurvy.

If such articular lesions were found in times past in frank scurvy cases, it is only logical to conclude that similar lesions of lesser degree, such as we now find in chronic rheumatic disease, may be etiologically related to deficiency of vitamin C. Our modern knowledge of this vitamin may thus provide the linkage between scurvy and these diseases. James Rinehart and Stacy Mettier (4) were the first modern writers to correlate deficiency of vitamin C with rheumatic disease. In animal experiments they found that prolonged deficiency of this vitamin in the diet produced functional impairment and anatomic changes in the joints. Throughout this research the concurrence of infection, superimposed on vitamin C deficiency, is stressed as being jointly involved in rheumatic etiology. The writer of this thesis adopts a modification of this concept in regarding both the infections and the arthritic phenomena as the sequelae of vitamin C deficiency.

Recently the author of this thesis has made therapeutic trial of massive doses of vitamin C (1 to 10 grams daily), intravenously and orally, in a number of cases of rheumatic fever. The patients made rapid and complete recovery in three to four weeks without cardiac complications. Similarly favorable results have been obtained in incipient arthritis. We therefore believe that the rheumatic diseases should no longer be regarded as of unknown etiology.

Intervertebral Disc Lesions

Eighteenth-century postmortems on victims of scurvy showed degeneration of cartilage resembling the condition of the cartilage in modern lesions of the discs of the spine. The doctor suggests vitamin C therapy for all cartilaginous lesions.

Our knowledge of the pathology of the intervertebral discs has been developed mostly within the last three decades. It is more than likely that lesions of these structures were equally if not more prevalent in earlier times, but were not generally recognized until x-ray technique became a major factor in physical examination.

The possibility of preconditioning factors, in the form of degenerative changes has been intimated by most writers, but the exact nature or cause of such changes has not been established. According to Beedle (5), "It is submitted as the most probable theory that certain faults in the texture of the cartilage matrix occur . . . and give rise to the rupture of the cartilage by minute traumatic influences that would have no effect on normal tissue." As degenerative changes advance in the disc structure the elasticity of the same lessens, and this loss of function is sometimes hastened by deposition of calcium, and the efficiency of the confining fibro-elastic network is lost. When the stage of rupture

[289]

and herniation is reached, the resultant lacerations are often accompanied by extensive hemorrhages, which further complicate the picture. That these lesions are not due to senile degenerative changes is shown by the age incidence; beginning in the second decade, it reaches its peak in the fourth, after which it gradually declines. Key (6) has reported intervertebral disc lesions in young children and adolescents.

From a carefully correlated study of the nutritional background of subjects of these lesions, and from the records of analogous postmortem findings regarding the condition of cartilaginous structures in scurvy, as cited by Lind in his treatise on this subject (1753), we are convinced that deficiency of vitamin C plays an important role in the etiology of these lesions, as well as in those of the semilunar cartilages of the knees, the sacroiliac synchondroses, etc. It seems obvious therefore that therapeutic use of the vitamin should be made as part of the nonsurgical care of all such cases. It is conceivable that such means might result in fixation of a slipping disc or cartilage and prevent rupture or herniation of same. "A stitch in time saves nine."

Pneumonia

In 1936 Gander and Niederberger (7) found that vitamin C favorably influenced the course of pneumonia. When the vitamin C status was brought up to normal saturation level early in the disease the temperature dropped abruptly to normal and the pain subsided. The pulse remained of good tone, and remarkable general improvement was made. In the same year Hochwald (8) independently reported similar results, his findings indicating that massive doses of vitamin C—500 milligrams every 90 minutes until the temperature drops to normal—exerted a curative effect

[290]

in croupous pneumonia as shown in lessened prostration and dyspnea, earlier return to normal temperature and to normal white-blood cell picture. More recently the author of this treatise had occasion to treat a case of bilateral pneumonia in a middle-aged man. The temperature was 104 and both lungs were almost filled with exudate. Treatment was begun with 1000 milligrams of vitamin C intravenously, followed by 500 milligrams orally with a half glass of orange juice every hour. On second call, 7 hours later, the intravenous injection was repeated. At that time the temperature was nearly normal. This same treatment was continued for three days, by which time the pulmonary exudate had practically cleared. On the fourth day the patient felt so well that he voluntarily resumed work with no adverse effects. In 1944 Slotkin and Fletcher (9) reported on the prophylactic and therapeutic value of vitamin C in postoperative pneumonia. They summarized their findings as follows: "Pulmonary complications in old debilitated patients requiring prostatic surgery is a common cause of death. The pulmonary lesions most noticed were bronchopneumonia, lung abscess and purulent bronchitis. Most of these cases were 'wet chests' due to capillary secretions. Ascorbic acid, which increases the tonicity of these capillaries, has greatly alleviated this condition and promptly restored normal pulmonary function." Slotkin (10) further reports that since publication of his paper on this subject "ascorbic acid has been used routinely by the general surgeons in the Millard-Fillmore Hospital, Buffalo, as a prophylactic against pneumonia, with complete disappearance of this complication." Terminal pneumonia is often the cause of death in scurvy, and the "rusty-brown" sputum of pneumonia may owe its origin to the hemorrhagic status of subclinical scurvy.

[291]

Vitamin C for Tuberculosis

Tuberculosis has long been clinically related to scurvy and vitamin C deficiency, and has been favorably influenced by concurrent vitamin C therapy. Richard Morton, one of the earliest writers on this disease, says in his famous *Phthisiologia* (1689) : "Scurvy is wont to occasion a consumption of the lungs." Harris (11) finds that the excretion of vitamin C is decreased in tuberculosis, that this deficiency reduces the resistance of guinea pigs in tuberculosis, and that similar effects have been observed in man. Bauer and Vorwerk (12) report vitamin C deficiencies of from 1 to 4 grams in tuberculosis cases. They state that there seems to be certain parallelism between the activity of tuberculosis and the extent of vitamin C deficiency. McConkey (13) reports that of 437 pulmonary cases admitted to a New York State Hospital for tuberculosis in 1926 and 1927, 47 developed intestinal tuberculosis; whereas, of 399 admitted in 1928 and 1929, who received a prophylactic treatment consisting of 3 ounces of citrus or tomato juice and ½ ounce of cod liver oil with each meal, only 3 developed intestinal tuberculosis. Furthermore, of 913 other patients admitted during 1930 to 1938, who received the same prophylactic treatment, only 9 developed intestinal tuberculosis. Borsalino (14) reports a study of 140 tuberculous patients, in which administration of vitamin C rapidly increased capillary resistance and stopped hemotysis, which reappeared when the treatment was discontinued. Moore *et al.* (15), in a recent survey of nutrition among the northern Manitoba Indians, report a very high mortality rate from tuberculosis and pneumonia (761 and 383 respectively, per 100,000). In the tribes covered by their study, the

[292]

death rate for tuberculosis in 1942 was 1400 per 100,-000. The figure for the white population of Manitoba at that time was 27 per 100,000. They found the daily per capita food intake most deficient in vitamin C—less than 1/71 of the recommended allowance. In conclusion they say: "It is not unlikely that the Indian's great susceptibility to many diseases, paramount amongst which is tuberculosis may be attributable to their high degree of malnutrition."

Coronary Thrombosis

Vitamin C deficiency, and consequent capillary hemorrhage, has been found in 81 per cent of coronary cases.

Coronary thrombosis first made its appearance in our vital statistics about 50 years ago. Since then its incidence has been steadily increasing until now it heads our mortality list in the vascular-disease group, and tops our mortality figures generally. The major clinical feature of this disease is the development of a thrombus on the intima of the coronary artery at a point of threatened breach, gradually building up until in the course of weeks, months or years it occludes the lumen of the artery. As this state approaches the patient suffers heart pains and shortness of breath, in many cases culminating in a fatal seizure.

Paterson (16), of the Ottawa Civic Hospital, in a series of autopsies on coronary cases, frequently found a capillary hemorrhage at the site of the thrombosis, which he regarded as an etiological prelude resulting from deficiency of vitamin C. In support of this conclusion he found that 81 per cent of his coronary cases had a subnormal level of vitamin C, compared to 55 per cent in a corresponding group of general public ward cases. Accordingly he suggested that coronary patients be assured of an adequate intake of this vitamin. Willis (17) has shown that scurvy (or extreme deficiency of vitamin C) in guinea pigs is prone to cause thrombotic lesions identical with those of the human disease.

Subclinical Scurvy and Cancer

There are strong clinical similarities between scurvy and cancer, and pronounced vitamin C deficiency has been found in cancer cases. Dr. McCormick speculates that disintegration of epithelial and connective tissue, because of lack of the vitamin, may be an important preliminary to cancer development.

As long ago as 1609, Martini (cited by Lind) stated that scurvy is nearly allied to the plague, as it occasions carbuncles, buboes and cancer. In an effort to clarify this relationship we published two papers (18) in which we advanced the hypothesis that deficiency of vitamin C, by bringing about disintegration of epithelial and connective-tissue relationships, owing to liquefaction (19) of the intercellular cement substance (collagen) and disintegration of the connective tissue of the basement membrane, results in breakdown of orderly cellular arrangement, thus acting as a prelude to cancer. Pirani and Catchpole (20) found that glycoprotein (collagen) thus liberated finds its way into the blood stream, resulting in an increased serum level. Wollbach (21) found that administration of ascorbic acid (vitamin C) in scurvy rapidly restores the normal consistency of collagen. Simkin *et al.* (22) report an increase of serum glycoprotein (collagen) in cancer. Studies by Wingler (1953), Greenspan (1954), Locky *et al.* (1956) and Lansing (1957) have confirmed this finding. A correlation of these findings gives support

[294]

to our hypothesis. As further evidence, a diagnostic test for cancer has been developed in Germany (the Whitting reaction) based on the blood protein picture (23).

Schneider (24) cites Eickhorn as finding a pronounced deficiency of vitamin C in cancer cases, averaging 4,550 milligrams by the saturation method, while his noncancerous controls averaged only 1,350 milligrams. Bodansky *et al.* (25) studied the vitamin C level of blood plasma and white blood cells in cancer cases compared to noncancerous cases. They found the levels in the former to be significantly lower. Russell *et al.* (26) report that recurrent periods of scurvy, interspersed with periods of lettuce supplementation to prevent death, resulted in a significant shortening in the time of appearance of induced cancer on guinea pigs.

In accordance with these observations, may it not be maintained that the degree of malignancy in cancer is inversely proportionate to the degree of connective tissue resistance, which in turn is dependent upon the adequacy of the vitamin C status? Scirrhous cancer of the breast is slow to metastasize and may remain inactive for many years; whereas the medullary (soft) cancer of the breast is extremely invasive. In the former, there is predominant connective-tissue stroma which cohesively binds the cells effectively, thus curbing metastasis; while in the latter the structure is mainly cellular and almost completely lacking in connective-tissue binder, thus favoring metastasis. This variation in invasiveness is usually attributed to some intrinsic property of the cancer cells; but our hypothesis relates it to the acquired connective-tissue resistance of the host. In other words cancer is a disease that we unwittingly cultivate or contract by perverse habits of life. The wise man Solomon said "The curse

[295]

causeless shall not come" (Proverbs 26:2). Ravdin, I. S. (27), has said: "While surgery and radiology are helpful, they do not attack the underlying biological defects . . . Some time, some place, the existing jigsaw puzzle will be properly put together, and we shall wonder why the correct answer evaded us for so long a time."

The implications from these observations strongly suggest that our major effort should be directed toward prevention of the cause of the cellular disarrangement —collagenous breakdown of epithelial and subepithelial connective tissues — as manifested in open sores or fissures that fail to heal readily, and unusual or easily produced hemorrhage. Such lesions may be early warning signs of future cancer. They likewise are early signs of scurvy. Advance indications of such conditions may be noted in female subjects who bruise easily, as shown by unaccountable "black and blue" spots. We have found that fully 90 per cent of our adult female population are so afflicted, and by chemical test are found to be deficient in vitamin C.

Our observations in this respect have led us to the conclusion that the major cause of vitamin C deficiency in our modern civilization may be the well-nigh universal tobacco addiction. The smoking habit not only militates against normal nutritional practice, but actually neutralizes or destroys to a great extent what little vitamin C is taken in food. We have found by clinical and laboratory means, in checking the vitamin C requirements of subjects while smoking and not smoking, that the smoking of one cigarette, as ordinarily inhaled, tends to neutralize in the body about 25 milligrams of the vitamin, or that contained in an ordinary orange (28). This reciprocal effect is due, we think, to the chemical action of ascorbic acid as

[296]

an oxidizing or reducing agent. Our findings in this respect have been confirmed by independent research in the United States (29) and in Europe. On the basis of our hypothesis these findings would help to explain the phenomenal increase in lung cancer and the current upsurge in the incidence of leukemia in newborn infants and young children, which we have dealt with in a recent treatise (30).

In further support of this new concept of etiology we cite Dr. Felix Pincus, Germany, on the subject of "Acute Lymphatic Leukemia" in Nothnagel's Encyclopedia of Practical Medicine (American Edition, W. B. Saunders & Co., Philadelphia, 1905), sub-section "Acute Lymphatic Leukemia, pages 552-574, as follows: "The most striking clinical symptoms of the disease are the hemorrhages and their sequelae. We refer especially to hemorrhages into the skin, the invisible mucous membranes and the posterior eye ground; and further the hemorrhages in the interior of the body—those that are recognizable during life by their clinical results, as of the intestine, the bladder, the brain, and the labyrinth of the ear. Sometimes large and deep necroses of the skin arise, which spread rapidly and show not the least tendency to heal. The teeth sit loosely imbedded in the spongy remains of the mucous membrane. Every touch produces hemorrhage, making a condition completely identical with that of scurvy. Especially interesting in this regard is the case of acute leukemia in a 17-year-old girl who never, or at most rarely, ate fresh vegetables, a deficiency always named among the primary causes of scurvy."

This close linkage with scurvy seems to have been completely overlooked by modern writers on leukemia, the major stress being given to genetic changes in

[297]

chromosomes, irrespective of possible adverse maternal contributory factors. Ingalls (1956) has this to say: "Congenital defects are not all determined at the moment of conception; many are acquired during the ensuing fetal development. The latter are usually fetal manifestations of critical stress on the mother during pregnancy. Just as the genetically determined defects have been studied in the fruit fly by breeding experiments, so the acquired defects have been studied in the gravid mouse by the use of hypovia (lack of oxygen) as a standard stress applied to the mother. A large class of congenital defects is therefore preventable."

This new theory of the relationship of vitamin C deficiency in carcinogenesis suggests the possibility that all physical and chemical carcinogens may act indirectly by bringing about or exaggerating a latent deficiency of this vitamin. A comparable situation has prevailed regarding alcohol. For many years it was thought that alcohol was the specific cause of peripheral neuritis in the alcoholic subject, but it is now known that deficiency of vitamin B₁ is the cause, the alcohol only increasing the requirement of the vitamin.

Conclusion

In conclusion, it would seem that an optimal body level of vitamin C offers the best natural means of assuring healthy connective tissue and building natural resistance against any and all the diseases referred to in this treatise.

CHAPTER 44

Vitamin C and Senior Citizens

Is IT POSSIBLE that, as we grow older, we need more vitamin C—much more? The question was asked as long ago as 1940 by a physician at the Warneford Hospital, Oxford, England. Dr. P. Berkenau was concerned with what happens to the brains of older people: the changes that come with age and those that are called "senile dementia"—a much more serious group of symptoms.

Older people have a tendency to forget. They have a tendency to ramble in their speech and tell the same story many times. They have a tendency to inquire about something, then forget they have been answered and repeat their question almost immediately. These are symptoms of old age, you might say, but undoubtedly they represent certain changes in the actual physical structure of the brain cells.

Senility is characterized by an almost complete removal from reality on the part of the senile individual, so that he or she is no longer "responsible" but must be taken care of like a child. Memory becomes so disordered that friends and family go unrecognized. Delusions of persecution are common: the senile patient thinks that everyone is against him. It would appear that symptoms like these must be the result of much more basic changes in brain cells than just the milder symptoms of aging. Does nutrition have anything to do with preserving these brain cells and keeping them well-nourished against these degenerative changes? We are convinced that it does.

So we were happy to locate the article by Dr. Berkenau which appeared in the (British) *Journal of Mental Science* (Vol. 86, p. 675, 1940), on the subject of whether or not older people, especially those suffering from senility, are lacking in vitamin C.

Dr. Berkenau says that the borderline between old age and senility is not a sharp one. There is no way of knowing at just what time any individual passes from one stage into the next. In the brains of old people without symptoms of senility have been found changes such as are found in senile patients.

Vitamin C Is Lacking in Ill Patients

Dr. Berkenau tested the urine of patients at his hospital for its vitamin C content. The procedure was to give the patient lots of vitamin C, flooding all the tissues until the "saturation" point was reached—that is, the point at which no more vitamin C can be taken up by the tissues. Then the vitamin begins to be excreted in the urine. Using this method, researchers can tell just how great has been the individual's deficiency in vitamin C.

Normal patients not suffering from mental disturbances began to excrete vitamin C within two to five days—showing that their tissues were completely saturated by this time. The mental patients did not excrete the vitamin until after 8 to 11 days. "Thus we get a deficit of about 2400 to 3000 milligrams of vitamin C. A deficit of 1000 milligrams or at the most 1500 milligrams may be regarded as pathological [disease-causing]," says our author.

In one case there was a sudden drop in the vitamin C content after a complete saturation had been reached, although the patient was still taking 300 milligrams of vitamin C. The researchers thought perhaps their methods had been faulty. But no. The next day the patient's temperature rose and two weeks later he died of pneumonia. "The increased consumption of vitamin C had been doubtless caused by the infection."

This delay in saturation of tissues shows definitely that these patients were extremely deficient in vitamin C, says our author. He goes on to say that he does not know whether or not the tendency to infections and the delayed healing of broken bones in older people are both due to vitamin C deficiency. But it seems to be quite within the realm of possibility. Vitamin C is the most important ingredient of the cement that holds cells together. A deficiency in it results in loss of healing power and strength throughout every tissue of the body.

Dr. Berkenau does not draw any conclusions about the relation of vitamin C to mental deterioration. But the patients he is discussing here are senile patients. And they showed deficiency in vitamin C—all of them. We know, too, that the diet of older people nearly always tends to be short on foods high in this vitamin. Fresh fruits and green leafy vegetables are harder to eat when you have lost teeth or wear dentures. Older folks living alone find it hard to market for fresh food

[301]

and tend to live on foods high in carbohydrates which can be stored and prepared easily.

The answer, of course, is to establish food habits when you are young so that you will not fall into this trap as you grow older. Make fresh foods the most important part of your diet. Shun canned and processed foods. Get out of the habit of using them.

CHAPTER 45

Vitamin C Is the Busy Vitamin

VITAMIN C IS probably the best-known and the most underestimated nutrient of all. The general public tends to dismiss ascorbic acid as a doubtful cold-fighter and little more. The truth is that this vitamin is active in more functions of more organs in the body than any other. Current researches show its effectiveness in such diverse areas as mental illness and reduction of excess cholesterol levels.

Efforts to improve the recovery rate of psychiatric patients with even the most modern methods fall far short of hopes. None of them is really dependable, and even where positive effects with drugs are achieved, the danger of serious side-effects during prolonged use is always a threat. One reason for the lack of success in treating mental illness is that no one is sure just what causes it. The tranquilizers and antidepressants don't even attempt to do more than modify the symptoms. They aren't aimed at the cause so they can hardly be

[303]

expected to solve the problem permanently. Dr. C. Milner, writing in the *British Journal of Psychiatry* may have a real answer. He believes that psychiatric symptoms are brought on by a vitamin C shortage. To prove it he demonstrated definite changes for the better in mental patients whose C intake was increased.

Improved Personality

Dr. Milner tested the blood of 40 male patients suffering from chronic psychiatric illness for ascorbic acid content. In every one there was a vitamin C shortage. They were given standard personality and psychiatric tests to record their mental state before treatment began. Then, following the double-blind procedure, half of the patients received 1,000 milligrams of ascorbic acid every day for three weeks. At the end of that time, "Statistically significant improvement in the depressive manic and paranoid symptom-complexes, together with an improvement in overall personality functioning was obtained following saturation with ascorbic acid," reports Milner.

The experiment underlined the need for regular vitamin C supplementation in mental patients. It took an average of 6 days with 1,000 milligrams daily to saturate the tissues of participants. It normally takes 24 to 48 hours. "Stress, anxiety and excitement accelerate the depletion of ascorbic acid," says the report, so it follows that, "Psychiatric patients are shown to have an unusually high demand for ascorbic acid."

The positive changes in these long-stay psychiatric patients through vitamin C should prompt the use of added C for all psychiatric patients, in or out of institutions.

How Does It Begin?

We cannot ignore the possibility that a vitamin C shortage is what disturbs mental balance in the first place. Mothers under stress with their children or fathers anxious about their jobs are quite likely using more vitamin C than their meals alone provide. Perhaps if more of our people made supplementary C a daily habit, less of them would end up in institutions or on psychiatrists' couches.

It was hardly expected that vitamin C would turn up in cholesterol control, but in Russia, the Minsk Medical Institute ran a test with 257 patients with high cholesterol levels, and found that ascorbic acid combined with choline chloride, lipocaic or rutin was the most effective agent for reducing blood cholesterol. Sunflower oil (60 grams a day), pyridoxine and B_{12} also had some value but none was as effective in helping the body to handle cholesterol as vitamin C.

Protein Metabolism

Another of vitamin C's chores, the metabolism of tyrosine, an amino acid, was uncovered by M. N. D. Goswami and W. E. Knox in the *Journal of Chronic Disease* (16, 363, 1963). Tyrosine is required by the body for the production of the hormones thyroxine and adrenaline, and it is also the source for the pigment melanin. Without it, then, one uses body fuel too slowly and the marks of cretinism (arrested mental and physical development) can be a consequence when the body engine, including the heart, works too sluggishly.

Goswami and Knox were able to show that the tyrosine interruption led to certain enzyme decrease. They concluded that vitamin C is also essential to the protection of certain enzymes from oxidation.

[305]

The enzyme action of ascorbic acid has made it possible to use an effective antimalaria drug by counteracting its dangerous side-effects. At first the drug, primaquine, when given to a susceptible individual, led to anemia within five to eight days, due to a 30-50 per cent loss of red blood cells. *Medical Tribune* (September 11, 1963) reports that 1,000 to 2,000 milligrams of vitamin C given daily, for a week before, and during primaquine therapy, will prevent this action, because of the vitamin's action on the enzyme system of the red blood cells.

Improves Enzyme Activity

Dr. Roger A. Lewis, a specialist in tropical medicine, explains that two enzymes are involved in preventing this loss of red blood cells. If either one of these is inoperative in an individual given the medication, and if the other is deficient, as often happens, the blood is adversely affected by the drug. Ascorbic acid will accelerate the activity of one of these enzymes (diaphorase), assuring the body's self-protection.

Enzyme activation might also explain the effectiveness of vitamin C against virus infections, as reported in *Clinical Medicine* (July, 1963). W. L. Dalton, M.D., used a preparation of vitamin C mixed with B vitamins against six cases of virus infection, including hepatitis, mononucleosis, virus pneumonia and bronchitis. There was prompt patient response, "in four of the patients improvement was considered dramatic." Dalton ventured the opinion that "vitamin C seems to be virtually nontoxic. Doses as high as 10 grams (10,000 milligrams) have been administered intravenously without ill effects."

Two Japanese physiologists, writing in the British journal, *Nature* (December 28, 1964), give ascorbic

[306]

acid credit for fighting the accumulation of poisons in the liver. These poisons can deplete the liver's supply of the essential sugar, glucose, and severe low blood sugar results. In experimental animals prostration and death follow. The value of ascorbic acid in such cases lies in its boosting of the liver's normal protective ability, rather than any specific action of its own against the poisons.

Bleeding and Bruising

Spontaneous bleeding and frequent bruising have both been traced to insufficient vitamin C in the system, causing fragile capillaries. Two investigators reporting in the *Lancet* (December 21, 1963) told of 20 patients suffering from one or both of these conditions without apparent cause except fragile capillaries. Ascorbic acid supplementation brought complete relief in 8 out of 9 patients with spontaneous bleeding and 4 out of 11 with bruising. The authors recommend increased ascorbic acid as a routine measure when either problem is present.

The plague of painful, spongy and bleeding gums is common among Americans, and is almost always a result of frank vitamin C shortage. The report of USPHS officer, Barbara S. McDonald, on a group of Navajos suffering from this ailment (*Journal of the American Dietetic Association*, October, 1963) reinforces this impression.

During a routine dental examination of students at a Utah Indian School, officers found frequent occurrence of gingivitis (sore gums) among the students (about 10 per cent). Studies of the students' diets showed that only 17 per cent were eating foods which would give them the recommended daily ascorbic acid allowance. Six weeks of supplementation with 300 milligrams of vitamin C daily brought tissue levels up to saturation. With this came a general improvement in the condition of the gums, confirming again the findings of other researchers over the past generation or two.

High-C Food

The ever-continuing search for high-C foods has led most recently to Peru, where the natives prize an acid fruit called camu-camu. The ascorbic acid content of this burgundy-red fruit exceeds that of oranges and lemons, America's most popular sources. Camu-camu has close to 3,000 milligrams of vitamin C per 100 grams of edible food; oranges and lemons have about 50. Unfortunately camu-camu is not yet available commercially in the States, although the *Journal of the American Dietetic Association* (January, 1964) describes experimental efforts at preparing juices and jellies. It is likely that growers will try raising camu-camu in the semi tropical areas of the States, and if they are successful, we may soon have a chance at a new, nutritious fresh fruit.

CHAPTER 46

Vitamin C—
The Universal Remedy?

There is abundant evidence that vitamin C is plentiful in the healthy lens of the eye. It is absent or nearly absent in the diseased lens. In the answer to a letter to the editor of the *Journal of the American Medical Association* (December 16, 1950), we find this information: vitamin C plays an important part in the nutrition of the eye tissues. The healthy lens is particularly rich in this vitamin, while eyes that have cataracts contain little or none.

In the *British Medical Journal* (November 18, 1950), there is a review of 51 cases of small corneal ulcers of the eye. About half of the patients received 1500 milligrams of vitamin C every day, while the other half received a tablet containing nothing of medicinal value. In those who received the vitamin C there was no significant difference in the healing of the superficial ulcers, but the deep ulcers healed much more rapidly.

In the *Eye, Ear, Nose and Throat Monthly* (Vol. 31, p. 79), a doctor gives his formula for preventing cataract and checking its progress once it is formed. He gives his patients a special diet which includes the tops of vegetables—in other words, garden greens, one pint of milk and two eggs daily. In addition, each of his patients got vitamin supplements—chlorophyll tablets and vitamins C and A.

Cataracts are a disease of later years. And we suspect that one very good reason why they form may be that older people get out of the habit of eating eggs, leafy green vegetables and other foods that are rich in vitamins and minerals. It's so much easier and cheaper to live on white bread, soft, starchy desserts and coffee or tea. Surveys show that older folks especially are deficient in vitamin C.

The Thyroid and Vitamin C

According to *Iodine Facts* (Vol. 1, 1940-1946), Sir Robert McCarrison, the famous British nutritionist, found in his researches in India that individuals who were deficient in vitamin C had a fourfold increase of iodine in the thyroid gland. Iodine is one of the ingredients of thyroxin—the hormone manufactured by the thyroid. When there is too little or too much iodine in this gland, we know there is something seriously wrong with the body metabolism. McCarrison's observation appears to show that vitamin C is most important for the good health of the thyroid gland.

Stomach Ulcers

Eddy and Dahldorf in their book, *The Avitaminoses* (William and Wilkins), tell us of a group of ulcer patients put on the usual bland ulcer diet. One third of these had capillary fragility within 16 days. In 70 per cent of these, vitamin C produced a cure. Another researcher found that of 18 ulcer patients, 15 had vitamin C blood levels far below normal. In another group of 20 patients, 18 were found to lack vitamin C in their blood. Is it because the diets they are eating are grossly deficient in vitamin C, or is it that they cannot utilize vitamin C properly? We think it is probably a combination of all three, but certainly the most important fact is that the usual ulcer diet is practically void of vitamin C. On the other hand, if a lack of vitamin C in the diet has had something to do with the formation of the ulcer in the first place—and we believe that it does—then how foolish it seems to prescribe a diet of milk, crackers, and soft bland foods in which there is little or no vitamin C!

The Adrenal Glands and Vitamin C

The adrenal glands, located just in front of the kidneys, are the source of adrenalin which is released into your body whenever you are under stress of any kind— fright, anger, pain, heat, cold, fatigue, things like that.

There is an abundance of vitamin C in healthy adrenal glands—a great deal more than you will find concentrated in any other part of the body. Why? Is it just stored there? This seems unlikely. Is it necessary for the proper functioning of the adrenal glands? It seems so. As long ago as 1940 several researchers reported that the hormone released by a certain part of the adrenals cannot be formed there unless vitamin C is present. This seems to us to be ample reason for getting enough vitamin C every day, even if the body had no other use for it at all.

In 1942 researcher H. W. Holmes made a report in *Science* (Vol. 96, p. 497) that gave promise of relief to hay fever victims. He gave daily doses of 200-500

[311]

milligrams of vitamin C for a period of a week. Then the treatment was stopped. If the symptoms appeared again, the vitamin was given again, in large quantities. Holmes declared that these massive doses of vitamin C protect not only against hay fever but also against food allergies and asthma.

Lack of vitamin C damages the liver. Researchers do not know exactly how vitamin C works to keep the liver in a healthy condition, but they believe that the normal mechanism in which the liver engages, turning carbohydrate and protein into a form that can be used by the body, is slowed down when there is not enough vitamin C present.

Frederick Reiss, M.D., writing in the *Journal of the American Medical Association* (March 10, 1951), describes a condition always associated with prickly heat which he says is connected with a vitamin C deficiency. He gave his patients 900 to 1000 milligrams of vitamin C which cured the condition. He says that small doses ranging from 200 to 300 milligrams were effective only when the hot weather subsided and perspiration decreased. This physician believes that hot weather depletes the body's store of vitamin C, through perspiration. Vitamin C is water-soluble, so it seems reasonable that the body would lose it in perspiration. Lack of vitamin C lost this way may be the main contributing factor to prickly heat.

Lancet (October 31, 1953), concluding an article on vitamin C in relation to anemia, says: "Thus good evidence has been provided that if the diet is deficient in ascorbic acid [vitamin C] for long enough, anemia will result. Slight deficiency of ascorbic acid is common enough and cases of true scurvy still turn up—especially in old people living alone . . . Clearly if this deficiency is unrecognized and untreated, the anemia may resist

[312]

the usual hemantics [medicine given to increase the hemoglobin in the blood]. It is good to know, too, that the habit of prescribing iron and vitamin C together has some scientific support." The article refers to the fact that iron, whether in food or medicine, is better absorbed by the body if it is given along with vitamin C.

It is interesting to note, in connection with capillary fragility, that several things are involved. According to Bell, Lazarus and Munro, writing in *Lancet* (August 10, 1940), "Apart from abnormal influences—fever and administration of heavy metals—two factors influence capillary fragility in health—menstruation and ascorbic acid. In women near the menstrual period, the petechial count will be raised." The petechial count involves the number of small blood vessels that break beneath the skin when it is subjected to pressure.

This comment implies that menstruation may cause a drain on vitamin C and perhaps vitamin P as well. Since capillary fragility is greater at this time it would seem to be wise for women to increase their intake of vitamin C as the time for their regular monthly period draws near.

E. Schneider, writing in *Deutsche Medizinische Wochenschrift* (Vol. 79, p. 15, 1954), relates how he gave vitamin C (1000 to 2000 milligrams daily), along with vitamin A, to about 100 early and advanced cancer patients. There was general improvement—a reduction in the size of the tumors, increase in body weight, lowered blood sedimentation rate, a better nutritional state, reduction in hemorrhage and ulceration. He did not cure the cancers with vitamin C. But he got as good results in improving the condition of the patient as others have gotten with potent measures that have had drastic aftereffects.

[313]

CHAPTER 47

"C" Is for Surgery

PHYSICIANS WHO WANT to improve chances of surgical success are being urged by University of Texas researchers to dose their patients with vitamin C before and even during a serious operation. In the past some surgeons have used vitamin C after the operation to promote fast wound-healing. Now studies show that this vitamin's action is even more important before surgery than after. Vitamin C is known as the antistress vitamin, and since surgery is an extreme form of stress, it follows that a vitamin C buildup is the best kind of preoperative protection a person can get.

The Texas researchers believe that preoperative saturation with vitamin C works to prevent exhaustion of the cells' supply at a crucial time. Any operation sets off the body's "alarm reaction," activating the pituitary gland which releases ACTH to combat the threat. This causes a direct loss of vitamin C, and the more serious the surgery, the greater the vitamin C loss. Doctors M. Fujino, E. Dawson and W. McGanity of the Department of Obstetrics and Gynecology at the University of Texas Medical Branch conclude that at least a week before the operation supplementary vitamin C should be included in the diet of a surgical patient.

In forming their opinions the Texas doctors observed several groups of women and checked on their vitamin C levels during and after surgery. The interesting thing was that ascorbic acid levels first rose during the operation and then took a sudden and enormous drop. The doctors explained that the first stress of the surgery calls out the vitamin C working in the cells all over the body, to cope with the current emergency. Once that large supply of vitamin C is exhausted, the body has nothing to fall back on and the vitamin C level recedes to a dismal low. It is during this low period that the danger from the stress of surgery is greatest. The stress response of ascorbic acid in the blood was most remarkable in major abdominal and major vaginal surgery, but less obvious when the surgical procedure was a minor one.

Known for Almost a Generation

While it fell to Dr. Fujino and others to show the exact values of ascorbic acid dissipated during surgery, the suspicion that major amounts of this important vitamin are lost during operations has been talked about in medical journals for more than 20 years. *British Medical Journal* editors were using this information when they answered a question on vitamin C for surgical patients in their September 18, 1954, issue. The inquiry: "Is there any justification for routine administration of vitamin C to surgical patients? If so, what

[315]

is the suitable dose? Are there any contra-indications?" The *Journal* noted then-current "abundant evidence both practical and from the laboratories" that an adequate vitamin C supply is necessary for healing wounds. They also volunteered the information that the population of England (and presumably America) did not eat a diet sufficiently high in vitamin C to insure rapid and sound healing of major wounds. So sure of this work are they that they remarked, "For practical purposes it is better to assume that there is likely to be a deficiency [of vitamin C] and to be sure of sufficient ascorbic acid to saturate the body before any major operation."

The *Journal* offered the following suggested dosage: "Patients who are apparently well-nourished should be given 500 milligrams of ascorbic acid daily for three days and then kept on a maintenance dose of 100 milligrams daily throughout the period of the operation and convalescence. These doses will have to be increased for patients suffering from malnutrition, from acute infections and from carcinoma; if the carcinoma is of the stomach, ascorbic acid should be given by injection, and the same applies, of course, to patients who are vomiting. There are no contra-indications to giving sufficient vitamin C to maintain saturation of the body throughout the period of surgical treatment."

In 1946, efforts to evaluate the effect of vitamin C in the shock of therapeutic procedures were described by Dr. H. N. Holmes. He told *Ohio State Medical Journal* readers then that 500 milligrams of vitamin C, given orally, within an hour before the operation, brought actual clinical evidence that the shock of the operation was considerably decreased. When patients were injected by Holmes with 500 or 1000 milligrams

[316]

of vitamin C, either before or after surgery, in a series of 50 major abdominal operations, the results were excellent.

Proper preparation (with nutritional supplements) of patients undergoing operations of the colon was described by R. B. Cattell in *Surgical Clinics of North America* (June, 1951). He held that such patients have long-standing nutritional deficiencies anyway, so he saturated them with ascorbic acid and vitamin B complex. In some cases vitamin K was included, because patients with ulcerative colitis are known to have trouble with blood clotting.

Nutrition Already Low

Because many patients who are suffering from operable disease are already low nutritionally, Dr. M. A. Hayes (*Annals of Surgery,* November, 1954) emphasized the importance of checking on nutrition before surgery. He described two patients who underwent surgery on the gastrointestinal tract, suffering from nausea, vomiting, lack of appetite and dehydration. Lab tests showed that they had thiamine deficiencies, liver trouble, anemia, negative nitrogen balance and faulty carbohydrate metabolism. In addition there were sores on the lip and tongue, typical signs of B-complex deficiency. After the operation he placed patients on a 2400-calorie high-vitamin diet, including 900 milligrams of vitamin C.

In ten days Dr. Hayes took more tests to see what the intense vitamin therapy had done for the patients. The carbohydrate metabolism had become normal and so had the liver function. The hemoglobin activity improved and the nitrogen balance became positive. The lip and tongue sores cleared and "an intangible but

[317]

readily apparent improvement in the clinical progress of the patient's convalescence was a characteristic of this phase of management . . . It appeared that the convalescent requirements for vitamins where they are parenterally [by injection] or orally given are about ten times those established as maintenance amounts for adults." Dr. Hayes wrote as a member of the faculty of the Yale University School of Medicine.

If the value of vitamin C before and during surgery is even greater than its postoperative value, it is valuable indeed. J. H. Crandon in the *JAMA* (May 28, 1955), stated that "ascorbic acid is the only nutrient lack of which has been proved to delay or prevent wound healing in man. . . . Because of its ample availability and rapid absorption by all routes, there can be little excuse for surgical complications resulting from ascorbic acid lack."

Patients in the surgical wards of many of our hospitals, and perhaps the doctors who are treating them, would be surprised to read Dr. Crandon's report that "studies of daily maintenance requirements of postoperative surgical patients for ascorbic acid, on the basis of minimal doses required to keep blood above deficiency levels, reveal a minimum requirement range from 100 to 150 milligrams per day for the uncomplicated gastrectomy to 400 milligrams per day for a patient with severe, ultimately fatal ulcerative colitis."

Other Vitamins Valuable

Surgical patients who have suffered for a long time from liver and gall bladder disease are especially likely to require additional vitamin A. They also require vitamin K, the vitamin essential to promote blood clotting, particularly when jaundice exists. Vitamin K is manufactured in the small intestines and is also contained in certain foods. Vitamin K in the liver helps to produce prothrombin which circulates in the blood plasma. When body tissue is damaged (a cut, for example), thrombin is formed and acts on fibrinogen to form fibrin strands that act as a net to trap blood cells and form a clot.

If the intestinal flora are altered in any way, as they can be by the prolonged use of antibiotics (frequent pre- and post-surgical procedure), there is a decrease in the production of vitamin A. Any disease which interferes with the formation or passage of bile to the small intestines also results in a deficiency of vitamin K. If the intestinal linings are damaged, they shut off the passage of vitamin K into the vital systems. If anticoagulants are being used on the patient, the job of vitamin K is doubled in difficulty. Therefore in any of these cases the need for more vitamin K, either in the diet or therapeutically administered, is obvious.

Most operating room accidental deaths are caused by a lack of oxygen. This is especially important for persons of mature age, because as the body grows older its ability to utilize oxygen declines, according to Dr. W. B. Kountz, assistant professor of clinical medicine at Washington University (1955). Vitamin E, available in supplements and in wheat germ oil, has a conserving relationship to the body's oxygen, allowing the body to function efficiently while burning a minimum of oxygen. It is not difficult to see the value of vitamin E, especially in the presurgical period.

While vitamin C appears to play the most immediate role in preventing and normalizing the dangerous effects surgery brings, it is obvious that all nutrients are necessary in helping the body to cope with an operation.

[319]

Health-conscious people make it their business to have a continual supply of fresh fruits and vegetables, and vitamin and mineral supplements are included in their mealtime schedules anyway. But we believe an extra effort must be made to pump up the body's nutritional resources when surgery is in the offing. Then, of all times, there must be no cake or pie, no sodas or cigarettes, nothing that can interfere with the body's defense mechanisms against stress. You have a part to play in making your operation a success. Don't depend on luck. It may not be enough.

CHAPTER 48

Vitamin C and Fluorides

CHRONIC FLUOROSIS — a crippling, organ-destroying and eventually deadly type of "mild" poisoning—is a problem of many common industries such as fertilizer manufacturing and aluminum fabrication. Fluorine, of course, is a deadly poison and its presence in the air, even in small quantities, is recognized as a definite hazard to an industrial worker. Our own industries tend to attack the problem by developing protective masks and other safety equipment for people who have to work in a fluorinated atmosphere. In Russia they have a different outlook. They try to find a protective diet that will enable the worker to survive such a poisonous environment.

We are not prepared to say that one approach is superior to the other. We are inclined to think it might be far better if both countries took both approaches. You can't have too much protection against fluorides. But we do consider it fortunate for us in the United

States, where 50 million people are being subjected daily to fluoridated water supplies, that the Russians have been exploring dietary means by which we can protect ourselves against the toxic effects of fluorides. What other hope do those of us who live in fluoridated communities have? Our local governments are not going to protect us.

So it is very good news indeed that two Russian public health officers, R. D. Gabovich and P. N. Maistruk, have found a dietary supplement which, they state, shows "marked protective action." What is this substance? Simply an old friend we have often shown is the greatest protection against all forms of toxicity that has ever been discovered. It is vitamin C!

The study was published in the leading Russian scientific periodical *Voprosy Pitaniya* (22, 1, p. 32, 1963).

Enzymes Affected

The experiment seems to have been an unusually thorough one. It was begun with a large number of guinea pigs that were divided into ten groups. These groups tested all possible combinations of the substances that were regarded as possibly protective against the damage done by daily exposure to fluorides. The substances were: ascorbic acid (vitamin C), niacin, riboflavin, thiamin, vitamin D and calcium derived from milk. One group was also kept as a control, receiving none of the protective substances.

In the control animals, the most marked effect that was consistently produced by exposure of the animals to sodium fluoride, was alterations in the enzymes of the carbohydrate metabolism, leading to a chronic abnormally high level of blood sugar—in other words,

[322]

an artificially induced diabetes. This effect was consistently neutralized and reversed in the group that was receiving vitamin C, the group that was receiving all the vitamins, and the group that was receiving a combination of vitamin D and calcium. The B vitamins alone did not show any ability to resist this degenerative effect of fluorides.

However, high blood sugar was not the only effect of the sodium fluoride administered to the guinea pigs. Another, and quite as deadly, was selective accumulation of the poison in the liver and in the hard tissues such as the bones and teeth. This caused definite damage in the control animals, while this damage was nullified in the vitamin C group and in the group receiving the combination of all the vitamins. A mathematical analysis demonstrated that vitamin C had by far the greatest protective effect.

Once the experiment had gotten this far, it was not dropped. On the contrary, the time had now come to determine whether it was meaningful in terms of human beings. A test was made on four groups of six people each, working in a factory with a mean daily concentration of fluorine gas in the air of only two thousandths of one part per million. Such a concentration of pure fluorine is known to be enough to induce chronic fluorosis in those who breathe it day after day.

Works for People

Of the four groups of laborers, one was used as a control, while the other three were respectively given daily doses of 50, 100, and 150 milligrams of vitamin C in addition to the amounts normally consumed in their diets. It was found that the more vitamin C there

[323]

is in the diet, the more fluoride is excreted in the urine every day. The significance of this excretion is as a demonstration that vitamin C detoxifies fluoride by carrying it right out of the system. This is another way of saying what we have often stated, that fluorides use up the body's supply of vitamin C. This is true. But in the course of this interaction, what is actually happening is that the vitamin C is using itself up to protect our systems by carrying the fluoride out of them.

The conclusion of the Russian investigators was: "Ascorbic acid [vitamin C] has a particularly marked protective action; fluorine deposition in the body was least with its administration. Administration of vitamin C completely prevented the development of symptoms of fluorine poisoning experimentally in animals administered fluorine.

"Observations on human subjects under factory conditions showed that addition of ascorbic acid to the daily diet in a dose of up to 100 milligrams stimulates the excretion of fluorine. Hence, it may be concluded that to prevent the toxic effects of fluorine compound, the daily diet of year-round workers in the fluorine industry should contain at least 100-120 milligrams vitamin C (in food products or separately administered)."

And may we add, the same is obviously true where one is compelled to drink fluoridated water. In addition, though this particular experiment did not find calcium lactate (calcium from milk) particularly helpful in guarding against fluorides, we have had occasion in the past to report that bone meal has been shown to have an excellent protective effect. Our recommendation is that every reader in a fluoridated area be especially careful to take full daily supplementation of natural vitamin C from rose hips and bone meal. Take more than enough to simply detoxify the fluorides you may be compelled to drink. You also want the nutritional advantages of these marvelous food supplements. And you can be sure that they will do more to provide your children with healthy teeth than could ever be done by the poisonous fluorides they will be causing to be excreted and not permitting to be deposited in the teeth.

CHAPTER 49

Is There Propaganda Against Vitamin D?

Dr. Helen Taussig is an eminent member of the medical profession, professor of pediatrics at Johns Hopkins University, and an accepted authority on the diseases of children. In June, 1964, speaking to the Ontario Medical Association at its annual conference in Toronto, Dr. Taussig warned the doctors assembled there that many members of the medical profession are giving too much vitamin D to pregnant women. While pointing out that "this theory is not supported by medical science yet," Dr. Taussig expressed the belief that excessive vitamin D, commonly administered or prescribed by doctors, is leading to an increase in aortic stenosis, a malformation of the heart with which some children are born, that is frequently associated with retarded mentality.

If the obstetricians who care for pregnant women knew half as much about nutrition as the obligations of their position morally oblige them to know, Dr.

[326]

Taussig's probably accurate warning should have been unnecessary. They should certainly know that synthetic vitamin D is an extremely dangerous drug and that even the natural vitamin, found largely in fish liver oils, should not be taken in excess of a few thousand units a day except in cases of unusual need.

There are obvious reasons for this. Vitamin D is partially responsible for the calcium metabolism. It is necessary to the absorption of calcium through the intestinal wall, it can increase the level of calcium in the blood serum, and it is partially responsible for the deposition of calcium into the bones. Any of these functions, obviously, can be overdone. They can be overdone easily if the calcium involved is not accompanied by sufficient minerals phosphorus and magnesium, both are indispensable to a proper regulation of calcium metabolism.

Vitamin D, if taken in excess, is stored by the liver. It is not eliminated like an excess of the water soluble vitamins, but is kept in the bank, as it were, for future use when needed. A daily excess keeps accumulating, and while there are advantages to becoming a millionaire in money, a vitamin D millionaire is running a great risk of disordering his calcium metabolism. This could theoretically lead to excess calcification of the bones, to the form of calcification that is involved in hardening of the arteries, and to the retarded mentality in children that is associated, through a mechanism not yet understood, with greatly excessive levels of calcium in the blood.

Yet the average obstetrician, not being fully aware of these interrelationships, tends to recommend to his pregnant patients large quantities of an isolated synthetic pharmaceutical preparation like calciferol, which

[327]

is just plain synthetic vitamin D unaccompanied by either the phosphorus or magnesium needed to regulate what the vitamin D may do to the calcium metabolism. And it is quite possible that Dr. Taussig is right and that aortic stenosis, hardly known 50 years ago, is now on the increase because of the way obstetricians administer vitamin D.

The Toxic Level

How much vitamin D does it take to induce a toxic reaction? The Merck Index says that the danger level comes at "prolonged daily use of 50 thousand international units or more. . ." This is a level of consumption you would find very difficult to reach on your own initiative, without a doctor's prescription. If, for instance, you were to take halibut liver oil, which is the highest potency combination of natural vitamins A and D available, you would find it very hard to find a capsule containing more than 5,000 units of vitamin D, with clear instructions on the label that only one capsule a day is to be taken. If you decided for some reason to double your dosage, you would get 10,000 units. You would have to take 10 such capsules to reach the level of 50,000 units a day, and it is beyond our conception that any sensible person could take 10 times the recommended dosage of anything without medical advice, and go on doing so day after day and month after month.

No, when toxicities occur it is almost invariably because medical patients have followed the advice of well-meaning but insufficiently informed doctors.

An enlightening report appeared in *Nutrition Reviews,* the publication of the food-industry-dominated Nutrition Foundation which publishes and discusses abstracts of articles on nutrition from scientific periodicals. The September, 1965, issue of *Nutrition Reviews* reported an article that had appeared in *Acta Paediatrica Scandinavica* describing the cases of five infants who suffered hypervitaminosis. "In four of the author's cases the excessive amounts of vitamin A (and D) were prescribed, while in the 5th the mother misread the directions." These infants, none of them more than three months old, were given preparations of vitamins A and D in which they received from 3,100 to 9,000 units of vitamin D and from 18,500 to 60,000 units of vitamin A every single day. These are obviously adult doses and far too much for newborn babies. Yet while these infants did develop vitamin A intoxication, in not a single one of these cases was there any bad effect from the vitamin D that they took.

Nutrition Reviews concludes its report of this Swedish article by stating that "vitamins are the great American placebo." A placebo is a useless substitute for medication that a doctor gives because his patients expect him to give something. And it is true that many doctors prescribe pharmaceutical vitamins, sometimes in excessive amounts, when they feel that no medication is really needed. And now, on the basis of the occasional reports of ill effects from this misguided practice of doctors, the Food and Drug Administration is proposing to so stringently limit the amounts of vitamin D that may be contained in food supplements and certain specified foods such as milk and milk products, that the total daily consumption will not exceed 400 units a day for any person.

It is also reported that the American FDA proposal has influenced the British health authorities to propose similar limitations for Britain.

[329]

The Innocent Penalized

Note the paradox here. There are occasionally a few reports (very few and very occasional) in the medical literature about intoxication from the liver-stored vitamins A or D when those vitamins are prescribed by doctors in excessive amounts. Do the authorities, therefore, propose to limit the amounts of these vitamins (usually synthetic) doctors may prescribe? Certainly not. A doctor must be left free to prescribe for his patients however he judges best, and his judgment can be questioned only by other doctors. Instead, because doctors have been injuring occasional patients by prescribing excessive amounts of vitamins, the health authorities propose to make it impossible for a private citizen to supplement his diet with reasonably substantial amounts of these vitamins unless he first goes to a doctor, pays a fee and gets a prescription for them. The rationale for this is the idea that we have already quoted from *Nutrition Reviews*—that vitamins are only a placebo anyway and supplements are not really needed.

Let's check on this. Let's take a look at the nutritional history of vitamin D, which is one of the two vitamins currently under attack.

It is stated by Richard H. Follis, Jr., M.D., in his authoritative text *Deficiency Disease* (Charles C. Thomas, 1958), that "the skeletal manifestations which characterize rickets have been recognized from earliest times." These skeletal manifestations are fragile and easily broken bones, and soft teeth extremely susceptible to decay. Their outward sign is bowed legs and bent backs. Cases of rickets in children used to occur not occasionally, but by the millions. As recently as 1942, it was reported in the *Bulletin of Johns*

Hopkins Hospital (December, 1952) the incidence of rickets in young children studied was as much as 90% during the first year of life with an overall average of between 67.7% and 71.9%. Rickets was classified as severe in 11.8% of white children and 36.3% of Negro children. In England, the incidence of severe rickets was so widespread that the government resorted to free distribution of cod liver oil for children.

To prevent or cure rickets you need adequate amounts of vitamin D, calcium and phosphorus in the diet.

Rickets occurs either because there is insufficient calcium in the diet, or because there is insufficient vitamin D to enable the child to absorb the calcium that has been eaten. Another cause of a slightly different type of the same disease is insufficient phosphorus and magnesium in the diet, preventing the proper deposition of the calcium into the bones and teeth. Although rickets still occurs, it is no longer the medical problem that it was even 30 years ago. That is because the world has become conscious of the need for vitamin D, whether in food, in food supplements or from sunshine. The ultraviolet light of sunshine does activate the fats under the skin and transform them into vitamin D. To the extent that children can receive enough sunlight on their bodies while avoiding an excess (cause of many skin problems from acne to cancer) they should require no other vitamin D fortification. But can children receive enough exposure to sunlight in England, let us say, where the weather is often cloudy and rainy and the summers are short? Can the millions of Negro children whose skin resists the penetration of ultraviolet light receive enough vitamin D activation from sunlight? Obviously not. That is why there are more Negro children than white with rickets today. And

these are some of the reasons why it has taken supplements of fish liver oil, providing several thousand units
of vitamin D daily, to eliminate rickets as a major
health problem. Are they trying to give our children
rickets again, in the name of protecting their health?

Wouldn't it be the height of the ridiculous to put
toxic sodium fluoride into drinking water in order to
improve the mineralization of children's teeth, and at
the same time make it difficult or impossible for them
to get enough vitamin D to properly mineralize their
teeth and bones with calcium, the basic building block
of these organs? Yet that is exactly what is being proposed in all seriousness today.

Rickets, it should be remembered, is far from being
the only disease requiring increased vitamin D. This
precious vitamin also has its effect on every function
of the body that utilizes calcium, for the obvious reason
that no matter how much calcium we consume, our
systems will never absorb it unless they contain enough
vitamin D as well. Therefore, any calcium deficiency
disease can be caused by insufficient vitamin D as easily
as by lack of calcium.

Calcium Deficiencies Related

Dr. Follis, previously cited, states some of the effects
of calcium deficiency: without calcium, the blood will
not coagulate properly. Calcium is vital "in maintaining the integrity of the contractile mechanism of the
heart." Calcium deficiency leads to "widespread hemorrhages, lesions in the gastrointestinal tract, cataracts,
parathyroid enlargement, and, of course, rickets."

Dr. Follis also points out that tetany (cramps) is
caused by lack of calcium and so is excessive irritability
of nerves and muscle. The most widespread result of
insufficient calcium or failure to utilize it properly is

[332]

osteoporosis, the demineralization of bones afflicting many mature and elderly people, leaving the bones brittle, easily broken and more difficult to mend.

Insufficient vitamin D may be the actual cause of many of these calcium deficiency diseases.

Now it is all very well to say that the average person does not normally require more than 400 units of vitamin D a day. But there are many reasons why a person may not be average and why his circumstances may not be normal. In the *Journal of the American Medical Association* (August 10, 1963) Robert E. Stone, M.D., wrote that "the adult is presumed to obtain sufficient vitamin D from exposure to sunlight and from the incidental ingestion of small amounts with food, such as fish and vitamin D fortified milk. Many adults probably fail to obtain optimum amounts of vitamin D because of their inadequate exposure to sunlight and because of dietary limitations. And perhaps a larger number, particularly of the elderly, fail to ingest adequate amounts of calcium and phosphorus." To this we would add that the cultivation of sun tans as well as hereditary dark skins make sunlight useless as a vitamin D source to many adults and children. More and more people are being discovered to have hyperactive parathyroid glands. When this gland, which removes calcium from the bones, is overactive, it can be countered only by consumption of additional amounts of calcium and vitamin D. And finally, many people are just not average and require larger than average amounts of one or another vitamin.

Why should you not make sure you are getting enough vitamin D by taking a good natural supplement of fish liver oil that will give you more than enough? Dr. Stone says that "generally there is a wide margin between the therapeutic or prophylactic dose and the toxic dose of vitamin D." When the National Institutes of Health made a study of people hypersensitive to vitamin D (*Drug Trade News,* May 25, 1964) it was found to take 10,000 units per day to induce a toxic reaction.

Manufacturers Profit

Then why the attempts to limit the consumption to a mere 400 units a day? As far as we can see, the only people who will be served by such a limitation are the food manufacturers, who have been coming under increasing criticism because their methods have been increasingly robbing our food supply of its natural vitamin content. If the public can be made fearful of getting too much vitamin D, it is not likely to complain that it is getting insufficient vitamin D in its food. We have no knowledge of any conspiracy, nor can we point the finger at any individual and say that this person is distorting the facts for any self-serving monetary reason. But a general picture of science today is a picture of commercial interest sponsoring so-called research for its own commercial purposes in all too many cases. When the research does not achieve the result desired by the commercial interest, the scientist who did the research finds it was part of his contract that the sponsor could refuse to allow publication. Thus, much of what is being discovered today by scientists of integrity is being buried. And the other research investigators learn very quickly which side their bread is buttered on.

If we could see any advantage in limiting the consumption of vitamin D to such a ridiculously small amount as 400 units a day, we would be the first to proclaim it. But we have shown that even unusually sensitive infants one to three months old were not

[334]

harmed by a daily vitamin D consumption of up to 9,000 units. We have shown that while excessive amounts of this vitamin can do damage to the fetus when taken by pregnant women, this is a matter entirely in the control of doctors and one that cannot be affected by such a limitation as the FDA proposes. We have also shown many times that most people in this world need more calcium in their daily consumption, rather than less. Yet what good will it do them to consume more calcium if they are not able to absorb it into their systems? And they cannot absorb it unless they take adequate amounts of vitamin D.

The only conclusion we can reach is that the current warnings against vitamin D are part of the general propaganda drive to discredit vitamins, so that people will not complain about the lack of vitamins in the foods their markets offer, and will not bypass the empty-calorie processed foods in favor of the more nutritious fresh meats and vegetables.

We suppose it can mean a lot of money if such propaganda can be put over on us. But we can't let it happen, because to us it means more than money. It means our health and our lives.

CHAPTER 50

Vitamin D and Those Vague Aches

IT IS NOT always the spectacular diseases, but more often vague aches and pains, that keep our citizens from enjoying life fully in their later years. Their doctors can handle something definite like a serious infection or gallstones. But they don't know what to do about the kind of generalized muscular tenderness and creeping weakness that can make a person miserable most of the time and rob him of all ambition. According to three prominent English physicians (*Lancet*, December 12, 1964), doctors can try vitamin D. Chances are that osteomalacia (softening of the bones) is at the bottom of the trouble, and a lack of vitamin D is a cause of this disease.

Osteomalacia in adults corresponds to rickets in children. The bones become soft and weak because they do not have the mineral content necessary for proper formation. Science believes vitamin D assists the body in assimilating phosphorus, a mineral which

[336]

combines with calcium in the body. If that is true, a lack of vitamin D almost certainly means a lack of phosphorus and calcium even though the diet has plenty of both of these minerals. Yet, for some reason, physicians are reluctant to attribute osteomalacia to a lack of vitamin D. They suggest an intestinal malabsorption of calcium, or kidney defects, but regard a dietary deficiency as most unlikely. Until 1962 only three cases of nutritional osteomalacia had been reported in Great Britain and America. Now the *Lancet* article tells of three patients seen and diagnosed at the Bristol Royal Infirmary within twelve months, and the authors suggest that the condition is much commoner than has been suspected.

The difficulty of D-deficiency diagnosis may be partly due to the vagueness of the symptoms. However the three cases described by K. R. Gough, O. C. Lloyd, and M. R. Wills in *Lancet* were confirmed in the laboratory, and they all improved under treatment with vitamin D. One patient complained of low back pain and aching thighs for years. Her usual daily intake consisted of two slices of bread and butter, a cracker and 13 cups of tea containing ½ *pound of sugar*. She seldom left the house. Her pains continued until she was unable to walk unaided. Samples of her bone examined under the microscope showed a calcium deficiency.

Pure Vitamin D

A normal diet was prepared with a high calcium content and some supplementary vitamin D. But there was no real effect. When calciferol was introduced in weekly intramuscular injections of 100,000 units, the symptoms were promptly relieved. Calciferol is a practically pure version of vitamin D prepared by the ultraviolet irradiation of ergosterol obtained from

[337]

yeast. The *British Medical Dictionary* tells us that "calciferol promotes the absorption of calcium and phosphorus from the bowel and is essential to the normal development of bones and teeth. When there is a deficiency, rickets and osteomalacia appear."

After three months of vitamin D treatment, the process of bone formation was reversed and normal new healthy bone was forming.

A 64-year-old widow was admitted to a hospital for the investigation of severe bone pains in her legs and back. She said she lived alone in a small dark country cottage and seldom ventured out of doors. Her average daily intake of calories included only 600 milligrams of calcium and 48 international units of vitamin D. Notable symptomatic improvement in her took place on weekly injections of calciferol. But here again most physicians would have passed over the possibility of a vitamin D deficiency. The only abnormal physical signs in this lady were generalized bony tenderness especially over the ribs and down the spinal column and a very slight impairment of sensation in the hands and feet.

In the third case, an 84-year-old spinster was admitted to the hospital with a fractured leg. Physicians attempted to pin the fractured bone but it was too soft to hold the pin.

She had complained of pain in the lower part of the back and thighs for many years, and because of it had been unable to leave her room for at least ten years. This situation was coupled with an extremely poor diet for many years, consisting largely of tea, bread and butter, and an occasional egg and milk pudding. After three months on a normal diet, the consistency of the bone has so improved that the fracture could be pinned.

[338]

Other Causes Excluded

The authors are very careful to state that the osteomalacia in each of the patients was of nutritional origin, because all *"other possible causes have been excluded."* The calcium content of the diet in each case was considerably lower than the 1,200 milligrams the normal adult diet seems to average, and the dietary intake of vitamin D in these patients was very low, prohibiting the body's full use of even the little bit of calcium it did receive.

American physicians make much of saying that no one eating a normal diet can be deficient in vitamin D. They fail to mention that science has yet to decide just what a vitamin D deficiency is! According to *Lancet,* "The precise daily adult requirement of vitamin D is unknown. . . ." In the *British Medical Dictionary* we read, "Some vitamin D is formed in the skin by the action of sunlight, and so the adult daily requirement from food is not known with certainty, and in fact must vary widely. Increased amounts are necessary in infancy and childhood, and during pregnancy and lactation, when up to about 1,000 units above the usual daily intake are advisable; larger doses are needed if there is evidence of deficiency. Much bigger doses have been used successfully in the treatment of lupus vulgaris, tuberculosis lymphadenitis and osteoporosis associated with parathyroid deficiency . . ."

Many people cannot depend upon haphazard intake of vitamin D to cover all their needs. Foods generally recognized as rich in vitamin D are milk, butter, fish, and egg yolk. There are great numbers of our citizens who go month after month without eating any one of these foods. As for vitamin D absorption from sunlight, it is useful to know that some of the effective rays for creating vitamin D from the skin secretions are absorbed by buildings and glass so that people who don't go outside, even though they might sit in brightly sunlit rooms, can fall short of their vitamin D requirements.

The Scare

Recently *Time* magazine shocked the nation with a story warning that excessive vitamin D can be responsible for mental retardation and other abnormalities in babies. Dr. Robert E. Cooke, at Johns Hopkins Children's Medical and Surgical Center, blamed vitamin D for abnormalities in thirteen babies seen in eighteen months at this hospital. Dr. Cooke was careful to point out that *for the vast majority of women and their babies, the prevailing intake of vitamin D does no harm.* In certain cases an excess over normal requirements can cause unnatural calcium deposits in the fetus. Its bones grow especially dense and chalky deposits narrow the aorta, a heart artery which can shut off the flow of blood to the kidneys and make the baby suffer from high blood pressure. Such stories touch off anti-vitamin-D campaigns. The first ones to give up vitamin D are those who need it most — pregnant women.

It is excessively unlikely that anyone taking fish liver oil gets too much vitamin D if he pays attention to suggested dosages on the bottle. More than 400,000 units daily are considered toxic for adults; 30,000 units or more a day over a period of time can produce symtoms of poisoning in babies; 50,000 units daily are dangerous for children. But if you are sure to take fish liver oil in the suggested dosage, and unless you live outdoors summer and winter, your body is likely to be grateful for supplementary vitamin D as it occurs naturally.

[340]

One reader wrote recently that he had been using a certain brand of fish liver oil for many years. He happened to notice the label one day and found to his amazement that this product now contained large amounts of *synthetic vitamin D,* and it was no longer just natural fish liver oil. The label stated that this change had been made to avoid any possibility of a "fishy" taste. Check the label on every bottle you buy to make certain you are getting a wholly natural product. Of course the finest possible companion for fish liver oils in your daily food supplements, bone meal, supplies calcium, phosphorus and other minerals which are the essential companions of vitamin D.

If you have vague aches and pains, the feeling that your bones are sore and tender, check your diet for vitamin D. Think about the foods you eat, the sunlight you are exposed to. The elusive osteomalacia could be working in you undiagnosed and unsuspected. Don't accept your friends' opinion that you are merely being cranky or neurotic when you complain of soreness; they can't know what you feel. Ask your doctor to check on the possibility that your bones are in bad shape. English physicians say it happens much more often than we realize.

CHAPTER 51

Is Vitamin E Necessary?

THE CHEMICAL NAME FOR vitamin E is tocopherol which comes from three Greek words—*tokos* meaning "child," *pherein* meaning "to bear" and *ol,* "alcohol." The name indicates vitamin E was first studied in connection with fertility.

There are several different kinds of vitamin E. The most important are alpha, beta, gamma and delta. These are the Greek letters corresponding to our a, b, c and d. So alphatocopherol is A-tocopherol, betatocopherol is B-tocopherol and so forth. Alphatocopherol is the most active biologically.

A number of years ago it was discovered that female rats on a diet of milk, yeast and iron were incapable of raising young. This aroused interest in what substance might be missing in such a diet. The result of this investigation was the discovery of vitamin E. Female rats conceive on a vitamin-E-deficient diet, but the embryo dies and is reabsorbed into the body rather than

[342]

developing and being born. K. E. Mason, in his book, *Vitamins and Hormones,* tells us that the cause of this misfortune is abnormality in the system of blood vessels, leading to thrombosis (the formation of blood clots). As the blood vessels contract, there is anemia and finally hemorrhaging which causes the death of the fetus. Even though the anti-hemorrhage vitamins K and C are administered, the embryo dies. Vitamin E supplies the missing substance in the diet, and conception and development of the embryo proceed normally if the diet contains ample vitamin E. In male rats permanent sterility results from a diet that does not include vitamin E. Male chicks and guinea pigs also suffer degeneration of the testicles when they are deprived of vitamin E.

In the case of rats on diets low in vitamin E, litters can be born, but the young rats often develop paralysis of the hind legs shortly after birth. This paralysis (much the same as muscular dystrophy in human beings) spreads rapidly to other muscles of the body. No one knows what exact chemical process is involved, but there seems to be ample evidence that vitamin E is closely related to healthy muscles. And, don't forget, the heart is a muscle!

A third indication of the necessity for vitamin E in the diet came with the discovery that ample vitamin E protects the body's store of two other vitamins—A and C. Both these vitamins are very sensitive to the presence of oxygen and may lose much of their value over a period of time. But the presence of vitamin E in the digestive tract protects them from oxidation. From this we might assume that, all other things being equal, you would need to take less vitamin A and C if you were taking vitamin E at the same time.

So far as human nutrition is concerned, experiments

[343]

on vitamin E have been conflicting. How is it possible, you might ask, that one group of researchers can perform an experiment in which vitamin E added to the diet produces a certain effect while another group of researchers might obtain exactly the opposite effect or no effect at all? The answer lies in the great complexity of all the chemical aspects of testing a vitamin. Scientist A, working over a period of many years, might be able to discover just one important scientific fact about vitamin E. Scientist B, working in another laboratory, might meanwhile be investigating some other aspect of vitamin E in human physiology. But all his work might be in vain if he performs it before scientist A has proved his one fact. And when scientist C uses A's method, he may get one result. If he uses B's method he may get quite a different result. And so forth.

Dr. Walter Eddy in his very valuable book *Vitaminology* (Williams and Wilkins Company, Baltimore), says of vitamin E and muscular dystrophy: "Some positive results have been claimed for vitamin E therapy in muscular dystrophy of certain types. Two are of particular interest in suggesting combination with other vitamin material for effective action.

"In 1940 a researcher reported treatment of five patients with muscular dystrophy; one with muscular atrophy following anterior poliomyelitis; one with muscle atrophy after an attack of multiple neuritis. He found that improvement took place in all cases and the addition of vitamin B to vitamin E appeared to give even better results."

Now this statement alone might very well answer our question about conflicting results in the use of vitamin E for human nutrition. One doctor giving vitamin E to patients might pay no attention to their diet, might

[344]

make no effort to see that they are also getting all the the other vitamins necessary for good nutrition. This doctor might not get any results from his vitamin E therapy. But another physician, aware of the great importance of one vitamin in relation to another, might check carefully to see that his patient is getting all the vitamins in abundance. And in this case the addition of vitamin E to the diet might work wonders!

Vitamin E for Many Disorders

We print elsewhere in this book a great deal of information about the Shute Clinic in Canada where the Shute brothers use vitamin E in curing heart disease. The Shute brothers are M.D.'s who carry on general practice as well as their work at the heart clinic. They use vitamin E as a medicine for sick hearts. That is, they study each individual case and prescribe exactly the dosage they feel will be most beneficial, then watch the patient carefully, changing the prescription if necessary, just as any physician does in treating a disease. We are told that other scientists have experimented with vitamin E for heart disease without results. What does this prove? That vitamin E has no effect on the sick heart? It may. Or it may prove only that the other researchers were not using the same methods the Shutes use.

Elsewhere we report on vitamin E in its relation to reproductive, circulatory and joint disorders. These facts were taken from reputable scientific and medical journals and they were simply reports on actual experiments made. Now if some other experimenter does not obtain these same results perhaps this means that vitamin E has really nothing to do with these disorders in the human being. Or perhaps it means that the vita-

[345]

min has everything to do with a healthy body and the researchers who got the good results knew exactly what combinations would bring about those good results.

A report in the *Texas State Journal of Medicine* for January, 1952, reveals that alphatocopherol was used for a group of surgical patients to prevent thrombosis or embolism (formation of a blood clot) after the operation. It was found to be very effective. Does this mean that vitamin E will always, under any circumstances, prevent thrombosis? Or does it mean simply that we have one more piece of valuable evidence as to the place of vitamin E in human nutrition?

How Vitamin E Is Destroyed

Vitamin E is inactivated by rancid oil or fat. So if there is rancid fat in the diet, all the vitamin E in the world will do no good. We know, too, that some of the inorganic iron compounds destroy vitamin E activity. Let's say a patient is being treated for anemia and is taking some kind of iron supplement containing ferric chloride. No amount of vitamin E in the diet will do this patient any good, because this particular form of iron will destroy vitamin E. In the same way mineral oil used as a laxative destroys vitamin E along with other fat-soluble vitamins in the digestive tract.

As you can imagine, with all this controversy over the rightful place of vitamin E in human nutrition, no one has decided yet what the recommended daily requirement of this vitamin is. Nutrition books tell us that it is present in many many foods. Yet actually the food richest in vitamin E is wheat germ—that part of the wheat we threw away when we introduced white, highly milled flour. Is it just a coincidence that heart disease mortality figures have climbed steadily during the past 50 years—that is, since we have been eating bread from which the vitamin E is removed? Is it just a coincidence that vitamin E works best in association with the B vitamins? Vitamin E and the B vitamins are both plentiful in the germ of grains. Does there not seem to be ample evidence that our refining of foods has worked this fatal mischief on our hearts, our joints, our muscles?

Dr. Henry C. Sherman of Columbia University says in his *Essentials of Nutrition* (Macmillan, New York) that vitamin E is plentiful in foods, "doubtless occurring very widely among food materials of both plant and animal origin *which have not been artificially refined.*" How many of us ever get any food these days that is not artificially refined, except, of course, for our fresh green vegetables and fruits? Glance at the chart at the end of this chapter which gives the vitamin E content of various foods. Corn oil, cottonseed oil, peanut oil, soybean oil, and wheat germ oil contain the largest amounts. How much of any of these do you or your family eat in one day? Of course, vitamin E appears too in small amounts in various fruits and vegetables. But, having destroyed our best source of vitamin E in the germ of the grain which we throw away in the milling, how can we be sure that any one of us is actually getting enough vitamin E to keep us healthy from day to day?

Should You Take a Vitamin Food Supplement?

We believe that the average American diet does not contain enough vitamin E for good health. All the evidence points in that direction. We should include in our daily fare as many foods as possible that are rich in vitamin E as prevention against those disorders that may result from a lack of vitamin E.

[347]

In addition, we believe you should supplement your diet with wheat germ oil and a natural vitamin E preparation. What is the difference? Wheat germ contains substances other than vitamin E. So you will not get as much vitamin E in wheat germ as in a pure vitamin E preparation, but you will get the other food elements present in wheat germ. These elements are extremely important, too. You need them as well as the vitamin E.

When vitamin E is taken from wheat germ oil and put into a separate preparation, you are, of course, getting nothing but vitamin E — in much greater strength than you get it in wheat germ oil. Now different kinds of wheat may have different amounts of vitamin E. This we call "potency." In addition, there are, remember, several different kinds of vitamin E—alpha, beta and so forth. The most potent of these is alpha-tocopherol.

How Much Vitamin E?

We cannot tell you how much vitamin E or wheat germ oil you should take. As we stated above, minimum daily requirements have not been set. Besides, if you are eating a diet rich in natural wheat germ, if you use a lot of vegetable oils and eat a lot of salads, you obviously need less vitamin E in a food supplement than somebody else might.

If you are already suffering from heart disease and want to use vitamin E, you should certainly consult one of the medical authorities, for this involves using very potent and very large vitamin E doses, just like a medicine. He may be able to recommend a physician in your locality who uses the Shute methods. Your own physician may agree to write to Dr. Shute about your case and learn how to treat you with vitamin E.

[348]

Foods Containing the Largest Amount of Vitamin E

Food	Milligrams of vitamin E
Apples	.74 in 1 medium apple
Bacon	.53 in about 10 slices broiled
Bananas	.40 in 1 medium banana
Beans, dry navy	3.60 in ½ cup steamed
Beef liver	1.40 in 1 piece liver
Beef steak	.63 in 1 piece steak
Butter	2.40 in 6 tablespoons
Carrots	.45 in 1 cup
Celery	.48 in 1 cup
Chicken	.25 in 3 slices
Coconut oil	8.30 in about 6 tablespoons
Cornmeal, yellow	1.70 in about ½ cup
Corn oil	87.00 in about 6 tablespoons
Cottonseed oil	90.00 in about 6 tablespoons
Eggs, whole	2.00 in 2 whole eggs
Grapefruit	.26 in about ¼ grapefruit
Haddock	.39 in 1 piece haddock
Lamb chops	.77 in 2 rib chops
Lettuce	.50 in 6 large lettuce leaves
Oatmeal	2.10 in about ½ cup cooked oatmeal
Onions	.26 in 2 medium raw onions
Oranges	.24 in 1 small orange
Peanut oil	22.00 in 6 tablespoons
Peas, green	2.10 in 1 cup peas
Pork chops	.71 in 2 chops
Potatoes, sweet	4.00 in 1 small potato
Potatoes, white	.06 in 1 medium potato
Rice, brown	2.40 in about ¾ cup cooked rice
Soybean oil	140.00 in 6 tablespoons
Tomatoes	.36 in 1 small tomato
Turnip greens	2.30 in ½ cup steamed
Wheat germ oil, crude	150-420.00 in 6 tablespoons
Wheat germ oil, medicinal	320.00 in 6 tablespoons

CHAPTER 52

We Can't Ignore Vitamin E

WHILE MANY AMERICAN medical men stubbornly hold
to their opinion that vitamin E is useless in the treatment of disease, the rest of the world avidly is taking
advantage of the remarkable curative powers of this
vitamin. Researchers and practicing physicians from
just about any country you can think of have rejoiced
in their success in treating circulatory disturbances,
problems of fertility and abortion, skin disorders and
many other conditions in which vitamin E has shown
its effectiveness.

As with most developments in nutritional research,
the information on vitamin E is sketchy, but that is only
because the isolation of this vitamin was accomplished
so recently that there hasn't been time yet to discover
all that it will do. New experiments every day show
vitamin E to be effective in cases in which its use was
undreamed of a few years ago. Some of these accomplishments are catalogued in the magazine published

by the Shute Institute, entitled *The Summary*. Evan
and Wilfrid Shute are two Canadian doctors who have
pioneered in the work with vitamin E being done in
North America, and who founded the institute which
bears their name for further research with this vitamin. They have collected data on the experiences of
doctors from many countries for inclusion in this
publication.

Americans Have Little to Do with Vitamin E

You will see few references in American medical
journals. Our doctors have been too busy commenting
on the uselessness of vitamin E to try it themselves.
The spirit of adventure which causes them to prescribe
and inject newly discovered and unproven antibiotics,
tranquilizers and stimulants into their patients, seems
to desert them, inexplicably, when vitamin E is mentioned. This attitude persists even though the side
effects of vitamin E can be completely discounted,
except in cases of high blood pressure, when large doses
can cause an increase in the pressure. Therefore, low
dosage (50 to 100 International Units or milligrams)
is recommended at the start of treatment when the
blood pressure is high.

However, reputable medical men of other countries
report success with vitamin E in treating diseases still
puzzling to us. We hasten to add that there is a handful
of doctors in the United States who are willing to
prescribe vitamin E as a treatment, but their number
is pitifully small. Chances are slim indeed that one in
10,000 of the people reading this could successfully
prevail upon his doctor to use vitamin E in treating
him. Perhaps a copy of *The Summary*, available from
the Shute Institute, London, Ontario, Canada, would

[351]

convince a skeptical doctor that vitamin E is worthy of his careful investigation.

Your Circulation Improves with Vitamin E

Vitamin E has achieved its greatest reputation in treating circulatory diseases. Its ability to help maintain a high level of oxygen in the blood has been held as a great boon to the more economic action of the heart. Since the blood, rich in oxygen, performs more efficiently on its trip through the body, less blood, hence less pumping, is required to do the same job. The increased level of oxygen retained in the blood is helpful in nourishing the body's tissues, in maintaining the body's reproductive powers, in slowing or halting completely the disintegration of certain organs of the body and in improving a good many other body processes.

Let us look at *The Summary* (1955 to 1957) and examine a few of the reports on vitamin E's effectiveness in treating diseases and malfunctions of all kinds.

Results for 44 Varicose Vein Patients

In *La Riforma Medical* (69, 853-6, 1955) we are told of 44 patients with types of varicose vein complaints who were treated with 300 to 500 milligrams of vitamin E daily for from two months to three years. Nine of the cases of varicose ulcers showed improvement within 30 days—7 were healed completely—and the other 35 all showed some improvement in relief of congestion, pain and edema. The author notes no side effects were observed.

Phlebitis, or inflammation of the veins, has shown an equally willing response to vitamin E. In the *Proceedings of the International Congress on Vitamin E* held in Venice, Italy, in 1955, a doctor reported on his

[352]

experience in treating 27 such cases with 300 milligrams of vitamin E daily, for 6 days, followed by 150 to 200 milligrams of vitamin E for another 6 weeks. There was notable to excellent improvement in 20 of the 27 cases.

Muscular Dystrophy Responds

Vitamin E has been seen in many experiments to be a factor in the mystery of muscular dystrophy. In observations related to the International Congress on Vitamin E (1955) by Dr. M. Aloisi, it was found that the disease could actually be duplicated experimentally in rabbits by merely creating an absence of vitamin E in their systems.

Another report made to the Congress (p. 53 of the *Proceedings*) by G. Cadeddu told of three muscular dystrophy patients given only 9 to 10 milligrams of vitamin E per day. Two of these showed improvement in motor activity, while the third showed no change, but was considered to have been under treatment for too short a time (15 days) for any definite results. Dr. Cadeddu said that the vitamin E therapy must continue for months, even years.

The Vital Organs Require Vitamin E

In some cases, diseases of the vital organs have shown a gratifying response to the administration of vitamin E. *La Clinica Terapeutica* (9, 1, 1955) tells of the general health improvement noted in 30 persons with chronic liver diseases when they received 200 milligrams of vitamin E daily for 40 days. Liver function tests showed an improvement in many of the cases, and those of enlargement of the liver responded particularly well.

[353]

Twenty-eight cases of kidney disease of various types were written up in *Medizinische* (1955, 1195-6). They were first treated with 50 milligrams of vitamin B₁ per day. When this was not effective, further treatment with vitamin E was instituted. The patients were given 300 milligrams of vitamin E per day (up to a total of 4000 milligrams). The result was improvement in all of the patients thus treated.

Similarly, it was noted in the *Calcutta Medical Journal* (no date) that 7 victims of nephritis, a kidney condition, were treated with vitamin E. The response was termed "good" in 5 of the cases.

Arthritis patients have found relief in vitamin E therapy, too. *Therapiewoche* (3, 467, 1953) carried the story of 50 patients suffering from a type of arthritis, *epicondylitis,* in which the rounded end of the bone becomes inflamed and calcium deposits are evident. Each patient was given 300 to 600 milligrams of vitamin E per day orally. After about 8 days the pain was seen to decrease, and in 3 or 4 weeks the calcium deposits ceased forming. The author also told of the use of vitamin E therapy in every patient with hip arthritis as a last resort before trying plastic surgery. Some severely inflamed stiff hips so responded that they regained full motion with no further treatment.

New Hope in Treating Bedsores

An exciting discovery for those long confined to bed due to illness was detailed in the *Canadian Medical Association Journal* (77, 125-128, 1957). The article told of the use of vitamin E in treating the bedsores which develop at points of pressure in patients who spend much time in bed and whose motion is limited. Often these sores eat deep into the body's tissue until bone and muscle are completely exposed. They spread rapidly and have a reputation for resisting most forms of therapy. The four cases included in this report had been treated with the standard methods to no avail. The physician who wrote the report says he was persuaded to use vitamin E only as a last resort, and he did so with no faith whatsoever in its effectiveness. The treatment consisted of 400 milligrams of vitamin E 4 times daily by mouth, and a spray treatment applied to the site of the bedsores once each 8 hours. In the doctor's opinion, vitamin E induced rapid healing of the sores and improvement of the general condition of the patients. The doctor termed the effect remarkable and recommended the trial of vitamin E therapy in treating other cases of bedsores.

Vitamin E's effectiveness in treating skin diseases might be attributed to its ability to hold a greater supply of oxygen in the blood stream. This oxygen plays a major part in revitalizing the skin's cells, helping them to resist the inroads of infection. This property was demonstrated in the case of three women who experienced severe attacks of psoriasis before each menstrual period. *Dermatologica* (112, 468-470, 1956) reports these women were given 400 milligrams of vitamin E per day and were completely cured in a period of 4 to 6 months.

Menstrual Problems Effectively Treated

The effectiveness of vitamin E in a case such as this is particularly understandable since it was concerned with the reproductive cycle. Experiments have shown time and again that vitamin E has a strongly beneficial effect on the reproductive organs and processes. In cases of menstrual difficulty we have the evi-

[355]

dence of the *Lancet* (I, 844-47, 1955), which carried the story of 100 women between 18 and 21 years of age who suffered pain and discomfort during the time of their monthly period. The authors divided the girls into two groups of 50, giving each of one group 50 milligrams of vitamin E per day for 10 days before the period began, and for the next 4 days. The second group was given a pill resembling the one containing vitamin E, but it contained nothing. None of the patients knew if she were getting the vitamins or not. The treatment was continued for 3 months.

In the third month improvement was noted in 76 per cent of the girls treated with vitamin E. Only 29 per cent of the girls who did not receive vitamin E noted any improvement in those 3 months. It was found that those women who had suffered the most before treatment began were those who experienced the most relief. They found that vitamin E seemed to have a cumulative effect and that the relief seemed to be more distinct by the third month than it had been at first. The patients found that there was a recurrence of their pain and discomfort two to six months after the vitamin E treatment was stopped. Obviously the diet these women were eating was not sufficiently endowed with vitamin E.

Stillbirths and Abortions Have Decreased

In the field of fertility the experiments with vitamin E have brought some gratifying results. Horses have been used as experimental animals, and *Schweizer Archiv Tierheilk* (90, 113-133, 1948) states that the conception rate of mares given vitamin E and serviced by proven stallions was increased by 5 per cent, and the number of live foals was increased by 7 per cent.

Stillbirths, abortions and early losses in foals were reduced by 40 per cent when vitamin E was used. It was further remarked that the sex urge of the stallions was found to increase with the inclusion of vitamin E in their diet.

This therapy was applied to humans and reported on in *Geburtschilfe und Frauenheilkunde* (16, 396-405, 1956). Involved were 20 cases of habitual abortion or infertility in marriages in which poorly developed sperm seemed to be the cause, or the women appeared to be sterile. The women were treated for 10 months prior to conception with 100 milligrams of vitamin E, at least every other day. The men were similarly treated for 3 months prior to conception. The quality of the sperm was seen to improve in each case, and "a good number of normal pregnancies resulted."

A Physician Reports on 32 Patients

The *British Medical Journal* (October 4, 1958), carried a letter from a doctor discussing his treatment for habitual miscarriages. He told of 32 patients whom he was treating at the time with vitamin E. All had had at least one miscarriage or more (usually two). One had 3 miscarriages and another 4. He instructed them to take 50 milligrams of vitamin E three times each day from the day the first period was missed. Nineteen of these 32 had already been successfully delivered and two were due at the time the letter was written. Three were 6 months pregnant, and 3 were 3 months pregnant. Two had moved from the area, and 3 of the patients had had miscarriages once again.

The writer concluded by commenting that hormones are not any more effective than vitamin E, and have been found to be more dangerous.

[357]

In women reaching the menopause, or change of life, symptoms such as dizziness, hot flashes, flushing, pain and discomfort were found to be relieved by treatment with vitamin E. *Therapiewoche* (4, 263, 1953-54) tells us that such relief resulted from doses of 150 milligrams of vitamin E per day, at first, then a reduced dosage of 50 milligrams about twice a month. In stubborn cases up to 300 milligrams of vitamin E per day were prescribed.

Vitamin E Used Against Many Eye Diseases

The Summary (8, 85-93, 1956) reports on 44 cases with a variety of ocular diseases that were treated with vitamin E for 2 to 7 months. Showing improvement reaching from increased vision to complete recovery were: seven of the 14 cases of hypertensive retinopathy (inflammation of the retina), all of the 3 diabetic retinopathy cases, 7 of the 9 cases of senile degeneration of the eyes, 1 of the 4 retinitis pigmentosa (hardening of the blood vessels of the eye), 1 of the 4 cases of glossy dimness of the eyes and one case of inflammation of the nerve behind the eyeball. There were no side effects. It was noted that glaucoma cases were not helped. In the *Practitioner and Digest of Treatment* (July, 1956) the details of a most enlightening experiment with vitamin E are recounted. Sixteen turkey hens were reared to maturity, then placed in separate laying cases and fed identical synthetic diets. Half were given vitamin E in addition and the other half kept on the diet deficient only in vitamin E. The hens were artificially inseminated weekly with pooled semen from the farm's toms. All care was taken to be sure that the hen turkeys ate and lived exactly alike, but for the difference made by vitamin E.

[358]

The eyes of 109 embryos taken from eggs laid by the experimental hens were examined. Cataract-like opacities were observed in 21 out of 54 vitamin E-deficient embryos; out of 55 embryos given vitamin E supplements, only two were found to show cataract-like films over the eyes.

Here is some more information on the work done with vitamin E taken from *The Summary* for December, 1960.

Burn Cases

What is usually done about serious burns? If the patient manages to survive at all, skin grafts are attempted often with small success.

In one case treated by Dr. Shute, the patient was a 6-year-old boy who had spilled scalding water over his chest and back nine weeks before the examination. Attempted skin grafts had not been successful, and when seen by the Shutes, ". . . his body was bathed in pus, and one could smell him 5 feet away." After 13 weeks of treatment by Dr. Shute, complete healing occurred. The procedure was 300 milligrams of alpha-tocopherol given orally and tocopherol ointment applied locally (each day, we presume). Nothing else was used except penicillin ointment applied to the infected wounds on alternative days of the first 10 days. None of the scars thickened or contracted, i.e. pinched together, as they formed; this seems to be a characteristic of alphatocopherol-treated wounds, and should prove especially valuable where scars of the face, neck or arms are involved.

Tocopherol Clears Up Second-Degree Burns

There is also the case of a 6-year-old boy who had a hot iron fall on his hand. The ensuing second-degree burn of the back of the hand and 4 fingers made his parents consider taking him to the best clinics for skin grafts. The Shutes gave 300 milligrams of alphatocopherol orally and applied sulpha ointment locally for the first 8 days, after which tocopherol ointment was applied to the fingers. After 15 days, the hand was clean and scabbed. After 31 days, it was healed completely and flexibility of the fingers was perfect.

Two cases of radiation burns caused by x-ray treatment for cancer and eczema are outlined. In the one instance the physician used only tocopherol ointment applied locally, and complete healing occurred in 91 days. In the second, the patient's doctor could do nothing, so the patient began the use of alphatocopherol on his own. The area was healed in 6 weeks.

Strong Effort Rewarded

Another case involved a boy of 14 years, who spent 17 months in the hospital, where skin had been grafted to severe wounds of his legs 5 times without success. His abdomen, from which the skin had been taken, had also not healed. He was emaciated and despondent, and had been sent home to die when Dr. Shute entered the case. Hopelessness made the patient uncooperative. He was given 450 milligrams of alphatocopherol a day, tocopherol ointment was applied to the wounds and pressure areas, and tocopherol was also sprayed on them. In the next 24 months his wounds were all healed and now he lives a normal life which includes participation in all sports, including swimming.

Then there was the 70-year-old man with arteriosclerosis which caused a leg ulcer measuring 15 x 7 centimeters in size. The stench from it was so bad that his co-workers refused to work with him. After 57 weeks on a daily oral dose of alphatocopherol (400

[360]

milligrams) the sore was healed. It remained healed thereafter, though such ulcers tend to recur.

Osteomyelitis is an ailment which frequently occurs in middle-aged people as a companion to diabetes. It manifests itself in unhealing ulcers or sores frequently found on the lower extremities. *The Summary* for December, 1960, describes 3 such cases successfully treated. Wouldn't vitamin E be an excellent preventive measure against such a consequence in diabetic patients?

A Civil Defense Measure

Dr. Shute notes that the application of vitamin E in healing superficial wounds is unusually effective and very quickly relieves the accompanying pain. The resultant scar remains flexible and desirably thin. This is especially important if the scar is at a joint.

Dr. Shute brings up a very interesting point which we never considered before now. He remarks upon the great value of a treatment such as alphatocopherol—it is cheap, self-applicable, easy to use, can be widely distributed when danger threatens. In nuclear war, for example, the majority of injuries would be of the very kind alphatocopherol handles best—burns, scars, open wound, ulcerations, etc. Dr. Shute says that in spite of his effort to call the value of vitamin E to the attention of civilian defense 11 years ago, nothing has been done about investigating its possibilities. In that time nothing else has been developed that would be as effective, and certainly the need to take such a precaution grows greater each day.

The value of vitamin E in fertility has been studied in animals and humans over the last decade. One of the most ambitious projects was a 5-year follow-up by F. G. Darlington and J. B. Chassels, D. V. M. (Nation-

[361]

al Stud Farm, Oshawa, Ontario) on a group of thoroughbred horses who had vitamin E included in their diet. The result was that a group of mares aged 17 (equivalent in age to a woman of 40) maintained a fertility rate higher than the national average for all fertile mares regardless of age. The only change in their care was the vitamin E added to the diet. The quality of the mares' offspring, sired by stud horses also taking vitamin E is testified to by the fact that one racing day at Toronto's Woodbine Track, 6 of the 8 winners were such horses. One of the acknowledged best horses ever bred in Canada, Victoria Park, was also one of these horses.

While breeding horses may not be the same thing as breeding humans, studies of this type do have a suggestive value as to the place of alphatocopherol in the management of human fertility. It should also be borne in mind that vitamin E therapy in humans has shown a power to increase fertility and to reduce the incidence of miscarriages in women who are prone to this difficulty.

The usefulness of vitamin E is obviously not a figment of the imagination. There are scores of reports similar to those carried in these pages appearing in medical journals throughout the world. If added vitamin E will sometimes cure these disorders, why shouldn't a regular intake of vitamin E help to prevent them?

CHAPTER 53

Is Vitamin E a Powerful Preventive Agent?

by DR. WILLIAM HALDEN

THE DEVELOPMENT of research work on vitamin E began with investigations by Dr. H. M. Evans and associates in California in 1922. A three-session symposium on vitamin E, organized by the late Sir Jack Drummond and Alfred Bacharach took place in London, in April, 1939, when the course of further research on this remarkable vital element was outlined by distinguished scientists. After 10 years, the Second International Congress on Vitamin E was held in New York under the chairmanship of Dr. K. E. Mason of the Department of Anatomy, University of Rochester, New York. The long series of communications and discussions at that Congress were published in the Annals of the New York Academy of Medicine. This volume contains a wealth of valuable information on vitamin E with many predictions on the future trend of research in this particular field.

[363]

The Third International Congress on Vitamin E was held in Italy September 5-8, 1955, under very favorable auspices. More than 250 participants from all parts of the world attended the official inauguration and the subsequent sessions at the famous Ani Foundation on the beautiful island San Giorgio Maggiore, opposite the enchanting panorama of Venice.

The history of vitamin E has gone through various stages, the most interesting one, without a doubt, being the present one. It is characterized by the conviction that tocopherols (the name given the 6 different types of vitamin E, called by the Greek alphabet letters alpha, beta, gamma, delta, epsilon, zeta), are very helpful agents in preventive and curative medicine.

The first lectures on vitamin E and metabolic processes were given by Dr. P. L. Harris, Chief of Research Laboratories, D.P.I. Rochester, followed by a comprehensive report of Professor K. E. Mason of the University of Rochester. Dr. Harris outlined the situation in the field of present research, documenting his remarks with over 1000 references to medical and scientific literature. One was astonished to learn from these and other American scientists about the wealth of biological and clinical information on this particular vitamin.

These findings would not have been possible without dependable analytical methods for determining the single tocopherols in natural sources of very intricate composition. It was chiefly the admirable work of Mary-Louise Quaife, which decisively contributed to the knowledge of the occurrence of various types of tocopherols in natural foodstuffs. H. R. Bolliger of Basel, Switzerland, gave a survey of the newest analytical methods and their use in the evaluation of tocopherols. Dr. Green from England also made valu-

[364]

able contributions to this field. Then there were lectures by British, Danish, French, German, Italian, South American, Swiss and other researchers which were of special interest for the problems around vitamin E and its relation to other vitamins, hormones and enzymes.

Most emphasis was given to the relation of vitamin E to the cardiovascular system (the heart and blood vessels) for of course there is great world-wide interest in this problem. Diet and circulation are intimately connected, especially from the standpoint of vitamin E administration, as was amply demonstrated in Venice.

Professor Henrik Dam of Copenhagen and his co-workers had found that the administration of large quantities of cod liver oil to experimental animals resulted in severe disorders of the skin and other organs if the diet of these animals was devoid of vitamin E. All signs of illness disappeared in a rather short time after the supply of sufficient amounts of tocopherols or vitamin E.

This strange happening occurs because cod liver oil contains highly unsaturated fatty acids, like the group of acids that make up the so-called vitamin F. Such fatty acids make it easier for oxygen to go by way of the blood stream to all cells, tissues and organs. You can easily understand, then, that these unsaturated fatty acids (vitamin F) have great importance for the respiration or oxygenation of our most vital organs.

The Danish investigators made another very important discovery in finding deposits of dark-colored peroxides of fatty acids in the arteries at various parts of the animal body *if there was not sufficient vitamin E in the diet*. The occurrence of such peroxides could be prevented by giving vitamin E or synthetic sub-

[365]

stances somewhat like vitamin E. One of these substances is methylene blue which produces some effects similar to vitamin E, when it is given in appropriate, small quantities.

Here one can see the difference between a natural vital substance such as vitamin E and a synthetic substance of the methylene blue type. When the supply of the methylene blue was raised over a certain limit, very severe disorders occurred in the bodies of the laboratory animals, clearly showing the unbiological effect of such a substance. Vitamin E, however, can be supplied in much higher doses than the usual ones without any undesirable reaction.

Take for instance some drug that may be given to you by a physician in a small dose, bringing you some comfort and help during a state of illness. If you should take such a poisonous agent tenfold it would badly harm you, and if you should take 20 times as much as the helpful dose it would probably kill you. In a similar way methylene blue can be applied in small doses to experimental animals in order to prevent severe disturbances caused by an oversupply of highly unsaturated fatty acids. The tenfold or twentyfold doses would prove disastrous to the animals.

On the other hand, the natural tocopherols which are normal constituents of plants as well as animals and human beings may be applied in concentrations of many *milligrams* (as they are contained in every 4 ounces or so of many natural foodstuffs) daily for preventive purposes up to daily doses of *grams* (1000 milligrams) without doing any harm. So, in other words, a thousand times as much vitamin E as you might get in food is not harmful, because it is a natural substance.

[366]

This fact has been emphasized by some researchers, especially by Drs. Evan and Wilfrid Shute of the Shute Institute at London, Ontario, Canada. These scientists have already written, in their papers on vitamin E in the treatment of hypertensive heart disease, that the "dosage of alphatocopherol varied with each type of heart disease and with each case within that type."

At the Congress in Venice, Dr. Shute again described a great many cases of successful treatment of cardiovascular diseases with tocopherols, showing the results of this medication with dozens of marvelous colored pictures which made a deep impression on the audience.

The clinical results of the application of vitamin E on severe cases of cardiovascular and nervous diseases, degenerative muscular dystrophies and myopathies (muscle diseases) described by other scientists of international reputation clarified the importance of vitamin E as a valuable tool in practical medicine.

The chief point of attack of tocopherols in the body seems to be intimately connected with the utilization of oxygen and therefore with cell respiration. As you know, oxygen is absolutely essential for every process that goes on inside our bodies, and it is believed that in many diseases one of the chief troubles is lack of enough oxygen in the cells.

The highly unsaturated fatty acids (such as vitamin F) act as biological "accelerators" of oxygen transport. That is, they make it easier to move oxygen from place to place in the body. It is easy to understand that the process of oxygen utilization can proceed too far and produce some unwelcome reactions. One of these might be the deposit of peroxides in the blood vessels and all of the disorders that might accompany such a state.

[367]

In order to avoid this condition, nature provides "moderators" that prevent the overactivity of all the various substances that promote the use of oxygen.

In the human body vitamin E plays this role of moderating, thus being able to counteract the too-rapid action of the other substances that are using up the oxygen. We might imagine it as a river in which the oxygen flows between two streams of those substances that accelerate and those that moderate like vitamin E. In this way the oxygen operates in the most effective manner, without going beyond the proper threshold established by vitamin E. True respiration must be harmonized in order to make the best possible use of oxygen without forming any deposits in blood vessels. If vitamin E is continually supplied to the human body in appropriate quantities as they occur in natural foodstuffs such as wheat germ and whole grains, almonds, nuts, oilseeds and oils pressed therefrom, then the most economical conditions for a normal circulation prevail.

Vitamin E and its natural sources are of course not the only requisites for a normal circulation and condition of blood vessels. Some authors are of the opinion, expressed also at the International Congress in Venice, that some vitamins of the B group as well as vitamins A and C form an auxiliary team of vital substances that help to accomplish the manifold roles the tocopherols have to play in the concert of vitamins, that accompanies the biological harmony of a well-balanced respiration, heart action and easy-going circulation.

CHAPTER 54

Reports from the Vitamin E Congress

AFTER THE Third International Congress on Vitamin E was held in Venice in 1955, a review of the proceedings was published. Most of the text is in Italian, but many articles have been translated into English. There are altogether 183 entries—that is, reviews of addresses made at the Congress by scientists, European and American.

We are sure that no one could read through this review and not be convinced of the absolute necessity of ample amounts of vitamin E in the diet. We are giving you a few samples of the kind of information that is being uncovered in research on vitamin E, the kind of information that was presented at the Vitamin E Congress. After you read it, we are sure you will agree with us that, considering the serious lack of vitamin E in today's refined and processed foods, it is absolutely essential for you to take this vitamin as a food supplement every day.

[369]

Here are reviews of some of the papers presented:

*   *   *

Authors E. Boschi and A. Gaspari have treated 90 cases of skin wounds with 100 milligrams of vitamin E given orally, in injections and applied directly to the wounds. They have obtained quite favorable results.

*   *   *

Seven years of clinical experience in a total of 508 cases have convincingly demonstrated that rheumatic and ischemic heart disease (that is, disease due to contraction of local blood vessels) respond well to vitamin E treatment if carefully planned and systematically carried out over a sufficiently long time, according to L. Schmidt of England. He says further that hardening of the arteries, widely believed to be the principal cause of this kind of heart disease, plays only an intermediary role and the direct cause is the serious upset in the normal balance of the blood caused by: 1. prolonged ingestion of more calories than the normal daily requirement; 2. the sustained lack of sufficient vitamin E in the diet. According to Dr. Schmidt, the individual who eats a rich diet, high in fat-producing calories, must take vitamin E if he would make himself a little less vulnerable to this disease. *The person who eats a low-calorie diet and takes large amounts of vitamin E is, for all practical purposes, immune to heart disease.*

*   *   *

The value of vitamin E in a variety of conditions of ill health is clearly indicated in a detailed study of 180 cases, presented by O. Connor and J. P. S. Hodges of England. The vitamin is especially beneficial in acute peripheral thrombosis (that is, a blood clot near

[370]

the surface of the skin), acute nephritis, acute rheumatic fever, hardening of the arteries and high blood pressure. Even more important is the new hope it offers patients with heart disease of all types or cerebrovascular accidents (strokes).

"The physician can now see his patients gradually getting better and returning to their work and normal life in most cases, whereas under the old treatments —and indeed, under many of the new treatments— they steadily become worse without having shown any evidence of real cure."

* * *

Drs. E. Bottiglioni and P. L. Sturani of Italy speak of treating successfully with vitamin E some cases of diabetic retinitis and a few cases of thromboangiitis (Buerger's disease).

* * *

Dr. A. Vogelsang of Canada relates his experience with vitamin E over 10 years. He gives 400 International Units of the vitamin daily with a minimum maintenance dosage of 300 units, for coronary thrombosis and coronary insufficiency; 600 to 900 units, with a minimum dose of 400 units, for Buerger's disease and arteriosclerosis; for acute thrombophlebitis he gives 600 units daily for a period of 3 weeks only. He believes, too, that vitamin E should not be given to hyperthyroid heart cases.

* * *

Vitamin E is uniquely valuable in the treatment of acute and subacute thrombosis of veins, according to Dr. P. Khoo of Canada. It is very safe, he says, permitting the patient to be out of bed without any fear of embolism or hemorrhage.

[371]

S. Tolgyes of Canada declares that vitamin E in high dosage is valuable in the treatment of early gangrene. Especially in diabetic patients, toes and feet that formerly would have been amputated may now be saved.

*　　*　　*

Menopause symptoms treated with vitamin E responded excellently, according to A. Raffy of Budapest who treated 200 patients with minimum doses of 30 milligrams on alternate days. There was considerable improvement in 65 per cent of the cases. He believes that the vitamin has a direct effect on the sex hormones produced at this time.

*　　*　　*

E. V. Shute of Canada reports on vitamin E in obstetrics. It is valuable, he says, in threatened abortion, miscarriage or prematurity. In cases of habitual abortion or miscarriage, it should be given to the father before conception and perhaps to the mother afterward. If the father takes vitamin E before conception, it seems to prevent the formation of many congenital defects in families where they tend to appear. It may decrease hemorrhaging after childbirth. It hastens healing of facial wounds in the newborn. It probably decreases brain damage to the child in difficult labor. It seems to reduce the number of stillbirths and the mortality among newly born infants.

*　　*　　*

Vitamin E assists the middle-aged eye to focus readily, good news for those of us who are contemplating glasses for close work. According to Dr. R. Seidenari of Milan, Italy, patients over 40 given vitamin E showed in tests and by their own statements that their far-sightedness had improved and they could once again read without spectacles.

[372]

Dr. E. Raverdino of Italy used vitamin E in cases of degeneration of certain parts of the eye, due to old age. He gave doses of 600 milligrams a day. In the majority of cases, except those in which the central vision was already completely destroyed, the results were favorable with a rapid return of vision and a reduction of the blind spot.

* * *

Clues as to why some researchers are not successful in treating disorders with vitamin E are suggested in the work of several investigators. M. Aloisi and V. Polanyi of Italy show clearly that laboratory animals kept on a vitamin E-deficient diet developed a paralysis due to lack of vitamin B_1 (thiamin) which they later found was also deficient in the diet. Giving the animals vitamin C (of all things!) cured the paralysis. In another paper read at the Congress, M. Aloisi describes the close association between vitamin E and vitamin C. Guinea pigs given muscular dystrophy by diets deficient in vitamin E show far greater damage to muscles when there is a lack of vitamin C in their diets, too. Could it be that researchers who get good results using vitamin E for human muscular dystrophy also make certain there is enough vitamin C in the diet, and those who fail, do so because they don't pay any attention to the rest of the diet?

* * *

C. Malatesta of Italy reveals the results of experiments in his laboratory indicating that lack of vitamin E alone causes severe degenerative changes in the retina and the lens of the eye. Detached retina and cataract are two rapidly increasing disorders of our time—could lack of vitamin E in the diet be partly responsible?

[373]

CHAPTER 55

New Experiments with Vitamin E

A 14-YEAR-OLD BOY destined for a most amazing change
in his life was brought to Ontario Hospital School in
Orillia, Ontario, on January 16, 1961. He had been
suffering almost constant pain since six hours after his
birth. The staff physician, H. D. Wilson, M.D., recognized at once the awful symptoms of epidermolysis
bullosa, a rare and painful skin disease that has always
defied satisfactory medical treatment. His decision to
try treating it with vitamin E and the results he
achieved made a kind of medical history. No other
literature on the subject till then describes more satisfactory results with epidermolysis bullosa than Wilson's
report in the *Canadian Medical Association Journal*
(June 6, 1964).

When the disease occurs, blisters develop that contain a fluid which can become infected. As the blisters
age they turn into painful crusted ulcers which leave
scars when they heal. Usually, before healing has taken

[374]

place completely, new crops of the blisters appear in the area and a vicious circle of healing and breakdown continues for months or years, often for life.

The boy's was a typical case, with extensive openings of the skin and the mucous membranes of the mouth, throat and the area surrounding the eye. "The condition of his skin, when the dressings were removed, can scarcely be described. It is difficult to imagine a more unpleasant sight, compounded with blisters of all sizes, scabs, scars and bloody purulent discharge . . . Personal experience in the treatment of chronic varicose ulcer with vitamin E induced me to make a trial of alphatocopherol in the boy's disease," wrote Wilson. "The varicose ulcer referred to healed readily, and has not recurred, and the patient has been active since. It seemed that what was so useful with one type of ulcer might be helpful in this particularly discouraging condition."

Many forms of treatment had already been used on the boy and he had spent most of his life in hospitals, including a home for incurable children. To test the effect of alphatocopherol on this patient, all other medication was discontinued except for a sedative given four times daily.

Tocopherol Treatment

On March 24, 1961, alphatocopherol gelatin capsules were administered in the amount of 400 units four times a day, and tocopherol ointment was applied to all affected areas twice a day. "Progress was soon evident. On July 1, 1961, the dose of vitamin E was increased to 800 units four times a day, in an attempt to find the optimum dosage . . . Improvement was progressive but slow. The color of affected areas faded from fiery red to a paler red or pink. The blisters con-

[375]

tinued to appear, but were smaller and did not tend to spread when pressure was applied.

"On August 1, 1961, a dosage of vitamin E succinate was increased to 1200 units four times a day in a further attempt to find the optimum dosage. Healing progressed, and on August 18, 1961, sodium amytal [the sedative] was discontinued because of the decrease in the amount of pain the patient was experiencing."

By January 1962, a year later, the number of blisters appearing per day had decreased and so had the size. The boy had gained weight, was attending school and was doing occupational therapy regularly.

At this point the doctors stopped giving vitamin E to see if the progress would be maintained. Almost at once the skin began to break down again and it continued to do so until vitamin E medication was started again in July. The starting dosage this time was 3200 international units of vitamin E per day, but still the progress was slow. It took 6000 international units per day to show an effect.

"Because the patient attends school and social functions, his hands, arms, feet and knees are bandaged for cosmetic reasons, to reduce friction, and to prevent infection. His general physical condition has been good and although he has had recurrences of lesions, these are of a temporary nature and his skin has a more normal appearance. The number of nursing hours required in his treatment is one per day compared to ten before treatment was started."

Success Confirmed

Dr. Wilson remarks that two other physicians have since had similar experiences in treating this disease with alphatocopherol, and they too have been gratified. "A number of communications have purported to confirm the original observations of Shute *et al.* on the value of alphatocopherol in the treatment of ulcers of various types, such as indolent, varicose, ischemic, topical, and those occurring after radiation, those due to burns—or even peptic ulceration."

Dr. Wilson's experience is one of a small flurry of reports on vitamin E's activity in the human system which have recently appeared in professional journals and in the late press. Of greater general interest and application is the estimate of Dr. Aloys L. Tappel, a biochemist at the University of California and Professor of Food Science and Technology at Davis College. In his opinion vitamin E can slow down the aging process in humans. "Aging," says Dr. Tappel, "is due to the process of oxidation, and since vitamin E is a natural anti-oxidant, it could be used to counteract this process in the body."

Aging Retarded

When oxidation occurs in the body, the result is the formation of very high-reaction compounds which can cause a breakdown and loss of function of proteins, the building blocks of the body. The debris from these destroyed proteins tends to pile up in cell membranes and accounts for the appearances and behavior which are characteristic of aging. "In normal humans vitamin E contained in the unsaturated vegetable fats acts to prevent the formation of free radicals and serves as a built-in protection against accelerated aging." Tappel suggested that extra vitamin E or some synthetic compound like it might be used from infancy to extend man's life span by decades.

This suggestion resembles one in an article in the *Journal of Gerontology* (July 1961), in which Denham Harman, M.D., Ph.D., discussed prolonging the normal

[377]

life span and inhibiting spontaneous cancer by the use of anti-oxidants. Harman suggests that aging may be due to the free radicals mentioned by Dr. Tappel which are produced by the body and lead to oxidizing the tissues. In his very first test, Harman was able to extend the life of experimental mice by 20 per cent merely by including some type of anti-oxidant in their diet. Certain of the anti-oxidant compounds "produced a marked decrease in the tumor incidence" of certain experimental mice.

The *Nutrition Review* for October 19, 1963, carried the discovery that a vitamin E deficiency could result in a serious type of anemia. This observation was first made in monkeys and scientists projected the possibility that if vitamin E deficiency could create anemia, persons already anemic might respond to treatment with this vitamin. A report in the *American Journal of Clinical Nutrition* described such an experiment using a series of 12 anemic children all treated with vitamin E. In every case and by all criteria available, these children responded to vitamin E favorably.

For years scientists have been flirting with the likelihood that vitamin E is one of the basic factors involved in the development of muscular dystrophy. J. S. Dinning (*Rev. Canad. Bio.* 21, 501, 1962) reported on young rhesus monkeys that were fed purified diets in order to bring about a vitamin E deficiency. From six months to three years were required to accomplish this but the result was universal. All monkeys fed the diet developed nutritional muscular dystrophy. "They became quite weak and with obvious loss of skeleton muscles. The histologic picture of the skeletal muscle appeared identical to that in vitamin E deficient rabbit muscle. A few weeks after the onset of the first signs of dystrophy, the animals were frequently unable to rise from their side. Vitamin E therapy resulted in dramatic recovery provided it was started before the very advanced stage of dystrophy."

Disease Prone

The journal *Pediatrics* (31, 324, 1963) has at last begun to recognize the essential quality of vitamin E in the diet. Subjects who are given low levels of serum tocopherol are admittedly more susceptible than others to certain types of disease, and "premature and full-term infants receiving heated milk or formulas of cow milk do not require supplementary administration of vitamin E except, possibly, when dietary intake of fat is markedly reduced, as is sometimes practiced in feeding premature infants. It seems desirable to provide dietary supplements of vitamin E to patients with prolonged steatorrhea (a form of diarrhea) from any cause."

Enlightened physicians and researchers are obviously beginning to take advantage of the possibilities in vitamin E therapy. Their impressive reports, which now appear with some frequency in well-respected journals both American and foreign, are nudging the everyday practitioners into a new attitude toward vitamin E. They are becoming curious and questioning, at the same time showing some respect for the undeniable results vitamin E has achieved in various fields of medicine. We hope that, like Dr. Wilson, more and more physicians will test vitamin E's ability to cope with diseases considered up to now to be impossible, or at best unlikely, objects for cure.

CHAPTER 56

Answer to Critics of Vitamin E

A MEDICAL DOCTOR WHO writes a widely syndicated column took up the question of vitamin E. Dr. Walter Alvarez, whose column is printed in, we suppose, hundreds of American newspapers, wrote:

"Many people write me asking if they should mortgage their home or borrow money and travel far to the institute they have heard about which advertises to cure some disease. I certainly would never think of going to such a place. Today a woman writes asking if she should take her very sick child to a place where marvelous cures are supposed to be worked with vitamin E. All I know is that a while ago I read a big book on the world's experience with vitamin E and the conclusion of the editors was that it was of no value on any known disease of man. We all of us get large amounts of vitamin E in all our foods. I know that there are many enthusiasts who have reported marvelous results from using vitamin E, but I know that other men, who have tried to confirm these results, have failed completely. It is very hard to decide if a drug is of value, especially if one is an enthusiast."

Dr. Evan Shute, of the Shute Clinic, London, Ontario, Canada, took up Dr. Alvarez' challenge and wrote him the following letter. We think it is a masterpiece, both for the information it contains and for its moderate, restrained and reasonable tone. This is the tone we think is most effective for letters to editors, Congressmen or public health officials. Be sure you have all the facts, then write with good humor but firmness, as Dr. Shute has. For those who regularly follow Dr. Alvarez' column—here, we think, is the best answer to his statements about vitamin E:

"Dear Dr. Alvarez:

"I often read your very wise and humane column which is carried by so many papers, but I must admit that both you and your column sank very low in my estimation today when I read your notes on vitamin E. They show so much bias, so much misinformation, and so little appreciation of current literature that I was astonished.

"There are now about 300 teams of medical 'enthusiasts' who have written papers emphasizing the therapeutic effectiveness of alphatocopherol (vitamin E) in cardiovascular disease, not to mention the numerous papers on reproductive difficulties. These include some of the great names in the profession, people whom you would be proud to have on the staff of the Mayo Clinic, for example. Their papers are what matters, of course, not any 'big book' of 'other men's pearls' (which, by the way, you gave no date for; it could have been 20 years old).

"I count myself among these 'enthusiasts' and I

[381]

know you will be interested to hear that I was asked to describe our studies on 'Vitamin E in Obstetrics and Vascular Disease' at the Pan-American Fertility Conference in Miami Beach two months ago, (their suggestion as to title, not mine), and am being asked to describe them to the doctors of Saskatchewan in a refresher course being sponsored by the Saskatchewan Board of Health a month from now. You know, surely, that I am listed in American Men of Science, belong to many international medical societies, and have served as president of a national society in one of my specialties.

"There are many overwhelming references which I could cite which would change your viewpoint, I am sure, but let me mention just three:

1. The study of Livingston, P.D., and Jones C. (England) — *Lancet,* 2:602, 1958 on intermittent claudication.

2. The study of Kawahara, on venous thrombosis —*Surgery,* Vol. 46, p. 768, 1959.

3. The study of Tolgyes, S., and Shute, E. V.— *Canadian Medical Association Journal,* 76:730, 1957 —giving coloured photographs of our results in treating early gangrene.

I would ask you to look particularly at figures 1, 2, 3 and 10, 11, 12 and 13, and ask yourself if any inert substance could produce a result like that.

"Surely you are aware that the last paper in the literature to cast doubt on our findings appeared fully 10 years ago!

"You point out in your column that we get 'large quantities of vitamin E' in our food. Dear Dr. Alvarez, surely you know better. This and all its relevant details were discussed by me in the last issue of *The Summary* which I am sending you, from page 51 onwards. I will

[382]

mention just one item in it to you now because I hope you will read the whole article at your first opportunity. It points out that the diets suggested by the National Research Council of the United States contain 6 international units of alphatocopherol per day. What anyone absorbs may be *much less* than this, but this is what is laid on his plate. It has recently been proven by Horwitt and others that the daily requirement is 30 International Units of alphatocopherol per day. What must your conclusion be?

"Finally, I am sending you a reprint which appeared a few weeks ago in the *Canadian Medical Association Journal* describing the intensive studies being undertaken in Russia at this moment on the value of this agent in cardiovascular disease. The Russians surveyed all the medical literature first, including any adverse opinion you could have uncovered, but looked at our evidence too. Then they decided to undertake this definitive study. You know how excellent Russian medicine is, as well as Russian nuclear physics. Didn't you speak too soon, Dr. Alvarez? Their results can make your country look foolish once again.

"I think and hope that you are an honest man as well as an able physician. I sincerely hope and expect that you will consider the points that I have brought to your attention, as well as the many others which are discussed in *The Summary*. Upon changing your views I will expect you to relate your change of heart in your column. If you fail to do so I shall know where you stand both by the ethical standards of our profession and by the still older standards of honesty to which all men subscribe.

Yours sincerely,

Evan V. Shute,
F.R.C.S.(C)"

[383]

CHAPTER 57

Do Doctors Study Vitamin E's Record?

EVIDENTLY, DR. ALVAREZ didn't follow the advice so ably given to him by Dr. Shute in the letter above, for, in another of Dr. Alvarez' columns which appeared in syndication on October 15, 1961, the question of the value of vitamin E as a therapeutic measure is revived once again. Under a subhead, "Vitamin E Has No Value in Treating Illness," Dr. Alvarez writes: "Beside me as I write is a big book on vitamin E. And the editor of it concludes by saying that, after reading the literature on this substance, his impression is that it has no value in the treatment of disease. . . . It [vitamin E] is found in so many foods that it is almost impossible to make up a diet that does not contain all the vitamin E that an animal needs."

Does it all sound familiar? For over a year Dr. Alvarez has sat with one big book on vitamin E which can tell him nothing new. How old is the book? He doesn't say. Could it have been written 20 years ago,

[384]

when there was little experimentation and evidence on the powers of vitamin E? Surely no authority on vitamin E could have read through the hundreds of reports on successful treatment of humans and animals with vitamin E since the 1940's and still contend that there is no evidence on the value of the vitamin in the treatment of disease. The evidence is overwhelming!

Furthermore, in spite of the information conveyed to him by Dr. Shute, Dr. Alvarez persists in keeping alive the myth that no one could possibly need more vitamin E than one gets in the average diet. If intake of vitamin E can reverse a disease condition in the body—and it most certainly can!—then it is obvious that that body was not getting the amount of vitamin E needed to prevent the disease. It is hard to believe that Dr. Alvarez has gone beyond the "big book" he keeps referring to, to do any serious research on the current standing of vitamin E. We have, however, and we know that Dr. Alvarez' conclusions on vitamin E are mistaken.

A Big Joke

Another columnist, Burton H. Fern, M.D., played vitamin E for laughs. In a copy of his column sent to us, he answered these questions: "Does vitamin E help varicose veins? How much should I take?" with this answer:

"Filled with vitamin E, varicose veins merely bulge more. So far, no one can prove that humans need vitamin E. In vitamin pills it merely calms worrywarts!"

We wonder if the "joke" got a good laugh in Dr. Fern's hometown. Would the folks still be laughing if they knew that, in spite of Dr. Fern's assertion that there is no proof for the need of vitamin E in humans,

[385]

the United States government ruled that such a need had definitely been established.

We would like to cite a few experiments with vitamin E, conducted by the world's scientists, which show that it does more, much more, than Dr. Fern says it can.

The basic disorder which causes varicose veins is circulatory. In the *American Journal of Physiology* (153: 127, 1948), Zierler, Grob and Lilienthal asserted their belief that alphatocopherol is vigorously antithrombic (fights clotting). This suggests to them that it may help prevent intravascular blood clotting. Alphatocopherol is recognized as an oxidative agent.

A Danish journal, *Acta Pathologica* (29: 73, 1951), carried a report on 8 patients with venous disease of the legs. The authors concluded that "a local deficiency of vitamin E" exists in certain types of chronic venous disease.

A study of 25 cases, most of whom had leg varices and who were given 100-150 milligrams daily of a special vitamin E preparation, plus a coumarin (anticoagulant) preparation was reported in *Lekarske listy* (7:549, 1952), a Czechoslovakian journal. The results were compared with similar cases of thrombosis seen in their clinic since 1946. It was found that the average number of days necessary before the patient was able to walk was cut in half. The combined treatment was preferable to the use of the coumarin derivative alone. The author, O. Bruchner, later used vitamin E as a preventive for similar disorders with success.

A Nine-Year Review

A review of nine years of experience with alphatocopherol appeared in the *Canadian Medical Association Journal* (74: 715, 1956). There were 327 cases of thrombophlebitis and phlebothrombosis treated. All were treated with nothing but alphatocopherol. Provided the dosage was adequate, the results were classed as dramatic and gratifying. Inflammation promptly subsided and the clotting dissolv.ed The heat, swelling and tenderness quickly disappeared.

Arizona Medicine (16: 100, 1959) carried an article by R. F. Bock in which he concluded that postoperative and postpartum thrombophlebitis respond well to 1100 International Units of alphatocopherol per day. The results often show themselves within 12 hours, and pain is relieved in 24 hours. Clinical results are apparent in 24 to 48 hours.

Varicose ulcers are also cured by alphatocopherol, says Bock. It can be used prior to surgery as a preventive against dangerous blood clots. It is characterized as safer and just as effective as dicumerol and heparin and never accompanied with hemorrhage complications. Bock saw no side effects from alphatocopherol use.

These are but a few of the many reports on the value of vitamin E in treating vascular disorders. If Dr. Fern has done any research on the question, he must have come across some evidence that is inexplicable, if vitamin E has no value and if he still insists that no one has shown that it is necessary to human life.

A Clue to Vitamin E Shortage

The obvious importance of vitamin E, and the mysteries which have yet to be solved before vitamin E is fully explained, are emphasized by a report in *Gastroenterology* (February, 1961). It told of the appearance of brownish-yellow coloring on the smooth muscle fibers due to deposit of certain granules when a vitamin E deficiency is induced in animals. What is interesting about this discovery is that 61 per cent of the subjects in this study who suffered from an inflammation of the pancreas, and 27 per cent of those who suffered from nutritional cirrhosis of the liver showed the same colored granule deposit. It was also present in the small intestine in nearly all the cases. Furthermore, 17 per cent of the patients with pancreatitis and 65 per cent with nutritional cirrhosis showed the coloring in the stomach, prostate gland, urinary bladder, bronchi, esophagus, gall bladder, colon and uterus. These findings raise the possibility that some of the gastrointestinal motor disturbances encountered in cases of inflammation of the pancreas and cirrhosis may be due to deposits of these granules caused by vitamin E deficiency.

Vitamin E in the treatment of diabetes was being used effectively in 1947, according to *Medical Record* (160: 667, 1947). M. B. Mololchick told of a 55-year-old man with diabetes melitus and angina pectoris. He was put on 200 milligrams of mixed tocopherols and the angina was gone in 3 weeks. Also, after 3 months of treatment with mixed tocopherols the patient's blood sugar was normal.

An Italian journal (*Gionale di Clinica Medica,* 31:1, 1950) carried U. Butturini's article telling of 50 diabetics treated with alphatocopherol. For 10 per cent there was no help from the treatment, 26 per cent were able to reduce their insulin intake somewhat and 64 per cent were taken off insulin entirely.

Skin Diseases Treated

Vitamin E, in the treatment of skin diseases is discussed in the Russian journal *Vestnik Dermatologii i. Venerologii* (32: 31, 1958) by Dr. M. E. Barabasch.

Twenty-eight patients were involved in the study. Eight had chronic ulcers of the leg and one had leg ulcers caused by x-ray. For these he used the preparation both internally and externally. For the other 19 patients, only external application was involved. This was accomplished by soaking a piece of cheesecloth in vitamin E concentrate and applying it to the sore part.

Of 11 psoriasis patients, nine experienced complete disappearance of the rash, and in the other two there was a considerable degree of improvement. The patients had been psoriasis victims for from 5 to 33 years. The vitamin E had shown complete or partial (in two cases) effectiveness within 3 months.

The patients suffering with leg ulcers experienced similar results. Some of these 10 patients had been treating their leg ulcers for as long as 12 years. The patients, using vitamin E internally as well as externally, took an average of about 1,000 milligrams per day. All were healed within two months, some in 30 days.

Two patients with x-ray ulcers started improving after almost two months on vitamin E, as was evidenced by a decrease in the size of the ulcer and a lessening of pain. Tuberculosis ulcers also started healing much faster than they had without vitamin E. The one scleroderma victim also showed definite improvement.

Aid in Withdrawal Symptoms of Drug Addicts

In these days of increased drug addiction, the report in the *Acta Medica Iran* (1: 215, 1956-1957) should be of great interest to city governments as well as medical men. Ten cases of opium addiction, of 4 to 14 years duration, were given 200-1,000 milligrams daily for 3 to 19 days. Abstinence symptoms improved along with ability to sleep and lessening of pain. The period of withdrawal treatment was shortened. The author suggests a maintenance dose of 100-200 milligrams daily for several weeks after recovery.

Perhaps addicts of other drugs would be aided in getting through the horrible period of withdrawal more easily and speedily with such treatment. We have seen no literature on such experiments conducted with vitamin E in the United States, where the addiction problem is becoming acute.

In *La Presse Medicale* (68: 855, 1959) the most common cause of myopia, an elongation of the front-to-back diameter of the eye, due to looseness of certain fibers of the coating of the eye, is discussed. C. and G. Desusclade have treated this affliction with vitamin E—100 milligrams each morning for 3 months of each year. This treatment is said not only to arrest the progress of this myopia, but has improved the condition in 15 per cent of the cases treated.

We believe vitamin E is important to maintaining good health. We believe that the average modern diet offers far less than the minimal amount needed by the body to function properly. It is quite understandable to us that so many common diseases of modern America respond to treatment with vitamin E. Obviously they occur because of a vitamin E shortage in the daily diet. We have said before that modern food processing has reduced the daily vitamin E intake by 100 milligrams. We believe it is essential that the diet be supplemented to that extent, at least.

[390]

CHAPTER 58

Pregnancy and Vitamin E

THE NEED for an increased intake of vitamins and minerals during pregnancy has become firmly established by now. Obstetricians routinely recommend supplements; and since it has become established that the B vitamins play a major role in preventing birth defects, more and more doctors are recommending a B complex supplement as well. Pregnant women are advised to increase their consumption of foods containing vitamins A and D for healthy growth of the child, and vitamin C to overcome the toxicities associated with pregnancy has long been known. Of all the known vitamins, it is only vitamin E that has been generally neglected in the efforts doctors make to keep pregnant patients and their unborn children healthy and normal.

Yet there is mounting evidence that in the process of pregnancy vitamin E is at least as important as any other essential nutrient, possibly most important.

[391]

Deficiency Causes Anemia

The latest information on the need for more vitamin E in pregnant women comes from two prominent Philadelphia pediatricians of the University of Pennsylvania Medical School. Dr. Lewis A. Barness, chairman of the Department of Pediatrics, and Dr. Frank A. Oski reported to a meeting of the American Pediatrics Society that "A vitamin E deficiency appears to be a common nutritional disturbance that manifests itself as a hemolytic anemia in the premature infant of low birth weight." Their report went on to describe their unprecedented success in quickly correcting such an anemic condition in eight infants at the University hospital.

Hitherto a mysterious disease of unknown cause, hemolytic anemia is characterized by rapid destruction of the red cells of the blood. Previous treatments, sometimes successful and sometimes not, have included such complex and dangerous procedures as surgical removal of the spleen, periodic blood transfusions and injections of antibiotics in the hope of eliminating some unknown bacterial agent that might be causing the anemia. In place of these drawn-out, perilous and distressing treatments, Drs. Oski and Barness used nothing but vitamin E taken by mouth and corrected the anemia conditions in eight premature infants in an average time of 10 days.

It is a development that not only promises sharp improvement in the mortality rate among premature infants, but also opens the door on new areas of inquiry that may well find vitamin E the answer to other puzzling questions about the health of newborn infants and their mothers. "Vitamin E, unlike other nutrients, does not readily cross the placental barrier to nourish

[392]

the fetus," Dr. Oski stated in a personal interview. This, he indicated, could readily become a problem if the unborn child has a less than normal ability to absorb the vitamin or if the mother is not consuming enough for the child's needs. In either case, the obvious answer would be for the pregnant woman to so increase her intake of vitamin E that the infant will be certain to get enough.

Although they have reached no conclusions as yet, the University of Pennsylvania researchers are also investigating possible relationships between vitamin E deficiency and other ailments of the newborn child, including brain damage and muscular dystrophy. Cystic fibrosis, another of the great scientific puzzlers that afflict newborn children, is also being investigated in other researches for its relationship to vitamin E deficiency.

Controls Oxygen Status

To us this new development is a heartening indication that medical research may at last be on the right track toward identifying and eliminating or reducing these major destroyers of young lives. It has long seemed apparent to us that there has to be an obvious and basic connection between the vitamin E status of the mother and the health of the new child. Vitamin E is the major antioxidant in nature, which means that it is nature's chief defense against the loss of oxygen by its forming into toxic compounds. Such compounds as hydrogen peroxide and carbon monoxide can be dangerous or deadly within the adult body. How much more perilous, then, must they be to the fragile embryo being formed into a person inside its mother's womb? Physiologically the womb provides superb protection against invasion of the child's body

[393]

by bacteria or viruses. But under no circumstances can oxygen be kept from the child if it is to stay alive. It is thus in the blood itself that the mother must supply the child with the means of preventing contamination of its oxygen. And the major means is vitamin E.

For these reasons, Doctors Woollam and Miller, writing in the British *Medical Journal* (June 2, 1956), attributed many miscarriages to deficiencies in vitamin E. They attributed those failures, and they are many, classified as "of unknown origin" to an insufficiency of pure oxygen in the blood supply.

Substitutes for Hormone

Another type of miscarriage is caused by the mother's shortage of progesterone, one of the female hormones, and in this type of miscarriage or threatened miscarriage, also, it has been found that vitamin E is of great value. Dr. Evan Shute, writing in the *Canadian Medical Association Journal* (January 9, 1960), reports that by routinely prescribing vitamin E for all his obstetric patients, he has reduced the rate of threatened miscarriage from 10 per cent to 5 per cent, and then with additional vitamin E therapy, has salvaged better than 80 per cent of the remainder.

The probable relationship of vitamin E to brain damage of the newborn child and such afflictions of the central nervous system as muscular dystrophy is equally strong. Dr. Lyon P. Strean, Ph.D., in *The Birth of Normal Babies* (Twayne, 1958), states that "Lack of oxygen for even short periods could produce brain damage to the fetus. General anesthesia for childbirth should be reduced to a minimum for the prevention of brain damage to both mother and child."

Yet general anesthesia now, seven years later, is even more popular than it was when Dr. Strean wrote these

[394]

words of warning. In a normal birth, the child is born already breathing. The motion-picture stereotype of the doctor delivering a spank to get breathing started is indeed a commonplace of the delivery room, but only because the anesthetics and pain-killing drugs used on the mother make it that much harder for the infant to breathe. It is our belief that a delay of even a minute or two before the newborn infant's breathing is started can be enough to effect serious changes in the brain that has been starved for oxygen for that long. And surely, for the infant having to rely for a whole minute on the residual supply of oxygen it has received from its mother, an ample supply of vitamin E with the consequent conservation of oxygen in its pure state can be all-important.

Taken all and all, it seems apparent to us that any pregnant woman who wants to assure her child of good health will add to her diet some supplement rich in vitamin E. She will have to improve her diet in other ways as well, of course, but those ways will be recommended by her obstetrician; while he may very possibly not yet have learned of the great importance of vitamin E. Since an ample supply of this vitamin is very hard to come by in the average diet, those who wish to be sure of getting enough take a good vitamin E supplement. Although not as rich or potent as the pure vitamin, wheat germ oil, wheat germ and sunflower seeds are also excellent sources. Their ready availability makes it inexcusable that any prospective mother should subject her child to the possible ill health that might result from a deficiency of this vitamin.

CHAPTER 59

Vitamin E and Fertility

DROOPING FIGURES for new births, added to the ballooning business fertility clinics do, support assertions that sterile marriages are on the rise in the United States. Even the latest remedial drugs and timetables fail in too many cases. Obviously something essential to the mating process is missing in some people. According to compelling evidence in an exciting new book by Herbert Bailey, *Your Key To a Healthy Heart: The Suppressed Record of Vitamin E* (Chilton Books, $4.95), what's missing is vitamin E. Its absence among the common medical tools used in obstetrics and pediatrics is an example of glaring neglect, says Bailey, and his evidence is hard to ignore.

Vitamin E was the answer for 100 childless couples included in an experiment by West German physician R. Bayer (*Wein. med. Wochschr.*, 109:271, 1959). More than half of the group were victims of "primary infertility"—couples were able to conceive, but there

[396]

were miscarriages in 100 per cent of the pregnancies. The couples had 144 pregnancies and lost all of them before vitamin E came into the picture. After that, in 79 pregnancies that occurred during treatment with vitamin E, only two women lost their babies. Before vitamin E therapy *all* women had aborted all their babies. Vitamin E was able to reduce the failure of pregnancies from 100 per cent to 2.5 per cent.

In a second group in which only 38 births had resulted out of 101 pregnancies, Dr. Bayer began the standard dosage of 100 milligrams of vitamin E daily for one month for the husband and 200 milligrams daily for three months prior to conception for the wife. The results were 100 *per cent* favorable. Out of 41 pregnancies in the second group, there were 41 births of healthy offspring.

Dr. Bayer was anxious to prove the effectiveness of vitamin E in these cases beyond a doubt. In both groups he lowered vitamin E intake to 1/3 of the former prescription. The result was that in the first group where failure had been reduced to 2½ per cent from 100 per cent, it rose to 33 per cent on the lighter dosage. In the second group the loss of babies that was 61 per cent without vitamin E and zero with it rose again to 21 per cent when the amount of vitamin E was reduced to 1/3 of the heavy amount.

An amazing footnote to Dr. Bayer's work: although there were hundreds of men, women and children involved in these experiments, not one in which the man and wife were under intensive vitamin E therapy ever resulted in the birth of a deformed baby or even a mentally retarded child. By all the laws of averages, there should have been several deformities and quite a few mentally retarded children among such numbers.

The reason is that vitamin E playing its many bene-

[397]

ficial roles in the body is able to improve the quality of the sperm in the human male, and likely alters the female's reception of the sperm and provides a good environment for the developing fetus. Additionally when the mother receives large amounts of vitamin E, it crosses through the placenta to nourish the growth of the fetus.

Supplementary vitamin E is important after delivery too. It enriches mother's milk so that a nursing mother is able to build up her newborn child's reserves of vitamin E in about seven weeks. Infants started on a cow's milk formula do not achieve similar levels of vitamin E for two years, writes Bailey. The fact is that most common ailments of premature and full term infants coincide with a serious depletion of vitamin E. More significant, when these infants are given vitamin E, the diseases usually clear up. These are the findings after exhaustive research conducted by Dr. F. Gerloczy of the University Medical School at Budapest.

In all of the infant and childhood diseases Gerloczy studied, ranging from scleroderma (a watery swelling, usually followed by an acute infection, frequently fatal to infants) to growth retardation in young children, the Hungarian doctor found vitamin E deficiency in direct proportion to the seriousness of the disease. And supplementary vitamin E therapy effectively cured or controlled most conditions.

Perhaps the most convincing study carried on by Dr. Gerloczy was one including 320 premature infants afflicted with scleroderma. Mortality was about 75 per cent before vitamin E therapy was begun; with it the mortality rate dropped to 27 per cent. The doctor explained that vitamin E's diarrhetic effect took the excess water out of the infants' bodies quickly and

[398]

safely. In this one area, at least, American researchers have corroborated Dr. Gerloczy's findings. Two teams of researchers working jointly at Mount Sinai Hospital and Johns Hopkins School of Medicine found vitamin E therapy greatly benefits infants and children with diseases of the liver. Dr. Beckman discovered that 300 milligrams of vitamin E given to women at the start of delivery reduces the incidence of brain hemorrhages in the child. He also recommends large doses of vitamin E for slow-growing children. All the researchers recommend supplementary doses of vitamin E for infants, particularly those not breast-fed.

This success story of the powers of vitamin E is one of dozens (all detailed in the language of the layman) contained in *Your Key To a Healthy Heart.* Still vitamin E is ignored by most American researchers and practicing physicians. Mr. Bailey believes this is the result of a suppression of vitamin E's record.

"I have found that the vast majority of doctors in this country have a distorted concept of vitamin E's efficacy. Why? Largely because the leaders of the organized medical fraternity have not seen fit to publish the favorable evidence in leading medical journals in the United States. Doctors who have been shown the evidence are amazed and cannot quite believe that such a dreadful suppression of the facts could happen here. . . . Throughout the past twenty years there have been hundreds of such studies; yet you will find that the majority of 'cardiac' specialists have never read the available world literature on the subject. If they have read anything on vitamin E, they consider it 'controversial,' and, therefore, not worthy of investigation. Unfortunately, in this country, the label 'controversial' immediately brands any medical evidence as undesirable and discourages any further inquiries

[399]

by individuals because they feel they must have complete professional approval."

Blame this lack of approval, at least in part, for 12 million Americans who suffer from an outright deficiency of vitamin E (*Journal of the American Dietetics Association*). The Federal Food and Drug Administration reluctantly admitted that vitamin E is essential to human nutrition in 1959, then set a figure for our vitamin E needs that is barely enough to deter obvious signs of outright deficiency. For vitamin E to treat or prevent disease, the amounts must be considerably greater.

Mr. Bailey's book explains that basically vitamin E is an antioxidant and an oxygen-conservator. This means that the cells of the body, because they are supplied with vitamin E, perform more efficiently on less oxygen. This frees more oxygen for cells and organs that really need it. An ailing heart, that needs less oxygen than before, does not have to pump as hard to get blood to the cells. With its work lessened, the strain is eased, an important factor in heart ailment. Vitamin E is also a vasodilator: it opens arteries so that more blood can flow through the circulatory system. Vitamin E also acts as an anticoagulant without harmful side-effects. It even hastens wound-healing.

As Mr. Bailey puts it, "thus we see vitamin E's essential role—or multiple role—at the most vital cellular level. We can begin to understand why the vitamin in therapeutic quantities should be effective in many ailments. Admittedly there is very little going on in this wondrously wrought mind-body-brain we call a human being that would not be afflicted by oxygen-conserving, clot-dissolving, wound-healing and blood-vessel normalizing."

The list of diseases against which vitamin E is effec-

[400]

tive is almost incredible. Mr. Bailey's remarkable book offers the details of experiments proving vitamin E's ability in treating diabetes, menopause symptoms, eye disorders and mental retardation in children and others. The researchers are world renowned, and their experiments have been reported in most of the major medical journals of the world. The professional journals of the United States scientists are notable exceptions.

Mr. Bailey believes that the citizens of this country are being deprived of a dramatic therapeutic agent which could save many lives now being lost and lengthen the productive years in others that are wasted in nursing progressively destructive diseases. Give a copy of this book to your physician to read. He cannot fail to be impressed with the evidence Mr. Bailey has marshalled. He may even be concerned enough with your health to try vitamin E.

CHAPTER 60

How Much Vitamin E Should You Take?

THE QUESTION of how much vitamin E to take recurs so often that we think it would be helpful to review some of the things said on this subject by a man who is undoubtedly the best authority in the world today on the subject of vitamin E—Evan Shute, F.R.C.S., of London, Ontario, Canada.

In *The Summary* for May, 1958, published by the Shute Clinic for Clinical and Laboratory Medicine, Dr. Shute takes up the subject of dosage in successful vitamin E therapy. When he began to use wheat germ oil in his early studies, he says, he used as low as 60 to 80 International Units of vitamin E, for he was treating threatened abortion and male sterility. Had he been treating chronic phlebitis or purpura (hemorrhages) where dosage is of a higher order, he would probably have become discouraged and decided that the treatment was useless.

Later when good preparations of vitamin E by itself

were available, Dr. Shute used higher levels of dosage. It was routine for years, he tells us, to use at least 300 International Units (or milligrams) of vitamin E as a daily dose for heart patients—all except the chronic rheumatics and the high blood pressure patients.

Higher Dosages Achieved Success

Doctors working with dosages like this achieved considerable success, and vitamin E became known in many different countries. But doctors at the Shute clinic were puzzled by some aspects of their experience with vitamin E. "We had always been much more interested in our failures than in our successes," says Dr. Shute. What was responsible for such failures? Was there a different level of need in different diseases or in different persons? In other words, should you give a certain number of units of vitamin E to all patients with a certain heart condition, but give a different dose to patients with phlebitis? Or should you vary the dosage according to the patient rather than the disease? Then, too, how could you know how much of what the patient was given was absorbed and used by him and how much was wasted because he was unable to absorb it?

Dr. Shute began to wonder whether he was using vitamin E as a vitamin, or was he using it as a drug? No one seemed to know, he says, what the adult human requirement of vitamin E was. Figures ranged between 20 and 170 units daily. Is it possible, he asks, that all the various conditions helped by vitamin E dosage were simply deficiency states—that is, patients acquired these diseases because they lacked this particular vitamin, just as they would get scurvy if they lacked vitamin C?

"It was easy to demonstrate," he says, "that people

[403]

in the Western nations were getting only 8 to 12 International Units of alphatocopherol (vitamin E) daily in their food, much of which they might not assimilate. What was the result of such prolonged semistarvation? Did it correspond in any way to the cardiac or muscular degeneration seen in all mammals that had been tested to date when they were deprived of alphatocopherol?"

Vitamin E Deficiency Undoubtedly Exists

There undoubtedly is such a condition as a deficiency of vitamin E, just as scurvy is the condition resulting from lack of vitamin C. But, says Dr. Shute, what is the effect of a prolonged *partial* deficiency in vitamin E which, he is sure, must be common? Heart disease and blood vessel disorders must often develop against such a background.

Even so, when you take vitamin E in what doctors call "massive doses," these doses are not related in any way to the amount of vitamin E that exists in food—even food very rich in the vitamin. But we use other vitamins in massive doses, too, and Dr. Shute mentions vitamin K used to counteract the effects of anti-coagulant drugs and vitamin C in massive doses to help wounds heal quickly and increase one's defenses against infections. Vitamin B and vitamin A have been given in massive doses for acne. So giving vitamin E in amounts that do not occur naturally in food is not something new and different.

"As our experience has increased, our doses of alphatocopherol have risen in parallel," says Dr. Shute. If there is something like a physiological "dam" which prevents the vitamin E from getting to the tissues, then his idea is to raise the level of vitamin E until it overruns the dam. "Our success with this procedure has been marked," he goes on, "notably in persistent an-

[404]

ginas, arteriosclerotic conditions, chronic leg ulcers, and chronic phlebitis." All sorts of patients receiving no obvious help from 300 to 400 units have been helped remarkably by 600 to 2400 units as a daily dose. Such doses crash through the dam, apparently.

Better to Overtreat

"Half a dose of alphatocopherol does not do half a job, as we pointed out years ago. One either uses the proper dose for that patient and his particular condition, or one is not using anything. Too small a dose is equivalent to half-treating a diabetic. Half the dose of insulin the latter needs leaves him still an untreated diabetic. When one is treating a claudication (numbness of the legs) or acute phlebitis, for example, and no obvious improvement occurs promptly, one should raise the dose to a level that proves helpful. If one is in doubt, it is safer and wiser to overtreat than to undertreat.

"Let us emphasize this point. If you use vitamin E, use enough."

The only people who must exercise care in taking large doses of vitamin E are those with high blood pressure. Large amounts of vitamin E may increase the blood pressure. So, in cases like this, it is best, of course, to proceed with great caution, very gradually increasing the amounts of vitamin E taken daily.

CHAPTER 61

The Unsaturated Fatty Acids

IN DETERMINING what food factors constitute a vitamin, certain general principles have been laid down by researchers. If the food factor is essential to good health and if a deficiency in this factor causes a deficiency disease, then the factor is a vitamin. This, in general, is the criterion by which we designate or do not designate certain substances as vitamins.

When a new substance is discovered which seems to have the properties of a vitamin, much research is done with animals. The animals are put on carefully prepared diets which include all necessary elements except the one being tested. If some disorder results, the substance in question is then administered to see whether it will cure the disorder. If it does, then it is fairly certain that such-and-such a food element is necessary for health—at least in the case of animals. With some substances, it seems that animal tests do not prove out in the case of human beings. It is then assumed that such-and-such an animal needs such-and-such a substance, but human beings do not. This has always seemed to us a most unsatisfactory way of doing things. Animal physiology is very much like our own. If it were not, there would be no reason at all for using animals in diet experiments.

It has always seemed to us that the very strict controls employed in animal experimentation may be the reason why some of these experiments do not prove out in regard to human beings. When a diet is decided upon for an animal experiment, nothing can be left to chance. There is no possibility for this rat or guinea pig to get out of his cage and go on a binge of eating forbidden foods. Temperature, rest, bedding, possible psychological irritants, family life, emotions, water, air, light—all these factors are most rigorously controlled, so that the animals' health cannot possibly be influenced either negatively or positively by any of these things. In planning diets for the experiments, the utmost case is taken to feed only those foods which have been shown to produce the ultimate in good health; vitamins and minerals, proteins and enzymes are supplied in ample quantities. Only the substance being tested is left out of the food for the first part of the experiment, then put back into the food for the latter part. And it is perfectly true that we know a lot more about what constitutes a healthful diet for a laboratory animal than for a human being. So, safe to say, these animals get the very best of everything that can be had.

Human beings do not live this way. No single human being lives this way. On this troubled planet, it is impossible to conceive of a human being who can live in the safe, unhurried, unstressful, relaxed, healthful atmosphere of one of these animals. Our human diets are full of all kinds of errors, no matter how careful we may be.

[407]

The air we breathe is full of pollution from industry. Our water is loaded with chemicals. Our lives are subject to stress, insecurity, frustrations, hurry, lack of proper rest, lack of exercise or possibly work that is too heavy and exacting. We try to keep up with the Joneses. Early in life we are endowed with a set of ideals that glimmers before us constantly from then on, inspiring us to try to achieve many things that may be far beyond our reach. Surely we need much more of the important food elements to carry us through this kind of life than a laboratory rat needs to live healthfully in his hygienically controlled environment.

The subject of this chapter is a set of food factors that were once spoken of as a vitamin. Animal experiments show that they are essential to the good health of animals. But we still do not classify them as vitamins in speaking of human nutrition. We want readers to know of these food factors and then to decide for themselves whether or not they should be included in a healthful diet for human beings. These food factors are the unsaturated fatty acids, once commonly called vitamin F. Specifically they are linolenic acid, linoleic acid and arachidonic acid. The names need not frighten you. The chemical names of most of our familiar vitamins are equally long and unpronounceable.

Unsaturated Fatty Acids in Animal Health

There is a disease which occurs in laboratory rats called "fat deficiency disease." By breaking down the different fatty elements of the diet, researchers have found that the disease occurs not from lack of fat— any kind of fat. It results only from lack of the unsaturated fatty acids. The rats show arrested or retarded growth, a raised metabolic rate (that is, they burn their food up very rapidly), changes in skin and hair,

[408]

kidney disorders and impairment of reproductive function. Rats who received no unsaturated fatty acids in their food ate just as much as the control rats, but they did not grow or put on weight; so apparently the food was simply burning rapidly without contributing anything to building the body. First over the paws, then over the face and gradually over the rest of the body a dryness and scurfiness (dandruff) spread. Cold weather—the kind that chaps hands—accentuated this condition. The rats developed kidney stones and many difficulties in reproducing. In the case of the female rats there was disturbance of the whole reproductive cycle. In many cases litters were not born but were reabsorbed. Or, if the mother rat finally had the litter, she had prolonged labor and hemorrhage and the litters were underweight and sickly. Male rats deprived of unsaturated fatty acids refused to mate and were sterile. It was found, too, that there was some relationship between efficiency of unsaturated fatty acids and pyridoxine and pantothenic acid, two of the B vitamins. A deficiency of any two of these factors caused a much worse condition than a deficiency of just one.

Now in regard to human beings, there are two extremely important aspects to this problem. First of all, human milk is rich in unsaturated fatty acids— far, far richer than cow's milk. If these acids are not vitally important to human nutrition, how could Mother Nature have made the mistake of including them in such quantity in mother's milk where every drop must count toward the nourishment of the child? Furthermore, it has been found that stores of fatty acids are built up in the heart, liver, kidney, brain, blood and muscle, and the body holds on to them tenaciously. In rats who were deprived of fatty acids for a long time, it was found that there was still some remaining when 76 per cent of the body fat of the rat had been used up. As soon as the unsaturated fatty acids were completely gone, the animal became very seriously ill. The body stores food factors it will need. And in cases of deficiency or starvation, it relinquishes first those factors which are not so important and until the very end hangs on to those things that are essential to life. So on this basis, too, we believe we are justified in assuming that the unsaturated fatty acids are important enough to be called a vitamin.

We are told that nothing is known about human requirements for the unsaturated fatty acids. Yet the National Research Council, which sets the standards and makes the decisions on matters of this kind in this country, says "in spite of the paucity of information . . . it is desirable that the fat intake include essential unsaturated fatty acids to the extent of at least one per cent of the total calories." Bicknell and Prescott, writing in *Vitamins in Medicine* (Grune and Stratton, 1953), tell us that only about one half this amount has been available in England since 1945. In this country there is no shortage of foods that contain unsaturated fatty acids, but do we realize how important they are and do we make every effort to include them in every day's menu?

Human Diseases That May Be Related to Deficiency

A number of human disorders appear to be related to deficiency of unsaturated fatty acids. Medical literature contains many instances of infant eczema that has been cured by including the unsaturated fatty acids in the infants' food.

Bicknell and Prescott suggest that the acids may be very important in any disease in which fat absorption is impaired. This includes diarrheal conditions of many

[410]

kinds. It may include many cases of underweight. Much of the research we did some time ago on acne seemed to show that acne patients are unable to use fat properly. Could a deficiency of unsaturated fatty acids be one of the causes of acne? Could it be one cause of the dandruff that appears on American scalps? Bicknell and Prescott tell us that the fact that the unsaturated fatty acids are so carefully stored and husbanded by the body may be why symptoms of deficiency are not more marked and severe. In other words, many of us may be suffering from a subclinical deficiency—not enough to make us definitely ill, but enough to prevent our being completely healthy.

The Lee Foundation for Nutritional Research, 2023 West Wisconsin Avenue, Milwaukee 3, Wisconsin, has contributed much to the study of unsaturated fatty acids in this country. Their booklets, *A Survey of Vitamin F* and *Vitamin F in the Treatment of Prostatic Hypertrophy*, present startling evidence of the importance of these substances in human nutrition. Harold H. Perlenfein, who wrote the first booklet, tells us that the unsaturated fatty acids reduce the incidence and duration of colds. He says that deficiency may be responsible for dry skin; brittle, lusterless, falling hair; dandruff; brittle nails; kidney disease. He states that the acids function in the body by cooperating with vitamin D in making calcium available to the tissues, assist in assimilation of organic phosphorus, aid in the reproductive process, nourish the skin and appear to be related to the proper functioning of the thyroid gland.

James Pirie Hart and William DeGrande Cooper, writing on prostate treatment, describe 19 cases of prostate gland disorder which were treated with unsaturated fatty acids. In all cases there was a lessening of the residual urine—that is, the urine which cannot be released from the bladder due to pressure from the enlarged prostate gland. In 12 of the cases there was no residual urine at the end of the treatment. There was a decrease in leg pains, fatigue, kidney disorders and nocturia (excessive urination at night). In all cases the size of the prostate rapidly decreased. Chemical blood tests showed a great improvement in mineral content of the blood at the end of the treatment.

Processed Foods Cause the Deficiency

Why should any of us be deficient in the unsaturated fatty acids? For the same reason we are deficient in so many other necessary food elements—food processing. Bicknell and Prescott tell us that in processed and stale foods, these acids have deliberately been destroyed to improve the keeping qualities of the food. Unsaturated fatty acids occur in vegetable and seed fats—such as corn oil, cottonseed oil, wheat germ oil, peanut oil and so forth. They may occur in animal fats, such as butter, depending on what the animal has been fed. They are destroyed very easily by exposure to air, and they then become rancid. This rancidity can be responsible for destroying other vitamins as well—vitamins A, D, E and K are destroyed in the presence of rancid fat. When fats are hydrogenated, much of the unsaturated fatty acid is changed into saturated fatty acids. This means that certain chemical actions take place which completely change the character of the fat and render it almost useless for the various conditions we have described. Hydrogenizing gives the fat a solid form, rather than a liquid form.

At present, much of the fat we use has been hydrogenized. Shortening such as we use for making pastry or for frying has been hydrogenized, margarine has been hydrogenized—little or no unsaturated fatty acids are left. In a family where the meal-planner depends on fried foods and pastries for fats and where margarine is consistently used, there is every possibility for deficiency of unsaturated fatty acids, unless a lot of salad oil is used, unheated, in salads. This is one reason why we feel certain that Americans in general may have a serious subclinical deficiency along these lines.

Here is the unsaturated fatty acid (or vitamin F) content of some of the common fats:

	Per cent of essential unsaturated fatty acids		
Butter	4.0	to	6.0
Beef fat	1.1	to	5.0
Lard	5.0	to	11.1
Mutton fat	3.0	to	5.0
Liver fat	3.0	to	7.0
Milk	.15	to	.23
Fish oils	traces		
Margarine	2.0	to	5.0
Barley germ oil	63		
Cocoa butter	2.0		
Coconut oil	6.0	to	9.2
Corn salad oil	70		
Cottonseed oil	35	to 50	
Linseed oil	72	to 83	
Maize germ oil	42		
Oat germ oil	31		
Olive oil	4.0	to 13.7	
Palm oil	2.0	to 11.3	
Peanut oil	20	to 25	
Rice bran oil	29	to 42	
Rye germ oil	48		
Soybean oil	56	to 63	
Sunflower seed oil	52	to 64	
Wheat germ oil	44	to 52	

Some of these foods sound exotic to us and, so far as we know, are not available to American consumers—such as oat germ oil, barley germ oil and so forth. But surely we have all heard enough about wheat germ oil during past years to realize anew that this extremely important substance (rich in vitamin E as well) should be a part of our diet. Corn oil, cottonseed oil and peanut oil are sold as salad oils in every grocery. So far as we can determine, nothing has been done to these oils in preparing them for the market that would destroy their content of unsaturated fatty acids. But we would advise crossing off your shopping list all hydrogenated fats, such as the shortening that comes in a can, and margarine.

See to it that your family eats plenty of vegetable or seed oils—in salads, as that is by far the best way of taking them. If you must fry something—and we take a dim view of frying anything—use liquid vegetable oils for the process. But keep in mind that the less heat you apply to any oils or fats, the better they are for you. In addition, we firmly believe that all present-day Americans should take wheat germ oil as a daily food supplement. This contains not only the unsaturated fatty acids we have been talking about, but vitamin E as well.

CHAPTER 62

Does Life Demand E and F—Together?

WE NEED VITAMIN F—Essential Fatty Acids—for the living membrane that holds our body cells together. This vitamin is indispensable for the health of our blood and arteries. There is no growth without it and teeth do not form properly. It is vital to healthy nerves.

Yet as much good as this vitamin does—as enormously important as it is to build and maintain health—it can be equally dangerous if we do not make sure of taking an ample amount of vitamin E at the very same time, and preferably in the very same food.

This inseparable relationship, now established as a fact beyond dispute, represents what we consider the most important advance of recent years in our knowledge of how to regulate our nutrition scientifically for superb health at any age. It holds out the hope and the likelihood that by this one simple regulation of our diets we can prevent atherosclerosis, keep our blood, skin and tissues youthful and healthy, and increase our

[415]

energy, nervous health and endurance. And all through relearning the lessons of nature, and restoring to our diets the precious foods the factories take from us.

Nature's Combinations

In nature, wherever we find a vegetable oil, it is rich in vitamin E. There is good reason for this, for "Vitamin E is known to be the major lipid antioxidant of nature," in the words of A. L. Tappel of the University of California in an article in the published symposium *Lipids and Their Oxidation* (AVI Publishing Co., Westport, Conn., 1962). Lipids are simply fats, or any substances containing fats. And an antioxidant is something that prevents oxygen from combining with another substance.

We ordinarily think of oxygen as a highly desirable and certainly necessary material for body processes. That is quite correct. But in order for our tissues to use oxygen, it must reach them in pure form. If its atoms link up with those of another substance in our digestive systems or blood, then we get compounds that our tissues cannot use and find highly toxic. Such compounds are called peroxides (one atom of oxygen in the molecule) dioxides (two atoms of oxygen) and so on. Peroxides, especially, cause toxic reactions, interfere with cell respiration, and are thought to be implicated in a host of diseases from cancer to dental cavities.

Vitamin E is an oxygen conserver because it prevents oxygen from forming peroxides or other toxic compounds. It is especially important to the lipids, because all fats have an especially strong tendency to form peroxides, developing an unpleasant taste and odor that we call "turning rancid." The more liquid (or unsaturated) a fat is, the greater is its tendency to turn rancid

[416]

quickly. But vitamin E protects it, preventing the peroxides from forming.

This is a rather technical matter that we have been compelled to spell out to make it clear just how wise nature was, in forming the nutritious vegetable oils, to make certain they always had a large content of vitamin E to prevent them from turning rancid.

But along come the food processors who are never content to leave things natural. Before they start extracting the oil of the soy bean, sunflower seed, corn, etc., they discard the germ which is hard to work with but happens to be the chief source of the vitamin E. Or else they "refine" it, destroying the vitamin E with heat. Then, having gotten rid of nature's chief antioxidant, they add chemicals to prevent the rancidity that only occurs as a result of their tampering. The result is indigestion and failure of the lipids in our diets to do the wonderful, necessary work they should be doing. They can even do serious damage, and frequently do, and all because man insists on tampering with nature without weighing the consequences.

Let's take a close look at these lipids, and see what they can do for us when we eat the Prevention way, with an awareness of the effects on our health.

Linoleic Acid

"The outstanding function of essential fatty acids . . . is structural, since they are required for the formation of cell membranes, mitochondrial membranes, and connective tissue, including cartilage and the matrix of bone." This is the statement of the famed Oxford University nutritionist, Hugh M. Sinclair, in the authoritative source book *Clinical Nutrition* (Harper and Row, 1962). It is a statement well worth closer examination.

[417]

When we talk of essential fatty acids we mean only *some* of the acids contained in fats—those that are actually essential within the human system for the processes of life, such as energy, growth and repair, to continue. Since they are not manufactured within our bodies, the only way we can get them is by eating them. This makes them nutrients. The combination of those two qualities — being an essential nutrient — is what makes a substance a vitamin, and is why the name vitamin F has correctly been given to the essential fatty acids.

There are a number of such acids in any vegetable oil, but the only really important one is linoleic acid. The others, such as oleic acid, are able to perform isolated functions if there is not enough linoleic acid in the system; but *linoleic acid alone will do every job that depends on vitamin F*. If you take in enough linoleic acid, you don't need any of the others, although you will probably get some of them in the same food.

We can define what is essential even more closely. The form of linoleic acid that has the greatest biological activity is its phospholipid (fat combined with phosphorus) form, which occurs in a compound fat substance called lecithin. It is those foods richest in lecithin, therefore, that will give us our best supply of vitamin F. The best one we know is soy oil, although good amounts of the precious vitamin are also to be found in corn, sunflower and wheat germ oil. A good day's supply of lecithin can be obtained from a tablespoon (14 grams) of soy oil, or from 1½ to 2 tablespoons of the other above-mentioned oils.

Vitamin F

We could not exist without vitamin F.

Through a series of complicated chemical reactions within the body, this vitamin combines with proteins and cholesterol to form structures so basic there is no life without them. One of them is the membranes that enclose every living cell. If such a membrane is absent, or weak, or faulty in structure, *the contents of the cell leak out and the cell dies.* If enough cells die, the body dies.

For healthy cell membranes we need vitamin F.

Through a different chemical transformation, vitamin F forms *myelin,* a fatty protein substance that sheathes the major nerves of the body, including the spinal cord. The nerves can only maintain good health when this sheath is in good health. Any damage to the sheath can impair the mentality and give rise to neurological symptoms or even the dread multiple sclerosis.

Is it possible that multiple sclerosis is a deficiency of vitamin F?

For healthy nerves we must have this vitamin.

One of the most fascinating facts about vitamin F is that it does most of its work by combining, within our bodies, with free cholesterol, which our livers manufacture. As long as we have enough linoleic acid in our diets, the cholesterol in our systems is put to work and does us nothing but good. It is only when we fail to utilize our cholesterol that it forms fatty plaques within our blood vessels and leads to that major killing disease, atherosclerosis.

Is it possible that atherosclerosis is a deficiency of vitamin F?

This vitamin, in ways that are not yet fully understood, regulates the coagulation of the blood so that it will be neither too fast nor too slow. By preventing fast clotting, it guards us against coronary thrombosis. It has been shown to be an effective agent against ulcers, asthma and other allergic conditions, dental cavities (vitamin F is one of the building blocks of teeth) and acne and other skin disorders.

Vitamin E

Yet even if we consume a very good supply of linoleic acid every single day, as we should, we will not benefit by its remarkable functions unless at the same time we take in a good supply of vitamin E. This is demonstrated very well by Dr. A. L. Tappel in *Lipids and Their Oxidation,* the previously mentioned symposium that collects the most advanced knowledge about these nutrients from many sources in a single volume.

Dr. Tappel shows that vitamin E is so necessary for the proper functioning of linoleic acid that the fatty acid can actually be dangerous if consumed without the antioxidant vitamin.

The simple fact is that linoleic acid combines so easily with oxygen to form peroxides that it can and does happen even during the passage from the stomach to the intestines.

Chemical preservatives may prevent rancidity on a store shelf, but there is only one substance that will keep linoleic acid from turning rancid within our bodies. That is vitamin E. It is one more incredibly important function of this neglected but utterly essential vitamin of which we can get enough only in supplement form.

We have already mentioned the danger of lipid peroxides. Dr. Tappel states that this damage is in the very "structural and functional components of the cell." As an example, he points out that such peroxides can destroy enzyme systems and break down the red cells in our blood, causing a serious form of anemia.

[420]

One of the enzymes destroyed by peroxides is catalase, which is thought to be important in our defenses against cancer.

It is easily seen then, that while it is absolutely necessary to health, linoleic acid is also a danger to health when we lack vitamin E.

The answer seems obvious. Make sure that you take a substantial amount of vitamin E right with the vegetable oil you consume every day. Take both of these vitamins at mealtime for the best absorption, and take them both at the same meal. Better still, take them at every meal.

That way, the only results possible will be good results. The benefits to health, energy and life itself will be enormous.

CHAPTER 63

They're Murdering Vitamin F

FROM FLUORIDATION to the spraying of insecticides, many are the crimes that are perpetrated against the human race with the excuse that they are really for our own good, if we only understood. But if statistics are to be believed, perhaps the greatest crime of all is the way that Vitamin F — the Essential Fatty Acids — is wantonly destroyed in every food that goes through the hands of the large commercial processors. For deficiency of this precious vitamin has been linked directly with the diseases of the heart and circulatory system, the major cause of death in the United States.

These days everybody is aware of the evidence that has been piling up for the past twenty years of the relationship between excessive deposits of cholesterol in the arteries and the incidence of hardening of the arteries and high blood pressure, leading to eventual stroke or heart failure. It is also known that something else called the unsaturated or polyunsaturated fatty

[422]

acids seems to be valuable in reducing cholesterol concentration.

As a result, a great deal of bad and nonsensical nutritional advice is hurled at us from the TV screens and the advertising pages of women's magazines. Brands of margarine and cooking and salad oils vie with one another in claiming to be highest in unsaturates. A new egg has been developed to contain less cholesterol. Everybody talks about cholesterol and polyunsaturates. Since they are apparently taken in by the deceptive claims made for foods that are nutritionally of very low grade, it is apparent that very few understand the meaning or significance of these terms that are being bandied about.

We will attempt to explain, and try not to get too technical about it.

The Fat Molecule

Fatty substances, like all other substances, are made up of molecules that combine atoms of the various chemical elements in a definite proportion. In fats, it is atoms of carbon, hydrogen, and oxygen that are combined. The unsaturated fats contain what chemists call double bonds—that is, points in their molecules that easily attach themselves to additional atoms. They are especially susceptible to the attachment of extra atoms of either oxygen or hydrogen.

If you attach enough atoms of hydrogen to a fatty molecule, so that it cannot hold any more, it is then said to be saturated. A saturated fat will be solid at normal room temperature, while the unsaturated will be liquid. This is the easiest and most obvious way to tell them apart.

Now let's take a look at the difference this makes within our bodies.

[423]

Since the unsaturated fatty acids have their double bonds which are like the open links in a chain, just waiting to attach themselves to some other substance, they are able to perform an enormous group of highly important functions in the body. One of these functions is to link up with certain amino acids and form the membranes that enclose each body cell and keep its contents from leaking out. Another function is to combine with oxygen within the cell to furnish energy. Still another is to form the sheathing of nerves. And yet another is to link with cholesterol into a combined fatty substance that is soft and can be broken down into forms in which the body uses fats for growth, for skin health, and for energy.

Cholesterol

Yes, indeed. According to Dr. Hugh N. Sinclair, the famous nutritionist of Oxford University, and according to many other top nutritionists as well, that old devil cholesterol can and should be a more useful substance in our bodies. The fact that it forms solid plaques that cling to the walls of arteries and congest them simply reflects that we don't get enough vitamins—especially E and C—and unsaturated fatty acids in our diets. We couldn't eliminate cholesterol from our systems, even if we never ate another drop of it. We manufacture it ourselves, or at least our livers do. And if we were so foolish as to try to regulate our diets in such a way as to consume no single drop of fat, either saturated or unsaturated, that would be a very good path to the development of atherosclerosis. Because our bodies would go right on manufacturing the saturated fat cholesterol, and would have no more vitamin F with which to handle it.

So what do we do about it? Do we buy the margarine that is advertised as being 60 per cent unsaturated, and solve the problem that way?

Not if we're wise, we don't.

As pointed out by Dr. Sinclair in *Clinical Nutrition* (Harper and Row, 1962), from the commercial point of view vitamin F is a troublemaker. The more unsaturated the fatty acid, the more useful it is within our systems. But also, the more easily it will link up with extra atoms of oxygen. When this linkage with extra oxygen occurs in an oil, the oil becomes rancid. So in order to preserve the shelf life of an oil, the first thing a food processor does is to "refine" it, removing as much as he can of the linoleic acid which is the most unsaturated of the polyunsaturates, the most valuable to us, but also the most liable to oxidation.

Without its linoleic acid, an oil may still be truthfully described as "unsaturated," yet it has been deprived of the greater part of its potential nutritive value for us. Then, to make doubly sure of avoiding spoilage while the margarine or oil is standing on a supermarket shelf, the processor will add a chemical anti-oxidant. This is the final blow. For while the essential fatty acids must be protected against oxidation until they have been absorbed into our systems, when they reach the cell or blood stream, they must then be able to be oxidized or they cannot do their work. But the chemical anti-oxidant, once incorporated into fatty acids, cannot be removed. And this, for all practical purposes, means the final destruction of whatever nutritive value was left.

That is how it is possible for margarines and refined oils to be advertised as rich in unsaturates, and yet be of no value for all the vital and indispensable jobs that our system requires of vitamin F.

[425]

Hydrogenation

An equally sure way of destroying the values of vegetable oils is hydrogenation. This is a process of bubbling hydrogen gas through the oils until all the double bonds have seized hydrogen atoms and become saturated. At this point, the oils have hardened to the consistency of butter and have become the vegetable shortenings that are sold to the American public by the billions of pounds a year. If you have ever been tempted to believe that these solid vegetable fats are actually any better for you than meat fats, now is the time to change your mind. Promise yourself that you will never buy another can of them. The simple fact is that chemically they have been transformed into meat fats before being put in the can. They have become equally indigestible, and equally useless to the body.

There is a way to preserve vitamin F without damaging its usefulness to the human metabolism. It is nature's way, and consequently food processors want nothing to do with it. But we can be wiser and gain for ourselves the superb health and freedom from illness that nature intended, by following nature's methods instead of abandoning them.

Vitamin E

As pointed out by Dr. A. L. Tappel in *Lipids and Their Oxidation* (AVI Publishing Co., 1962) "Vitamin E is known to be the major lipid antioxidant of nature." This vitamin, which is invariably found in conjunction with the unsaturated fatty acids in vegetable oils, prevents those double bonds from combining with oxygen almost as effectively as any laboratory chemical can do it. What is more, vitamin E has a special selec-

[426]

tive action that no chemical preservative has ever been able to duplicate.

What happens in our bodies is that the vitamin F, if accompanied by enough vitamin E, will not oxidize in our stomachs or in our intestines. Its double bonds are kept available to do their work. The fatty acids are absorbed through the intestinal walls into the blood stream and then, in that marvelous chemical laboratory we each have within us, vitamin B_6 (pyridoxine) acts upon the linoleic acid and other unsaturates in such a way as to transform them into arachidonic acid. At this point the vitamin E leaves the fatty acids, and the arachidonic acid which is formed is free to oxidize within the individual cells.

Through this complicated but understandable process, the end product, arachidonic acid, is free to combine with cholesterol and put it to use instead of letting it clog the arteries. It is free to strengthen and form new cell membranes, to maintain healthy nerve sheathing, to preserve the youth and beauty of the skin, and a hundred other important jobs.

And all these jobs are prevented if we try to get our vitamin F from refined oils or any other commercial products. That is why we recommend supplements— particularly soy oil, which is richest in linoleic acid— that are fortified with vitamin E; and that is why we recommend sunflower seeds, soybeans, eggs, vegetable oils generally, all of which are foods rich in linoleic acid and other unsaturates with enough vitamin E and vitamin B to assure them of proper processing within our bodies.

There is no reason to go looking for cholesterol to eat. You don't need it. Your own body will always make enough. But if and when you do eat it, and it can hardly be avoided, there is nothing to worry about so long as you make sure that every day you consume as well an adequate supply of unrefined vegetable oil such as you will get in a good food supplement, in sunflower seeds and in wheat germ, and make sure that you take plenty of vitamin E. Don't let the food processors sell you the dead ghost of what used to be vitamin F. It's easy enough to make sure that you are getting the real thing.

CHAPTER 64

The Fat Content of Food

WHICH ARE THE FOODS that contain valuable fats and which are the harmful ones? If you want to concentrate on nuts as a source of the valuable fats, which nuts contain the most of this kind of fat? What salad oils should one use? Where do cereals and dairy products stand so far as their fat content is concerned?

The answers to the above questions are not simple. We do not know, as yet, enough about fats in general and their relation to health to be able to state categorically exactly how much of which kinds of fats each of us should have every day.

However, there seems to be a definite pattern emerging from all the research being done. It appears that animal fats and processed fats (that is, hydrogenated ones) contain so much of the saturated fatty acids and so little of the unsaturated fatty acids that they should be cut down to the smallest possible level in one's diet. Fats from vegetable origins seem to contain

[429]

so much of the natural unsaturated fatty acids and so little of saturated acids that we should, undoubtedly, include in our diets more of these healthful foods.

Briefly, research seems to show that the vegetable fats are more healthful because they do not contribute a fatty substance called cholesterol to the body, and they do contribute some substance that helps the body to use cholesterol properly, so that it does not collect in gall bladders, arteries, etc., making deposits that mean trouble.

It is agreed among nutritionists that the substance in question (plentiful in vegetable fat and not so plentiful in animal fat) is some part of what is called the unsaturated fatty acids.

The Department of Agriculture has recently compiled a listing of the various fats in foods which we think you will find helpful. We are reprinting here some information from this list. A brief word of explanation is in order. In the first column we present the total amount of the saturated fatty acids in 100 grams (or an average serving) of each food. These are the fats generally agreed to be harmful if too much of them is consumed.

Unsaturated Fatty Acids Held Good for Health

In the second column we present the total amount of the unsaturated fatty acids in each food. These are the fats generally agreed to be the healthful ones. One of these, linoleic acid, is believed by many researchers to be the most valuable of all—the helpful substance that is the best preventive of fatty deposits that may cause hardening of the arteries, stroke, heart attacks, gall bladder stones and so forth. We give in the third column the amount of this fatty acid in each food.

How can one best interpret the chart and use it in

[430]

planning meals? First of all, look at the first column and you will see that, in general, the foods at the top of the list contain considerably more of the saturated fatty acids than the foods at the bottom of the list.

Notice, as you go down the second column, that almost the opposite is true. Those at the bottom contain more of the healthful unsaturated fats than those at the top. This suggests at once that one should be very careful to balance one's meals so that plenty of the seed, nut and oil foods are included in every day's meals. Remember, too, that one cannot use very much of the salad oils compared to the amount of a solid food one might use. The measurements given are for 100 grams. Now, 100 grams of avocado pulp or soybeans would be an average serving. One hundred grams of salad oil is about 7 tablespoons—lots more than one would need for salads during the day. This suggests using liquid vegetable oils or salad oils for all cooking rather than using butter, so that you get as much of the unsaturated fatty acids as possible, indirectly.

Some Surprising Aspects of Linoleic Acid

As you study the chart further, you will find some rather surprising things relating to linoleic acid—supposedly the most valuable of the unsaturated fatty acids. There is little of it in animal fats except for poultry, suggesting that it would be a good idea to serve poultry frequently. While the unsaturated fatty acid content of olive oil is high, it does not contain very much linoleic acid. But it is very low in the harmful saturated fats. Perhaps this might mean that if you are very fond of olive oil and use it always, you should change off and use sometimes others of the salad oils that have more linoleic acid—safflower or sunflower, for instance.

[431]

We are sure that readers will find many uses for the chart in preparing and planning meals. And once again let us repeat the caution we can't state too often— shun the processed shortenings, the white solid ones, and margarine. These fats have been hydrogenated to solidify them. This process destroys unsaturated fatty acids. We are convinced that it also brings about other undesirable characteristics in the food which will undoubtedly be discovered later. The less any food is processed, the better it is for you.

Charts of Saturated and Unsaturated Fatty Acids Including Linoleic Acid

	Total Grams Saturated Fatty Acids	Total Grams Unsaturated Fatty Acids	Grams Linoleic Acid
Meats:			
Beef	48	47	2
Buffalo	66	30	1
Deer	63	32	3
Goat	57	37	2
Horse	30	60	6
Lamb	56	40	3
Luncheon meats	36	59	7
Pork			
Back, outer layer	38	58	6
Bacon	32	63	9
Liver	34	61	5
Other cuts	36	59	9
Rabbit, domesticated	38	58	11
Milk Fat:			
Buffalo, Indian	62	33	1
Cow	55	39	3
Goat	62	33	5
Human	46	48	7
Poultry and Eggs:			
Chicken	32	64	20
Turkey	29	67	21
Chicken eggs	32	61	7

	Total Grams Saturated Fatty Acids	Total Grams Unsaturated Fatty Acids	Grams Linoleic Acid
Fish and Shellfish:			
Eel, body	23	73	36
Herring, body	19	77	19
Menhaden, body	24	71	3
Salmon, body	15	79	26
Tuna, body	25	70	25
Turtle	44	51	31
Separated Fats and Oils:			
Butter	55	39	3
Lard	38	57	10
Codfish liver	15	81	25
Halibut liver	17	72	
Whale blubber	15	41	21
Cereals and Grains:			
Cornmeal, white	11	82	44
Millet (foxtail)	31	61	35
Oats, rolled	22	74	41
Rice	17	74	35
Sorghum	12	81	44
Wheat flour, white	14	76	42
Wheat germ	15	77	48
Fruits and Vegetables, including seeds:			
Avocado pulp	20	69	13
Cantaloupe seed	15	79	53
Chickpea	9	87	36
Chocolate	56	39	2
Olives	11	84	7
Pigeon pea	33	57	46
Pumpkin seed	17	78	41
Rape seed	6	89	14
Sesame seed	14	80	42
Soybeans	20	75	52
Squash seed	18	77	42
Watermelon seed	17	78	59
Nuts and Peanuts:			
Almond	8	87	20
Beechnut	8	87	31
Brazil nut	20	76	26
Cashew	17	78	7

	Total Grams Saturated Fatty Acids	Total Grams Unsaturated Fatty Acids	Grams Linoleic Acid
Coconut	86	8	Trace
Filbert (hazelnut)	5	91	16
Hickory	8	87	18
Peanut	22	72	29
Peanut Butter	26	70	25
Pecan	7	84	63
Pistachio	10	85	19
Walnut, black	6	90	48
Walnut, English	7	89	62

Separated Fats and Oils:

	Total Grams Saturated Fatty Acids	Total Grams Unsaturated Fatty Acids	Grams Linoleic Acid
Cacao butter	56	39	2
Corn oil	10	84	53
Cottonseed oil	25	71	50
Margarine (varies widely depending on fats used)	26	70	9
Olive oil	11	84	7
Palm oil	45	49	9
Peanut oil	18	76	29
Safflower oil	8	87	42
Sesame oil	14	80	42
Shortening, animal and vegetable (varies widely	43	53	11
according to fats used)	23	72	7
Soybean oil	15	80	52
Sunflower oil	12	83	63

CHAPTER 65

The Miracle of Coagulation

THE BUILT-IN MARVELS of the human body usually function so smoothly that one is seldom aware of them until they break down. One such little-noticed miracle is the automatic thickening of the blood that stops its flow through a break in the skin by forming a scab. This process is known as coagulation, and it is brought about only when exactly the proper combination of body chemicals is present. If this combination is upset or unbalanced, a nosebleed can be fatal, a skinned knee a cause for transfusion, an operation practically impossible.

The mechanics behind the phenomenon of blood clottings are as fascinating as they are complex. Though the process cannot be observed completely, it is the general opinion of scientists that coagulation occurs in the following way: a substance in the blood called prothrombin combines with a substance called thromboplastin, and, with calcium, forms an enzyme called thrombin. This thrombin reacts with still another substance, fibrinogen, causing the blood to coagulate or clot.

It has been discovered that an essential element in the production of one of the ingredients (prothrombin) is vitamin K. Vitamin K was found by a Danish scientist named Dam. It was named after its property as a coagulant, K for "koagulation" (the Danish spelling of our word). The 20 or so years since then have been a short time for uncovering even a small number of the secrets involved in vitamin K's function in the body. It is not unusual nowadays to see notes in the newspapers and magazines on new discoveries concerning vitamin K.

It is reassuring to know that the body does not wait for science to discover its needs. A good natural diet would supply them all. In the case of vitamin K, this is especially true since the body can synthesize, or manufacture, its own K in the intestinal tract. However, this process requires the presence of certain intestinal flora. In recent years the heavy use of antibiotics, which can destroy these beneficial flora, has made the manufacture of vitamin K in the body less reliable than it was heretofore. Antibiotics users should be certain to get sufficient vitamin K from foods because of the body's inability to make its own.

Deficiencies of vitamin K are accurate indications of several serious disorders:

1. If, due to disease, bile is not present in the intestine, no amount of vitamin K in the diet will be utilized, for bile is essential to the absorption of this vitamin.

2. If the intestinal walls are damaged or diseased, as in severe cases of diarrhea, sprue or ulcerated colitis, vitamin K will not be absorbed.

[436]

3. If the liver is damaged and cannot function properly, the whole process of forming thrombin in the blood will be hindered, since it is done in the liver. It is safe to say then that a shortage of vitamin K in the body points to a disease of the liver, intestinal tract or bile duct.

Useful in Pregnancy and Childbirth

Extra amounts of vitamin K have been shown to have therapeutic value in certain cases. The most common therapeutic use is for pregnant women. The *Practitioner* (November, 1952) carried an article which could mean a great deal to many pregnant women who suffer from nausea and vomiting due to their condition. The article stated that this condition is believed to be caused by a transfer of a vomiting factor from the placenta to the mother. The investigation in this experiment attempted to decrease the placenta's porousness and thereby decrease the transfer of this factor. A combination of vitamin C (25 milligrams) and vitamin K (5 milligrams) was given to the expectant mothers daily by mouth. Of the 70 women who comprised the test, 64 had complete relief within 72 hours. Three of the remaining 6 were relieved of vomiting but the nausea persisted, and 3 were not benefited. As an important footnote, the author added that the use of either one of these vitamins without the other failed to give satisfactory results.

Experimental observation of animals has shown that those deficient in vitamin K suffer from frequent miscarriages. It is also known that the time required for blood to clot is longer (a low prothrombin level) and the vitamin C level is lower in women who habitually have miscarriages.

The use of synthetic vitamin K on newborn babies could have serious consequences, causing a disease called kernicterus. Because an ingredient in the synthetic formula has been found to be responsible, natural vitamin K might be safely used. The vitamin is given to the babies to counteract any possibility of hemorrhage, a frequent occurrence due to the thin capillaries in the newborn.

Lancet (February 24, 1951) describes an experiment in which the mother, not the child, was given vitamin K. The vitamin was given to 31 mothers before delivery, and the effect was that the prothrombin level of each of the babies was similar to that obtained by giving vitamin K to the infants at birth. It is possible, though not so stated, that the dangerous element in synthetic vitamin K would be filtered out by the placenta if the mother took the vitamin K. Thus the child would derive all the benefit without the risk if the vitamin came to it through the mother.

Although this method is not universally accepted, many doctors are convinced of its usefulness. The *Lancet* article quotes a Dr. Pancher who said in 1942: ". . . . it can be definitely stated that if oral preparations [of vitamin K] are given to a normal pregnant woman 12 to 24 hours before she goes into labor, or if vitamin K is administered daily before delivery, the prothrombin time of the infant will be normal and there will be no untoward effects on the mother. . . ."

Even livestock have been helped in their infancy by vitamin K. An Associated Press dispatch reported a discovery to control a disease known as scours which takes the lives of many newborn cattle deprived of nursing from their mothers. It is a combination of dried cattle serum, vitamin K and pedigreed milk solids—the serum to fight infection, vitamin K to combat hemorrhage and the milk solids to supply early nourishment.

[438]

Vitamin K and Anticoagulant Drugs

A great use for vitamin K was occasioned with the increased use of anticoagulant drugs for heart cases. The idea behind these drugs is to maintain a thin consistency in the blood, thus avoiding the likelihood of a blood clot developing and shutting off the flow of blood to the heart. As in so many drugs, absolute control of its effects is not possible so that the blood sometimes becomes so thin that hemorrhage is a danger. The attempt to cut down the clotting factor backfires, so to speak, and makes clotting difficult even at times when it might be vital. Carefully measured doses of vitamin K are administered to these people to raise the pro-thrombin level slightly, while not allowing it to completely counteract the effect of the anticoagulant. As can be imagined, the arrangement is a very tricky one, and rather dangerous, too. This is another example of those drug-powered merry-go-rounds that call for the administration of a second drug to counteract the effect of the first drug, which, in turn, might have to be administered once more to avoid serious consequences from the second drug, etc. At least the vitamin K involved can have no other side-effect that would be harmful, which is often not so when other drugs are involved.

While speaking of vitamin K and its use in heart cases, it is interesting to mention an experiment related in the *Proceedings of the Society for Experimental Medicine and Biology* (March, 1944). The observers artificially induced hypertension or high blood pressure in a group of rats. It was shown that vitamin K is capable of lowering blood pressure in a way similar to that of kidney extract.

While we have seen no more literature describing

[439]

further findings in this field, *Science* magazine (Vol. 92, p. 11, 1940) tells of a possible relationship between the body's protection against cancer and its prothrombin level. Cancer-inducing coal tar substances were neutralized by interaction with compounds like prothrombin. It was considered that one of the functions of prothrombin might be protection of the body from cancer-causing substances.

As a Preservative

The heavy use of dangerous preservatives in so many of the things one eats makes the news that vitamin K can be used in this way particularly welcome. At least one can rest assured that its use will not be toxic in any way. *Food Processing* magazine (August, 1954) designates vitamin K as a good preservative to control fermentation processes without influencing flavors. In comparison with sulfur dioxide, a compound commonly used in this way, vitamin K's advantages were enumerated as the following: no strong pungent gas, no unpleasant odor, does not alter taste, has no bleaching effect when added to naturally attractive colored fruits and berries, is more stable and more effective and will retain its strength for months. Why use anything else as a preservative when such advantages are present in a substance we know to be a nutrient?

If you should feel that for some reason your vitamin K intake is not what it should be, you can check your intake of these high-K foods: spinach, kale, alfalfa, cabbage, cauliflower, green peas, carrot tops, blackstrap molasses, liver, egg yolk, soybean oil and fish liver oil. Try to include one or more of these foods in your diet daily.

SECTION VIII

The Bioflavonoids (Vitamin P)

CHAPTER 66

How the Body Uses Vitamin P

THE STORY of vitamin P is the best we know to illustrate the superior value of natural vitamins over synthetic ones. Vitamin P is a substance that occurs along
with vitamin C in foods. So when you take synthetic
vitamin C made in a laboratory, you don't get any vitamin P of course. But when you eat foods rich in vitamin
C or take vitamin supplements made from natural
foods such as rose hips or green peppers, the vitamin P
comes right along with the vitamin C. And we have
discovered that in countless situations where vitamin C
alone is not effective, the combination of the two will
work wonders.

In February, 1955, a meeting was held in New York
to honor Nobel Prize winner Albert Szent-Gyorgyi for
his outstanding work on vitamin C and vitamin P. At
the meeting researchers spoke on their experiences with
vitamin P, or, as they called it, "the bioflavonoids."
Actually we should not speak of the bioflavonoids as

[441]

a vitamin until their status has been clarified. Our official scientific body which determines terminology like that has decided that the bioflavonoids are not a vitamin.

What are the bioflavonoids? They are brightly colored substances that appear in fruits, along with vitamin C. They have also been called citrin, hesperidin, rutin, vitamin C_2, vitamin P, flavones, flavonols, flavonones and so forth. These names are important to biochemists but do not have to concern us. It's up to the researchers to separate and sort, study and test these various substances. We need only to be grateful for the work they are doing, and make the most we can of their discoveries.

At the meeting in February, Charles E. Brambel of Mercy Hospital, Baltimore, spoke on the use of the bioflavonoids in anticoagulant therapy. Because of the tendency of blood to coagulate too easily in certain heart and vascular diseases, doctors give medicines that they call "anticoagulants," designed to prevent blood clots or thromboses. Coumarin is one of these. Coumarin keeps the patient's blood in such a state that it cannot clot and stop up a blood vessel. But you can see that such a medicine might cause some difficulty. What if it keeps the blood in such a free-flowing condition that the patient has hemorrhages instead? Dr. Brambel studied 2000 patients using anticoagulant medicines. Five per cent of them developed bleeding complications. One hundred milligrams each of hesperidin (bioflavonoids) and vitamin C were given 4 times daily. The hemorrhage areas cleared rapidly. Dr. Brambel tells us that hesperidin and vitamin C together accomplish this, whereas neither of them alone will do the job.

Treating Rheumatic Fever and Miscarriages

Dr. James F. Rhinehart of the University of California spoke at the meeting on the subject of rheumatic fever. It is his belief that vitamin C and the bioflavonoids have considerable value in the treatment of rheumatic fever. Dr. Carl T. Javert of Cornell University spoke of using vitamin C and bioflavonoids to prevent miscarriages. In a study of 1334 patients, he found that 45 per cent of 3 groups tested were deficient in vitamin C. This is in contrast, he says, with normal nonpregnant women, *only one-third of whom are deficient in vitamin C*. Giving large doses of vitamin C and the bioflavonoids to 100 pregnant women with histories of habitual abortion, he achieved a successful pregnancy in 91 per cent. These patients took a diet rich in vitamin C (350 milligrams) plus a supplement containing vitamin C and the bioflavonoids—making a total of 500 milligrams of vitamin C per day. The vitamin C or the bioflavonoids alone did not do the job. But the combination of the two worked the miracle.

Dr. Robert Greenblatt of the Medical College of Georgia also reported on using vitamin C and the bioflavonoids for habitual abortion. A group of women who had never been able to carry their children and bring them into the world alive were examined to determine the state of their capillaries—that is, the tiny blood vessels that spread through every inch of our bodies. It was found that they suffered from capillary fragility—that is, the walls of these tiny vessels burst easily, causing bruised areas. Vitamin C and the bioflavonoids were given to them with excellent results. Eleven of 13 patients with two previous abortions delivered live infants.

[443]

Dr. George J. Boines of Wilmington, Delaware, spoke on using these two food substances for curing polio. He said tests indicated that all 400 patients with acute polio were found to have abnormal capillary fragility, indicating that they needed vitamin C and the bioflavonoids. They were given 600 milligrams of vitamin C and 600 milligrams of hesperidin daily until the state of their capillaries improved. Eight per cent responded in the first five weeks. Appetites improved within the first week and by the second week there was increased warmth to touch in the involved arm or leg.

Bioflavonoids and Infections

Vitamin C and the bioflavonoids have been used successfully in the treatment of colds. A group of nurses at Creighton University School of Medicine were given tablets containing the two substances and then checked for a year against another group which got nothing. The treated nurses had fewer colds by about 55 per cent and their colds lasted only an average of 3.9 days compared with 6.7 days in the untreated group. In the *American Journal of Digestive Diseases* for July, 1954, Morton S. Biskind and W. C. Martin reported on 22 patients who had respiratory infections varying from a simple cold to influenza. Twenty of them recovered in an 8-to-48-hour period after treatment with the bioflavonoids and vitamin C. The patients got 600 milligrams of each of the two substances every day. Vitamin C alone or the flavonoids alone did not produce results. But together they did.

How Can You Get Bioflavonoids in Your Diet?

Where are you going to look in food for the bioflavonoids? The substance used by many researchers comes from citrus fruits—it is contained in the white

[444]

skin and segment part of the fruit, not in the juice. We are told that the edible part of the orange contains a tenfold concentration of bioflavonoids, compared to the quantity in strained juice. In the fresh peeled orange there are 1000 milligrams of bioflavonoids and about 60 milligrams of vitamin C. In the strained orange juice there are only about 100 milligrams of bioflavonoids. Here we have one excellent reason for not juicing citrus fruit; eat it instead. And when you eat it, don't do as the cookbooks tell you to do and remove all the white layers under the skin and around each segment of fruit. That's where the bioflavonoids are. Lemons, grapes, plums, black currants, grapefruit, apricots, cherries and blackberries also contain flavonoids. You will probably get enough to maintain health if you eat lots and lots of fresh raw fruit, especially if you can eat it fresh from the tree or vine.

CHAPTER 67

Rutin

ONE OF THE MANY subjects for investigation in cases
of hypertension (high blood pressure) has been rutin
—a substance found most plentifully in buckwheat.
Rutin is a part of vitamin P. Apparently vitamin P,
like the other vitamins has many parts called "flavones." All of them are more or less related and have
many of the same properties so far as human health
is concerned, but some parts appear to be more effective in the treatment of certain disorders.

High blood pressure brings with it certain dangers,
not the least of which is hemorrhage—including
cerebral hemorrhage which we speak of as a "stroke."
In cases of stroke, the small blood vessels or capillaries
rupture because of the pressure upon them, and the
hemorrhaging of the blood from this ruptured vessel
brings about the unconsciousness and other symptoms
of stroke. Doctors sometimes refer to strokes as
"cerebral accidents."

[446]

It would seem that more is involved in this rupturing of a blood vessel than just the pressure being put on it by the blood. Perhaps, researchers have reasoned, part of the fault may lie in the weakness of the actual walls of the blood vessels, or capillary fragility. Interest in rutin was aroused by the discovery that apparently it had a lot to do with maintaining the walls of the blood vessels so that they do not become fragile and hence are less likely to rupture and cause serious illness or death.

Immediately, a whole series of problems in research presented themselves. First of all, how can the fragility of the blood vessels be measured? It is relative to the blood pressure, of course, and the higher the blood pressure goes, the more hardy the vessels must be not to rupture. One may assume that the blood vessels of a person with a stroke were indeed fragile, but how can one discover this *before* the accident takes place so that the patient can be treated for fragile blood vessels and perhaps never have a stroke? The problem of measuring the fragility of blood vessels has never actually been solved satisfactorily, and this is one reason for the doubt and confusion about the whole subject of rutin for high blood pressure patients.

With laboratory animals there are several methods of measuring fragility of capillaries and these have been used in experiments. H. K. Hellerstein, M.D., and his colleagues at several hospitals in Illinois and Ohio experimented by producing in animals blood pressure high enough to cause hemorrhaging from the blood vessels. To one group of animals they gave rutin 10 days before inducing the high blood pressure. Another group received no rutin. As reported in *American Heart Journal* for August, 1951, all of the animals died as a result of the high blood pressure, but those

[447]

which received rutin did not show any evidence of hemorrhaging as the other animals did.

Vitamin P for Hemorrhagic Disease and Cancer

It is well known that patients exposed to x-ray may hemorrhage, supposedly because the x-ray has affected the walls of the tiny blood vessels. John Q. Griffith, M.D., and James F. Cough, Ph.D., writing in the magazine *Blood,* for June, 1951, describe experiments in which they gave rutin to rats before they were exposed to x-ray. The rats which received the rutin did not hemorrhage, while those which did not receive rutin suffered the usual hemorrhagic disorders. Boris Sokoloff and his associates at the Florida Southern College in Lakeland, Florida, tested various vitamin P compounds on rats and found that the mortality from x-ray was reduced to 10 per cent in the group of rats receiving the vitamin P as against a mortality of 80 per cent in those rats which did not receive the vitamin. These authors say, in commenting on their experiments in the *Journal of Clinical Investigation,* April, 1951, "capillary injury is by far the most frequent cause of clinical hemorrhagic disease," and this injury "may be due to infection, drugs, toxemia, allergy or nutritional disturbance." Increased capillary fragility appears to come, they say, from some defect in the intercellular cement—that is, the substance between the body cells which holds them together. They say, too, that vitamin P factors (rutin among them) appear to "affect the capillary system directly perhaps participating as a principal in the 'wear and tear' of a part or all of the capillary system, inhibiting its degeneration and taking part in its regeneration, specifically as far as the intercellular cement is concerned."

In another article in the *Archives of Pathology* for

[448]

September, 1951, Dr. Sokoloff and his fellow workers discuss the effect of vitamin P on experimental cancers. They note that many years ago researchers mentioned the possibility that the intercellular cement might be an important factor in the occurrence of cancer. In their experiment, they gave a vitamin P compound to animals with cancer and discovered that it had a moderate effect on the growths—that is, it decreased them. They also noted that the vitamin P had apparently no bad effects at all.

Bicknell and Prescott, in their book *Vitamins in Medicine* (Grune and Stratton, 1953), relate a number of experiments having to do with vitamin P in cases of high blood pressure. In one case rutin was given in a dose of 20 milligrams 3 times daily for periods up to 4 years. In 75 per cent of those tested, capillary fragility became normal. In the majority of cases the blood pressure was not reduced by the rutin. The authors are careful to point out that *rutin is not given to lower the blood pressure*. It is given to prevent accidents in which hemorrhages might occur in high blood pressure patients. In other words, it seems that rutin prevented the possibility of "stroke" in 75 per cent of these patients. It did not cure their high blood pressure.

Bicknell and Prescott give numerous other examples of vitamin P being used successfully in the treatment of cases involving hemorrhaging due to disease or due to drugs which the patient was taking for some disease. Hemorrhages due to drug poisoning, for instance, can be relieved by giving some vitamin P compounds.

Rutin was also administered to a group of patients with glaucoma—the tragic eye disease in which the pressure inside the eyeball rises. Among 26 patients who received 20 milligrams of rutin 3 times a day,

17 noticed a fall in the pressure inside the eye, in 4 the results were not definite and 5 subjects noticed no change.

We found an extremely interesting article on the use of rutin in ophthalmology by L. B. Somerville-Large in the *Transactions of the Ophthalmological Society of the United Kingdom* (Vol. 69, pp. 615-617, 1949-1950). Dr. Somerville-Large states that "in the eye we have what appears to be the only opportunity the human body affords of actually observing lesions (disorders) associated with capillary dysfunction. We must, therefore, forgive our medical colleagues for their caution in recognizing the value of rutin." He goes on to tell us that the tiny blood vessels in the eye can be studied by the ophthalmologist. It is actually the only place in the body where blood vessels can be directly observed. These tiny capillaries in the eye are packed closely together and they have a wider "bore" than other capillaries in the body.

He says that the commonest conditions in which the capillaries seem to be out of order are diabetes, toxic and inflammatory conditions, high blood pressure and hardening of the arteries. Although hypertension (high blood pressure) of itself has no relation to capillary fragility, he says, 6 to 10 per cent of those hypertensives who do have increased capillary fragility suffer from hemorrhages in the retina of the eye, and cerebral or brain hemorrhages. He gives doses of two 60-milligram tablets of rutin 3 times a day making a total dosage of 360 milligrams daily. "I find," says he, "that the larger doses give a more rapid and more complete negative result to capillary fragility tests." Incidentally, he always combines the rutin with 200 milligrams of vitamin C daily.

It is interesting to note that throughout the discussion

of vitamin P and rutin in medical literature, it is suggested that vitamin P and vitamin C work closely together and better results are always obtained when they are given together. Note, too, that Dr. Somerville-Large gives quite a large dose of vitamin C—200 milligrams. At the present time the official recommendation for the minimum daily intake of vitamin C is only 70 milligrams and it is believed that most of us don't even get that much! Does it not seem reasonable that two or three times this amount of vitamin C every day might do a lot to prevent the capillary fragility which is responsible for so much distress today? Remember that vitamin C is also involved in keeping the intercellular membranes healthy.

In conclusion, Dr. Somerville-Large states that in his experience he has not yet "met a case in which the capillary fragility skin test has not been reduced with rutin to well within normal limits." In speaking of the length of time it is necessary to continue taking the rutin, he says, "To me at the present time it looks like a life sentence. Whenever rutin has been discontinued the capillary fragility has again increased. Also if the rutin is discontinued and the vitamin C alone persisted with, again the capillary fragility increases."

How Much Vitamin P Are You Getting?

Just like vitamin C, vitamin P is destroyed by cooking in an open vessel. So, much of the vitamin P value of food is lost in cooking. Once again we are faced with the absolute necessity for eating plenty of fresh raw fruits and vegetables, for it is in these that vitamin P is found in the largest amounts, along with vitamin C. The rutin concentrate used by doctors in treating hypertensive patients is made from buckwheat. Rutin occurs chiefly in the leaves of buckwheat, which may

[451]

contain as much as 7 or 8 per cent of rutin. It is rapidly destroyed when the leaves are dried slowly, so they must be processed with the greatest care. After the leaves are completely dried, there seems to be no further loss of rutin.

If you are suffering from high blood pressure and your doctor advises taking rutin to avoid any possibility of a stroke, we would certainly go along with his advice, on the basis of the evidence we have collected. If you are perfectly healthy and interested in preserving the state of your blood vessels so that you will not suffer from these disorders later on, then by all means see that you get, every day, plenty of the foods in which vitamin P (hence rutin) occurs, along with vitamin C.

Here is a list of foods that are rich in vitamin P and we have given you their vitamin C content as well. We hope you notice that, just as rose hips are many, many times richer in vitamin C than any other food, so too they are especially rich in vitamin P.

	Vitamin P Content in Units	Vitamin C Content in Milligrams
Apricots	75-100 in 8 apricots	4
Blackberry	60-100 in 3/4 cup	3
Black currant	200-500 in 1 cup	150
Cabbage (summer)	100 in 1 cup, raw	50
Cherries, black	60-100 in 12 large cherries	12
Grapes, black	500-1000 in 1 small bunch	3
Grapes, white	500-1000 in 1 small bunch	4
Grapefruit	100 in 1/2 grapefruit	45
Lemon juice	450-750 in 8 tablespoons	25
Orange	300-500 in 1 medium orange	50
Parsley	130 in 1 cup	70
Plums	50-200 in 3 medium plums	5
Prunes	300-400 in 8 medium prunes	4
Rose hips	240-680 in 100 grams	500 to 6000

BOOK III

VITAMINS AND DISEASE

CHAPTER 68

The Rheumatic Diseases and Vitamin C

ARTHRITIS—TORMENTOR of millions of Americans and crippler of millions more—can it be caused by something we do or do not eat?

Certainly it is not the result of eating or not eating any one food. But it has seemed to us for a long time that arthritis and all the other rheumatic diseases must be related to patterns of eating—habits that lead one into all the wrong paths, dietetically speaking.

Confirmation of our belief comes in an article by W. J. McCormick, M.D., of Toronto, "The Rheumatic Diseases," in the *Archives of Pediatrics,* April, 1955. Dr. McCormick tells us that only recently have we classified these diseases according to the way they manifest themselves—rheumatic fever, rheumatoid arthritis, primary osteoarthritis, rheumatoid spondylitis, bursitis, synovitis and so forth. The one thing all these diseases appear to have in common, says he, is that the cartilages involved in joints and the connective tissue surrounding them disintegrate. So it seems that, if one could explain this one symptom, one could get to the bottom of the matter.

Dr. McCormick believes that the early writers on scurvy gave the most significant clues to the cause and cure of arthritis. Scurvy? How is it possible? Scurvy is a disease of long ago, before we knew the value of fresh raw foods in the diet. Nobody in our enlightened era ever has scurvy! Or do they? Listen to Dr. McCormick's reasoning and make up your own mind.

He quotes James Lind, who wrote medical treatises in 1753, as saying that in scurvy the muscles are so lax and tender that they readily fall apart during autopsies. He said, too, that scurvy affected the cartilages of the ribs so decidedly as to sometimes separate them entirely from the breast bone. He had no explanation for the fact that "scurvy seats itself so commonly in the joint of the knee."

Lind reviewed the findings of earlier writers on scurvy, who had observed that the bones of the scurvy patient cracked when he moved, "in some we perceived a small low noise when they breathed. . . . The ligaments of the joints were corroded and loose. Instead of finding in the cavities of the joints the usual sweet oily mucilage, there was only a greenish liquor. . . . gout is known to proceed from scurvy."

It is well to remember that 200 or 300 years ago medical students had ample opportunity to study scurvy. It was nearly as common as colds are today. So, from many autopsies, they knew the symptoms of this disease, then so puzzling, which we know today is the result of a deficiency in vitamin C.

"The most definitely established function of vitamin C is that of assisting in the formation of collagen for the maintenance of integrity and stability of the connective tissues generally, and this would include the

[456]

bones, cartilages, muscles and vascular tissue," says Dr. McCormick. Collagen is the substance that is so important in all connective tissue—the material that makes gelatin when you boil bones and cartilages. "In a deficiency of this vitamin (C)," Dr. McCormick continues, "instability and fragility of all such tissues is believed to be caused by the breakdown of inter-cellular cement substance, resulting in easy rupture of any and all of these connective tissues," which would include the discs of the backbone, the ligaments and small sacs in the interior of the joints and the cartilage which helps in the movement of joints. The vulnerability of these joints may be, then, the common cause for the rheumatic diseases, says Dr. McCormick.

Rheumatism in Animals

Coming up to modern times, we find two researchers, Rinehart and Mettier, who correlated deficiency of vitamin C with rheumatic disease. In an article in the *American Journal of Pathology* (Vol. 10, p. 61, 1934), they relate that they found impairment of the joints in animals deprived of vitamin C. When the animals were subject to some infection, the joint symptoms became worse. Those animals which were subjected to the same infection while on a diet rich in vitamin C did not develop the joint disorders.

Extending these researches further, Rinehart found that the amount of vitamin C in the blood of arthritic and rheumatic fever patients is extremely low. He believes that the important basic cause of rheumatic disease is infection, superimposed on a vitamin C deficiency. Dr. McCormick believes that both the infection and the rheumatism are direct results of vitamin C deficiency.

Infection and lack of vitamin C do go hand-in-hand.

[457]

In this article, we find reference to many different examples—a mouth infection associated with rheumatic fever which was shown to be due to vitamin C deficiency; a streptococcus and pneumonia epidemic in a naval training school which did not affect students who were taking liberal doses of vitamin C; a report on a less-than-usual excretion of vitamin C in rheumatoid arthritis patients who were getting plenty of the vitamin in their diets, seeming to indicate that the vitamin was being used at a faster than normal rate.

Rinehart, in a paper read before the California Heart Association, May 6, 1944, told of his findings that vitamin P (the flavonoids), used in conjunction with vitamin C, had a favorable influence on the condition of the blood vessels in infections. It seems to us that Rinehart may have the answer right here—that is, that natural vitamin C, which occurs along with vitamin P in foods, may be what the rheumatic tissues lack—not just vitamin C as it appears in synthetic preparations, unaccompanied by any of the other food elements.

Dr. McCormick, a great believer in the use of vitamins for prevention and for cure, tells us that he has given massive doses of vitamin C in injections and orally in a number of cases of rheumatic fever. "The patients made rapid and complete recovery in 3 or 4 weeks without cardiac complication." The usual hospital treatment may go on for 3 or 4 months, with cortisone or aspirin being given and a high rate of heart complications. Dr. McCormick has also given massive doses of vitamin C in cases of "incipient arthritis"— that is, arthritis which is just beginning—with "similarly favorable results."

What does he mean by "massive doses"? From one to ten grams daily; that is, in terms in which one buys natural vitamin C products, from 1,000 milligrams to 10,000 milligrams a day. Is it necessary for the average person on an average diet to take this much vitamin C in order to prevent arthritis? We believe not. These are curative doses for patients who already have the symptoms of disease. However, we do not think it is possible to get too much vitamin C in your diet these days, and it is likely that most of us are getting far too little.

How does this happen in an age when fresh vegetables and fresh fruits are available year-round? Too many other foods are available, too—worthless foods—soft drinks, pastries, candies, cakes, etc. Every mouthful of these foods that your family eats means that they can eat less of fresh foods. Just in the case of children, how much of their diet consists of worthless foods compared to their daily intake of fresh, raw foods?

Why We Lack Vitamin C

An article from the *Journal of the American Dietetic Association,* May, 1954, gives us part of the answer. In a survey of 131 children with rheumatic fever, compared with 131 carefully paired children who did not have the disease, it was found that the rheumatic fever children were eating less of vitamin-C-rich foods than the healthy children. The sick children did not get even one serving per day of foods that contain even moderate amounts of vitamin C.

In another survey, 35 per cent of the children of one parish in Louisiana ate *no fruits or raw vegetables at all!* In another survey, it was found on autopsies of infants dying at Johns Hopkins that 6 per cent of them suffered from scurvy. In another survey, reported in the *Journal of the American Dietetic Association,* it was shown that of a group of school children studied, 47 per cent had a low intake of vitamin C and 53 per cent had a low blood level of the vitamin. College students eating at dining halls were found to be eating meals that were 62 per cent deficient in vitamin C.

In another survey of institutional inmates over the age of 50, it was found that 87 *per cent were deficient in vitamin C*. Dr. McCormick tells us that he has examined more than 500 patients with particular reference to their vitamin C status, and has found that less than 10 per cent of them have had the optimum amount of vitamin C in their blood at any time.

Remember, too, that vitamin C is most perishable, so that even today, with our wonderful methods of transportation and marketing, the fruits and vegetables you buy may have lost much of their vitamin C by the time you buy them. Storing and cooking destroy much more of it. The poisonous substances to which you are exposed day after day use it up. Cigarette smoke is an enemy of vitamin C in your tissues.

If, indeed, lack of vitamin C is responsible for initiating rheumatic troubles of all kinds, is it any wonder that the medical journals report dolefully that practically everybody over the age of 40 has or shortly will have arthritic symptoms?

CHAPTER 69

Vitamin P and Vitamin C and Arthritis

"THERE IS A tendency to pay exclusive attention to the heart and the blood vessels. It is often forgotten that the sole function of the heart, the arteries and the veins is to maintain an adequate rate of blood flow through the capillaries. It is in the capillaries that the essential business of the circulatory system is carried on."

At first glance, these words seem astonishing. Capillaries are the tiny blood vessels that crisscross all our tissues. Through their walls food and oxygen are carried to cells and waste material is carried away. Is it possible that we have missed the point in concerning ourselves exclusively with the heart and blood vessels and largely ignoring the health of tiny capillaries?

Still, come to think of it, the function of the heartbeat and the pulsations of the arteries is to circulate the blood to every cell of the body. Getting it there is important, but what happens after it gets there is just as important. And this happens in the capillaries!

The words we quoted above are from an article in *Clinical Medicine* (Vol. 52, p. 157, 1945). We found them in an article on the treatment of arthritis with vitamin P and vitamin C. Four researchers studied 42 patients with rheumatoid arthritis and 17 patients with osteoarthritis over a period of 7 years to discover how their health could be improved if they took quite large doses of these two vitamins every day. The story of their findings, as reported in the *Journal of American Geriatrics,* June, 1956, is amazing. We owe a debt of gratitude to the authors for their work in following up 59 patients over such a long time. The authors are Peter J. Warter, M.D., and Henry L. Drezner, M.D., of McKinley Hospital, Trenton, New Jersey, Dominic A. Donio, M.D., of Sacred Heart Hospital, Allentown, Pennsylvania and Steven Horoschak, B.S., of the National Drug Company.

The authors remind us that we are all troubled with minor injuries during every day. We bump our ankles, pinch our fingers, stumble over cracks in the sidewalk, hit our heads on the cellar stairs and so on. Usually we pay no attention to these knocks except for a casual, "Oh, I wonder where I got that bruise." "That bruise" means that capillaries have hemorrhaged. You are bleeding internally, even if ever so slightly. Our authors tell us that these bleedings might well develop into something serious in a defective capillary system, made so by poisons of various kinds—drugs, for instance, or tobacco.

Furthermore, they tell us that rheumatic fever is believed to be a disease of the blood vessels, involving fragility of these small capillaries so that they burst easily. High blood pressure, or hypertension, is another disease in which the stability of the capillaries is of utmost importance. Patients who have fragile capillaries often have strokes, hemorrhages in the retina of the eye and other serious disorders. So it seems certain that disorders of the capillary system are at the bottom of many chronic diseases.

Vitamin C, Vitamin P and Capillaries

What are the capillaries made of? Cells and intercellular material. We know positively that the intercellular material is kept in repair by vitamin C. In scurvy, the disease of vitamin C deficiency, there is a breakdown of this intercellular material which can be reversed almost magically by giving vitamin C. Walter H. Eddy in his book, *What Are the Vitamins?* (Reinhold, 1941), says he thinks that "country rheumatism" which develops at the end of a long winter is nothing more or less than hemorrhaging capillaries in the joints, as a result of vitamin C deficiency.

Later researchers have shown that vitamin C cannot function well in the absence of vitamin P or the bioflavonoids, as they are sometimes called. Then, too, vitamin P does not take its part in body processes without vitamin C being present. So, in testing the effect of vitamin C on arthritic patients, the authors felt it necessary to add vitamin P as well.

They tested the rheumatoid arthritis patients for capillary fragility and found that it was almost universal. In other words, pressure on the capillaries caused them to burst. These folks consistently have bruised themselves from everyday bumps. Blood pressure was low in these patients, the heartbeat was rapid. The 17 osteoarthritis patients were obese and had high blood pressure. In the most severe cases of the rheumatoid arthritis patients, as much as 600 to 1000 milligrams of vitamin P-vitamin C (in equal amounts) were given daily in divided doses. Gradually, the dose was reduced to 300 milligrams daily. For milder cases, 400 to 600 milligrams were given at the beginning and these were then reduced to 300 for a "maintenance dose." In the osteoarthritic patients, the treatment was begun and maintained with 300-milligram doses. The reason given for the larger doses in rheumatoid arthritis is that there is inflammation in this disease which taxes the capillary resistance to a greater degree.

What were the results obtained? In the rheumatoid group, normal capillary resistance was established in 6 to 8 weeks. That means no more bruises for them. These patients apparently utilized their food better, too, for protein and vitamin B supplements brought a gain in weight and an increase in red blood, to combat anemia. This did not happen in patients who were not taking the vitamins. The blood pressure in most patients soon came to normal range. Some of the patients who had been subject to colds voluntarily reported that they had much more resistance to cold, even though the researchers were not testing for this angle. The arthritis, which improved steadily, flared up again when the vitamins were discontinued for several months in the case of a few patients. There were no strokes or other blood vessel disorders.

In the osteoarthritic group, those who bruised easily developed resistance to bruising within 6 weeks. Six patients with high blood pressure brought their pressure down to normal. The authors admit that rest and diet may have played some part in this, but they believe the vitamins should get some credit. The arthritic symptoms improved. Even though damage to joints could not, of course, be repaired, the patients had less fatigue, less discomfort in the joints and general improvement.

The conclusions of the authors are that the combination of vitamin P and vitamin C has the capacity to

[464]

correct abnormal capillary fragility and permeability, and thus enhances the effectiveness of therapy directed against the rheumatic diseases.

It seems apparent that anyone who wants to prevent conditions of this kind will see that he gets ample amounts of these two vitamins. Where can you get them? Actually the substance used in the rheumatism experiment was a combination of hesperidin and ascorbic acid—just these two. Now vitamin P is a conglomeration of "elements," as the chemists call them, all of which are apparently important. Hesperidin is one of these elements.

The only way to get all of the elements—both vitamin P and vitamin C—is to eat foods that contain them all and to take natural food supplements rich in them all. The foods you should be sure to get in ample quantity are mostly raw fruits. Grapes, plums, black currants, apricots, cherries and blackberries are good sources of vitamin P; also the citrus fruits, which we think should be eaten sparingly, due to their citric acid content. Other foods rich in vitamin C are broccoli, Brussels sprouts, cabbage, dandelion greens, melons, cantaloupes, tomatoes, mustard greens and green peppers.

CHAPTER 70

Vitamin D and Arthritis Patients

VITAMIN D FOR arthritis seems to be a treatment that carries little, if any, risk and one which can be applied with a good chance of success as a preventive measure.

We found, in a 1935 medical journal, the account of the treatment of a number of patients with vitamin D. Two physicians, Dr. Irving Dreyer and Dr. C. I. Reed of the University of Illinois Department of Medicine, writing in the *Archives of Physical Therapy* (Vol. 16, p. 537, 1935), have this to say, "In general, the results suggest that this material may prove an efficient form of therapy, as well as a valuable aid in the study of the fundamental nature of arthritis."

They treated 67 patients suffering from a variety of arthritic afflictions. Forty-four of these showed clinical improvement, 13 showed none and 10 cases were uncertain. About 200 other cases being treated privately showed approximately the same results. The doctors gave massive doses of synthetic vitamin D.

[466]

Since vitamin D is one of the two vitamins (vitamin A is the other) which has been known to produce toxic results if taken in too large a dosage over a long period of time, it is interesting to know that these arthritic patients were started on a daily dosage of 200,000 units of synthetic vitamin D. This dosage was given daily for a month. If there was no improvement and no indication that any harm had been done by this quite large dose, it was increased by 50,000 to 60,000 units each week, until there was some improvement or indication of overdosage. In some stubborn cases, it was found necessary to increase to 600,000 units or even to 1,000,-000 for a few days and then reduce again to 200,000. "Most of our results have been obtained with daily doses of 300,000 to 500,000 units," say the authors.

Are Massive Doses Dangerous?

Drs. Dreyer and Reed tell us that they do not believe vitamin D in such enormous doses poses any greater risk than many preparations used daily by physicians. And, they say, one knows within a few weeks if symptoms of overdosage are present. When the vitamin is discontinued, the symptoms disappear.

It is interesting, too, to note that some patients who could not take massive doses of vitamin D found that they could manage perfectly well if large doses of brewer's yeast were given at the same time. This is not successful in every case, they say, but they tell us of one woman patient who on 3 successive occasions, with intervals of 2 to 3 weeks between, took 300,000 units daily for 10 days, but became nauseated on the eleventh day. Nausea is one of the first symptoms that too much vitamin D is being taken. When she took 6 grams of brewer's yeast 3 times daily, she was able to take up to 600,000 units of vitamin D daily for 3 weeks

[467]

without becoming nauseated, or suffering from other unpleasant symptoms.

"The total number of human subjects to whom large doses of viosterol [synthetic vitamin D] have been administered for all conditions now numbers approximately 700," say our authors. They continue, "Of these, 63 have, at some time, manifested evidence of toxicity. The actual size of the dose producing toxicity varies in different individuals. Human subjects have received as high as 3,000,000 units daily for 5 days. Single large doses have been given by others. It is apparent, however, that toxicity is more likely to occur after prolonged administration of moderate amounts than as a result of brief administration of large amounts."

Let us compare the amounts the investigators are talking about to some of the all-natural vitamin D supplements. The all-in-one combination food supplements average between 1200 to 3200 units of vitamin D. Individual vitamin A and D preparations from fish liver oil provide around 1,000 units of vitamin D per capsule. The labels of such products carefully state what the recommended dosage is and give also the daily minimum requirement of each of the two vitamins.

Vitamin A is suggested in amounts of 5,000 units daily for adults. No daily minimum has been set for vitamin D for adults, as the official board which decides these things does not believe that adults in general need additional vitamin D. It's a vitamin for children, they say, whose bones are growing and who must have vitamin D so that the calcium and phosphorus can be used properly for bone growth.

It seems unlikely, then, that anyone could possibly get too much vitamin D taking natural food supplements where the source of the vitamin is fish liver oil.

[468]

It would be foolish, we believe, for anyone to try to give himself massive doses of this vitamin by taking natural food supplements, because he would be bound to get too much vitamin A at the same time, since the two are both present in fish liver oil. Of course, we do not recommend using synthetic vitamins at all.

Adults Benefit from Taking Vitamin D

So what lessons can we learn from the work that was reported on vitamin D for arthritis cases? It seems to us that we should learn that vitamin D is indeed essential for adults and, perhaps, lack of it may be a definite factor in the cause of arthritis. Apparently no one knows why the vitamin brings relief in those cases where it does. Couldn't it be simply that there was a lack of the vitamin? Vitamin D is almost completely lacking in food. Our chief source of it is sunlight which, falling on our bare skin, produces a substance the body then changes into vitamin D. Doesn't it seem quite likely that people who spend most of their time indoors could very definitely be lacking in vitamin D, especially in the winter months when sunlight is weak and infrequent?

We had never heard before of any relationship between the taking of brewer's yeast (rich chiefly in vitamin B and minerals) and protection against the possible toxicity of large doses of vitamin D. But it seems to indicate again that one is safest to take whole foods and to take all the important vitamins and minerals in natural food supplements, like brewer's yeast. Who knows? There may be many more important functions performed by brewer's yeast that we do not know anything about as yet. If it protects against toxicity of large doses of vitamin D, perhaps it also acts to protect

[469]

us against many other unknown poisons in our environment.

We would not suggest that you attempt to cure arthritic conditions by using massive doses of vitamin D as the doctors at the university hospital did, unless you are taking these doses under the supervision of a capable doctor who understands just what the symptoms of overdosage may be.

CHAPTER 71

Does B Complex Prevent Birth Deformities?

PHOCOMELIA (literally, seal limbs) and other types of physical deformity in newborn children have become the new terror that haunts the young woman of child-bearing age as well as the doctors responsible for the health of her offspring. Teratogenicity—the birth of malformed children — has for a long time been a mounting problem that the medical profession kept very quiet indeed, until the scandal of thalidomide burst upon the world. Suddenly, with thousands of limbless and otherwise deformed babies being born in Europe and North America as a result of their mothers being given thalidomide, public health authorities have been forced to recognize that the indiscriminate administration of drugs involves terrible hazards.

More recently the *British Medical Journal* for November, 1962, reported that two mothers who had taken an appetite-suppressing drug called Preludin had given birth to deformed babies. Promptly, the Italian

Health Ministry banned the drug. A week later the ban was rescinded. In Sweden, during the same week, Postafen and two other drugs were banned by the Swedish Medical Board because they were suspected of causing birth deformations. In the United States, however, our Food and Drug Administration does not ban drugs suspected of being harmful to the public but demands that their harmfulness must be rigorously proven before removing them from the market and cutting into the profits of the makers.

Even in the United States, however, authorities are becoming greatly concerned, and quiet but intense investigations are going on in the effort to reduce or eliminate the horribly deformed births that are occurring with increasing frequency.

Best Defense—B Complex

And here is the great and reassuring news: The best protector the young woman of childbearing age has against the possibility that her child will be born deformed is a high consumption of the B complex vitamins. Those who regularly take diet supplements of desiccated liver and brewer's yeast can be sure that of all the women in the world, they have the least chance of ever giving birth to deformed children.

This cheering fact emerges from a survey that was made by *Medical Tribune*, a weekly newspaper of medical news, on the subject of teratogenicity. Nine of the world's top medical experts working in this field were sent a series of questions by *Medical Tribune*. Their answers were published during the months of November and December, 1962. Many of their comments were enlightening, and if this were a sane world, would end for all time the efforts of our governmental

[472]

authorities to reduce the public's consumption of vitamin and mineral supplements.

Here is one comment made by Professor Bruno Filippi of the Maggiore Hospital of the University of Turin, Italy: "We have shown that many malformations of the fetus due to the administration of drugs such as the antibiotics to pregnant animals occur only when the latter are fed on diets deficient in the vitamin B complex. The malformations do not occur if the animals receive an adequate supply of the vitamin B complex which seems to exert a protective action.

"We have shown this in a controlled trial. One group of animals, given the antibiotics and no vitamin B complex in the diet, produced deformed fetuses; the other group was given the antibiotics and added vitamin B complex and had no deformed fetuses."

Dr. Charles Loux, embryologist of the faculty of medicine of the University of Paris, said: "There is some interrelationship between the vitamins and teratogenicity. Thus, the teratogenic effects of riboflavin deficiency are increased by a concomitant pantothenic acid deficiency." This refers to the fact, well-known by now, that the first established cause of these terrifying birth defects was a deficiency in riboflavin. It was not known until recently, however, that riboflavin in combination with pantothenic acid acted as a positive protector against the action of drugs causing birth deformities.

Drugs Damage Embryos

This new knowledge is beginning to point more and more inexorably to the idea that it is not just a few specific drugs that cause birth deformity, but more likely it is a large proportion of the entire field of pharmaceuticals, all of which have their toxic side-effects on the human system. According to Dr. F. Clarke Fraser, professor of genetics at McGill University, in a statement made to a recent seminar on birth defects at Ann Arbor, Michigan, "there are hundreds of agents, extrinsic factors, that are harmful to the mother and damage the embryo." He listed these as including radiation, which acts by killing cells or breaking chromosomes; rubella and other viruses; and a variety of drugs, including salicylates and steroids. Dr. Fraser suggested that somebody ought to experiment and find out whether even aspirin does not cause such birth deformities. As yet, it has not been incriminated, he pointed out, perhaps merely because it has not been investigated. Other salicylates closely related to aspirin have definitely been involved. The steroids, of course, are cortisone and allied compounds.

This statement of Dr. Fraser's, it will be apparent to *Prevention* readers, echoes what we have been pointing out for many years. No matter how harmless a drug may seem, it is always a poison, and always develops toxic reactions in the body. In normal circumstances, the body may be strong enough to fight off these reactions. But there are always abnormal circumstances in which the results of taking drugs or any kind of foreign and unnatural matter into the body will be unpredictable and terrible. Early pregnancy is one of those circumstances in which both the mother and the newly developing embryo are especially vulnerable. And since taking such foreign matter into the body is sometimes unavoidable in our chemical-saturated environment, the only real protection that we have is to keep our resistance always at its peak by keeping our tissues saturated with all the vitamins, and not merely supplied with the minimum amounts that prevent

[474]

deficiency diseases in normal persons in normal circumstances.

Malnutrition

With regard to teratogenicity, this is especially important, for Dr. Fraser pointed out that dietary deficiencies in themselves are enough to cause deformities in the newborn. "It used to be thought that the mammalian embryo was well protected from the harmful effects of the environment, but this is not entirely so," he said. He pointed out that it was erroneous to believe that even though the mother may have a deficient diet, the embryo will be sufficiently nourished. Studies show that starvation of a pregnant mouse for 24 hours will cause abnormality in the offspring, Dr. Fraser said. Such deformities, he believes, can be caused not only by the well-known riboflavin deficiency, but also by deficiency in vitamin A, vitamin E, or folic acid.

It must be remembered that the study of the causes of deformed births is only at its beginning. It is by no means unlikely, for example, that a year from now some other researcher will establish that vitamin C deficiency can also leave the young mother especially vulnerable and her infant subject to the shocking abnormalities of development that have lately been terrifying the world.

Strangely, vitamin A, when taken alone in enormous doses such as are administered therapeutically by physicians, can also cause such birth deformities. The experts queried by *Medical Tribune*, however, stated that this is never the case when an adequate supply of the B complex vitamins are taken at the same time. "These lesions occur only if the drug is given during a certain period of the pregnancy, and only in association with lack of the B complex vitamins," was the statement of

[475]

Dr. Philip Filippi. The special effect of vitamin A, given in the astronomical dose of 60,000 International Units daily to white mice, was to produce cleft palate. This dose, of course, is the equivalent of well over a million units of vitamin A daily administered to an adult human being. It is absolutely no reason to fear vitamin A in the kind of dosage that it is possible for us to get from our food supplements, which we always take in conjunction with all the other vitamins. The vitamin A we take this way is completely harmless and beneficial.

Dr. Filippi's cleft palate theory experiment, however, does suggest that when occasional human children are born with cleft palate, there might be some connection with an unbalanced diet of the mother. We think some qualified investigator should look into the question of whether mothers producing children with cleft palate have not had diets generally deficient in vitamins, while they drank abnormal quantities of milk, ate large amounts of butter, and in other ways consumed an inordinate amount of vitamin A without balancing it with the other vitamins. It has already been established that even in the huge amounts used by Dr. Filippi, vitamin A did not have this effect when a sufficient amount of the B complex vitamins were also present. As Dr. H. Woollam of Cambridge University stated it, "We assume that the vitamin B complex definitely protects against the teratogenic action of massive doses of vitamin A given between the 8th and 13th days of pregnancy. The B complex was injected every time the animals were dosed with vitamin A."

The conclusion to be drawn from the *Medical Tribune* survey is simply that deformed births are a product of vitamin deficiency, the administration of any of many kinds of drugs, or a combination of the two. Almost uniformly the experts condemned the wholesale administration of drugs that is today's common medical practice. "Drugs with no reported teratogenic action may be given," said Dr. Roux of France, "but greater care must be exercised by physicians now than in the past. Too many drugs are administered without adequate appraisal first. Physicians are induced to give new preparations by drug firms and by patients themselves. They should hesitate to give new and potent drugs to women in the childbearing age. The greater the activity of the drug, the more it should be viewed with suspicion as a possible teratogen. Many drugs introduced in the last 20 years belong to this class. The new drugs should be given only when absolutely necessary."

"The use of all drugs during pregnancy should be restricted to the absolute minimum," echoed Dr. Professor Heinz Ruebsaamen of the University of Freiburg, Germany.

Dr. Sidney Cohlan of the New York University Medical Center, went a step further. "The general principles of careful drug therapy remain the same, whether a woman is pregnant or not," he stated. "The placental panic generated by the unfortunate thalidomide tragedy does not alter the basic teaching of responsible drug administration. It should hopefully serve to re-emphasize the oft-repeated precept that promiscuous use of drugs for vague indications is unjustifiable, and that especially during the child-bearing age, even well known drugs should be administered only on absolute indications. The widespread use of newer preparations(often with unproved effectiveness) for minor complaints is an unnecessary risk."

Amen, we say. And since the chances are that your

[477]

own doctor will never have read the survey, and just loves to prescribe a fancy new drug every time you get a headache or a broken fingernail, we say make sure that you always have the best protection known against the dangerous effects of medical drugs—a system saturated with all the vitamins, taken in proper combination. And if you happen to be a woman of childbearing age, be especially careful, whatever else you may do, always to take your desiccated liver and brewer's yeast supplements. As long as you have enough of these wonder foods in you, you and your child have little to fear.

CHAPTER 72

Vitamin C and Backaches

A PERSON SCHEDULED for surgery to relieve severe back pain might do better with daily doses of vitamin C, according to Dr. James Greenwood, Jr., of Baylor University College of Medicine. He reports that the vitamin has helped a number of patients with back, neck and leg pain due to spinal disc injuries to avoid surgery in seven years of testing. Anyone who has ever put in time with massages and heat pads to ease occasional backache knows how welcome this news must be to chronic sufferers.

Dr. Greenwood's work was the result of efforts to relieve ten years of back pain in himself. In 1957 he began to experiment with vitamin C personally, and has since worked with over 500 people, most of whom find relief with 500 milligrams of ascorbic acid a day taken in two doses. If there is any heavy exercise such as hiking or sailing or strenuous games, the dose is upped to 1000 milligrams per day. Even ordinary muscular soreness seems to be greatly relieved by large doses of vitamin C, he reported in the *Medical Annals of the District of Columbia*. It took only four months on the ascorbic acid therapy before Greenwood himself was "quite comfortable" and could do extra exercise with little difficulty.

Dr. Greenwood believes that the official estimates of the need for vitamin C are based largely on the amount needed to prevent absolute scurvy, "a severe deficiency."Actually a smaller deficiency might account for spinal problems which have put him and others flat on their heating pads, says the author. "With the exception of monkeys, guinea pigs and man, all species maintain their vitamin C at saturation point in tissues." There is no indication in medical literature that any harm can come from large doses of ascorbic acid, said Greenwood, except in combination with steroid drugs such as cortisone and ACTH.

Surgery Out of Style

A few years ago Dr. Greenwood's evidence on the value of vitamin C in treating backache would have made little headway. Surgery was almost standard procedure for serious low back pain and sciatica in the postwar years. This was true in spite of an estimate in *Lancet* (February 3, 1951) that only one in forty cases of this type actually requires surgery for a cure. Now the outlook has reversed so that orthopedic surgeon Dr. H. R. McCarroll was able to tell an American Medical Association meeting in June 1963 that approximately 90 percent of the patients with low back pain can be managed satisfactorily without surgery.

Some physicians are returning to the tried and true methods of massage for relief of low back pain. Mayer

S. Deroy of the University of Pittsburgh said that orthopedic surgeons should be best at this treatment of low
back pain because of their knowledge of anatomy,
physiology and the pathology of the muscular system.

What Discs Do

Doctors guess that there are about 50 types of stress
that can cause back pain, but most lower back troubles
can be traced to the spinal discs. The discs are a type
of shock absorber, made of cartilage around a jelly-like
center, which fit between each of the 33 vertebrae.
When all of the discs are in place, they absorb the
shock between the bones and prevent their scraping
together. Sometimes a little of the disc protrudes
through a small tear in the surrounding tissue (ruptured disc). These protruding discs squeeze out from
between the vertebrae and press against nerves that
emerge from the spine. When they do, the pain is
excruciating and the body automatically goes into a
muscular spasm. This reflex discourages unnecessary
movement of the injured portion. The muscles may
remain in tight and painful spasms for hours or even
days. Pain begets more pain, the muscles in spasm
produce pain and the pain produces more spasm.

A weak back due to a lack of exercise and muscle
tone causes the backache problem. How can abdominal
muscles, notoriously flabby in most of us, help to support the spine, as they are intended to do? Women,
instead of exercising the abdominal muscles, simply
wear girdles to hold themselves in. Men don't even do
that much. Without help from the abdominal muscles
to hold the spine erect, the whole load falls on the back
muscles, and they tend to weaken. With these main
supports gone, the ligaments take over like steadying

wires, but they have no real strength. They stretch as the job becomes too much for them, and the spine becomes wobbly, like a very tall bamboo pole. If it bends too far, the pressure near the bottom can push a disc right out of place. Anything can trigger it— bending to pick up a shoe, twisting to talk to a friend behind you in the car, jumping lightly down a step or wo from the front porch.

A Case for Prevention

An occasional twinge of back pain should serve as a warning that more serious complications are on the way unless you do something to prevent it. In 1963 the AMA blamed low backache largely on the "soft aspects" of modern American living (ill-fitting or inappropriate shoes, lack of exercise, super-soft mattresses and low chairs with little back support). Dr. Greenwood says it can be due to vitamin C deficiency. Likely it's both. This puts backache smack in the center of preventive medicine. In short, if you get backache, it's your fault and you can probably provide the remedy.

The first thing, check your diet for a rich vitamin C intake (do you take rose hips?) so you can be sure of the healthy tissues necessary for strong muscles and ligaments in your back and abdomen. These are the instruments you must have first to keep your spine erect and to pamper the discs between the vertebrae. Get a bed board if you have a mattress too soft to keep your spine on a straight level. As you go through an average day, choose straight back chairs for long periods of sitting. (A soft deep chair bends the spine and increases the strain on the muscles of the low back.) Above all get some exercise in the abdominals and the back muscles. (Any library will have a book with a good selection of these.)

If you aren't convinced that it's worth all this trouble to avoid back pain, ask someone who suffers from it. They will tell you that nothing is too much trouble. Adjusting your intake of vitamin C, firming your mattress and doing a small amount of regular exercise are a cheap price indeed for a strong back that will get you through the day without the constant ache that can make work and play a misery.

CHAPTER 73

Vitamin E and Buerger's Disease

IT IS SELDOM THAT medical men have as clear-cut and final a cause and effect setup in dealing with any disease as they have in the case of smoking and Buerger's disease. Not absolutely everyone who gets Buerger's disease smokes, but by far the largest majority of them do. Not absolutely every patient who stops smoking in time will be cured of Buerger's disease. But medical men everywhere are generally agreed that patients with Buerger's disease dare not smoke. If they stop smoking, symptoms generally improve, only to become worse again if the patient goes back to smoking.

Aside from the fact that smoking appears to have a great deal to do with it, no one knows what causes Buerger's disease. Its other name is thromboangiitis obliterans. Dr. Leo Buerger made an intensive study of the disease about 30 years ago, so it is called after him. It is a disease of the blood vessels, in which the inner linings of both arteries and veins become inflamed. There is also clogging of the blood vessels due to blood

[484]

clots. In general, the disease affects the legs and feet. It may start with pain in the legs on exertion. As the blood vessels become more and more inflamed, the pain becomes more severe and continuous. In the acute stage, there is great pain after walking a short distance. As the disease progresses and becomes chronic, the pain becomes so severe that the patient is unable to sleep. Eventually a spot develops on a toe or under a toenail and gangrene is on the way. It may take a year or ten years, but the epilogue to a case of Buerger's disease is generally amputation of a foot or leg to save the patient's life.

Relationship Between Smoking and Buerger's Disease

Just in case there should be any doubt in the minds of smokers as to the relationship of tobacco to the disease, here are some quotes on the subject. An editor's answer to a reader's question in the *British Medical Journal* for December 22, 1951: "As a general rule, however, withholding cigarettes has a beneficial effect on Buerger's disease." In the *Journal of the American Medical Association* for May 18, 1946, appeared a warning about diabetics smoking: blood vessel disease of a kind that incapacitates the patient with pain and weakness in his feet and legs so that he cannot walk or that leads to ulcers and gangrene afflicted significantly more smokers than nonsmokers in a group of 301 diabetic men. Smoking constricts the blood vessels. A patient whose vessels are constricted already may have them further constricted by using tobacco.

Another article in the *Journal of the American Medical Association* for June 12, 1954, indicates that filter cigarettes will be just as bad for the Buerger's disease patient as the ordinary cigarette. Dr. Irving Wright of New York told of a patient with Buerger's disease who had not smoked since 1940. So long as he did not smoke and followed treatment, he was free from symptoms. In 1954, impressed with the ads for the new filter-tip cigarettes, he began to smoke them and almost immediately his disease appeared again and soon he was faced with the prospect of gangrene in his toes. Says Dr. Wright, no one has ever found a tobacco that does not have an effect on the blood vessels. And it is believed that the dangerous element in tobacco may not be the nicotine at all, but may be something else, at least for persons who are sensitive to tobacco, as Buerger's disease patients appear to be.

In *Risk Appraisal,* published by the National Underwriter Company, we find some appalling statistics on smoking and health. The smoking of one cigarette by a person who inhales produces a 5 to 20 increase in pulse, a rise of 10 to 25 in blood pressure, a drop from 3 to 6 degrees Fahrenheit in the temperature of the fingers and toes. Twenty per cent of Buerger's disease patients have diabetes, too. Thirty-five per cent of them have hypertension or high blood pressure. There are many more males than females among the victims of this disease. And many more smokers than nonsmokers.

In one series of 1000 patients studied by one physician, every patient was a smoker. In another series of 948 cases in which the average age was 42, there were only 68 who did not smoke. In 401 of these incidentally, the disease became so bad that amputation eventually was necessary.

Until recently practically nothing could be done for the Buerger's disease patient. If he could not stop smoking, and sometimes even if he did, he was a candidate for amputation. Since the disease is a disorder of the blood vessels, it seemed logical to try vitamin E in its treatment. In the large file of material from the medical journals on the subject of vitamin E, we find that, sure enough, it has been used with success in treating Buerger's disease. An article in the *Medical Record* (Vol. 161, pp. 83-89, 1948), by A. B. Vogelsang, and the Shute brothers, tells us that symptoms of Buerger's disease have been relieved, as well as symptoms of other vascular conditions where better circulation of oxygen can improve disease conditions. These researchers found that the dose of vitamin E was extremely important and might be different for each individual. Small doses were not effective. In general, doses of about 500 milligrams were used to begin with; they were reduced to about 200 milligrams as a "maintenance dose" thereafter.

Dr. E. V. Shute in *Seminar,* Vol. 1, 1949, describes a series of 23 consecutive cases of Buerger's disease treated with vitamin E. Of these only 4 got no relief and two were doubtful. Seven patients were under treatment for a year or longer and all remained improved. In more recent medical literature we find an article by W. R. Cameron in the *Summary,* Vol. 3, 1951, describing 35 persons who had had Buerger's disease for an average of 6 years. They were treated with vitamin E and for 4 years the researchers kept in touch with them. Eight of these patients did not follow the directions. Of the others, 15 got good results, 5 got only fair results and 5 got poor results. Two received no benefit. Says Dr. Cameron, "thus alphatocopherol therapy is the best, safest and simplest treatment for Buerger's disease and deserves an intensive trial before other medications are used or before surgical measures are attempted."

The *International Record of Medicine* for July, 1951, reports on the use of vitamin E for Buerger's disease. Of 18 patients treated with vitamin E, 17 were cured, only one was not. It was found that the medication had to be continued indefinitely.

The *Journal of Bone and Joint Surgery,* Vol. 31B, 1949, has an article by A. M. Boyd, A. H. Ratcliffe, R. P. Jepson and G. W. H. James on 3 different kinds of arterial disease of which Buerger's disease is one. The authors conclude that alphatocopherol (vitamin E), 400 milligrams daily, is the only substance that has given consistently good results in treatment of these disorders. Of 72 patients, 27 were completely relieved and 32 were markedly improved. The consistency with which there is a lag period of 4 to 6 weeks before improvement was most striking. After a few months of treatment, there was obvious improvement in the appearance of the feet of the patients.

Advantages to the Use of Vitamin E

These are but a few of the many references given in medical literature on the treatment of Buerger's disease with vitamin E. Do these samples indicate that any and all cases of the disorder will respond to vitamin treatment? Not at all. They do show that in many cases it works. This is all that is expected of any treatment. The miracle drugs and all the various hormone, antibiotic and pain-killing treatments used by the medical profession today have no better record than this. Sometimes they work. Sometimes they don't. And most of them have serious aftereffects which means that the patient must be watched very closely to make sure that the cure is not worse than the disease. But there are no harmful aftereffects in the use of vitamin E, because it is a food substance. So its use is surely to be preferred to that of drugs. In addition, there are apparently no drugs that are the least bit effective in Buerger's disease! Two further notes on Buerger's disease that came to our attention: Dr. Julius Kaunitz of New York, addressing the American Medical Association convention on June 24, 1954, presented the theory that eating too much rye bread might possibly lead to Buerger's disease. Ergot, a poisonous fungus that grows on rye, might be responsible, he said, for the symptoms of Buerger's disease. Even though grain in this country is closely watched for evidence of ergot, it is conceivable that just enough of the fungus escapes detection so that there is a small but fairly constant amount of it in rye bread. This wouldn't affect you, of course, if you eat rye bread only occasionally. But if you are a confirmed eater of rye bread, eat a lot of it every day and eat no other kind of bread, perhaps you would do well to cut down. (Editor Rodale recommends removing all bread from the diet.) Dr. Kaunitz mentioned that Buerger's disease has a high incidence among the Jewish people of New York who are known to be heavy consumers of rye bread.

We do not deal in cures for diseases. We are interested in preventing disease. It seems to us that Buerger's disease is surely an outgrowth of our modern way of life. It seems completely possible that lack of vitamin E in the diet may be responsible for predisposing individuals to the disease. Smoking increases this susceptibility.

How then to prevent the disease? First, decide to stop smoking if you are dedicated to that habit. Then take vitamin E as part of your daily food supplements. In former days, before food was refined, we used to get enough vitamin E in our meals. Nowadays we have to watch our diets closely to make certain we are getting any at all. In addition, we should, all of us, take a protective, preventive amount of vitamin E each day —about 50 or 100 milligrams.

SECTION XIII

Cancer

CHAPTER 74

Vitamin B Deficiency and Cancer

MANY PEOPLE COMPLAIN about troubles with their mouths, tongue, lips, gums. They have burning sensations, they have ulcers, boils or patches of inflammation on their gums; white spots may have appeared on the gums or insides of cheeks, their tongues are smooth and shiny or swollen and deeply fissured, the corners of their mouths have cracks or sores.

Experts have found that many such symptoms are what they term "precancerous." This does not mean that cancer is caused by these disorders. It means simply that often the bodily condition that produces such disorders in the mouth may later produce cancer. It was thought for a long time that such conditions were caused by irritation of some kind. And it is believed that cancer is often the result of irritation superimposed on just the right combination of ill-health factors to make the body susceptible to cancer.

We can report some conclusive work which seems

to show that a deficiency in vitamin B is responsible for most such mouth disorders. People who suffer from them can take heart, for not only is there a good possibility that plenty of vitamin B will bring back good health, but the fear of cancer can be permanently disposed of. Such mouth conditions need not be "precancerous" if you get plenty of vitamin B.

"In most cases of intra-oral cancer, there are in addition to the primary lesions, definite degenerative changes in the oral mucous membranes which obviously have antedated the malignant growth. It has long been noted that such degenerative tissue changes are found in a majority of patients with mouth cancer, and, therefore, they are commonly referred to as precancerous," says Hayes Martin, M.D., and Everett Koop, M.D., in an article in the *American Journal of Surgery* for August, 1942. Here are the medical names for some of the changes they are talking about: leukoplakia, subacute or chronic inflammation, vascular injection, atrophy or hypertrophy of the papillae, erosion of the epithelium. Most of them can be produced by chronic forms of irritation—tobacco, venereal disease, badly fitting dentures and so forth.

It is well known, these authors say, that the B vitamins are important for mouth health. In studying 300 patients at Memorial Hospital, New York, they found that those who were suffering from mouth disorders, ranging all the way from the slightest irritation to advanced cancer of the mouth, were short on vitamin B. They found, too, that, in general, other symptoms of vitamin B deficiency accompanied the mouth symptoms in these patients. Depression and malnutrition went hand-in-hand with constipation and other digestive disorders. Interestingly enough, Drs. Martin and Koop mention fragility of fingernails as one of the most easily recognized symptoms of vitamin B deficiency. A tendency for nails to break easily, and ridges that extend lengthwise or horizontally are further indications of lack of vitamin B.

Some Actual Conditions

Here are some of the actual mouth conditions that prevailed: *glossodynia* (a burning sensation of the tongue); chronic inflammation of the mucous membrane lining of the mouth; ulceration of the tongue, cheeks or gums; atrophy and hypertrophy of the papillae of the tongue (this means a decrease or increase in the size of the little knobs on the surface of the tongue, so that the tongue may be partly or wholly bald); fissure folding (this is a condition in which the tongue has become too large and is compressed into folds which look like crevices or fissures in its surface); leukoplakia (consists of white spots on the inside of the mouth. Incidentally, our authors tell us that about 50 per cent of all men and about 10 per cent of all women over the age of 45 have some degree of leukoplakia); gingivitis (bleeding from the gums); salivary changes (the mouth becomes dry and the scanty saliva becomes sticky and thick); Plummer-Vinson disease (inflammation of the esophagus, anemia, inflammation of the tongue).

Since these are the visible changes in the lining of the mouth, our authors state that undoubtedly, farther along in the digestive tract where we cannot see them, similar disorders are prevalent. "The evidence is plain," they state, "for at least a tentative diagnosis of lack of vitamin B when an inflammatory oral mucosal lesion is associated with one or more of the following symptoms: malnutrition, mental depression, dermatoses

[492]

(skin trouble), nervousness, insomnia, constipation and irregularities of the fingernails."

Which of Us Is Deficient in Vitamin B?

What is a vitamin B deficiency? Can you pick one person out of a crowd and say that he is deficient in vitamin B and pick out another and say that he is not? According to our authors, "It would be impossible to separate a group of individuals into two definite classes, one with conclusive evidences of vitamin B deficiency and the other with no evidences whatsoever. No laboratory test has been devised which furnishes an accurate basis for this determination. For this reason, there is as yet no method of determining the absolute incidence of lack of vitamin B in mouth cancer or precancer. The proof of such dietary inadequacy is found in the fact that a large percentage of patients with mouth cancer do manifest one or more of the general and local abnormalities. And that these are almost always improved by administration of vitamin B."

Then, too, there is the complicating factor that people who start out with some mouth disorder generally end up with rather serious vitamin deficiencies as well as other forms of malnutrition for the simple reason that it is so hard for them to eat. In spite of any encouragement, they avoid most carefully those fresh raw foods which would contribute most to curing their deficiency—fruits and vegetables.

Drs. Martin and Koop took careful dietary surveys of hundreds of patients while they were collecting material for this article. It is, of course, difficult to find out exactly what people eat unless they are under constant and very close supervision. But the several

[493]

case histories they give in the article show extremely bad dietary habits. For instance, there was one woman who lived almost completely on gin. And, although she eventually died of "alcoholism," the doctors are quite sure that her main difficulty was a lack of vitamin B and she could have been saved, had she been given massive doses of the B vitamins.

Wide Survey Made by Physicians

Giving brewer's yeast as the best source of the B vitamins was done uniformly throughout the experimental period. And we mean large doses of brewer's yeast. The average dose was 3 tablespoons a day. In one case a man who was being treated for cancer of the tongue was given liver and yeast. Within two months he had gained a badly needed 25 pounds in weight. About a year and a half after treatment was begun he appeared to be losing ground even though he continued to take the yeast and to eat large quantities of vitamin-B-rich food. So the daily intake of yeast was increased to 8 tablespoons daily, "a dose which few patients can tolerate without marked nausea and diarrhea." There was tremendous improvement in his condition almost at once. From then on, so long as he maintained this enormous daily intake of yeast he remained healthy and the condition of his mouth remained good.

"These cases in which massive doses of vitamin B must be taken in order to maintain health can be explained on the basis of marked individual variations in ability, either to absorb or utilize ingested vitamins," say the authors. Among patients they studied whose diets contained apparently enough B vitamins to keep them in fairly good health, there were some who were definitely suffering from deficiency. Although their intake of B vitamins was not far below normal, their requirement was abnormally high. It is well to remember in this connection the theories of Dr. Roger Williams of the University of Texas, who believes that alcoholism is a disease of persons who require far more vitamin B than the average person and just don't get it, no matter how good their diet.

"Fad" Diets Actually Worsened Conditions

How did people fall into the practice of eating the diets that were notoriously bad? According to Drs. Martin and Koop some of these diets were prescribed by doctors for such diverse conditions as ulcer, gall bladder disease, obesity, colitis, and so forth. Some patients had blindly followed completely inadequate diets for many years, firmly believing that some disorder of theirs could be cured by "dieting." Instead, they had brought on a worse condition than the one they had started out to cure. In some cases, a deficient diet brought about such loss of appetite and interest in food that the patient progressively restricted his diet still further to "those substances most easily and cheaply obtained, mainly pure carbohydrates." For instance, there was a wealthy eccentric who ate only breakfast and then took beer and onions whenever he got hungry during the rest of the day. A woman voluntarily went on an "ulcer diet" along with her husband who actually had an ulcer. A beer salesman drank beer when hungry. A traveling salesman ate only sandwiches because he was afraid of dirty food in restaurants. A woman avoided pork, fruit and eggs because certain members of her family were allergic to these foods.

The most frequent underlying cause of an inadequate vitamin intake lies in personality factors such as peculiar dietary prejudices based on family customs.

Often deficient diets are encountered because of fear of overweight. "In most city dwellers," say our authors, "there is a tendency to eat at 'quick lunches' and drugstore counters, where green vegetables and fresh meats are replaced by carbohydrates in the form of sandwiches, ice cream, malted milk and pastry."

According to these researchers, there is little storage of excess vitamin B in the body and deficiency symptoms occur *within a few days* after withdrawal of the vitamin source. For this reason, correcting such a deficiency must be done on a daily basis. "We have found it advisable," they go on, "when using natural concentrates such as yeast and liver, to provide from 5 to 10 times the normal minimum requirement of thiamin and riboflavin or 30 to 45 grams (two to three tablespoons) daily of granular yeast. In exceptional cases the maximum relief cannot be obtained unless inordinately high therapeutic doses are consumed, as for instance, one of our patients who ingests about 240 grams (2 teacups) of brewer's yeast a day and who insists that unless this amount is taken, marked asthenia and mental depression occur."

It is noteworthy that these doctors do not give synthetic vitamins for treatment of vitamin B deficiency. They say, "In some instances the administration of a single fraction of the vitamin B complex (thiamin, riboflavin, niacin, etc.) may cause marked improvement, but combinations of the known fractions almost always give better results." Discussing the kind of yeast to take, they deplore the use of brewer's yeast *tablets* for, they say, it is almost impossible to get enough brewer's yeast for a good big dose when you take tablets. It would require about 70 ten-grain tablets to make up the equivalent of three tablespoons of yeast.

"It would be easier to impress both physicians and

[496]

the laity," say our authors, "if it could be maintained that there is one sole cause for cancer and precancer, and that there is one simple remedy which, taken in pill form, so many times a day for a few weeks, would effect a lasting cure and a preventive of the basic abnormality. *In order to relieve avitaminosis [deficiency in B], however, the mode of life must be permanently modified, that is, the intake of vitamins must be increased and maintained as long as the patient lives.* Such a permanent regime will, in many cases, become tedious since it is not supported by the emotional stimulus which accompanies a shorter, more intense course of therapy."

The italics are ours. We put them there because this seems to us to be the key sentence in all this discussion. There is no quick and easy way to good health. There is no pill you can take to relieve any physical condition or any vitamin deficiency. Being healthy is a way of life. And if you have allowed yourself to fall into a state of diet deficiency—and most of us have—you must make a permanent change in your way of life—nothing less than this will accomplish what you want. Vitamins are something you need every day and, if you would cure a deficiency, you must decide to take vitamin supplements permanently.

Drs. Martin and Koop tell us in their summary that degenerative changes are found in the lining of the mouth in most cases of mouth cancer. The most frequent reason for these changes is a deficiency in vitamin B. Most patients are already suffering from a marked deficiency when they go to their doctor. This is aggravated by the necessarily restricted diet during the painful stage of any mouth disorder. Supplementary vitamin therapy is one of the most important factors in the successful treatment of mouth cancer

[497]

or conditions that are called "precancerous." There is much evidence suggesting that the mouth symptoms are repeated farther down in the digestive tract, so it seems logical that what we say here about mouth cancer applies equally to stomach and intestinal cancer as well.

Remember We Need B Vitamins

Most of us are deficient in B vitamins. Many of us may need extremely large amounts of them to stay in good health. The evidence above illustrates well the reasons for taking brewer's yeast or some other purely natural food supplement rather than synthetic vitamins. Since Drs. Martin and Koop wrote their article, several more B vitamins have been discovered. They could not have been put into synthetic vitamin preparations at the time this article appeared, for their existence was unknown. But they were already in the brewer's yeast and the liver preparations, and these patients benefited from them, even though they had not been discovered.

Don't be afraid to take large quantities of brewer's yeast and other completely natural food supplements rich in B vitamins, like desiccated liver and wheat germ, especially if you have distressing symptoms in mouth or digestive tract. And eat a diet high in B vitamins, too. Meat, fish, eggs, wheat germ and fresh vegetables and fruits are the best source.

CHAPTER 75

B Vitamins and Cancer

THE TREATMENT for cancer developed by Dr. Max B. Gerson is described in an official statement of the American Cancer Society as being "essentially that of diet. The principal ingredients stressed are liver, vitamins and fresh vegetables and fruit juices." The statement concludes that the cancer society "has found no acceptable evidence that treatment with the Gerson method results in any objective benefit . . ."

We would like to call the attention of the cancer society to a recent paper by Dr. H. F. Kraybill, Ph.D., of the National Cancer Institute. Published in *Clinical Pharmacology and Therapeutics* (4, 1, January-February, 1963), this paper coming from our top agency involved in cancer research has marshaled considerable evidence that nutritional treatment is of value both preventively and therapeutically, and that there may be a great deal more to Dr. Gerson's theories than was thought possible ten years ago.

What is the Gerson theory? It was best stated by Dr. Gerson himself in his book *A Cancer Therapy,* currently being published by Groton Press. "Cancer is not a single cellular problem; it is an accumulation of numerous damaging factors combined in deteriorating the whole metabolism, after the liver has been progressively impaired in its function. Therefore, one has to separate two basic components in cancer: a general one and a local one. The general component is mostly a very slow, progressing, imperceptible symptom caused by poisoning of the liver and simultaneously an impairment of the whole intestinal tract, later producing appearances of vitally important consequences all over the body."

The Liver Is the Key

In other words, it is the liver and its health that Dr. Gerson considers the core of the body's ability to resist cancer, and it is the malfunctioning of the liver that he believes is responsible for the weakening of the body's defenses and the ability of cancer to take hold. He states that "the damage is done by a permanent daily poisoning brought about by our modern civilization. This starts with the soil which is denaturalized by artificial fertilizers and depletion, thus gradually reducing the top soil. In addition, the soil is poisoned by sprays with DDT and other poisons. As a consequence, our nutrition is damaged . . . Furthermore, the food substances are damaged as they are refined, bottled, bleached, powdered, frozen, smoked, salted, canned and colored with artificial coloring. Carrots are sold in cellophane bags after having been treated for better preservation. Other foods contain damaging preservatives; finally, cattle and chickens are fed or injected with stilbestrol to

[500]

accumulate more weight and be quickly ready for market."

Although the Sloan-Kettering Foundation has just begun to establish the fact that in a truly healthy person there is a cancer immunity and even the implantation of living, active cancer cells will quickly be overcome, this was something that Dr. Gerson knew and published in his book many years ago. He believed that the source of immunity was a healthfully functioning digestive tract, particularly the liver. And his diet was directed toward cleansing the liver of accumulated poisons and building its health through a proper selection of nutrients.

Even though Gerson was called "one of the most eminent medical geniuses in the history of medicine" by Dr. Albert Schweitzer, most of the medical profession, at least in the United States, considers that Gerson has been discredited. Yet if we are to judge by Dr. Kraybill's paper, some of today's cancer investigators may be engaged in rediscovering, slowly, methodically and painfully, just what Dr. Gerson was trying to tell them if they would only have listened.

Here are some of the discoveries that Dr. Kraybill has gathered together into his truly impressive paper:

Vitamin Value Documented

"Yeast is particularly effective [for the prevention of liver cancer] since the level of 15 per cent of it is almost completely protective, and any high quality protein diet and B vitamins, especially B_2, are defensive mechanisms in inhibiting formation of such neoplasms."

"According to Cramer, certain precancerous lesions of the gastric mucosa such as gastric polyps, atrophic gastric ulcer and chronic atrophic gastritis have been attributed to deficiencies in vitamin A, riboflavin, and

[501]

nicotinic acid. These lesions may advance into neoplasia in the presence of a carcinogen."

In the next paragraph, it is pointed out that it was necessary to deplete an experimental diet of thiamin and riboflavin in order to induce brain tumors with a chemical carcinogen.

"Perhaps the most interesting observations are those of Japanese and American investigators on liver neoplasia in which riboflavin-rich diets inhibited tumor formation. This preponderance of evidence on hepatomas associated with low B vitamin diets can probably account for the high tumor incidence among the Bantus and certain Asiatic groups.

"Hepatic tumors have also been reported to occur in rats when a choline-deficient diet was administered to a strain of rats having a high choline requirement. In general, the injury of liver cells resulting from a nutrient deficiency may impair normal growth of cells, and carcinogens may then readily induce hepatomatous nodules."

It will be noted that the nutrients pointed out by Dr. Kraybill as having a cancer-preventive effect are all foods that are directly concerned with the health of the liver. Thiamin, riboflavin and choline are all used principally in the liver, both for digestive functions and detoxification of the blood. When they are deficient, not only can the liver not function properly but it also deteriorates. Yeast, of course, is one of our most potent sources of the B complex vitamins. And it may also be presumed that there are other, still undiscovered food elements that are also necessary to liver health and may be deficient in many diets. That is perhaps why Dr. Gerson found that he got his best results by directly feeding raw liver, containing known and unknown necessary liver nutrients, to his patients.

Additives Incriminated

When it comes to identifying those elements in food that may or may not be responsible for causing cancer, Dr. Kraybill again sounds remarkably like Dr. Gerson. He points out that "A consideration of food intake in carcinogenesis is not restricted to nutrition per se but must also include additives, contaminants, or processing degradation products which may play a more important role in tumor induction." And he then goes right down the list from heated or processed fats to spices, plastics, petroleum by-products and food colors and flavor additives as established or probable causes of cancer. These are all materials known to have toxic effects on the liver; and they are all materials that Dr. Gerson attempted to keep out of the diets of his patients.

Dr. Kraybill cites 75 references, no less, all the authors of which have worked, established, and published these facts for which Dr. Gerson only ten years ago was being called a quack and a faddist.

We find it especially interesting that while Dr. Kraybill does not cite Dr. Gerson and nowhere refers to the Gerson conclusion that the liver is the key organ in the body's resistance to cancer, just about all of his material deals with food elements that have a direct connection with liver health. The pesticides, food preservatives and colors, and the heated fats that occur in cooking all have their toxic effects on the liver and quite conceivably may gradually diminish the body's resistance to cancer in this manner.

Certainly the 75 studies on which Dr. Kraybill based his paper as well as the pioneering work of Dr. Max Gerson give us every reason to believe that if we can keep our livers in good health, we are greatly improv-

[503]

ing our chances of being able to resist and overcome any incipient cancer. It is the belief of *Prevention* that the very best food for liver health is liver itself. Liver, particularly when it has not been altered in any way by cooking, obviously would contain all those nutrient elements that are essential to liver function. These include a rich supply of the B complex vitamins, and several extremely important mineral elements such as phosphorus and magnesium. In desiccated liver, which is vacuum dried at comparatively low temperatures, all these elements are retained fully. And this is why desiccated liver is one of the most valuable food supplements that can be included regularly in anybody's diet.

Yet when you get right down to it, the liver has so many functions in relation to health, from digestion to purification of the blood stream and addition to the blood of various food elements as they are required, that there is no nutrient that does not have some importance to the living, functioning liver. Brewer's yeast, a rich source of vitamin B and high grade protein, is certainly of enormous value. So are the A and D vitamins and there is recent evidence that the antioxidant functions of vitamins C and E are equally important.

CHAPTER 76

Is Vitamin C Deficiency Related to Cancer?

AN ARTICLE on the possible relationship between a deficiency in vitamin C and susceptibility to cancer, written by W. J. McCormick, M.D., appeared in *Archives of Pediatrics,* October, 1954. Now Dr. McCormick has written another article in the same magazine, enlarged on his theory and brought it up to date with new research.

It is such a simple and easily understood theory that we marvel that it has not achieved more prominence among medical researchers. Perhaps it is too simple. Perhaps the solution to our cancer problem by a change in diet and environment that would bring all of us ample supplies of vitamin C is just such a simple everyday thing that the majority of our learned researchers will not even consider it.

Dr. McCormick tells us that the injury that precedes cancer (whether it is an actual physical injury or a chemical injury) produces a certain condition result-

[505]

ing in the formation of what some researchers call "pseudo-elastic tissue." He quotes Dr. T. Gillman and colleagues, writing in the *British Journal of Cancer* (Vol. 9, pp. 272-283, 1955), as saying that such tissue is regularly encountered in sites of chronic injury to connective tissue in the skin as well as in other parts of the body—arteries and gall bladder, for example.

This tissue, which is preceded by and associated with an invasion of dermal cells by epidermal cells, can consistently be produced in human beings who have injuries. The British researchers go on to say, "It is shown that similar elastotic degeneration of collagen [tissue] is invariably present in the dermis in many degenerative skin conditions which may and frequently do become precancerous." They believe that such a degeneration of this layer of cells may play an important part in causing cancer.

Dr. McCormick then quotes a researcher who wrote in 1908 (long before vitamin C was discovered) that precancerous tissues always show a loss of connective tissue. The edges of the cells in the epithelium (the lining of all parts of the body) are frayed. Yellow elastic tissue disappears. *And it is in this de-elasticized area where connective tissue has disappeared that the first beginnings of cancer occur.*

How Vitamin C Protects Intercellular Cement

We know that the cement holding cells together can be manufactured only if vitamin C is present in ample quantity. This cement becomes watery in an individual suffering from scurvy which is the disease of vitamin C deficiency. The protein contained normally in this cement disappears into the blood. In cancer patients, recent tests have shown that there is an increase of this particular protein in the blood. When vitamin C is given, almost immediately the intercellular cement begins to reform in its normal consistency.

More evidence. Several researchers have found that there is a pronounced deficiency of vitamin C in the blood of cancer patients, compared to that of healthy persons. It has been found that guinea pigs suffering from scurvy and given just enough vitamin C to be kept alive are far more susceptible to cancer and get it sooner than healthy guinea pigs.

Dr. McCormick believes that all this evidence shows definitely that the degree of malignancy of an illness is determined inversely by the degree of connective tissue resistance. And this, in turn, is dependent on the adequacy of vitamin C intake. In other words, the less resistant the connective tissue is, the more serious the trouble is likely to be. And lack of vitamin C is perhaps the basic cause of lack of resistance.

Hard Cancer Spreads Slowly

To illustrate this point, he tells us that the scirrhus or hard cancer of the breast is slow to metastasize or spread throughout the body. It may remain just as it is, completely inactive for years. On the other hand, soft cancer of the breast is "extremely invasive." That is, it spreads rapidly to other parts of the body. In the former there is plenty of connective tissue which binds the cells together more effectively. In the second kind of cancer, mainly only cells and the connective tissue is lacking.

It may be, says Dr. McCormick, that cancer cells, which are known to move around in the body, may do so because of an inherent propensity which becomes manifest solely because they have lost their connective

[507]

tissue anchorage as a direct result of vitamin C deficiency. The teeth become loose in an individual suffering from scurvy. This is because the cementing substance holding them in has liquefied because there is not enough vitamin C to keep this cementing substance in good repair.

So cancer may not be a "malignant" disease, striking its victims like a bolt of lightning out of the blue, but rather, says Dr. McCormick, it may be an ailment that we cultivate all during our lifetime by our habits.

Preventing Cancer Is the Important Thing

We should, then, direct our attention to preventing the cause of cellular disarrangement—that is, the breakdown of connective tissue. What about sores or fissures that fail to heal? What about unusual and easily produced hemorrhages—not necessarily with visible blood as in a nosebleed, but the bruises so many of us take for granted?

Dr. McCormick tells us he has found that fully 90 per cent of our adult female population show bruises or "black and blue marks," yet little or nothing is ever done about it. No one should ever show bruises unless he is in an extremely serious accident. The bumps and knocks we get in everyday living should never produce bruises. They are as easy to prevent as the nearest vitamin C tablet and a glass of water.

Easy bruising is one of the earliest—hence one of the most important—symptoms of vitamin C deficiency. And, make no mistake about it, bruising is a serious symptom. As Dr. McCormick has suggested, it may be your first and most valuable warning of a predisposition to cancer.

Dr. McCormick believes that one reason we moderns are so likely to be deficient in vitamin C is the almost universal habit of smoking. Smoking destroys or neutralizes to a large extent what little vitamin C is taken in food. The smoking of one cigarette, as ordinarily inhaled, tends to neutralize in the body about 25 milligrams of vitamin C, or the vitamin C content of an average orange. This fact alone would do much to explain the terrible increase in lung cancer in recent years.

But poisons other than nicotine are counteracted by vitamin C in the body. And the vitamin C is used up in the process. We know of many. Could it be that all physical and chemical carcinogens (causes of cancer) may act by using up the body's supply of vitamin C, thereby destroying the connective tissue and leading the way to cancer that spreads rapidly through the body?

Who Is Susceptible to Cancer?

The Sloan-Kettering Institute conducted a test on live, virulent cancer cells. These were transplanted under the skin of the forearm of 15 advanced cancer cases. In every case the transplanted cancer tissues grew vigorously and spread for from 6 weeks to 6 months before they were removed by surgery. On the other hand, the same cells transplanted to the forearms of normally healthy and cancer-free volunteers, were destroyed by an overwhelming defense reaction on the part of these individuals.

No study was made, unfortunately, of the nutritional background or living habits of the subjects. Such a study would certainly have thrown a lot of light on the subject of susceptibility to cancer. However, the test surely shows that cancer is a disease of the whole body. Therefore, it seems reasonable to suppose that it can be prevented by keeping the body healthy.

[509]

Vitamin Status Study Advised for Middle-Aged

Dr. McCormick suggests that all persons of middle age or over should have a study made of their vitamin C status. Your doctor should be able to do it.

Or, as a general overall test, ask yourself these questions: Do your gums bleed or do you have some loose teeth? Do you bruise easily? Do you get colds easily? Do open sores heal slowly? Are you exposed to tobacco regularly, or smoke, or fumes of some materials like solvents, fresh paint, etc.? If you answer yes to any of these questions, better get concerned about your vitamin C status. Now, before there is any possible chance of a serious deficiency that might mean a predisposition to cancer.

A natural vitamin C food supplement is your best assurance that you won't be short. In addition, concentrate on getting as many fresh raw foods as possible in your diet every day.

SECTION XIV

Colds

CHAPTER 77

Can Vitamin A Help Prevent Infection?

WHEN VITAMIN research was younger than it is today, a great deal of interest was aroused by the discovery that animals in a state of vitamin A deficiency were more susceptible to infections than animals on a well-rounded diet. A whole series of experiments followed, to determine just how and why this was true. An Italian physician, Di Salvatore Princi wrote in *Bollettino della Societa Italiana di Biologia Sperimentale,* July, 1942, on the action of vitamin A on the influenza germ. Dr. Princi worked with two groups of mice on an identical diet, except that one group obtained, in addition, a daily quantity of a vitamin A preparation. All the mice were injected with a lethal dose of influenza germs. All the animals in both groups died, but those who had received the vitamin A survived an average of 89.9 hours while those who were deficient in vitamin A survived only 69.3 hours, showing that the vitamin resulted in additional disease resistance.

[511]

Dr. Torsten Lindquist in the German medical publication *Klinische Wochenschrift,* September, 1937, announced the results of the action of vitamin A in 45 cases of croupous and bronchial pneumonia. Dr. Lindquist found that the vitamin A content of the blood was drastically lowered during even the first five days of illness. When the patient began to convalesce, the level of vitamin A rose rapidly even though no additional vitamin A was added to the diet. One week after the crisis of the disease passed, the level of vitamin A in the blood was 3 times as high as before the crisis. This evidence appears to indicate that the vitamin A was engaged in combating the infection, in some way or other, until the crisis passed and hence was used up rapidly, restoring itself when the patient began to get well.

Writing in *Romana Medicala,* two Romanian physicians, D. Hagiescu, M.D., and Gh. Bazan, M.D., discuss the use of vitamin A and D in pulmonary tuberculosis. We are encouraged by the fact that they used the two vitamins, rather than just one, for, as you know, we believe that all of the vitamins are necessary for health and that any one of them functions best when the others are also present. These two researchers remind us of the possible reasons for vitamin A deficiency —not enough food which contains this vitamin; an infectious disease which uses up the vitamin A, thus bringing about a deficiency; defective absorption of the vitamin or defective assimilation in the intestines because of liver trouble or digestive disorders.

They also point out that calcium is important for the cure or prevention of many diseases and is especially important in the treatment of tuberculosis patients. As vitamin D is necessary for the assimilation of calcium, these doctors decided to administer to the

[512]

tuberculosis patients both vitamin A and D together to see what results they would obtain. The vitamins were not used as a "cure" for the disease. Other regular treatment was going on at the same time and the vitamins were given simply to see what additional benefits might be noticed. As a special precaution, the vitamins were injected rather than taken by mouth, for many of the patients suffered from indigestion and it was feared that this might interfere with proper absorption of the vitamins.

The results were:

1. All patients tolerated the injections perfectly.
2. The weight of all patients showed an increase, which continued after the injections were stopped.
3. Appetite increased in all patients.
4. Blood count improved in some patients.
5. Rate of sedimentation of blood improved.
6. In children even greater improvement was noted than in adults.

The authors believe this was because of the greater vitality and powers of resistance of children in general. The physicians also used A and D together with excellent results in cases of anemia, loss of appetite and malnutrition.

Vitamin A and Disease-Resistant Powers

An article by H. J. Jusatz, M.D., in the German medical publication *Zeitschrift fur Immunitatsforschung und experimentelle Therapie,* August 4, 1937, describes the results of feeding animals on a vitamin A deficient diet, then testing their blood to determine its power to form antibodies—that is, its power to fight off the germs of infectious diseases. It was found

[513]

that after a lengthy period of feeding the deficient diet, the germ-inhibiting power of the animals' blood became extinct. They could no longer resist disease, but would become ready prey for any germ that came along. Vitamin A was then added to their diet over an extended period of time, and the tests were made again. There was no improvement in the formation of antibodies. Vitamin D in small amounts was then given with a resulting increase in the germ-inhibiting index of the blood. But when the vitamin D dose was increased to such an extent that the animals were receiving an overdose, the blood immediately reacted by a decreasing number of antibodies. This author concludes, then, that neither vitamin A or D has the power of preventing infection by increasing the disease-fighting bodies of the blood.

From summarizing all these various articles, it seems we are safe in concluding that vitamin A and to some extent vitamin D make the body more resistant to disease. But they do not accomplish this by changing the character of the blood. How then do they work?

How Vitamin A Prevents Infection

Curiously enough, we found what appears to be the most logical and reasonable interpretation and solution in—of all places—*Veterinary Medicine* for September, 1944. J. Lavere Davidson, Lt. Col. V. C., tells us how he believes vitamin A works in the human body to prevent infection. Of course, the vitamin does not itself kill germs (cold, flu or distemper germs, for example), says Davidson. Instead, "by direct action vitamin A preserves the normal physiological functions and anatomical structure of the mucous membranes and also aids in the regeneration and restoration of these membranes in the event they become injured or de-

[514]

stroyed." The surface of the normal mouth, nose and bronchial membrane is covered with cilia, which look under a microscope like tiny hairs, constantly in motion, waving in one direction. With this waving motion the cilia sweep foreign matter, including germs, toward the pharynx where it can be expectorated or swallowed. In addition, these various mucous membranes secrete a substance called lysobyme which is powerful against bacteria. In an individual who is not getting, or absorbing, enough vitamin A, a change takes place in the mucous membrane. The cells with cilia gradually disappear and are replaced by scaly, hard cells which do not have cilia. The substances secreted by the membranes are cut off and the dryness increases. So this individual now has two counts against him—the cilia are no longer wafting germs out of his respiratory passages and the antiseptic secretions of his nose and throat are no longer functioning. When the germ comes along, there is no defense against it.

Hence, says Lt. Col. Davidson, the action of vitamin A against colds is an indirect one. This vitamin preserves the strength and health of the cells of the mucous membranes. It also rejuvenates and replenishes these cells when they have been destroyed or injured by attacks of germs. In children there is a twofold demand for vitamin A—they need it for growing and they need it to safeguard the health of their tissues. Might not a deficiency of vitamin A be the reason for so many colds among school children? Lacking the vitamin A which they use up in their growing process, they do not take even the few precautions adults take against sudden chilling, drafts, dry air in overheated rooms and other factors which affect the mucous membranes of the respiratory passages.

A survey conducted among the school children of

[515]

New York City revealed that slight vitamin A deficiency was the most common diet deficiency found among all the children.

Recommendations For a Cold-Free Winter

Our conclusions and recommendations, then, are as follows:

1. Vitamin A is protective against infections—not directly by killing off the disease germs, but indirectly by providing for the health of the mucous membranes which the germs attack. Ample amounts of vitamin A should be provided in one's diet and, in addition, one should make certain that the supply of vitamin A is not being lost through lack of assimilation due to digestive disorders.

2. Since the evidence is positive and emphatic showing that vitamin A preserves the health of the mucous membranes, do not wait until you have a cold or an attack of grippe before making sure of your vitamin A supply. By this time the susceptible tissues of your nose and throat will be weakened and much more likely to succumb to a secondary, or even chronic, infection. Begin now to build up your store of vitamin A against the rigors of the cold weather ahead. Remember that food containing vitamin A (greens, sweet potatoes and so forth) contains much less vitamin A in the winter than in the spring and summer, for it has lost the vitamin in storage. So count on using food supplements of natural vitamin A in addition to the vitamin A foods you eat at every day's meals.

3. Some foods containing large amounts of vitamin A are: carrots, beet greens, cantaloupe, collards, dandelion greens, whole eggs, endive, kale, lettuce, fresh calf and beef liver, mustard greens, parsley, alfalfa leaf meal,

dried peaches, green peppers, spinach, winter squash, sweet potatoes, tomato juice, turnip greens, watercress and, of course, fish liver oils, which contain many times more vitamin A than any other food. In general, you can be guided by the yellow color of foods. This yellow comes from carotene which changes to vitamin A after it is eaten. So it's best to include at least one yellow vegetable in each day's menu, along with plenty of greens and eggs.

4. In spite of the best intentions, however, it is often impossible especially during winter months to obtain enough vitamin A. This is why we believe that adults and children alike should use natural vitamin A as a food supplement every day. Natural vitamin A is easiest to obtain in fish liver oil capsules, which also contain vitamin D, another vitamin that is scarce in winter when the sun's rays are short. As you have seen from the facts above, we are just beginning to realize how important the whole family of vitamins is to the proper functioning of any one of them. In treating the tuberculous patients the doctors used vitamin D along with vitamin A. Other researchers have found that vitamin C is also important for the proper use of vitamin A in the body.

So we recommend that the very best preventive of sniffles, colds, grippe and other troublesome respiratory infections during the winter months is to begin now to eat a diet ample in all the vitamins, and to supplement this diet with fish liver oil capsules for vitamins A and D, brewer's yeast for vitamin B, desiccated liver for vitamins A and B, rose hip powder for vitamins A and C and wheat germ oil for vitamin E.

[517]

CHAPTER 78

Vitamin B and Colds

VITAMIN B HAS BEEN shown to be effective against invading germs. Dr. A. E. Axelrod of Western Reserve University, speaking at a meeting of the National Vitamin Foundation on April 4, 1952, described an experiment in which he deprived rats of 3 of the B vitamins, and found that the animals were severely impaired in their ability to build up antibodies with which to fight disease. Another experiment reported at the same meeting involved human beings.

Young men, on an ordinary diet, were immersed in cold water for 8 minutes, and this stress, although brief, produced chemical changes in the blood and urine, as well as in the temperature, blood pressure and heart rate. There was a significant increase in two substances in the blood—the granular red blood cells and the circulating white blood cells, which are the disease-germ fighters of the body.

Then, for 6 weeks, the men were built up with large

doses of a member of the vitamin B group and again given the cold-water experience. Tests identical with the former showed that the changes in the blood and urinary components were less than before, and that this occurred because the vitamins had strengthened the effectiveness with which the adrenal glands produced various hormones, possibly including cortisone. These adrenal outpourings help the body to overcome physical strains and thus the B vitamins increase the bodily capacity for resistance.

Two articles from the *Proceedings of the Society of Experimental Biology and Medicine* (Vol. 67, 1948, and Vol. 62, 1946), describe experiments on animals made deficient in pyridoxine, thiamin and biotin—all B vitamins. In all cases, the rats who were deficient in the vitamins were able to produce fewer antibodies in their blood, for fighting off germs.

Experiments with Multiple Deficiencies

Finally, let us examine an article in the *Journal of Laboratory and Clinical Medicine,* Vol. 30, 1945, in which L. J. Berry, J. Davis and T. D. Spies discuss the influence of the B vitamins on the resistance of rats to infection. These researchers tell us that "single vitamin deficiency studies are important in elucidating the metabolic function of the vitamins, but single deficiencies seldom occur naturally." That is, in terms of human nutrition, a person who suffers from a lack of one B vitamin is certain to lack the others, too, for they occur mostly in the same foods. And they react with one another in the body. Someone who lacks vitamin B will probably lack vitamin C as well. If a person does not get enough vitamin A in his food, he almost certainly will not get enough of the other fat-soluble vitamins—D and E—for they occur in many of the same foods.

In their experiment, these nutritionists decided to place one group of rats on the diet commonly eaten by many of the patients who visited their clinic in Birmingham, Alabama. They divided the rats into 10 groups— two of which received only the basic diet as eaten by families in the neighborhood. Two other groups received the basic diet plus casein (a protein). Two other groups received the basic diet plus casein and minerals. Two other groups ate the basic diet plus casein and B vitamins. The final two groups received the basic diet plus casein, minerals and B vitamins.

The basic diet consisted of corn meal, white flour, pork fat and cane sugar. Yes, this was the diet the researchers had discovered their clinic patients were eating every day. The animals were permitted to remain on the diets for two months before they were checked. The pictures taken at that time indicate more clearly than any words what condition the rats were in by then. Those on the basic diet were small, scrawny, weak. Their coats were rough and ugly. As the various elements were added to diets, the appearance of the rats improved. The final picture shows a handsome, sleek, healthy-looking rat who was, of course, eating the minerals, vitamins and proteins, as well as the basic diet.

Laboratory tests showed that the leucocytes (disease-fighting blood corpuscles) *decreased steadily in the rats on the deficient diets.* As the diets became progressively better, the number of leucocytes increased, and the total number of leucocytes was normal only in the rats on the best diets. "These studies support the working hypothesis that resistance to bacterial invasion may be depressed by inadequate nutrition," say these investigators. "Their importance is enhanced by the fact that the animals were eating the same diet that gives rise to the mixed deficiencies seen in patients in the clinic. . . . Therefore, in mixed deficiencies, the importance of restoring the organism to a balanced nutritional regime becomes apparent if that organism is to be able to defend itself against the onslaughts of bacterial invasion."

Now how can we use the information from these experiments to prevent colds? To us they seem to indicate that an abundance of vitamin B in the diet, as well as vitamins A and C, will help the body's defenses against germs. So, when you feel a cold coming on, what should you do—go to your doctor and ask for an injection? We think not. We believe you should use vitamin B, along with other vitamins, every day, as protection, so that you simply do not contract colds.

Your diet should include the following: meat or fish every day (organ meats like liver at least once a week), fresh vegetables and fruits in abundance, especially during the winter (and be sure to include green leafy vegetables and yellow vegetables every day). Omit all foods made from white flour or white sugar, for they rob your body of B vitamins. And finally, just to make certain, take desiccated liver and/or brewer's yeast every day for B vitamins. It's simple, really, to adjust your diet along these lines—and inexpensive, too.

CHAPTER 79

Vitamin C and Colds

COLD WEATHER MAY mean you need more vitamin C! Yes, it's true, at any rate for guinea pigs, who are the only creatures, aside from apes and human beings, who cannot manufacture their own vitamin C inside their bodies. Jolliffe, Tisdall and Cannon, in their monumental book, *Clinical Nutrition* (Paul B. Hoeber, Incorporated, 1950), tell us that rats exposed to cold weather develop more vitamin C inside their bodies to protect them from this stress of cold. Those rats who for some reason cannot produce the required amount of vitamin C may begin to show a decrease of vitamin C in their tissues, which may indicate that the cold actually uses up their store of vitamin C. Guinea pigs, who, like man, cannot make their own vitamin C, must depend on an increased intake in their food if they are to be able to survive cold weather. The lower the temperature, the more vitamin C is required.

An amount of vitamin C that is perfectly adequate

for a guinea pig at room temperature is reported to be completely inadequate at a temperature of freezing or 32 degrees Fahrenheit. The small animals can adapt themselves to cold and manage to live healthfully only if their supply of vitamin C is increased. In studying the guinea pigs, it was found that this vitamin C supply was in the tissues of the bodies, especially the adrenal glands, of those which managed to survive. And when their supply of vitamin C was discontinued, those who had taken a large supply of the vitamin previously were found to survive longer than those who had not.

In our file on colds we found a letter from the *British Medical Journal,* April 21, 1951, written by John M. Fletcher and Isabel C. Fletcher, expressing surprise that more material does not appear in medical journals on the potency of vitamin C in protecting against cold germs. These two physicians state that, in their own practice, they have found vitamin C an excellent preventive of colds. Perhaps, they say, the general disregard of the vitamin as a cold preventive results from the difficulty among the experts in reaching agreements as to what actually is the daily requirement of vitamin C. With adults, they say, the disease of scurvy will occur when the adult is getting less than 10 milligrams of vitamin C daily. But, they continue, this represents far less than "saturation level." By this they mean that, to soak all the tissues of the body in vitamin C, a much larger amount than 10 milligrams a day is necessary. In cases of fever or hard physical exertion, the body uses up vitamin C much faster than usual. So it is not ever possible to set one figure as the absolute daily requirement for all people under all circumstances.

The Fletchers go on to tell of a number of experiments in Holland, Germany and Australia in which colds were prevented by the administration of vitamin

[523]

C. In the German experiment, there was a marked decrease in illness over a period of 8 months among factory workers given 100 to 300 milligrams of vitamin C daily, a benefit not found when they were given 20 to 50 milligrams. N. W. Markwell, writing in the *Medical Journal of Australia* (Vol. 2, p. 777, 1947), describes giving vitamin C in cases where cold symptoms have just begun to appear: the colds were frequently, but not always, dispersed within a few hours and the aftereffects and complications which often accompany common colds were nonexistent. The Fletchers conclude: "We believe that, unlike the outcome of the antihistamine trials, the results may show considerable benefits can arise from ascorbic acid (vitamin C) treatment given in sufficient quantities at the right time."

Cowan, Diehl and Baker, writing in the *Journal of the American Medical Association,* Vol. 120, 1942, describe their giving vitamin C to ward off colds. One group of people took 200 milligrams of the vitamin every day. The others took no additional vitamin C but depended on what was in their food. The first group averaged 1.9 colds a year and the second group averaged 2.2 colds.

In the *British Medical Journal* (Vol. 2, p. 617, 1942), Drs. A. J. Glazebrook and S. J. Thompson report an experiment in an institution in England caring for boys. At this institution, the handling of food—that is, the way it was stored, prepared, served and so forth—had resulted in a vitamin C intake of 15 milligrams per boy per day—just barely enough to prevent symptoms of scurvy. Part of the boys were given vitamin C for 6 months. The other boys went on eating their regular diet. During the brief period of 6 months, there was no appreciable difference in the incidence of colds in the two groups, *but* the boys who had the vitamin spent only an average of 2½ days in the infirmary, whereas those who had received no vitamin C spent an average of 5 days being sick. So the additional vitamin C, even for this brief period, apparently strengthened the children's resistance to germs so much that they were able to throw off the effects in half the time it took the untreated children.

There is a very good physiological basis for the use of vitamin C to prevent infectious diseases such as colds. It acts to maintain the strength of the capillary walls, and these tiny blood vessels, when damaged, are the portals through which colds can enter the system. If they become weakened at the same time infection is in the air, your chances of contracting a cold are very good, says I. J. Sobel, M.D., in the *Journal of the Medical Society of New Jersey* (October, 1959).

In his article he describes the action of these infectious organisms which can and do release enzymes that weaken the all-important capillary walls. Once these have been penetrated, it is easy to see how the virus is passed on to other parts of the body as the blood circulates. The capillaries might be described as many tiny little cross-pipes leading off from the main vessels to bring blood to and from body tissues at the extremities. The proper functioning of these capillaries has been shown to depend upon the mucous cement substance which coats the pores of the capillary walls.

This substance or covering which protects the capillary walls requires vitamin C and the bioflavonoids in its manufacture by the body. The fortification the body builds against colds depends largely on its supply of vitamin C which can be called upon to manufacture more of this vital element.

In his *Journal* article, Dr. Sobel describes further how he tested the value of vitamin C and the bioflavonoids in relation to their effect on colds. He treated 176 patients by giving them 400 milligrams of the bioflavonoids and 400 milligrams of vitamin C every four hours. Of the 176 cases, "160 responded promptly. As a rule a complete abatement of symptoms occurred in 24 to 72 hours in most of those cases apparently uncomplicated by bacterial involvement . . . the overall response obtained from the bioflavonoid therapy in this series of 176 cases gave us a definite impression of a salutary effect."

Bioflavonoids Plus

Dr. Sobel's next effort was directed toward testing the protective or preventive effects of the bioflavonoids: 62 patients were given 400 milligram capsules of bioflavonoids twice daily for from one to two years. These 62 patients were selected for the study because of a past history of susceptibility to colds and influenza. Twenty-two of the patients did not have a single attack of a common cold or influenza while on this preventive therapy. Of the remaining 40, each had but one cold, "which was very mild and subsided within two or three days." While the colds these people experienced previously had been of long duration and frequent occurrence, the few colds that did develop after the therapy were so mild that they did not interfere with daily activities.

Vitamin C and Other Infections

Discussing vitamin C in relation to infections, Rhinehart, Connor and Mettier, in *International Clinician* (Vol. 2, 1937), and the *Journal of Experimental Medicine* (Vol. 59, 1934), tell us they found that guinea pigs suffering from scurvy (vitamin C deficiency), who were infected with a streptococcus germ, developed a condition similar to rheumatic fever and rheumatoid arthritis in human beings. They suggest that a "subclinical" degree of scurvy may make up the rheumatic tendency which, with an added factor of infection, causes the development of rheumatic fever. This means, simply, that infections develop more readily in animals (and why not also in persons?) who lack vitamin C—not to the extent of producing scurvy, but just to the extent that most of us lack it—a "subclinical deficiency."

It has been found that diphtheria susceptibility is greater in guinea pigs who lack vitamin C. And children with scurvy are more susceptible to diphtheria. Lawrynowicz, in the *Journal de Physiologie et de Pathologie Génerale* (Vol. 29, 1931), suggests the scurvy may so reduce the resistance that a diphtheria carrier may become the victim of the bacteria which it previously carried without any ill effects.

Vitamin C—A "Super-Antibiotic"

An experiment in a tuberculosis sanitarium showed the potency of even small amounts of the vitamin against tuberculosis symptoms. The patients were grouped in pairs. One patient was given a daily orange, while his control, in the other group, received a pastry. It seemed that the addition of vitamin C, even in such small amounts, assisted in healing the tuberculosis symptoms.

S. W. Clausen, writing in the *Physiological Review* (Vol. 14, 1934), throws light on the subject from the point of view of natural products supplying the vitamin. In testing guinea pigs, several researchers have found that an abundance of fresh green fodder, which contains, of course, natural vitamin C, has protected against infections. In a study of 400 animals, one scientist (Wamoscher in *Zeitschrift fur Hygiene und Infek-*

[527]

tionskrankheiten, Vol. 107, 1937) showed that subacute scurvy—that is just a slight case of scurvy—predisposes to spontaneous pneumonia. Cure sometimes followed the administration of vitamin C in orange juice.

F. R. Klenner, M.D., of Reidsville, North Carolina, has used vitamin C successfully in the treatment of many serious diseases. He describes his point of view in a paper presented before the Annual Meeting of the Tri-State Medical Association of the Carolinas and Virginia, February 19 and 20, 1951. He compares the action of vitamin C with the antibiotics. "It has been reported," he says, "that one of the mold-derived drugs [antibiotics] is a super-vitamin. Conversely, we argue that vitamin C, besides being an essential vitamin, is a super-antibiotic." Dr. Klenner believes that it is the capacity of the vitamin as an aid to oxidation that makes it valuable against germs. Apparently it unites with the toxin or virus in the body.

He describes the case of a patient with chills, fever and head cold for 14 days and severe headache for 3 days. She had been given sulfa, penicillin and streptomycin without effect. Vitamin C injections were given. Within 72 hours, she was "clinically well of her pneumonia." In 3 other cases of pulmonary virus infection, results were equally good, using vitamin C injections.

In a person suffering from a virus infection, says Dr. Klenner, vitamin C is not only absent from the urine, but is also missing from the blood. So it seems that, as the infection gets worse, the patient's need for vitamin C becomes greater, for his body tissues are depleted and what vitamin C he obtains from his food is rapidly used up in fighting against the virus. This is why Dr. Klenner gives massive doses of the vitamin in cases of serious illness. "Hippocrates declared the highest duty

[528]

of medicine to be to get the patient well. He further declared that, of several remedies, physicians should choose the least sensational. Vitamin C would seem to meet both these requirements," says Dr. Klenner.

Why We Suffer from Colds

Perhaps many of us suffer from frequent colds for two reasons: first, we are not careful enough to choose foods that contain vitamin C and second, we may not know how to preserve the vitamin C in foods until the time we eat them. Vitamin C is the most perishable vitamin there is. It is lost when foods are stored or cooked. It seeps away into the water when foods are soaked.

So choose vitamin C rich foods year-round. In general, this means fresh fruits and vegetables. In the wintertime especially, make sure of enough vitamin C by taking rose hips or one of the other natural vitamin C food supplements. If you should feel the symptoms of a cold coming on, double or triple the amount of natural vitamin C you take daily. It can't possibly harm you. Any excess which your body does not need will be excreted harmlessly.

CHAPTER 80

Vitamins and Minerals, and Constipation

BRAN RELIEVES CONSTIPATION, not alone because of the large amount of cellulose it contains, but mostly because it is a rich source of B vitamins. Treating alcoholic neuritis with B vitamins has resulted in regularizing the intestines. Giving rice bran or rice polishings has relieved constipation—again mostly because of the B vitamins.

G. Spiegel, M.D., *La Clinique,* Paris, March, 1939

* * *

In the majority of pellagra cases, the patient is constipated. Patients complain of abdominal pain, discomfort and distention especially after meals. Pellagra is a disease of vitamin deficiency—a lack of B vitamins. As an experiment, thiamin, one of the B vitamins, was withheld from a group of individuals. Loss of appetite, nausea and vomiting followed. Constipation was the rule. Young men subjected to hard physical work and living on a diet deficient in B vitamins, especially thiamin, were victims of easy fatigability, apathy, muscle and joint pains, lack of appetite and constipation.

> Jolliffe, Tisdall and Cannon, *Clinical Nutrition* (Hoeber)

* * *

Experiments with animals reported by Dr. Clive McCay of Cornell University showed that powdered brewer's yeast (rich in B vitamins) and the pulp left from making tomato and citrus juices (vitamin C and P and a wealth of minerals!) might help many older persons suffering from habitual constipation.

> *Science News Letter,* November 19, 1950

* * *

There is a great disturbance of the movements of the intestinal tract in vitamin B deficiency. The stomach and intestines are relaxed and sluggish. The emptying time of the intestine is twice as long in vitamin B deficient animals. And such animals respond with a greatly improved activity of the intestine when vitamin B is added to their diet.

Robertson and Doyle (*Journal of Nutrition,* Vol. 9, p. 553, 1935) showed that animals fed on a diet low in minerals were noticeably constipated while other animals fed the same diet, but with added minerals, were not.

Vitamins A, C, B_1 and B_2 are all needed to keep the mucous lining of the digestive tract in healthy condition. Constipation and many ill-defined digestive disorders frequently clear up when additional amounts of these vitamins are given.

> L. Jean Bogert, Ph.D., and Mame T. Potter, M.A., *Dietetics Simplified* (Macmillan Company)

[531]

The need for vitamins and minerals to prevent constipation is not generally appreciated. For instance, the lack of thiamin produces many and varied disorders of the stomach and intestines. For patients who cannot take the rougher vitamin-carrying foods (he means bran here, we suppose), brewer's yeast is a valuable food.

> James S. McLester, *Nutrition and Diet in Health and Disease* (Saunders)

*   *   *

In an experiment on deficiency in thiamin (vitamin B_1) it was found that the persons in the experiment who were eating a diet from which all thiamin had been removed suffered, among other things, fatigue, lack of appetite and constipation. Other symptoms were loss of weight, nausea and vomiting, backache and sore muscles, numbness, burning feet, mental depression, headache, very little digestive juice in the stomach and so forth. The diet which produced these symptoms was: polished rice, tapioca, cornstarch, sugar, white bread, butter, cottage and American cream cheese, egg white, cocoa, tea and white raisins. We are told that, had the diet been unknown, their physician would probably have told these individuals that they were suffering from chronic nervous exhaustion.

"The high-vitamin diet has wide application in the treatment of disease." Among conditions for which a high-vitamin diet should be prescribed are chronic gastrointestinal disorders — constipation, colitis, diarrhea, gastric atony, hypochlorhydria (lack of hydrochloric acid in the stomach), visceroptosis (fallen abdominal organs), ulcer, sprue, pellagra.

Laboratory work with animals shows that deficiency of thiamin (vitamin B_1) and/or pantothenic acid (another B vitamin) and probably other members of the B complex as well causes loss of intestinal tone and decreased movement of the intestines. It is not easy to confirm these findings in human beings because relief from constipation often occurs after the taking of very bulky food. And one does not know whether it was the bulk or the B vitamins that did the trick. However, we know that our American diet is deficient in B vitamins. Hence brewer's yeast should be included in the diet. Wheat germ is another good food to include.

Bridges Dietetics for the Clinician
(Lea and Febiger)

*   *   *

Dr. Gustav Martin and co-workers at the Warner Institute of Therapeutic Research studied the effects of different B vitamins on the intestinal tract. Separate vitamins were given and the researchers studied the movements of the intestines as each was taken. Only inositol (a part of the vitamin B complex) caused a marked increase in the intestinal movements. Poor appetites became normal and constipation was relieved. Of course, more and better absorption of food occurred, as intestinal movement increased. One of the richest sources of inositol is blackstrap molasses.

Patients taking synthetic vitamin preparations are likely to become constipated because the imbalances of B vitamins created by such preparations can produce shortages in the very vitamins needed to protect against constipation.

A partial deficiency of potassium in animals causes constipation and gas formation. (Potassium is plentiful in fresh fruits and vegetables. Sodium—table salt—in the diet causes your body to lose potassium. Cooking fruits and vegetables brings about great losses in potassium.)

[533]

If so much fat is eaten that it cannot be absorbed, both fat and calcium are lost, for they combine to form a soapy substance which is excreted. This often becomes hardened in the intestine causing constipation.

Lack of calcium can cause spastic constipation. Plenty of calcium in the diet prevents cramps and spasms. Spasms in the intestines, called by physicians spastic colitis or spastic constipation, can be relieved by getting plenty of calcium in the diet.

Enough protein in the diet is necessary for healthy intestines. The walls of the stomach and intestines are muscles which contract and relax alternately. When there is not enough protein in the diet, these muscles cannot function as they should and the flabbiness resulting may cause the entire intestinal structure to "fall," so that organs are displaced and constipation results. Food remains undigested when the flabby walls of the intestine cannot contract normally.

Adelle Davis, *Let's Eat Right to Keep Fit*
(Harcourt Brace and Co.)

SECTION XVI

Epilepsy

CHAPTER 81

Vitamin B₆ and Epilepsy

EPILEPSY IS ONE of the few illnesses still surrounded by medieval fear and superstition. Epileptics are perfectly normal mentally, and 9 out of 10 are able to hold normal jobs. Epilepsy is not inherited, although some states still prohibit epileptics to marry, and some even reserve the right to sterilize an epileptic against his wishes. The term "epilepsy" is Greek for "seizure." The only difference between an epileptic and a non-epileptic is that at various times—perhaps several times a day, or once each few months—the epileptic will experience one of four types of seizures:

Grand Mal: Meaning "great illness." The patient loses consciousness, tightens muscles, and falls; may cry out or groan, emitting saliva from the mouth; twitches violently for a minute or so, then falls into a state of sleep or drowsiness.

Petit Mal: Pronounced "petty-mahl" and meaning "small illness." The patient is affected only for a few seconds, may twitch slightly, stare vacantly, then resume his task of the moment, sometimes unaware of his seizure.

Psychomotor: Patient appears to be conscious, but will remember none of his actions after the seizure. May resemble either grand mal or petit mal, but patient functions during seizure, may act strangely or irrationally. It can be mistaken for ordinary "nasty" behavior. Relatively rare form.

Jacksonian: A modified grand mal. Patient is conscious, experiences a twitching, shaking, or numbness on one side of the body, which gradually spreads until consciousness is lost; indicates an irritation of a specific part of the brain, and can often be surgically cured.

By far, the greatest problem of the epileptic is not his seizures, but the social problems which arise when he is known as an epileptic. It is not uncommon for the epileptic—even though his seizures are controlled by drugs or by vitamin B$_6$—to be denied admittance to a school or university, to be refused jobs he could handle perfectly well, or to be viewed with constant suspicion and apprehension by friends and acquaintances. His problem will be solved partly by medical advances, such as the one reported here, and partly by an extensive public information program which will wipe away the mystery of epilepsy by bringing forth the truth.

Vitamin B$_6$ can prevent epilepsy. A deficiency of B$_6$ can cause epilepsy.

This startling discovery, the result of the work of several isolated medical teams from different parts of Europe and the United States, has given new hope to the 1½ million epileptics in America and to millions of others throughout the world. It may mark the begin-

[536]

ning of the end of one of the most feared and least understood illnesses man has ever known.

Vitamin B₆ (pyridoxine) was isolated for the first time in 1934—not so very long ago. And, up until World War II, its role in the body was thought to be minor. Some years ago, medical men believed the outstanding effect of B₆ deficiency was certain skin disorders. During the war, however, researchers had a chance to study deficiency effects on human beings, especially when it was found that the K rations used by American soldiers in the field were severely short in pyridoxine content.

By the early 1950's it was generally accepted in medical circles that pyridoxine could, and did, have strong effects on the central nervous system, and that it was clearly related to epileptic convulsions in infants.

Before that time, medical researchers discounted the idea that epilepsy could be caused by a vitamin shortage. Until then, most researchers worked only with the standard laboratory rat in experimenting with vitamin shortage. The rat reacted to a B₆ deficiency by exhibiting pellagra. Later it was found, however, that other animals reacted in quite a different way. When pyridoxine was withheld, the dog, the calf, and the pig reacted with epileptic-like seizures. This news was exciting, and researchers followed it up rapidly. Dr. R. H. Reilly, in a 1953 issue of the *Journal of the American Medical Association,* showed that convulsive attacks produced in animals by administration of I.N.H. (a substance which destroys pyridoxine) were halted by administration of pyridoxine. These experiments were corroborated by the work of Dr. S. Shintani, reported in a 1956 issue of the *Journal of the Japanese Pharmaceutical Society.* In more recent experiments, Shintani produced epileptic convulsions in an animal by administering hydro-xmethyl-pyrimidine. He then gave the animal doses of vitamin B₆. The attacks stopped. Further, when the animal's diet was sufficiently high in B₆, even the hydro-xmethyl-pyrimidine could not produce convulsions. Vitamin B₆ had proved to prevent epileptic attacks in this instance, and gave promise of doing the same in humans.

The discovery of desoxy-pyridoxine, another destroyer of B₆, allowed researchers to conduct deficiency experiments on volunteer human beings. Drs. W. W. Umbreit and J. Wadell, discoverers of desoxy-pyridoxine in 1949, carried out experiments wherein they destroyed B₆ in volunteers. The subjects responded with peripheral nervous afflictions, including polyneuritis, and some malfunction of the central nervous system manifested in convulsions.

Epilepsy in Infants

Around the time of the new discoveries, researchers noticed references in various journals citing the appearance of convulsive attacks in babies receiving artificial milk formulas deficient in B₆. Mother's milk contains ample amounts of natural B₆, while processed formulas, unless synthetic pyridoxine is added, often are deficient. All formula makers immediately added pyridoxine to their mixtures.

Clinically, the pattern of B₆ deficiency in infants is always the same. The baby is born at full term, of a normal pregnancy, and develops normally until about 4 months old. Attacks of epileptic convulsions then appear suddenly, repeating many times a day. When vitamin B₆ is administered, the condition is improved rapidly, and the attacks end with the regular inclusion of B₆ in the diet. When the B₆ is again removed from the formula, the attacks resume. Three researchers,

[538]

Drs. Besey, Adam and Hansen in 1957 found that infants prone to epileptic attacks require a higher daily dose of B₆ than normal infants. Reporting in a 1957 issue of *Pediatrics* they found that a daily dose of 5 to 10 milligrams is required to stem convulsions in nursing babies prone to attacks. It is important here to note that B₆ cannot "cure" epilepsy, as such, but in these instances can prevent or mitigate seizures.

Research is now expanding in an attempt to discover new ways of utilizing B₆ on patients with other neurological disorders. Dr. David G. Coursin reported in a 1954 issue of the *AMA Journal* that he gave a dosage of 100 milligrams of B₆ intramuscularly to 100 patients with various illnesses relating to the central nervous system. There were some spectacular results, particularly in patients with brain disorders.

Dr. M. Calvario, reporting in a 1958 issue of the Italian journal *Acia Vitaminologica,* made very complete studies on the relationship between vitamin B₆ shortage and epileptic convulsions. The work of Calvario has been effective on 40 illnesses showing epileptic symptoms. Of these, 45 per cent showed a deficiency of B₆.

Where Does It Lead?

This basic research on vitamin B₆ and epilepsy has two major sets of ramifications. One, of course, is vitally important to the epileptic. For him, the new work with B₆ holds promise of a new life, free—or nearly free—from the embarrassing and dangerous seizures to which he is subject from time to time. Should he find that he can control seizures with an increase in his vitamin B intake, either through daily foods or through food supplements such as brewer's yeast, his world will become a new and brighter one.

For all readers who follow the Prevention method, this news is yet another affirmation of the soundness of their nutritional plan. The infant who is started on mother's milk is far less likely to be subject to epileptic seizures, even should he be born with a proneness to epilepsy. After weaning, the child who is given a sensible diet, rich in natural and unprocessed foods, supplemented by natural vitamins, stands the best chance of avoiding convulsions associated with epilepsy.

Dr. Coursin, writing in *Drug Trade News,* May 28, 1962, suggests that "a large segment of the world's population may have some degree of B_6 deficiency." He goes on to indicate that not only is B_6 sometimes hard to get, but that it is hard to hold onto.

Although the well-balanced diet will contain sufficient amounts of B_6, says Dr. Coursin, "with marginal dietary intake, illness, pregnancy, and aging, the dietary supply of B_6 may not be adequate for all normal cellular enzyme activity.

"In foods containing vitamin B_6," he continues, "it is possible to have the content altered by some technological factors in processing. Several examples of such changes have been described in the treatment of milk with heat. The prolonged heating of milk with increased temperature and pressure may result in partial destruction of its B_6 content." It seems that this would apply both in dairy pasteurization of the milk and in heating the milk before giving it to the infant.

Dr. Coursin further suggests that various factors within the body may prevent full utilization of the B_6 which is ingested. It is possible that various alterations of the enzymes which are necessary for the body's utilization of B_6 may further depreciate the body's B_6 level.

In pregnancy, the need for B_6 is greater than ever, since so much is demanded by the growing fetus. While the recommended adult intake is 2 to 3 milligrams, the recommended amount for pregnant women is from 10 to 15 milligrams. Others whose physical situations call for higher than normal amounts of B₆ include persons with liver disease, hypothyroidism, leukemia, diabetes, oxalosis with stone formation, and those persons who carry an inborn error of metabolism which deprives them of B₆. These persons, chronically short of B₆, suffer from convulsive seizures which are halted with heavy doses of B₆.

How Much B₆?

The diet of the average American family is sadly lacking in vitamin B₆. At one time, bread was the main source—sometimes the only source—of this vitamin of the B complex. Today, however, according to a 1957 *British Medical Journal* article by Dr. H. M. Sinclair, "We now remove from bread and flour much of the vitamin B₆ they contain." This is accomplished through many steps of refinement which bread is subject to in the mill and bakery. The foods richest in pyridoxine are seeds, nuts, and legumes, providing they are unrefined, and the family which includes plenty of these foods in its diet is most likely to maintain a high level of B₆. Among food supplements, brewer's yeast is the best source of B₆, and it is vitally important that, to be sure one is getting enough, this supplement be taken regularly.

We are happy that this wonderful medical research again confirms the Prevention method of nutrition. If, for example, 10 years ago a mother would have stated that her epileptic child has had no seizures since taking brewer's yeast, her doctor might have discounted the reader's experience as coincidence, telling her that she is throwing away her money on fad foods, because experiments on rats showed that epilepsy has absolutely no relation to vitamin shortage. Today, he may take a different approach. The important point is, however, that if we fortify our bodies with ample amounts of *all* the vitamins in natural form, through a sound diet and regular supplementation, even though we be taking many times the so-called "minimum daily requirement," we may be preventing ills for which cures or controls will be found in years to come.

SECTION XVII

Eye Diseases

CHAPTER 82

Do Your Eyes Need Vitamins?

"IN ANY ILLNESS, and as the result of fatigue, over-strain or malnutrition, the eyes being part of the body become affected as do the other organs of the body." This is the opening sentence of a chapter on nutrition and the eyes, as found in the book, *The Preservation of Eyesight* by Sir Arthur Salusbury MacNalty, M.D. (The Williams-Wilkins Company, Baltimore, Maryland).

The truth of this statement is evident when we think of the sunken, inflamed and lusterless eyes of those who are, or have recently been, ill. The patient himself might have noticed that his vision was less acute and that his eyes burned and were sore to the touch. These are all strong symptoms of a lack of nutrition in the eye, yet most of us are inclined to let the eyes get along as best they can and concern for their nutrient supply is the last thing to enter our minds.

As your energy is sapped by serious illness, your eyes

suffer with the rest of you. The energy needed by the eye muscles for the quick adjustments they must make almost every second is not there. If you are too weak to lift your head or sit up as you normally do, how can you expect your eyes to adjust to bright and dim light, skim back and forth across a page, accommodate for far and near objects, large and small print, as they do under normal conditions?

Various Nutritional Elements Needed

Each part of the eye has its individual make-up. Each chemical it needs must be contained in the body so that the eye can draw on it when necessary. For example, the cornea and sclerotic coat are made up of simple protein, collagen, water and chemical salts. The collagen in a thickened state forms sclerotic tissue, less dense collagen forms the transparent cornea. Vitamin C assists in the formation of this valuable material, and vitamin C is one of the first nutrients to be depleted in times of physical stress. The lens also is made up of protein, along with water and salts. Cataract is said to be caused by an imbalance of these ingredients.

The vitreous humor forms a large part of the eye. It is almost all water, but about one per cent of its mass is accounted for by a starchy solid. It is this which transforms the water into a jelly-like solid, accounting for the shape of the eye and holding the retina in its proper position.

The retina, which takes care of the eye's response to light, contains many fine blood vessels. From this supply of nourishment, the retina is able to manufacture visual purple. This substance, composed of protein and a substance chemically related to vitamin A, is extremely sensitive to light. Visual purple is built up in the dark

[544]

and depleted upon exposure to light. The importance of visual purple lies in its aid to the eyes in adapting to dusk or dim light. A lack of this ability is known as night blindness.

The aqueous humor (a liquid) flows constantly over the front surface of the cornea. It is the function of this liquid to maintain the pressure inside the eyeball at a constant level and to nourish the lens and the cornea. The aqueous humor is made up of glucose, dissolved oxygen, various chemical salts, simple nitrogenous substances (proteins) and vitamin C.

Vitamins A and C Show Dramatic Results

As can be seen from the analyses of Dr. MacNalty, vitamins A and C are important to the health of the eye, as is protein. As you would suppose, the diet deficient in vitamin A is likely to result in night blindness, xerophthalmia and keratomalacia. Xerophthalmia is a dry and thickened condition of the conjunctiva or eye tissues which sometimes follows conjunctivitis or a disease of the tear glands. Keratomalacia is a softening of the cornea.

It is known that the normal retina and the choroid (an eye membrane) contain enormous amounts of vitamin A. Apparently vitamin A is necessary for the process that goes on inside the eye when your body moves from darkness to light, or from light to darkness. So a lack of vitamin A would hinder this process.

It has been found that night blindness resulting from vitamin deficiency may be accompanied by scotomata —dark spots in the field of vision. We know that both these conditions are caused directly by too little vitamin A and can be cured by increasing the amount of vitamin A available for the use of the body.

[545]

Often night blindness is accompanied by dryness of the cornea and the eye tissues, with silver gray, shiny triangular spots called Bitot's spots after the physician who first studied them. The area that is affected by this dryness feels gritty, as if there were grains of sand on the eyeball; it cannot be "wetted."

Keratomalacia is an advanced and much more serious state than either or both of these two first conditions. Dryness is first noticed, followed by a softening of the cornea which becomes gray, dull and cloudy. Since this condition is an indication of severe vitamin A deficiency, other tissues in the body also suffer and may finally be so starved for vitamin A that the patient dies.

Vitamin B Is Important Too

It seems that most of the B vitamins, as well, are necessary for eye health, and that even partial deficiency in one or more of them results in symptoms that can be recognized by physicians. Serious lack of thiamin (one of the B vitamins) may bring on beriberi or neuritis. In the eyes, this takes the form of retrobulbar neuritis, or pains behind the eyeball. There may also be many dark spots on the field of vision, probably near the center of this field.

Riboflavin, niacin, pyridoxine, pantothenic acid and folic acid, other B vitamins, are also concerned in eye health. In certain forms of pellagra, for instance, giving just niacin will not cure the disease. These other members of the B family of vitamins are necessary as well. In pellagra there is inflammation of the eyelids and loss of eyelashes, erosion of the eye tissues and clouding of the cornea. When riboflavin is lacking in the diet, the eyelids may smart and itch, the eyes may grow tired, vision may be poor and cannot be improved by

[546]

glasses, it may be difficult for the individual to see in dim light and there may be extreme sensitivity to light. This does not mean that the patient cannot stand any light at all, but rather that he suffers actual physical discomfort in the presence of bright light.

Adelle Davis in her book, *Vitality Through Planned Nutrition,* gives more details about eye conditions that result from lack of riboflavin. Dr. Day at Columbia University produced cataract in rats who were deficient in riboflavin. If they were not given riboflavin, they eventually became completely blind. Dr. Sydenstricker of the University of Georgia studied 47 patients who lacked riboflavin. They suffered from a variety of visual disturbances. They were sensitive to light, suffered from eyestrain that was not relieved by wearing glasses and had burning sensations in their eyes and visual fatigue. They were sensitive to light and their eyes watered easily. Six of them had cataract. Within 24 hours after the administration of riboflavin, symptoms began to improve. After two days, the burning sensations and the other symptoms began to disappear. Gradually all disorders were cured. When the riboflavin was taken away from them, the symptoms gradually appeared again and once again were cured by riboflavin.

Vitamin C Is All-Important for Eye Health

Vitamin C is often mentioned in connection with cataracts (a cloudy film which forms over the lens of the eye). It has been shown that the lenses over which cataracts have formed have little or no vitamin C, though this vitamin should be present. In experiments with laboratory rats upon whom cataracts had been induced, the growth of the cataracts was inhibited by increasing the vitamin C intake of the animals. One

[547]

function of this vitamin is to repair the cement between the cells, and it is suggested that, due to a lack of vitamin C, the cells have degenerated and formed into the cataract.

Protein, the tissue builder, is always in demand throughout the body. It is significant, however, that analyses of several parts of the eye are largely made up of protein and little else. Therefore, it is easy to see the importance of a high protein intake (lean meat, fish, eggs) for health of the eyes.

Temporary Blindness

In another interesting chapter Dr. MacNalty discusses temporary blindness. Apparently this condition occurs with amazing frequency. It can be caused by excessive doses of quinine, as used by malaria patients. The quinine contracts the blood vessels and reduces the normal supply of blood to the retina. Eyesight usually returns with the elimination of the quinine. Smoking can also produce a failure of eyesight. The victim can see only through a glimmering mist, due to an inflammation of the optic nerve. Again, the cure lies in eliminating the use of tobacco. Alcohol can have exactly the same effect. It should be mentioned that both vitamin C and vitamin B, needed for eye health, are depleted by the use of tobacco and alcohol.

Nervous blindness is a terrifying symptom which sometimes occurs in persons suffering from neurasthenia (high susceptibility to fatigue from physical or mental exertion), hysteria, neuroses and nervous states. The sight of these persons just leaves them quite suddenly and they might be blind for days or weeks, though sight might return when they really make an effort to see. These cases are illustrative of the eyes' dependence upon the proper working of the body's

nervous system. This system, in turn, is heavily dependent upon a good supply of the B-complex vitamins. As
with all other organs of the body, the eyes are strongly
influenced by the health and nutrition of the rest of
the body. Remember sunflower seeds as a help in avoiding eye problems. They contain vitamin A as well as
other elements valuable in maintaining healthy eyes.

SECTION XVIII

Gangrene

CHAPTER 83

Vitamin E and Gangrene

AN ARTICLE ON the use of vitamin E in the treatment of small areas of gangrene brings us much valuable information about vitamin E and why we should take it every day of our lives.

Did you know, for instance, that vitamin E can and does produce new blood vessels around the site of an obstruction in a vessel, so that the blood can continue to circulate there? In some cases it has been found that the new artery is as large and sound as the old, obstructed one. Did you know that vitamin E has the power of dilating the veins? That is, if they are narrowed by deposits so that the blood has trouble getting through, vitamin E widens them. Did you know, too, that vitamin E is an antithrombin? This means that it has the power of retarding or preventing the coagulation of blood—a good guarantee against a clot in the brain or heart artery. It does not, however, predispose one to hemorrhages, as many of the anticoagulant drugs do. Finally, did you know that vitamin E makes the tiny capillaries stronger so that hemorrhaging is unlikely?

The authors of "Alphatocopherol in the Management of Small Areas of Gangrene" (*Canadian Medical Association Journal,* May 1, 1957) are Stephen Tolgyes, M.D., and Evan Shute, M.D. They go into the story of arteriosclerosis or hardening of the arteries with a most unusual theory. They quote a recent researcher, J. B. Duguid, who believes that the "hardening" that appears on the walls of arteries may be just an accumulation of old blood clots. It seems that a careful examination has shown that this troublesome substance does indeed contain fibers of blood protein. Is it the result of blood clots attaching themselves to the walls of the arteries? If this is indeed correct, then the role of vitamin E becomes even more important, for it may do much to prevent the formation of such clots.

Then, as perhaps its most important function in the body, vitamin E "enjoys an unrivaled role among physiological agents in its ability to improve tissue utilization of oxygen," according to our authors. All of us know the importance of oxygen to good health. Conserving oxygen and helping tissues to utilize to best advantage what oxygen there is becomes an increasingly important function of vitamin E when you contemplate the ever lessening amounts of oxygen in an atmosphere polluted day and night, in homes that are well-insulated and stuffy and often blue with tobacco smoke.

Treating Gangrene with Vitamin E

In treating gangrene with vitamin E, the authors handled patients with arteriosclerosis, diabetes and thromboangiitis obliterans or Buerger's disease. They

[551]

saved a good percentage of 48 patients from pending threatening amputation.

The first patient whose case history they give, aged 30, had gangrene patches on the fingers of the left hand. He was given 500 units of vitamin E by mouth and a vitamin E ointment was applied. No other treatment was given and within a little more than two months healing was complete.

The second case, a woman of 85, was an unsuspected diabetic. Gangrene of one of her toes had spread down the inside of her foot. Treatment with vitamin E and insulin, along with a low-calorie diet brought about complete healing within 4 months.

A third patient smoked heavily. She was urged to stop smoking but did not. It is well known that smoking is at least one of the causes of Buerger's disease, if not the leading cause. The usual story in cases of Buerger's disease is that the disease can be halted so long as the patient does not smoke. In this case the vitamin E treatment halted the progress of the gangrene, even though the patient did not adhere to the diet she was given and did continue to smoke heavily.

The pictures that accompany the article by Drs. Tolgyes and Shute are even more convincing than the text. It is hard to believe that the hideous purple and black patches of degeneration on these patient's limbs can be changed into normal pink tissue, with no other treatment than the taking of a vitamin.

Most Successful in Diabetic Gangrene

In discussing these and other cases, the authors say that while vitamin E cannot cure every case of gangrene, it appears that it can "save many toes and feet that otherwise would be sacrificed." It is most successful in cases of diabetic gangrene. In 50 per cent of these cases the insulin requirement was subsequently decreased. This often happened long before there was noticeable change in the gangrene, and in two cases it happened within 3 days of beginning the vitamin E treatment.

Patients with Buerger's disease may find that treatment with vitamin E brings pain as the blood returns to the area that has been gangrenous, in much the same way that a frozen toe or finger aches when feeling returns. The authors recommend that vitamin E be used on frostbite and on feet or fingers suffering from long immersion in water.

If vitamin E can work near-miracles like these with the horribly degenerated tissues of gangrene where the only alternative may be amputation, what can it not do to strengthen healthy tissue? Now, while you are healthy—now when there is no fear of gangrene or blood clots or any other affliction in your circulatory system—is the time to take vitamin E in supplement form as well as getting plenty of it in everyday meals.

It is most plentiful in whole grains—real whole grains, vegetable and cereal oils, legumes, brown rice, eggs and salad greens.

SECTION XIX

Heart Disease

CHAPTER 84

Vitamin B$_{15}$ and Your Heart

UNTIL NOW, practically nothing has been known about vitamin B$_{15}$ and its role, if any, in human metabolism. The latest edition of the *Merck Index,* an authoritative encyclopedia for pharmacists, chemists, and doctors, merely describes the chemistry of this vitamin, but has nothing to suggest as to what it may be useful for. In fact, pangamic acid (B$_{15}$) has been called a vitamin only by virtue of its having been discovered in certain foods that are sources of the B complex vitamins—notably, brewer's yeast and seeds.

Pangamic acid is one of those substances that the "nutritional authorities" of the Food and Drug Administration consider of no value in human nutrition, because they don't know of any such value, and they like to think that what they know about nutrition is all that there is to know and all that will ever be known. This arrogant attitude, of course, is the reverse of that of many nutritional authorities, such as J. I. Rodale, who have faith in the wisdom of nature and know that a substance like pangamic acid, nontoxic and part of the B complex of vitamins, must have a purpose even if it is not yet discovered.

This, of course, is one of the basic reasons why we have always recommended vitamin supplements, like brewer's yeast, made of the whole foods that contain the vitamins, as superior to purified vitamin substances. That our point of view is the correct one and the necessary one for any person interested in peak health is once more borne out by a Russian research study published in *Reports of the Academy of Sciences, U.S.S.R.* (144,3, 1962).

Retards Asphyxiation

It is only a preliminary report that has been published so far, yet it was able to arrive at the definite conclusion that "our results indicate that vitamin B_{15} increases general and myocardial resistance to hypoxia." Coming from a team of prominent Russian scientists (Dokukin, Konstantinova, Chechulin, and Bukin), this conclusion is in itself important, and opens a door to further investigations that might be of prime significance.

Hypoxia simply means an insufficient supply of oxygen to living tissue. The myocardium is the muscle tissue of the heart, tissue that makes a continual, strong demand for oxygen and that quickly fails when the oxygen supply is inadequate. There are many reasons why, at any given time, the heart and other tissues might not receive enough oxygen. There might be an anemic condition of the blood, causing hypoxia at a time of unusual physical effort such as unaccustomed running or shoveling snow. There is sometimes difficulty in starting the breathing of a newborn baby, and until the breathing actually begins, there is hypoxia. Carbon monoxide poisoning—almost a chronic condition in the polluted air of large cities—will induce hypoxia. Failure or weakness of the respiratory system, whether temporary or chronic, will have the same result. It is not a problem that occurs for everyone, but it occurs enough times for enough people so that any substance that increases our ability to survive such a crisis becomes an important substance for that reason alone.

That, it seems, is just what pangamic acid does for us.

Experimental Proof

The Russian scientists carried out their experiments on large numbers of mice, rats, cats, and dogs. The animals were given dosages of vitamin B_{15} in amounts of from 150 to 500 milligrams for each kilogram of weight. Then the animals were placed in sealed containers and the process of gradual asphyxiation was observed.

(Though the knowledge gained from these experiments was important, we do not condone the cruelty that was involved in the experiments themselves. It seems to us that scientists capable of conducting brilliant experiments could well apply some of their brilliance to devising more humane methods.)

Twenty minutes after the start of the experiment, it was found that 9% of the control (no pangamic acid) animals had died, as compared with only 3.3% of the animals that had been fortified with the vitamin. Under these asphyxiating conditions, animals that had received vitamin B_{15} survived on the average 10 minutes longer than the controls. That was the average, while individual cases survived up to 50 minutes longer

[556]

than the animals that had not received any of this vitamin.

The Russian scientific team offered a persuasive explanation of why this should be so. The direct action of pangamic acid, they say, is to stimulate the hypophysis of the suprarenal glands. These are glands located in the body just above the kidneys, hence the name. The hypophysis is a kind of bump on each, which the Russian investigators state has an important detoxifying function. By stimulating this activity, they believe, pangamic acid retards the accumulation of toxic waste that results from an insufficiency of oxygen. Thus the hypoxia does less damage, and a longer period of time remains for normal oxygen metabolism to be reestablished without fundamental damage to the organism.

The Russians offered this preliminary report to urge the use of pangamic acid as a drug in heart surgery, when for a time the flow of blood to the heart must be cut off and hypoxia results. Certainly it should be of value for this purpose.

Nutritional Need?

How about vitamin B_{15} in nutrition, however? In Russia, that cannot represent any great problem. Sunflower seeds are eaten in large quantity by practically everyone. These seeds contain a rich supply of vitamin B_{15}, and we may assume that most Russians get a sufficiency of the vitamin in this way. Improved ability to endure the oxygen-depletion of heavy exercise could well be a partial explanation for the superior stamina and physical condition of young Russians as compared to young Americans, a matter that has received a great deal of comment lately.

Unlike Russians, most Americans eat neither seeds

[557]

nor brewer's yeast for fear of being considered food faddists and health nuts. We can assume, therefore, that the American diet is generally deficient in this vitamin. It is not even included in most vitamin supplements, unless they are natural supplements. Its dietary sources are very few, indeed. Aside from seeds and brewer's yeast, the vitamin is found also in horse liver, ox blood and rice bran. None of these is exactly a staple on the American table.

We must, therefore, assume that most Americans get little or no pangamic acid. This means that Americans have less ability to survive temporary conditions of oxygen insufficiency. The inevitable result would seem to be a larger number of heart attacks and less ability to recover from such attacks. Can this be the reason, or one of the reasons, why the rate of cardiac deaths in the United States is sharply on the increase?

Here is a field wide open for investigation. Without irrefutable scientific evidence, we cannot say that it is so. But it seems a reasonable conclusion from the facts that have already been scientifically demonstrated. Having learned these facts, we urge our readers to protect themselves with a good intake of pangamic acid.

You may be sure that in the sunflower and pumpkin seeds and in the brewer's yeast, you will also be getting other protective factors that have not yet been discovered or whose values are still unknown, but which will go ahead and work for you regardless of whether or not they have been sanctioned by the Committee on Nutrition of the AMA.

CHAPTER 85

Cholesterol and Nicotinic Acid

THE CONDEMNED anticholesterol drug MER/29 was used by at least 400,000 patients before the government blew the whistle on it as a cause of blindness, falling hair, skin disease and a loss of sexual desire. The doctors could just as easily have been prescribing nicotinic acid, a B vitamin, known to be more effective and safer than MER/29 or any other drug used to cut cholesterol. But doctors rarely use a vitamin when a drug is available to treat the same thing, and they didn't use nicotinic acid very much.

Laymen find this hard to understand since nicotinic acid, according to reports by a number of investigators, is at least as effective against cholesterol as any dangerous drug. Dr. William B. Parsons, Jr., director of research at the Jackson Clinic and Foundation, Madison, Wisconsin, has been urging that a major long-range test be given to nicotinic acid therapy in control of high cholesterol to settle once and for all its superiority in the field. A study to be supported by the National Institutes of Health, planned as early as March, 1961, has yet to be begun.

Why is it that there is so little interest in nicotinic acid among medical men, and indeed among government officials who know what a threat circulatory diseases are to the American people? In *Medical Tribune* (November 28-29, 1964) Dr. Parsons suggests that interest would be more active if the B vitamin could be patented. Drug companies, without the incentive of large profits from a new drug, aren't too interested in promoting "just a vitamin." Although several of the companies did develop new versions of nicotinic acid with additives that could be patented, their product often caused serious side effects that were never present in the plain nicotinic acid.

MER/29 certainly did not have the drawback of being an old, unprofitable, tried and true compound. It was introduced to the American Medical Association by a University of Texas doctor, Arthur Ruskin. At the June, 1960, convention of the nation's doctors, he rose to announce that on the basis of one year of study, MER/29 was "a step forward in the simple control of blood and liver cholesterol without modification of diet or danger to the patient." Doctors snapped at the drug, no questions asked. The press was cholesterol-conscious anyway, but the William S. Merrell Company of Cincinnati set fire to a publicity campaign planned to make the whole nation aware of MER/29, and it succeeded. In two years the company sold $12,-000,000-worth of the drug. This was a nice return from a 1.9-million-dollar advertising budget.

Doctors are amazingly consistent in their concern about side effects where *nutrients* are used in medicinal doses. Mention a vitamin or a mineral as a treatment for disease, and physicians become terribly concerned about the possibility of flushing, loose stool, mild nausea, etc. They would rather risk liver damage, cataract, serious skin disease or even cancer from a drug sold by a big-name manufacturer than take a chance on a vitamin.

Dr. Parsons demonstrates this attitude: "Doctors keep asking me, 'Isn't there an awful flush?'" The so-called flush consists of a warm feeling, accompanied by a redness of the face and upper part of the body that lasts for twenty minutes to half an hour after each large dose of nicotinic acid early in the treatment. This effect usually disappears after the first few days on the treatment, and few of the patients are ever concerned enough to make more than a passing reference to it. Compared with the effect from almost any commercial drug compound, it is negligible.

In a test with 90 patients, doctors found that a "significant minority" developed changes in the liver enzyme function test after long-term therapy. When the patients were studied more closely, the abnormal liver tests were shown due to the synthetic *aluminum* nicotinate only, and this side effect was eliminated when the medication was stopped, or when *plain nicotinic acid was substituted* in the same dosage. Nausea has shown up, but again it was because aluminum nicotinate was used in place of simple nicotinic acid. Dr. Parsons said even the aluminum nicotinate side reactions are minor and should not discourage investigators from using the drug. But apparently plain nicotinic acid is even better.

Medical Tribune reported early studies at the University of Saskatchewan where Drs. Altschul, Hoffer and Stephen lowered cholesterol concentrations in rabbits as well as in humans with nicotinic acid. In sev-

[561]

eral cases visible cholesterol deposits (in skin or in tendons) were eliminated by nicotinic acid, and results were achieved in periods ranging from a few months to a year or so.

No one knows exactly what the mechanism for nicotinic acid's effect on cholesterol is. We do know that the vitamin causes a widening of the blood vessels but this itself does not explain everything. Perhaps a high cholesterol level is an early warning of nicotinic acid (niacin) deficiency.

Doctors are reluctant to believe this because few patients with excess cholesterol show symptoms of pellagra (a serious B vitamin deficiency disease). But why wait for that? In many cases of vitamin shortage, subtle changes of health occur before a serious deficiency disease is obvious. For example, a shortage of vitamin C creates problems in bruising and healing, long before out-and-out symptoms of scurvy appear.

Most diseases can be prevented by adequate nutrition. We think people are much less likely to develop cholesterol problems if they have a high intake of vitamin-B-rich foods (all of which include niacin) and avoid saturated fats whenever possible. Brewer's yeast, wheat germ and desiccated liver are all good sources of nicotinic acid. If they are consciously added to one's diet, they provide insurance against a pileup of cholesterol. If you include vitamin B supplements in a regular diet, it won't be necessary to concentrate on large amounts of a specific B vitamin as a treatment.

It is not the amount of cholesterol which one takes but the body's readiness to handle cholesterol as it should that is important. A normal healthy body is bound to have a normal healthy cholesterol level and it won't need dangerous drugs to achieve it.

[562]

SECTION XX

Iatrogenic Diseases

CHAPTER 86

Vitamins Versus Toxic Drug Effects

A MONTHLY NEWSLETTER issued to the medical profession by Hoffman-La Roche, Limited, of Montreal, Quebec, Canada, the *Courier,* carried an interesting two-part series in its February and March, 1959, issues. The series dealt with the use of vitamins in the treatment of toxic side effects of drugs. It has been shown that many drugs deprive the body of its nutrients, often without a visible and pronounced side effect. However, sometimes the antivitamin effect of certain drugs is so strong that it must be classed as an iatrogenic (medicine-caused) disease. The *Courier* acknowledges this fact, but remarks that, "Often they [side effects] must be accepted as the lesser evil when balanced by therapeutic value of the preparation." Of course, it is true that one would be foolish to hesitate in using a drug, because of a rash it might cause, while one's life hung in the balance. But side effects are often more serious, and the drugs are used less judiciously than that.

If a drug is the only answer, we say use it, of course.

But to spare yourself possible side effects, always increase your vitamin intake and cut down on those habits and environmental situations such as smoking, drinking, stress of temperature or emotional situations, etc., which cost the body nutrients. Drugs take more vitamins from the body than you can afford. If you put them back as quickly as possible, the body can continue to function with some efficiency; if you do not, the lack will quickly show itself as actual poisoning. It is for treating this poisoning that the *Courier's* article was written. Any disease that responds to nutritional therapy need never have occurred if a sufficient amount of that nutrient had been present in the first place. Never take the chance of permitting a vitamin shortage to exist in yourself.

Why Vitamins Are Helpful

The exact reason for the salutary effect of vitamins in cases of drug toxicity is not certain, but one explanation is offered by the *Courier:*

"As biocatalysts, the vitamins have a variety of regulatory functions in the metabolic processes. Sometimes they form part of enzymes, sometimes they act as redox [oxidizing] agents, protecting biologically important substances from inactivation. . . . Under these circumstances, it seems quite plausible that such substances should exert a favorable influence on iatrogenic disturbances, as they are able to compensate the dysmetabolism [upset in the body's use of nutrients] by their regulatory activity."

A common cause of toxicity is anesthesia. Certain of the anesthetics are almost sure to make the patient vomit or have a headache. Sometimes an anesthetic is as likely to cause death as the disease or the operation employed to correct that disease.

Postanesthetic symptoms are caused by an overloading of the blood with acid metabolites, principally pyruvic acid. The levels of this acid are always highest in the blood of those with the severest postanesthetic illnesses. Markees, *et al.* (*Schweizerische Medizinische Wochenschrift,* 80, 1079-81, 1950), found that if these patients are given vitamin B complex or cocarboxylase (thiamin pyrophosphoric ester), the pyruvic acid levels fall rapidly, accompanied by an improvement in the patient's comfort.

W. Hugin, in another German publication, *Anaesthesist* (2, 193-96, 1953), told of giving patients 3 intravenous injections of 100 milligrams of cocarboxylase during the first 24 hours after operation. Patients receiving this treatment felt much better than untreated controls and were less frequently sick. Another researcher, Stieve, is cited as describing cellular damage in a dog, caused by anesthesia, which was sometimes incurable and which could be prevented by administering B vitamin complex.

Some researchers experienced excellent results in postoperative situations by using vitamin B6 (pyridoxine). One doctor, K. Wedel, reported in *Anaesthesist* (4, 122-23, 1955) that he used 100 milligrams of pyridoxine, injected subcutaneously (under the skin) after surgery. No vomiting was seen as a sequel of ether anesthesia in 79 per cent of this group, while only 49 per cent of those who were not treated with the vitamin escaped postoperative nausea.

Antibiotics Not Without Dangers

Leaving the discussion of anesthetics, the *Courier* tells us that the use of antibiotics "is not without its dangers—toxic effects such as hearing impairment, neuritis and digestive disorders, to name only the most

[565]

important. They occur despite careful supervision, because toxicity varies from patient to patient. In postantibiotic entercolitis [inflammation of the large and small upper and lower intestinal tracts], neither onset nor severity of symptoms is dependent on dosage."

It is for this reason that we issue a strong warning against indiscriminate use of antibiotics. Here is a drug manufacturer who admits in his own bulletin that it is impossible to predict the reaction of an antibiotic drug on an individual. It is the height of foolishness for a patient to insist, for example, on a shot of penicillin to knock out a cold—and it is worse for the doctor to agree to such a request. Antibiotics can control life or death and should be used with that in mind.

Why antibiotics react so strongly upon the body has yet to be fully understood. It could be due to any of these: disturbance of the balance of the intestinal flora; prevention of vitamins combining properly; the development of resistant strains; moniliasis (an infectious disease of the skin, nails, bronchi, lungs, etc.); disturbance of progressive cell metabolism; and bacteriolytic endotoxins (destruction of bacteria working from within the cells).

Bacterial or fungus super-infection (staph, for example) leads to the suppression of certain organisms, giving rise to intestinal upset, or malfunction. To prevent or lessen such disorders, H. P. Kuemmerle (*Medizinische,* 1957, 715-19) recommends a combination of panthenol, ascorbic acid and acidophilus baccilli, plus the natural components of sour milk.

Treatment for Antibiotic-Induced Digestive Disorders

The *Courier* offers these principles for the treatment of digestive disorders induced by antibiotics: administration of the all-important vitamin B complex (oral administration if absorption and serum protein levels are normal, otherwise injections of the B vitamins until a normal absorption of protein state is arrived at). Oozing intestinal hemorrhage in the absence of other causes implies vitamin K deficiency and should be treated by vitamin K preparations, orally or by injections.

The usefulness of streptomycin sulfate has been restricted by its toxic effects on the acoustic nerve. Therapeutic amounts could not be given without running the risk of injury to the ear. However, when mixed with the B vitamin, pantóthenic acid, the toxicity of streptomycin was reduced greatly. This applies, as well, to neomycin and viomycin. When either is mixed with pantothenic acid, the therapeutic result is as good and the drug is safer.

Vitamin A is also used to reduce or prevent the acoustic nerve injury by streptomycin and neomycin. The dose of A used to accomplish this is high—300,000 International Units daily.

One of the most frequently used of the antituberculosis drugs is Isoniazid, which may cause toxic inflammation of the nerves in high dosage. The symptoms— paresthesia (tissue abnormality), feelings of deafness, burning and weakness are probably due to a disturbance in pyridoxine metabolism. Daily doses of this vitamin largely or entirely relieve the symptoms. If the pyridoxine is given in amounts of 50 to 450 milligrams per day from the beginning of Isoniazid treatment, the neuritis never occurs at all!

Barbiturates are increasingly common on the American scene, in the form of sleeping pill preparations. Their danger does not seem to limit their popularity. Only those who have experienced the awful consequences of prolonged use of barbiturates seem to fear them. It is known that they may impair the oxidative

[567]

processes in the tissues of the nervous system and else-where. The body's use of carbohydrates is chiefly affected. The electrical impulses of the brain also suffer interference when barbiturates are used in excess.

But here, too, it has been shown that the vitamins of the B complex are of great value in neutralizing the toxic effects. Interference with brain waves due to barbiturate therapy are relieved by use of the B complex. In acute stages of barbiturate poisoning the prescription in the *Courier* is as follows: "Intravenous infusion or injection of 1.5 grams vitamin C, 1.0 grams B_1, 200-400 milligrams nicotinamide (nicotinic acid—a B vitamin), 20 milligrams B_2, 100-200 B_6 and 25 milligrams pantothenic acid, in addition to the usual measures, leads to rapid regression of the symptoms and earlier recovery of consciousness. Such injections may be repeated every 4-8 hours if necessary."

There is much to be done in the field of vitamin therapy, but those who are wise are anticipating the findings by fortifying themselves before and after surgical and antibiotic therapy with vitamin-rich foods and natural food supplements. Especially valuable are brewer's yeast, desiccated liver, rose hips and flavonoid-C. We wonder that more doctors are not aware of this good news to pass on to their patients. Perhaps it would help to reverse the procedure. Maybe the patients should pass on the good news to the doctors.

CHAPTER 87

Vitamin E and a Blood Vessel Ailment

A DISORDER CALLED by doctors "intermittent claudication" involves the legs chiefly. It becomes noticeable when one is walking, and it consists of disagreeable sensations like "pins and needles" followed by pain, shaking and excessive perspiration. It is said to be caused by arteriosclerosis or, as we commonly call it, "hardening of the arteries."

From what we know of vitamin E and its benefits for heart and vascular conditions, it would seem that this might be helpful for such a condition. An article in the *Lancet,* September 20, 1958, confirms this point of view. Written by Peter D. Livingstone and Clifford Jones, the article first reviews past experience with vitamin E for this condition. These reports are conflicting. Some researchers got good results and others claimed that they got none at all. But in most cases the treatment with vitamin E was continued for quite a short time.

[569]

Drs. Livingstone and Jones decided to test two groups of patients at their hospital, giving vitamin E to one group and a "dummy" tablet to the other group. Neither the patients nor the doctors themselves knew throughout the test which patient was getting the vitamin E, for a procedure was worked out whereby the patient was given his tablets according to a number system and the key to this system was not divulged until after the test was over. This, of course, was to make certain that no patient thought he felt better because he knew he was taking a medicine and the doctors did not diagnose any patient as being better because they wanted the test to succeed.

The 40 patients who took part in the test ranged in age from 40 to 57, and both groups of 20 were equally divided as to age. They were all men. In all cases the symptoms had been noticed *for at least 5 years* and in all cases the pain was felt in the calf of the leg.

It was difficult to decide on a way of testing improvement in the patients, since this is one of those conditions in which the symptoms are "subjective," that is, the doctor cannot tell whether there is improvement. The patient is the only one who knows. He must decide whether the pain and numbness are better or worse than they were the day before.

The doctors decided on an exercise tolerance test. The patient climbed up and down a series of steps 18 inches high until pain made him stop. The number of steps taken by the patient was counted each time and also the length of time taken to recover from the pain and feel normal once again. By using this test the doctor had a measure of the patient's actual improvement apart from his own opinion as to whether he had improved or not.

It was decided to give large doses of vitamin E.

Each tablet was 200 milligrams and the usual daily dosage was 600 milligrams—that is, each patient who was taking vitamin E took 3 tablets a day. We assume that he took one tablet in the morning, one at noon and one at night.

Those who were taking dummy tablets also took 3 a day, so that no one knew which group was getting the vitamin E.

Results of the Test

Thirteen of the 20 patients taking vitamin E thought they had improved, at the end of the test. In all these cases, the walking test on the steps indicated, too, that they had improved. In the 20 patients taking the "dummy" tablet, two thought they had improved and actually had. Two of the members of this group of 20 thought they had deteriorated.

Three patients dropped out of each group before the end of the test because of other ailments or death. Of the 4 patients who did not respond at all to vitamin E, the first had very extensive disease of the arteries, and both his legs were in grave danger of gangrene. The second had extremely high blood pressure. The third was grossly overweight, smoked heavily and refused to cooperate in any way so far as restrictions in diet or habit were concerned. In the fourth patient there seemed to be no reason for failure.

Of the patients who improved on vitamin E treatment, 7 were able to continue walking indefinitely at a slightly slower pace than usual. Four were able to walk any distance up to half a mile and do their full work. Two showed slight but definite improvement and were quite certain that they were more active than they had been and that the pain was less severe.

Of the patients who took the dummy tablet, two

[571]

recovered enough to walk a useful distance. One of these made a spontaneous and complete recovery after suffering severely for many years. All the other 15 members of this group had no relief.

The authors say in conclusion that there can be no doubt that vitamin E was responsible for improvement in 13 of the group of 17 patients. These patients are now carrying on their work with ease and enjoying their leisure. All of them had undergone certain forms of therapy before trying the vitamin E and had been disappointed. The fact that it took a number of months for them to improve seems to rule out the possibility that psychological factors played any part in their improvement.

The experiment seems to show definitely that large doses of vitamin E are necessary and that there is considerable delay before any response can be noted. The authors believe that treatment should be carried on for at least 3 months before being abandoned. Their test was conducted for 40 weeks or about 10 months.

Remember, if you suffer from intermittent claudication, the investigators in the article we describe above found that large doses of vitamin E were required and there may be considerable delay before improvement is noted. So don't give up too soon if improvement is slow in coming.

CHAPTER 88

Can Kidney Stones Be Prevented?

A CENTURY OR SO AGO kidney stones were an important
cause of illness, especially among young people. Today
kidney stones are far less prevalent in this country and
the emphasis has shifted from youth to age. But in some
parts of the world this problem exists among most of
the population. Such a background cannot help but
lead one to believe that the development of kidney
stones is related to poor nutrition.

No one knows exactly how or why the stones are
formed, but it is generally agreed among the experts
that diet plays a part. It is known for instance that
stones formed chiefly of calcium oxalate may be related
to a high content of oxalic acid in the diet. In *Bridges'
Dietetics for the Clinician* (Lea and Febiger, 1949),
the editor, Harry J. Johnson, M.D., F.A.C.P., says,
"It is a matter of common observation that calcium
oxalate sediments will appear in the urine of nearly
every patient in a ward after ingesting oxalate-rich food

as spinach and rhubarb." Now most of us don't eat enough spinach and rhubarb to cause this kind of trouble. But there are other foods rich in oxalic acid that we do eat in quantity, perhaps every day. Chocolate, for instance, and cocoa both contain lots of oxalic acid. Plenty of children (and adults too) have a cup of cocoa for breakfast, chocolate milk for lunch and dinner and possibly a couple of chocolate bars or chocolate cupcakes between meals. So it is well to keep in mind this possible cause of stones. In *Today's Health* (August, 1959), it is reported that vitamin B_6 has been found to inhibit the production of oxalates. It seems fair to assume, then, that a good, steady supply of vitamin B_6 would keep one safe from the danger of kidney stones.

Dr. Johnson goes on to say, "Vitamin deficiencies probably contribute to the formation of calculi [stones]; the effect of vitamin A on epithelial surfaces [the cells lining various passages in the body such as the urinary passage] is well known and an adequate amount must be ingested in order to keep the urinary mucous membrane in good condition . . . attention has often been called to the frequent occurrence of urinary stone following peptic ulcer therapy and the concomitant dietary restrictions involved."

Rose's *Foundations of Nutrition,* a classical nutrition textbook (The Macmillan Company, 1944), has this to say: "When animals are kept for some time on diets low but not entirely lacking in vitamin A, kidney and bladder stones are frequently found. They have not been found in animals on other types of deficient diets. . . . According to McCarrison there are certain areas of India, particularly in the northwest, which are known as 'stone areas' because of the prevalence of kidney stones among the people. It is a 'poor man's disease' occurring among those whose chief dietary staple is cereal of some sort, but is most frequent where vegetation is relatively scanty, where grazing for cattle is poor, and where wheat is the chief food crop. Mc-Carrison has produced calculi in rats in 90 days from weaning time on diets low in vitamin A and consisting chiefly of wheat."

W. J. McCormick, M.D., of Toronto, who has done matchless work on vitamin therapy, has something further to contribute in the way of dietary prevention of stones—whether they form in kidneys, bladder, gall bladder or elsewhere. Dr. McCormick points out in an article in the *Journal of the Canadian Dental Association,* August, 1946, that vitamin A was the only vitamin known during some of these early investigations. Hence researchers who had removed all the vitamin A from the diet of their laboratory animals might think they had the answer, when as a matter of fact, they had also removed other necessary vitamins at the same time. He says McCarrison found that if vitamin C were also removed from the diet, kidney stones were more likely to be produced. He reminds us that the diets of the Tibetans, the people of West China, India, Labrador and Newfoundland are almost completely lacking in vitamin C, and among these people kidney stones are common. Easterners live on rice, barley flour, butter and tea with few or no vegetables and fruits. In Labrador and Newfoundland white flour, fish, game, lard, oatmeal, tea and sugar make up the bulk of the diet, and here again fresh fruits and vegetables are all but unknown.

Retarding Calcium Deposits with Vitamin C

Dr. McCormick tells us further that the teeth of people living on these diets are covered with tartar.

Even very young children have heavy tartar deposits on the teeth. This might happen, he says, because lack of vitamin C leads to a breakdown of the body tissues, including those of the mouth. The mucous lining scales off and, mixing with remnants of food, creates the unsightly and unhealthy deposit that clings so tenaciously to the teeth, resulting in pyorrhea and inflammation of the mouth tissues which have already been seriously weakened by lack of vitamin C.

Is it not possible, he asks, that the urinary tract goes through the same process when there is not enough vitamin C in the diet—the mucous lining scales off and forms the nucleus of the stones? And if this is true of kidney stones, might it not also hold true for gall bladder stones, and stones in the appendix, pancreas, prostate gland, mammary glands, uterus, ovaries and even the calcium deposit that brings about hardening of the arteries and arthritis?

Observing his own patients, Dr. McCormick found that cloudy urine containing phosphates (which constitute some kinds of kidney stones) and pieces of sloughed-off mucous from the walls of the urinary canal accompanied vitamin C deficiency. By giving large doses of vitamin C (much larger than one would get even in a daily diet relatively high in vitamin C) he could clear the urine within a matter of hours. During this treatment his patients reported to him that the tartar deposits were clearing from their teeth and dentures. Nurses in hospitals reported that patients whose urine had formerly caused calcium deposits on the urinary utensils now found that the utensils remained free from deposits. He interjects at this point a reminder that these particular patients were also getting a diet and dietary supplements high in the complex of B vitamins, but his investigations seemed to

[576]

show that it was the vitamin C that was responsible for the change in the appearance of the patients' urine.

If Dr. McCormick is correct in his theory that ample vitamin C in the diet prevents the formation of stones and tooth tartar, how should we interpret the fact that Americans as a whole have less trouble of this kind than formerly, and the age accent has shifted from youth to middle age? It's very simple, says Dr. Mc-Cormick. American mothers these days have had it drummed into their heads that their children must have vitamin C. Summer and winter, infants and youngsters must drink their orange or tomato juice and eat other fresh raw fruits. But how many of their fathers and mothers get a sufficient amount of vitamin C? Adults today are subjected to hundreds of substances that rob them of vitamin C. Smoking, drugs, insecticides, minor infections, sleeping pills and scores of present-day industrial products (such as lead, paint and benzene) are enemies of vitamin C. So, while we protect our children from scurvy by giving them fresh fruits and vegetables, we forget that adults need vitamin C in even larger amounts than children. Might this not explain very satisfactorily why the incidence of kidney stones has shifted from children to adults?

Correcting Vitamin C Deficiency May Be the Answer

McCormick quotes J. W. Joly in his book, *Stones and Calculus Disease of the Urinary Organs* (C. V. Mosby Company, 1929) : "I believe the hypothesis that stone is a deficiency disease is the most plausible and probable that has yet been advanced. It explains not only all the principal features of the condition today, but also the changes in incidence during the past years. I believe that vitamin starvation acts primarily on the renal epithelium [the lining of the kidneys] and through

[577]

it on the colloidal mechanism of the urine; also that once this mechanism is deranged, stone formation must follow as a direct result of the laws of physical chemistry."

Since the time of the early Roman scientist Pliny, physicians have been searching for the cause of kidney stones, looking generally for some medicine that could be taken orally that would dissolve the stones. Pliny's remedy was the ashes of snail shells. One of the main causes for surgery during the past century, stone formation has been so common a disorder that there are in medical dictionaries some 80 words beginning with "lith" which is the prefix referring to stone formation.

Yet how simple the answer may be! And not just for kidney stones, but, as Dr. McCormick suggests, for every kind of unhealthful calcification process that takes place in the body! At first glance it may not seem easy to get enough vitamin C. The vitamin is extremely perishable. Yet, if you should decide that from now on you are going to get enough vitamin C, it isn't really an impossible task. Fresh raw fruits and vegetables are the answer—and the sooner you can eat them after they are picked, the more vitamin C you will have. Broccoli, mustard greens, kale, green peppers, turnip greens. watercress, parsley, strawberries, Brussels sprouts and cabbage are good sources.

Pyorrhea and deposits of tartar on teeth are so common in this country as to be almost universal. No one has ever been able to find that you can get too much natural vitamin C. So why not get rid of that ugly scum on your teeth right away and prevent the possibility of pyorrhea and stones forming later on, by being sure you get many times more than the accepted daily minimum requirement of vitamin C which is about 75 to 100 milligrams.

SECTION XXIII

Liver Disease

CHAPTER 89

Vitamin C and Liver Health

WE THINK OF VITAMIN C in connection with the health of the skin, teeth and gums, blood vessels and other tissues. We know it is related to eye health and helps fight infections and poisons from the outside. We know, too, that it is rapidly destroyed in the process of fighting poisons. In other words, the more chemicals, sprays, insecticides and other poisons you are subjected to, the more vitamin C you need to stay healthy.

Vitamin C is extremely important to good health for another reason, too—one we would never have suspected. It is necessary for the well-being of the liver—that most important organ of all, the organ without which no one has ever lived longer than a few moments.

The researchers who discovered this fact tested carefully to make certain that some other element in the diet might not have influenced their conclusion—one of the B vitamins, for instance, like choline, which is very important for liver health. Choline prevents livers from becoming "fatty," so it is spoken of as a "lipo-tropic" substance—that is, something which is attract-ed to fats and hence is useful in helping the body to manage them properly.

G. C. Willis, in the *Canadian Medical Association Journal,* June 15, 1957, tells us that early researchers showed that the liver was affected in scurvy, the disease of vitamin C deficiency. Later on, the subject of vita-min C in relation to the liver was somewhat neglected, mostly because scientists were using for their dietary experiments animals that can make their own vitamin C. (They all can, you know, except guinea pigs, man and the ape family.) Research with the B vitamins showed clearly that fatty degeneration of the liver occurs when choline is lacking in the diet. Several other circumstances have been investigated, too, in regard to fatty liver—the amount of vitamin E in the diet, the degree of unsaturation of the fatty acids in the diet, any antibiotics used by the patient, thyroid and anti-thyroid drugs being used. None of this uncovered any further information about vitamin C and the liver.

So Dr. Willis set up an elaborate experiment in which he fed a total of 115 guinea pigs different diets, to take care of all the different combinations he wished to try —diets that would produce scurvy but were rich in the B vitamins, scurvy-producing diets to which certain B vitamins had been added, etc. By this means he believed he could finally discover whether vitamin C alone is necessary to prevent fatty degeneration of the liver.

It is. Passing over all the elaborate calculations made and the many examinations of the condition of differ-ent livers, we see that there can be no doubt that a lack of vitamin C in a diet which is otherwise healthful can and will produce a fatty liver. It also appears to be true that giving ample quantities of vitamin C causes the harmful deposits of fat to disappear rapidly. Furthermore, Dr. Willis showed that fatty degeneration of the liver can occur in as little as three weeks from the onset of a diet *low in fat* but deficient in vitamin C.

Note the kind of diet given—one *low* in fat, so you could not possibly assume that too much fat in the diet brought about the trouble in the liver. Giving the animals choline, the B vitamin which orders fats around like a top sergeant in the body, did not relieve the condition. Giving vitamin C did. So we can conclude, says Dr. Willis, that vitamin C and choline have two entirely separate functions so far as fat is concerned.

"This is not the first time it has been shown that ascorbic acid has lipotropic properties," he goes on. Then he quotes an earlier research showing that the deposits of cholesterol present in human hardening of the arteries can be dissolved by vitamin C.

Lack of vitamin C in the liver apparently causes the same condition this deficiency causes in other parts of the body. The intercellular material begins to dissolve and collapse. Giving vitamin C immediately causes the liver to begin to reconstruct these cells once again. Dr. Willis tells us medical literature contains a reference to a seven-month-old child who suffered from scurvy and who had an extreme case of fatty degeneration of the liver. Incidentally, the child had been given milk since birth, but it was obviously milk from which all the vitamin C had been removed by processing or by boiling.

Now you can be even more confident about the benefit you reap from taking great care about this one aspect of your diet. If you are getting plenty of vitamin C, there is far less chance that you are going to develop hardening of the arteries with all its accompanying effects on the heart and the blood vessels.

[581]

CHAPTER 90

Can Vitamins Aid in Relieving Menopause Problems?

AMONG THE CLASSIC problems menopause presents for many women are leg cramps at night, frequent bruises and nosebleed. Anne Horoschak, M.D., writing in the *Delaware State Medical Journal* (January, 1959), stated that each of these symptoms could be traced to capillary weaknesses, that is, weaknesses in the walls of the capillaries, which are the tiniest of the blood vessels.

In the case of leg cramps, Dr. Horoschak believes that the pain could be caused by a shortage of oxygen in the muscles, due to poor functioning of the capillaries supplying those muscles. High susceptibility to bruising, usually found in women of fair complexion and thin-textured skin, is probably caused, she says, by the thin-ness of the skin, abnormal fragility of the smaller blood vessels and defective cushioning of the deep vascular bed. Dr. Horoschak is convinced that spontaneous nose-bleeds are the result of a capillary system not properly strengthened by needed nutrients.

The answer to these problems, then, is to reinforce the capillary resistance to stress and injury. Long known as active agents in this area are vitamin C and the bioflavonoids. The bioflavonoids are known to act in connection with vitamin C and to help the body retain this quickly lost vitamin for longer periods of time. Aside from the increased fragility of the capillaries in deficiency cases of the bioflavonoids, pain in the extremities at any effort, and laziness, also follow as a result of a shortage of this nutrient.

As A. Szent-Gyorgi states (*Annals of New York Academic Science,* 61:732, 1955), "There can be little doubt that flavonoids are not only useful therapeutic agents in conditions of capillary fragility, but have many diverse actions in the animal body." G. J. Martin adds, in *Experimental Medicine* and *Surgery* (12: 570, 1954): "It [combination of bioflavonoids and vitamin C] is to be regarded as supplemental therapy of value in virtually all disease states and specific in action with respect to some."

With such opinions in mind Dr. Horoschak entered into an experiment to determine the effect of a mixture of hesperidin (a bioflavonoid) and vitamin C on 40 patients with various of the 3 symptoms outlined above: 14 had leg cramps at night, 15 showed easy bruising and 11 spontaneous nosebleeds. The patients were an average of 51 years old, and none had any diseases which might have caused the complaints. Most of them had been "doctoring" and had received various medications, but with no apparent effect. All of the symptoms were more pronounced during the time when the patients would have had their menstrual period.

The treatment was divided into two phases. The first consisted in nothing other than establishing an amicable relationship between the doctor and the patient. It was considered important that the patients understand that such ailments are frequent in menopause and can be remedied, and that a full and productive life can and should continue through, and follow after, menopause. The patients discussed their problems freely and received advice when they asked for it. The whole procedure was intended to relax tension and relieve anxiety, and as a result cooperation of the patients was freely given.

The hesperidin-ascorbic acid (vitamin C) capsules contained 100 milligrams of each. At the beginning all patients received two capsules after each meal and two at bedtime for two weeks, then one capsule 4 times a day for 4 weeks. As improvement was noted, the patient was directed to lower the dose. When all symptoms disappeared, the patient took a maintenance dose of two capsules a day, then none.

Of the 14 suffering from nocturnal leg cramps, 4 were under control within two weeks, and the rest within an average of 7 weeks.

Of the easily bruised patients, 11 out of the 15 showed a resistance to bruises after only 8 weeks of treatment with 8 capsules, then with two capsules daily. The remaining 4 took 8 capsules a day for 16 weeks before their resistance was evident.

Nosebleed, a source of concern to 11 patients, stopped within 6 to 11 weeks in the 8 moderate cases. They began with the regular 8 capsules, and then went on a maintenance dose of two capsules a day for a year.

Three of these 11 patients had severe nosebleed, and they responded less positively. One of the 3 was under control in 3 months, and stayed that way on a maintenance dose of two capsules a day. The condition was lessened in the other two patients, but never completely controlled, until it stopped suddenly in the fourth year.

It is not surprising to us that so simple a device as vitamin C and the bioflavonoids in a capsule would be effective in treating these problems. A shortage of these and other nutrients is most likely to occur during the menopause. The female system receives a tremendous shock at this time, for the body shuts down a set of hormones which have been operating, and affecting every part of the body by their operation, for 35 or more years. Now a shifting of gears is required. The body must learn to operate without the intimate influence of these hormones. This new learning places a stress on the body and such stress uses nutrients from everywhere else to keep the body going. These nutrients must be replaced by diet and supplements. When they are not, things go wrong—the things that many doctors simply designate as "menopause problems" for which they have no cure. So many middle-aged women find themselves condemned to 3 or 4 years of headache, cold sweat, cramps, backache, irritability, nervousness, etc. —all because no one considered replacing the nutrients used so extravagantly in meeting the needs of these stressful years.

Prevent Deficiencies

If a disease can be cured with nutrients, it is only logical to assume that a deficiency existed. Such deficiency can be prevented by more careful intake of all the nutrients, and the disease is automatically prevented, too. Special attention should be paid to food supplements at the time of menopause. Extra amounts of vitamin C—the stress vitamin—should be added to keep the skin healthy and well supplied with nutrients

[585]

through strong arteries and capillaries. Easy and long-lasting bruise marks are the result of little else than a shortage of this vitamin. It also prevents infections at a time when the body is most susceptible to them due to lowered resistance.

Vitamin E, to keep needed oxygen in the blood longer, is essential to treating many menopause symptoms including leg cramps, hot flashes, etc. The B-complex vitamins also deserve special attention, for they are most active in preserving the full health of the nerves which are often the cause of headaches and irritability at this time.

Menopause is a perfectly natural process, and should cause no more difficulty than any other basic bodily function. The key is, of course, a healthy body to begin with. Such a body can only result from healthful eating, proper rest and exercise. The time to prepare for menopause is long, long before it arrives!

CHAPTER 91

Menstrual Difficulties?
Have You Tried Vitamins?

IF HOMES AREN'T actually broken due to menstrual tension, they are certainly sorely tried because of it. The wife can't explain her irritation at little things, and her husband is likely to tire of putting up with her irritability. The result is a loud argument and a strained household for a few days.

Symptoms of premenstrual tension may appear as early as two weeks before menstruation (the bleeding phase of the menstrual cycle), increasing in intensity until they reach a peak shortly before menstruation begins, then disappearing completely with the beginning of the flow.

Symptoms include mild depression, irritability, anxiety, nausea, headache, tiredness or agitation, abdominal bloating, swelling of extremities, dizziness, blurred vision, swelling and tenderness of the breasts, cravings for certain foods, etc. The list is endless, and can be extended by almost every woman who notices a change in her emotions and physiological make-up prior to menstruation. It is important to make it clear, however, that such mental stresses and physiological manifestations are not necessarily to be expected in a healthy woman. Women should not be willing to resign themselves to physical discomfort and psychological tension just because they are due to have their monthly period. In many cases, premenstrual and menstrual problems can and should be treated.

The Mechanics of Menstruation

Science has tried to discover just what it is about the natural process of menstruation that should create such difficulties for so many — not all — women. To understand the proposed treatments perhaps it would be best to start with an analysis of the actual mechanics of the menstrual cycle. What actually occurs in menstruation, and why?

The average menstrual cycle lasts about 28 days. The schedule of just what occurs in this time runs approximately like this:

The first day of bleeding begins slowly, and builds to a maximum flow on about the second or third day. By the fifth day, menstruation usually ends. The blood which flows carries with it the lining of the uterus which was intended to act as a bed for the egg, should it have become fertilized. The unfertilized egg is ejected, too. Meanwhile the ovary begins to produce a follicle containing a new egg.

As the follicle matures, it produces a hormone, estrogen, which stimulates the growth of a new lining for the uterus—a lining intended once more for implantation of a fertilized egg. This process goes on for about 14 days, at which time the egg follicle bursts, discharging the fully developed egg into the Fallopian tube.

[588]

Now the egg waits for possible fertilization by a male sperm. If this should occur, the fertilized egg implants itself in the wall of the uterus to grow for the 9 months of gestation. If fertilization does not occur, the egg travels down the uterus to be expelled when the menstrual flow begins again.

In the meantime, the follicle which held the egg has been transformed into a solid yellowish ball which secretes two hormones: estrogen and progesterone. (The latter produces a swelling of the lining of the uterus intended to prepare for the development of a fertilized egg.) If pregnancy has taken place, the egg has implanted itself on the wall of the uterus, and the uterine wall will not slough off. This means, of course, that menstruation will not occur. If the egg has not been fertilized, uterine bleeding, characteristic of menstruation, begins again.

The Troublesome Stage

The stage of the menstrual cycle that takes place between the 14th and the 28th day is the one which seems to create most problems for women. It is during this time that the previously described distressing symptoms appear. It is suspected that the cause lies in the fact that two very powerful hormones, estrogen and progesterone, are secreted in irregular patterns of supply, which are as yet little understood by scientists. Both of these hormones affect a number of glands and organs in the body, and should there be any deviation from the proper ratios of secretions it would undoubtedly show itself in some kind of discomfort.

The emotional problems of menstruation, say some doctors, are aligned with a varying degree of basic emotional instability in the individual woman. It is not the direct cause of the problem of premenstrual tension, but unstable emotions may act to make one woman react more violently than another to the monthly menstrual stress. Women who react emotionally to ordinary situations with which they are confronted can be expected to react in the same way to the physical strain presented by the menstrual cycle. This emotional reaction to the physical symptoms may result in increased output of the very hormones which caused the original physical discomfort.

The treatments offered by most doctors take cognizance of the hormonal factor. They either treat to step up or decrease bodily hormone secretions. They use sedatives, pain killers, tranquilizers, diuretics, etc. Even psychiatry is resorted to in cases of extreme emotional upset.

Why Should a Natural Process Be Painful?

We believe that premenstrual tension is not a necessary and normal part of the menstrual cycle. The fact that the problem is so common has convinced many suffering women that they might as well resign themselves to the pain and stress they experience and consider it as a part of the unfair burden of their sex. The fact that many women do not suffer at all is enough to dispose of that theory. Why should suffering be involved with a natural bodily process? We believe the answer to menstrual difficulties lies in our nutrition and environment.

In March, 1955, the *Medical Journal of Australia* carried a summary of the work done by A. P. Hudgins in which he showed the relationship between nutrients and premenstrual pains. He used only those patients, in his research, who had cramps severe enough to require bedrest, heavy sedation or time loss from work. The test included 220 women who suffered in this way.

[590]

Each was given a basic dosage of 100 milligrams of niacin every morning and evening, and 100 milligrams of the same every two or three hours during the period of actual cramps. Dr. Hudgins stated that each dose may be increased by 50 to 100 milligrams or more to maintain flushing for maximum effect.

The effectiveness of niacin, the B vitamin, was improved by adding a combination of rutin (60 milligrams) with 300 milligrams of ascorbic acid (vitamin C). The theory was that the blood vessel dilating effect of the niacin was made more effective by the improvement in capillary permeability brought about by the two added nutrients.

In most cases the niacin was effective if it had been taken 7 to 10 days before the onset of the menstrual flow. The effectiveness of the therapy continued for several months after therapy was discontinued. This led Dr. Hudgins to conclude that the problem is nutritional in origin. The effectiveness of the therapy is evident in the fact that 90 per cent of the patients studied were relieved of cramps.

Vitamin A Found Effective Against Tension

As far back as June, 1951, the *American Journal of Obstetrics and Gynecology* carried a report on the role played by vitamin A in menstruation. Dr. Allesandro Pou of Uruguay told of using a solution of vitamin A in olive oil on patients with premenstrual tension and delay of the menstrual period. The tension was characterized by edema, nervousness, tenderness of breasts, etc.

The patients received 150,000 International Units of vitamin A per day, orally, for 15 days prior to menstruation. The treatment was followed for from 3 to 6 months. In 13 of 24 patients thus treated (54.17 per cent) the results were termed "very good." The symptoms had completely disappeared.

In 7 of the remaining 11 patients the results were termed "fairly good." Symptoms were partially relieved in 4 of them, but in 3, though there was remarkable improvement, there was still some discomfort.

The last 4 patients could discern no change, and one of the women showed a remarkable intolerance to vitamin A.

Over all it was concluded that improvement was obtained in 83.34 per cent of the patients. Further, it was seen that stopping the administration of vitamin A led to an immediate reappearance of the symptoms in 8 of the 20 patients, 40 per cent, who had shown improvement.

Vitamin K was employed to regulate the menstrual cycle by Richard Gubner and Harry E. Ungerleider, and they wrote of their experiments in *Transcript of the American Therapeutic Society* (April 9, 1954).

Vitamin K for Cramps and Prolonged Flow

A synthetic vitamin K preparation was given to a total of 43 patients. These people were employees at an insurance company's home office who regularly presented themselves at the infirmary for treatment and rest periods due to chronic prolonged menstrual flow, some with clotting and some with severe menstrual cramps.

The authors theorized that prolonged bleeding could be due to an impairment of the clotting mechanism. It was suggested that a malfunction of the liver is indicated when profuse bleeding occurs in menstruation. The liver is the original site of prothrombin mechanism, the tool for blood clotting. Vitamin K is intimately involved with prothrombin formation and

[592]

its administration is indicated where a prothrombin deficiency exists.

In view of this possibility, vitamin K was given to these patients in dosages averaging about 25 milligrams over a 5-day period. The vitamin was given one or two days before menstruation began, or on the first day of the menstrual period. This was the only medication given.

Of 12 cases with a history of prolonged menstrual flow, lasting 6 days or longer, the duration of the flow was reduced by one or more days in 8 cases, and was unchanged in 4 cases. Twenty-six of the cases studied usually had clots in the menstrual discharge. Of these, the clots disappeared or diminished in 16 cases, were unchanged in 8 cases, and increased in 2 cases.

All of the 43 patients studied by Drs. Gubner and Ungerleider suffered from moderate to severe menstrual cramps. Of that total the cramps were lessened or abolished in 28 cases, and unaffected in 15 cases.

E and A Combine to Give Relief

The *Bulletin, federation societe gynecologie et obstet, langue franc.* (10, 3-7, 1958), carried a report on 54 patients experiencing chronic premenstrual tension. They were each given 90,000 International Units of vitamin A, plus 210 milligrams of vitamin E daily. Results were termed "good" (i.e., complete disappearance of symptoms) in 73 per cent of the cases and "intermediate" (i.e., symptoms were lessened) in 10 per cent of the cases. The most frequently observed symptoms—breast congestion, depression and abdominal tension—disappeared in 80 per cent of the cases. Nervous agitation and premenstrual pain were markedly relieved.

This is some of the evidence that convinces us of the

[593]

need for a healthful diet as a preventive against menstrual problems. We feel that if one's diet contains sufficient of the B vitamins and vitamins K, E and A, there will be no need for treatment during menses. And, of course, fresh, unprocessed foods, properly prepared, are the best guarantee that one's meals will supply the proper intake of nutrients.

If one is already suffering with a difficult menstrual cycle, we believe that the above-quoted experiments should act as an excellent guide to possible therapeutic measures to be taken. Consult your doctor, and ask him at least to try vitamin therapy before resorting to hormones and tranquilizers as a means of relieving the distress. These can have dangerous side effects which are as bad or worse than the original distress. The nutrients, on the other hand, pose no such problem. The possible exception is vitamin A, which can be toxic if taken in massive amounts.

Above all, don't suffer in resignation when plagued with menstrual disorders. Check your diet and your natural food supplementation. If you are certain that you are getting the nutrients you need, see a doctor to make sure yours is not a serious physiological problem.

SECTION XXVI

Mental Illness

CHAPTER 92

Vitamin B₁₂ Deficiency and Mental Illness

THE WHOLE QUESTION of mental disease, its causes and treatment, is taking on a new look. The psychiatrist's couch is being displaced by the laboratory. The chemical make-up of the blood has been proven to have a very definite effect on the health and operation of the brain, and it is in this field that the greatest advances against mental illness have been made. Strangely enough, the doctors who deal with mental disorders seem reluctant to take advantage of these new developments, in spite of the fact that the more commonly used treatments are obviously ineffective in most cases, can be dangerous and often lead to recurrence. We have seen startling evidence of the effect an unbalanced blood sugar level can have on the mind; the lack of a proper amount of thyroxin in the blood has been seen to cause mental disorders; treatment with nothing more than a potent vitamin-mineral supplement has brought about amazing results.

[595]

The findings of Drs. James Wiener and Justin Hope, as printed in the *Journal of the American Medical Association* (June 27, 1959), are another example of the relationship between mental health and nutritional deficiency. Research has shown that mental illness and pernicious anemia (which is largely the result of a vitamin B₁₂ shortage) often go hand in hand. This connection was first suggested in 1902. In 1915 Pfeiffer recorded an unquestionable case. By 1927 McAlpine was able to write, "Mental changes occur not uncommonly in pernicious anemia. They range from states of depression accompanied by loss of mental energy, to definite psychosis. They, like the nervous symptoms, may precede the characteristic changes in the blood by many months." In other words, the patient might become ill mentally long before his doctor could discover, from tests, that he had anemia.

Little Consideration in Standard Textbooks

The *Journal of the American Medical Association's* article calmly states that the cerebral (mental) manifestations of a vitamin B₁₂ deficiency have received little consideration in standard textbooks. In other words, a doctor would probably never hear of this possibility in medical school. After graduation he probably would have missed it, unless he came upon the 1927 reference of McAlpine, until June, 1959. Imagine the number of patients who have consulted doctors on mental trouble who might have needed B₁₂ and nothing more, yet were pronounced hopeless.

The effectiveness of the B₁₂ therapy depends largely on the duration of the deficiency before beginning the therapy. The importance of early diagnosis is apparent in the report by Holmes quoted in the article. Holmes treated 14 patients for a B_{12} deficiency, all of whom had well-marked mental symptoms. In all but two, the mental symptoms disappeared, or were greatly relieved after intensive treatment. The two patients who did not respond had been psychotic patients at a mental hospital for several months before treatment. Psychosis, in these cases, had developed and progressed over a period of 7 or 8 years.

Diagnosis Difficult

The diagnosis of mental problems due to pernicious anemia is often difficult because they may occur without the changes in the blood usually expected when anemia is present. However, the article describes two tests for vitamin B_{12} levels in the blood which are helpful in such cases. It is also worth noting that tests show consistently low values of oxygen consumption in the brain in patients with mental disturbance due to pernicious anemia, as compared with normal people and those with anemia due to blood loss.

When mental symptoms occur along with the classic symptoms of pernicious anemia—weakness, sore tongue, an increase in the size of red corpuscles, absence of digestive juices in the stomach, etc., diagnosis is easy. However, these are often absent, and the mental symptoms are not consistently characteristic. They range from mild moodiness, with difficulty in concentrating and remembering, to violent maniacal behavior, severe agitation, stuporous depression and hallucinations.

The common nervous symptoms of a B_{12} deficiency are different, and not connected with the mind at all. They include pins and needles sensations, numbness, stiffness, feelings of heat and cold, local feelings of deadness, tightness and shooting pains. If any of these

[597]

are present with the mental symptoms, the diagnosis is again made somewhat easier.

The Treatment Is Simple

In the actual treatment of mental illness resulting from a deficiency of vitamin B_{12}, much larger doses are needed than in the treatment of simple blood count conditions of anemia. The treatment outlined by Wiener and Hope in their article is extremely simple: intramuscular injection of 1,000 micrograms of B_{12} for the first treatment, followed by 500 micrograms twice weekly for one month, then 100 micrograms of B_{12}, intramuscularly, once a week for 6 months. The authors tell us that results can be expected in 3 to 6 months.

Now this is certainly a worthwhile avenue of investigation for the doctor confronted with a puzzling case of mental illness. Determining a B_{12} deficiency is not an involved procedure. Each patient can be tested for this possibility. Such testing for all nutrients should be a matter of course when any physical problem presents itself. This is especially true, when a precedent has been set through responsible treatment, given by a respected physician, with good results. The tragedy of mental illness requires us to use any means we have to combat its appearance and development, and we see no reason why proven nutritional therapy should not be given a chance to show its effectiveness.

Note that injection is used in all these cases. The reason is simply that, by the time such conditions have appeared, the stomach does not contain any, or possibly enough, of a certain substance which must be present to absorb vitamin B_{12}. So vitamin B_{12} taken by mouth would be wasted. Injecting the vitamin into the patient's blood or muscle assures its absorption since it does not pass through the digestive tract at all. Of course, injection of a vitamin must be done by a physician. Meanwhile, to insure oneself against the ever-increasing threat of mental illness, include some food and food supplements rich in B vitamins (including B_{12}) such as beef liver, and other organ meats, brewer's yeast and desiccated liver in your regular diet. Remember, if B_{12} can be used to cure mental disorders, it should also be an excellent preventive.

CHAPTER 93

Vitamin E and Mental Disorders

In the *Summary* (June, 1961) we saw what will probably be, for many, the most valuable and hopeful information yet. A letter from Dr. Alfonso del Guidice, Chief of Child Psychology, National Institute of Public Health, Buenos Aires, Argentina, is quoted in full, and it tells of the success of vitamin E as a treatment for mental defects in children. Let us quote for you his initial remarks:

"Dear Sir:

"Our extensive experience with vitamin E therapy in children has taught us a good deal about the management of psychosomatic [physical disorders of mental origin] aspects of their problems.

"We use dosages of alphatocopherol which vary with the age of the patient and the gravity of his disease, as well as the time permitted for treatment. However, the guiding principle has been massive dosage and continuous administration, never omitting a single day in

[600]

our effort to achieve and maintain tissue saturation—one continuous course of treatment, until one sees the child's mental state improve.

"We have treated many complications in our infantile psychotics, such as the ophthalmological [visual disorders] where we have had brilliant results in myopia [nearsightedness], nystogmus [involuntary, rapid movement of the eyeball], strabismus [crossed eyes], cataract and other conditions, as will be noted in more detail below (case histories following the letter). No child remained unimproved when properly treated.

"Generally we have begun treatment with 200 to 300 milligrams of vitamin E daily, increasing over a period of as long as 6 months to doses approximating two grams daily—depending on the age of the child and his type of disease.

"Vitamin C was also given in doses of 500 to 1500 grams [most likely a misprint for milligrams] daily. It was added because of my belief that it reinforces vitamin E—it being clear, always, that the latter is the basic item. Vitamin C seems especially indicated in organic deficiencies and old cataracts."

Dr. del Guidice then presented a group of short case histories. We think his results with vitamin E are most gratifying and certainly deserve the attention of doctors in the United States. What doctor or parent would allow the opportunity of using a healthful nutrient therapeutically to slip by, if he could hope for such results as Dr. del Guidice describes?

Epilepsy Responds to Vitamin E

The first case concerns epilepsy, a not-too-rare problem in children. Its control is largely confined to rather powerful drugs which are given on an increasing scale,

[601]

as required, until their side effects become so intolerable that some other form of therapy must be introduced.

Epilepsy occurs in two general forms: petit mal (minor sickness) and grand mal (severe sickness). Petit mal is more common in children. These seizures are frequent, but last only a few seconds and are often not noticed at all. The child may drop whatever he is holding, or may fall and immediately get up. There may be twitching of the facial muscles. Petit mal attacks are usually at their peak in the morning hours, and they usually diminish in frequency and seriousness as the child grows older. Grand mal is what most of us think of when we mention epilepsy. The patient becomes unconscious and falls. Saliva may appear on his lips, as his body tightens into violent convulsive spasms and twitchings, and this state lasts for a minute or two. Afterward he may feel dull and drowsy for a time, or he may go to sleep for hours.

Judge for yourself if the epilepsy cases treated by Dr. del Guidice could have merely disappeared in so short a time, or if vitamin E is the answer.

Case I: A little girl aged 3. She had experienced a severe fall at 9 months, and the epilepsy was attributed to that. She had her first seizure at the age of two. It lasted 4 minutes, with unconsciousness, spasm and frothing at the mouth. Afterward, the child suffered with a violent headache and other slight disturbances for 6 hours. She was unable to speak for the first 1½ hours of that period.

She fell frequently thereafter, wet the bed, was restless in sleep, was nervous, had crying spells and did not get on well with other children. Tocopherol medication was begun as her sole treatment. In 3 months time she had improved, was far more tranquil, played with other children, had no more convulsions.

After 10 months of treatment she still had had no more convulsions, or seizures, had conquered her bed-wetting problem, had become quite friendly and calm, had gained weight, slept well, rarely cried and was a happy child.

Case II: A 9-months-old boy who after electroencephalograph tests (ECG) was diagnosed as an epileptic. He had convulsions several times daily during which his eyes pulled to one side, his neck retracted and became rigid and he lost consciousness. There was great instability in his movements and he was nervous while awake and restless in sleep.

His previous treatment had consisted of hormonal preparations and sedatives, but to no avail. Previous medication was halted by Dr. del Guidice, and the boy was given tocopherol only. After several months he lost his convulsions, excitability and instability of motion. After 5 months' treatment, he had no more convulsions, slept peacefully and was much quieter.

Both of these cases of frank epilepsy responded to treatment with vitamin E when other treatments had failed. This is not an infrequent course of events. We do not know if such results could be achieved with adult epileptics. Dr. del Guidice does not discuss any patients but children, but we can see no reason for not trying vitamin E to treat adults as well.

Why Does Vitamin E Work?

The fact that vitamin E can prolong the retention of oxygen in the blood stream is probably the key to its effectiveness in treating mental disorders. The brain needs an optimum supply of oxygen if it is to function

[603]

properly. Perhaps in some systems, the demands for oxygen elsewhere in the body exhaust the supply before the blood reaches the brain. This could be the result of an inadequate supply of oxygen in the first place, or because of an inability to retain it in the blood long enough to meet all necessities. Vitamin E could be very effective in preventing or reversing such a situation.

Dr. del Guidice gave 20 more case histories in his letter to the *Summary*. In each of them mental disorder was effectively treated with vitamin E. It is not true that all of them were completely cured with vitamin E, but all were benefited sufficiently so that the change was clinically observable.

Here, briefly, are some of the other cases discussed by Dr. del Guidice: A 12-year-old girl, a congenital idiot, exhibited aggressive impulses which called for restraint of her arms by her parents almost all the time. She shouted and cried for no reason, and was extremely moody. The girl could not speak properly, could not comprehend questions and was unable to manage her own toilet routine. For 6 years of medical treatment there had been no improvement.

After 40 days of tocopherol therapy she had made more progress than in all of the previous 6 years. At the end of a year she was fairly subdued, sat correctly and watched her surroundings calmly. She lost her babbling, crying and aggressivness, sat at table and ate by herself for the first time.

Case 12 was a female, aged 3, who stuttered and had a severe inferiority complex. Her mother was almost unaware of what the child's voice was like. She couldn't even play with her little brothers and sisters. On the third day of tocopherol therapy she was improved. In 3 months of tocopherol treatment she was completely free of stammering, could recite 3 verses of a poem with ease and fluency, and played happily with other children.

Psychosomatic Paralysis and Blindness Yield

Case 14 concerned a 5-year-old girl whose both legs were paralyzed, and her mind deficient. She had never talked, could not balance herself on her feet, did not walk and had had no result from any of the considerable medical treatment taken since birth. After 7 months on tocopherol she began to walk and talk, articulating some words clearly. Four months later, she could walk well, even run, and her mentality was improved.

This is an obvious case of so-called psychosomatic illness, the type in which the mind is largely responsible for a physical disability. The child's legs were certainly able to function, had she willed them to do so.

A case much like this was number 15, a 23-year-old man who had physically normal eyes, but suffered from a mental deficiency and "blindness." Though he was equipped with normal visual apparatus, the man could not see. Eight years of treatment under his own physician had been futile.

In less than two months on vitamin E, he could vaguely count the fingers on a hand almost 7 feet away, and recognize people 10 feet away, with his left eye. With his right eye he saw a little less, but he could now dress and feed himself, travel alone on a train and walk through city traffic. He was mentally improved as well.

Of special interest to us were several cases, described by Dr. del Guidice, in which vitamin E proved an

[605]

effective cataract treatment. In one instance, a 10-year-old girl who had been born with cataracts on both eyes was totally blind; she could not distinguish light, even after an operation on her right eye. She was depressed and extremely quiet. After 6 months on tocopherol, her personality had changed for the better, and she could detect light. The cataracts were less dense, and the corneas more brilliant. In the right eye the pupil was now visible.

Another child of 10, also born with cataracts of both eyes which had been operated on unsuccessfully, tried vitamin E. In 8 months the child could see small objects at short distances.

A boy of the same age had congenital cataracts of the right eye and other defects of both eyes. He was also mentally deficient. In 1955 vitamin E therapy was begun. His mental capacity increased, and the congenital cataract disappeared, as the Opthalmological Institute which had been watching him testified. His vision improved in both eyes. (The slow disappearance of the cataract began as soon as the tocopherol treatment started.)

These cases are of more than passing interest. If the results obtained by Dr. del Guidice can be repeated by other doctors, surely vitamin E is at least a partial answer to one of our most vexing problems, mental illness. And if all cataracts will show a similar response to vitamin E, many inoperable cases can hope for relief.

It is to be hoped that more work will be done along the lines of Dr. del Guidice. We hope other clinicians will be sufficiently impressed with the doctor's position and prestige to listen to him when he tells of his results of vitamin E, and use the treatment themselves. If there had been no Dr. del Guidice to use vitamin E

[606]

on them, would those patients about whom he wrote have progressed as they did? No one really knows, but the record would indicate against it. Treatments of as much as 6 and 8 years along conventional lines had done no good. Several weeks or months with vitamin E had been rewarded with strong indications of improvement or complete recovery.

Will Our Children Have a Chance?

Will our children be given a similar opportunity for recovery? Will an American doctor who sees progressive epilepsy or some other mental involvement in a child try vitamin E? Will he do so in the case of congenital cataracts? Will he try to *cure* nervousness instead of merely tranquilizing it?

Dr. del Guidice's experiences are monumental in the field of treatment for emotionally disturbed children, an increasingly common disorder in modern society. We can only guess why vitamin E is so effective in this area, but it apparently does work, so why not make the most of it? We are using drugs which merely dull symptoms and do not reach the causes of illness at all. Vitamin E is a nutrient, and if it is effective, it is effective because it fills a need which has not been met by diet. Meet this need and you have conquered the problem, not merely pacified or disguised it. Modern medicine seems satisfied to pacify disease instead of curing it. Aspirins don't cure headaches, they merely help to dull the pain; cortisone doesn't cure arthritis, it merely dulls the symptoms; phenobarbitol doesn't cure epilepsy, it merely quiets it. But this is the kind of treatment doctors prescribe. Why should we settle for temporary relief without trying for a possible permanent cure?

[607]

CHAPTER 94

Brain Surgery and Vitamin B

PREFRONTAL LOBOTOMY is a brain operation performed on longterm, violent mental patients. It has been likened to "inserting a knife in a pumpkin and sawing up and down." The surgeon attempts to sever fibers leading to an area of the brain that stores undesirable past associations. If the scalpel slips, the uncontrollable maniac that was wheeled into surgery emerges as an even more pathetic human vegetable. But even if the operation is a complete success, destructive personality changes follow: healthy concern about the future disappears, and with it initiative and drive necessary for normal living. Dull, unimaginative placidity has been the fate of thousands submitted to the operation. And now it turns out, according to Dr. K. G. McKenzie, one of Canada's pioneers in neurosurgery, the patient is no better off with the operation than he would have been without it.

Dr. McKenzie's opinion, appearing in the *Canadian*

Medical Association Journal (December 10, 1964) is especially startling since he performed this operation more than any other Canadian surgeon. He never knew, until the recent results of the first controlled study of lobotomy patients, that he was wasting his time. At an Ontario hospital, 183 patients who submitted to the hour-long operation were compared with a less radically treated control group, for adjustment to society, readmission to hospital, and discharge rate after five years, etc. The appalling fact is that the operation made no significant difference.

Doesn't it seem strange that surgeons and psychiatrists, so anxious to treat mental illness that they will resort to unproven brain surgery, all but ignore the encouraging evidence of nutrition's impressive record in this field? One cringes at the possibility that the brains of thousands of the mentally ill were mangled by useless surgery when they might have been restored to normal by simple nutritional supplementation. Certainly the first step in the treatment of any mental disorder should be a careful check on the nutritional status of the patient.

Well-Kept Secret

It is unfortunate that the effect of poor nutrition on mentality is not more widely publicized. Americans are aware that insufficient rest, sudden shock and certain types of injury can cause mental illness, but the danger to mentality of poor nutrition is one of the better kept secrets of modern research. The *Journal of the American Medical Association* (June 27, 1959) admitted as much: "Mental changes resulting from vitamin B_{12} deficiency are among the least publicized aspects of this condition. The cerebral manifestations of this disorder have received little consideration in

[609]

standard textbooks on the subject. The milder symptoms may be a slight mood disturbance or mental slowness with difficulty in concentrating and remembering. The symptoms may be much more severe, however, with violent maniacal behavior, severe agitation, stuporous depression, paranoid behavior, or the presence of overt visual and auditory hallucinations. . . . When present these mental status findings make it difficult to distinguish this condition from schizophrenia."

A group of researchers who reported in the *Bulletin of the Staff Meetings of the Mayo Clinic* (Vol. 14, pp. 787-793, 1939) on an experiment with mental patients demonstrated nutrition's effect on the mind 20 years earlier. Patients deprived of thiamin (vitamin B₁) changed their behavior within ten days to five weeks. They became confused, uncertain of memory and generally weak. They were all irritable, depressed, quarrelsome, uncooperative and fretful of some impending disaster. Two actually threatened suicide. The missing thiamin ruined the patients' manual dexterity, and brought headaches and painful menstruation instead. They could not sleep and were excessively sensitive to noise.

Thiamin worked in reverse for Dr. Tom Spies. In the *Association for Research on Nervous Disorders* publication (1943, Vol. 22, 122-140) he told of 115 patients eating a diet low in thiamin. They were described as timid and depressed people; but within 30 minutes to 20 hours of receiving supplementary thiamin, they became pleasant and cooperative.

Among 194 children suffering from pellagra (a disease brought on by vitamin B deficiency), Dr. Spies found that brewer's yeast and good diet along with a supplement of niacin (another of the B vitamins) brought immediate relief of symptoms such as irrit-

[610]

ability, fright and fretfulness, lack of appetite, and disinterest in the normal activities of children (*Journal of the American Medical Association,* Vol. 113, 1481-1483).

All Nutrients Essential

Although B vitamins seem to be the most obvious need, we know that all the nutrients are essential to mental health. Researchers have found, for example, that any serious psychological stress causes a sudden and extreme decrease in the body's supply of vitamin C. Elderly patients suffering from mental deterioration are especially likely to need added vitamins. C. W. Clinibal (*Hippocrates,* Vol. 22, 481-482, 1951) found that with supplementary vitamin E he could cut excessive nervousness and irritability in children. (Dr. Spies also recorded a form of nervous upset which responds to vitamin E therapy.) Calcium deficiency is frequently associated with instability of the nervous system, since this mineral is required to transmit impulses along the nerves. If calcium is involved, so are vitamins A and D and phosphorus—all necessary to calcium's assimilation.

Dr. George Watson, whose report appeared in the *Journal of Psychology* (1957, 43, 47-53), decided that unless one specific nutritional deficiency can be pinpointed, mental cases are likely to be the result of a multiple deficiency. Therefore he worked out a formula including generous amounts of all the vitamins and minerals known or believed to be important in human nutrition.

Watson tested his formula on a group of 19 emotionally disturbed patients. Each patient received a placebo (dummy pill) for the first one to two and a half months to establish any reaction to the mere psychology of using a pill. After that each received an experimental capsule of nutrients for an average period of 2.9 months. Of the 19, all but 3 improved significantly; one got worse and two showed no change. An enviable record.

Difficult Cases

The type of cases that did respond is impressive. They could hardly be dismissed as simple neurotics. Any of them could have been committed to a mental institution without question. Another doctor might have ordered straitjackets, insulin shock treatments, heavy tranquilizer therapy—perhaps lobotomy.

One, a young man of 19, was psychotic because of a skin disease on his face. He would not leave his room or talk with his family. He was depressed and afraid to meet anyone. On the placebo the boy got worse. But after only one month of treatment with the actual vitamin capsule, he began to change. The family was surprised to find him joining them in the living room to watch television. He began to have long confidential talks with his father, whom he had especially ignored before. His score in a psychological test given at the end of the treatment was normal. According to his mother, "his recovery, frankly, is more than we had hoped for."

A hostile and slightly depressed 26-year-old man was so emotionally uncontrolled that he once attempted to kick in a television set because his father asked him to change the station. Once the vitamin treatment began, the father said his son's condition was better than ever. He was more at ease and more alert. He even attempted to find a job, and succeeded, whereas before he couldn't get interested in anything.

[612]

Among the other patients was a woman too depressed to get a job, who spoke with a slow, childlike voice pattern and seemed mentally confused. After a month on the vitamin treatment, she re-enrolled in school and her voice became normal. In three months, she had a job and was completely calm and relaxed. A 53-year-old woman showed flights of anger and excessive hostility. Her doctor had been treating her with a tranquilizer for months. After one month on the vitamin treatment, her irritation was gone. After four months she appeared normal and obtained a job as a saleslady in a department store.

Help Yourself

You can use all these astonishing facts to protect yourself and your family from mental illness. Though the rest of the public may be uninformed, at least you are aware that a full quota of nutrients can relieve and prevent mental problems. Dr. Watson gave his patients "large quantities of all the vitamins known or believed important in human nutrition." To prevent mental breakdown, we think everyone should get the vitamins by concentrating on fresh, unprocessed foods and natural food supplements. The important B vitamins, particularly, are almost completely lacking in modern diets. If you eat white bread and refined cereals; if you eat too few fresh fruits and vegetables and favor pastries, desserts and between-meal snacks; if you don't eat enough meat, fish, eggs, nuts and seeds, you probably have a deficiency in B vitamins and most of the other ones important to mental health as well.

Revise your diet. Add B-rich natural food supplements—especially brewer's yeast, desiccated liver and wheat germ. See that the organ meats have a prominent part in your weekly menus. Concentrate on fresh fruits and vegetables. For the calcium so necessary to the health of the nerves, use bone meal, eggs and nuts.

If a member of your family should be so unfortunate as to suffer from a form of mental illness, show your doctor this article. Ask him to send for a copy of Dr. Watson's paper describing exactly what he did and the formula he used. Urge him to try nutritional therapy, alone or in connection with his regular treatments. It can't do any harm. It might be all that's needed to restore someone you love to a normal, happy existence.

SECTION XXVII

Miscarriage

CHAPTER 95

Does Vitamin E Have a Role in Preventing Miscarriage?

IN THE *Canadian Medical Association Journal* (January 9, 1960), Dr. Evan Shute presents an interesting discussion of a question of concern to all who are capable of becoming parents. What should be done in the case of spontaneous abortion or miscarriage, that is, the spontaneous interruption of pregnancy up to the twenty-eighth week? Can it be prevented? Should it be prevented?

It is the view of many physicians that spontaneous abortion is nature's way of rejecting a fetus which has been poorly formed, or had an unhealthy start, from the beginning. They say if spontaneous abortion, or miscarriage, begins it is best to let it run its course, rather than to try saving a fetus to full term which will be born abnormal.

Dr. Shute is not of this opinion, and quotes figures to show that it is far from the rule. He refers to E. S. Burge who, in the *American Journal of Obstetrics and*

[615]

Gynecology (44: 973, 1942), remarks that, of the threatened abortions in 12,000 cases, no more than 1.5 per cent ended in the birth of major defectives. On that percentage Dr. Shute suggests that of 100 mothers threatening to abort, 98.5 should produce babies free of any major defect. Such odds offer every reason for attempting to avert threatened abortion, says Dr. Shute. It is not at all a rule that congenital defects are bound to appear in infants whose spontaneous abortion was reversed.

Dr. Shute then goes on to tell of his 25 years of experience, in which he has administered vitamin E routinely to every private obstetrical patient registered with him from the beginning to the end of the pregnancy. He has administered alphatocopherol to every patient with threatened abortion (except two special cases in which estrogen was used). The doses have ranged from two drams of wheat germ oil 25 years ago to 50-450 milligrams of alphatocopherol (vitamin E) per day at present.

Half the General Average of Abortions

Of 4,141 private, consecutive, unselected cases, all given alphatocopherol, there have been 134 recognized abortions and miscarriages, an incidence of 3.2 per cent. Dr. Shute suggests that this percentage be raised to 5.2 per cent to account for abortions reported over the phone before there has actually been time for an office visit, and for incidents casually mentioned at a later office visit. The 5.2 per cent figure is still only about half of that reported in literature generally. Surely, this fact lends support to the idea that alphatocopherol is helpful in preventing abortion in a large number of cases treated both preventively and therapeutically.

[616]

Of Dr. Shute's 4,141 patients, there were 139 threatened abortions and 98 threatened miscarriages (the term differs only to designate the first 3 or second 3 months of pregnancy), and the abortion or miscarriage was reversed in 76 per cent and 96 per cent respectively. Therefore, 182 normal children were born, in a ratio to 13 abnormal children, 6 of whom died at birth.

Dr. Shute further holds that the administration of alphatocopherol just before or just after conception is helpful in the prevention of congenital defect, and this theory has been borne out in literature concerning animals made vitamin E deficient by special diets. The placenta is the foundation of good circulation for the fetus. Presumably, if there is a good foundation, a good infant will develop and the mother will remain normal. On the other hand a defective placenta may alter the whole pregnancy and its product for the worse.

The placenta provides the embryo with nutrients of all types, but especially oxygen. Alphatocopherol has been shown time and again to be an oxygen-conserving agent. This alone would make it a valuable agent in pregnancy.

The placenta can also be regarded as a great sponge, a net of capillaries. Their being kept intact is vital to the life of the fetus. Alphatocopherol has unique properties for preserving normal capillary strength and in maintaining their proper width.

We believe that the evidence Dr. Shute presents on behalf of the use of vitamin E in pregnancy is indeed convincing. It is obvious that vitamin E is effective in maintaining the health of the fetus, as well as in providing the fetus with the best possible atmosphere for normal development. Of course, whether or not to attempt to reverse a spontaneous abortion is a question

[617]

to be decided by the attending doctor and his patient. However, scientific warning on the possible malformation of a child which threatened to be aborted does not seem to scare most people. Doctors and patients usually do all they can to see that such a pregnancy continues to term. It would seem, from Dr. Shute's figures, that such an attempt is justified, since the tragedy of serious malformation follows in only a very small percentage of these cases. It is of great interest to see that the use of vitamin E as a means of preserving the fetus is effective in threatened miscarriage—76 per cent in the first 3 months, and 96 per cent in the second 3. But even more important is the low incidence of this problem, in Dr. Shute's practice, for which he credits vitamin E. We believe that everyone should be taking a vitamin E supplement daily, but especially pregnant women.

Aside from vitamin E, the B vitamins, notably B_1 and niacin, and vitamin C, have shown themselves to be of value in maintaining a normal, comfortable pregnancy. A diet which is rich in foods containing these nutrients, as well as supplementary dosage, is the best guarantee a woman can have for a successful pregnancy.

SECTION XXVIII

Myopia

CHAPTER 96

Vitamin E and Myopia

MYOPIA IS NEARSIGHTEDNESS, a condition in which the
individual can see clearly things right beneath his nose,
but cannot see things farther away—across the street,
for instance. The myopic eye is like a camera permanently focused for a close-up.

Myopia generally becomes apparent when one is a
child or perhaps in the teens. It is caused by an abnormal enlargement of the eye in the diameter from front
to rear. This greater length of the diameter of the eye
causes the image of what is being seen to be focused in
front of the retina rather than on it. As the child grows
older, this enlargement process gradually ceases.

Many things are blamed for myopia—posture, light
used for reading, heredity, diseases and diet deficiencies. According to an article in *Coronet,* September,
1959, more and more children are found to be nearsighted. In 1925 only about 20 per cent of high school
and college students wearing glasses were nearsighted.

[619]

Today more than 30 per cent have been diagnosed as myopic.

The article quotes Sir John H. Parsons, an English ophthalmologist, as believing that in days to come myopic sight will be considered "normal." Our eyes are adapting to modern conditions, he says. Whereas our forefathers had to scan horizons, look out over wide fields, seas and rivers, we must spend our lives in narrow rooms, peering at something on our desks in the way of reading material—lists, charts, books, blueprints, reports or something of the sort. This must be why there is so much more myopia among our young people than there used to be, in the opinion of several experts.

It seems to us that this is a very shallow argument indeed. For it suggests that the body is able to readapt the focusing of its eyes within about 50 years, whereas for thousands and thousands of years before this, the eye has been adapted for far-seeing. It does not seem possible to us that such a big change could possibly take place within so short a time. Our bodies are not equipped to make this kind of change in adapting to our environment within a space of time so short. Changes like this take many generations.

Aside from this is the fact that there are still millions of people who must use their eyes largely for seeing at great distances. Have they or their children also begun to experience more myopia? We are not told and we doubt that anyone has done an investigation of this.

It seems to us, rather, that exactly the same things in our environment are responsible for increased myopia as those which are causing our children's jaws to be too small for their teeth, causing degenerative diseases like cancer to take a terrible toll among young people and causing almost 50 per cent of our young men to be rejected for military service for physical and psychological reasons—namely, our processed and devitalized modern diets.

We were delighted to find in a French medical journal, *Presse Médicale,* April 25, 1959, an article by two Paris physicians who have been giving vitamin E to their myopic young patients with remarkable success. Drs. C. and G. Desusclade tell us that they have been giving vitamin E for over 10 years and that they can generally stop the process of the disease, or maladjustment, so that the young patient does not become any more nearsighted. Checking on their early patients after 8 years, they found that the effects are lasting.

Not satisfied with mere success, they then decided to find out why vitamin E produces these results. For this, it would seem to be necessary to understand how and why myopia occurs. They had long known, they tell us, that vitamin E can be used to treat diseases of the connective tissue—the collagen diseases. Could this be what was involved in their treatment of myopia? They believed, they tell us, that the collagen fibers of the eye may lose part of their physical qualities and become abnormally distended so that they cannot give the support they should. In other words, the ligaments become lax.

In 1956 another researcher, Garzino, using an electron microscope, discovered that the fibers of collagen in the eye of a myopic individual have a smaller diameter than those of the normal eye and that they are bathed in a more abundant liquid than is present in the normal eye. The two Paris doctors think this is ample proof of their theory that vitamin E helps in cases of myopia because myopia is a disease of the connective tissue. Their conclusion is that myopia is something which has a mechanical *and nutritional* base.

[621]

They tell us that myopia is due to the feebleness of the conjunctive "shell" of the eye. This feebleness may have been acquired in some cases before birth, during growth inside the womb, but usually it is acquired during childhood and adolescence.

"What is the cause? Lack of vitamin E or perhaps an exaggerated need for this vitamin or a lack of ability to assimilate the vitamin properly," they declare. They continue, "Proof of the vitamin E treatment lets us verify not only the complete stoppage of the development of a case of myopia, but also the improvement of those little, more general symptoms that are so often associated with it—little disorders of the joints, slight glandular upsets, retarded development of puberty."

How Much Vitamin E Will Prevent Myopia?

The treatment they give their young patients is as follows: one or two 50 milligram tablets of vitamin E (alphatocopherol acetate) first thing in the morning every day for 3 months. After this 3-month treatment, a lapse of several weeks is allowed and then another 3-month series is given. According to Drs. Desusclade, this stabilizes the improvement. It is well to repeat the treatment every year, they believe, while the child is growing up.

Our authors warn against the installation of atropine in the eyes, and the use of eye exercises. They say that while some good results are obtained through exercise, they believe that they are dangerous. Exercises done before treatment with vitamin E may pull on the delicate tissues of the eye, since they are unused to this kind of exercise. After the treatment, however, Drs. Desusclade believe that eye exercises are helpful, for they permit the now strengthened muscles to help in

[622]

shortening the too-long diameter of the eyeball which has been causing the trouble.

In stressing how important it is to discover myopia and begin treatment with vitamin E at once, the authors remind us that certain kinds of myopia may lead, in later life, to detached retina which can be a cause of blindness. Myopia is not, then, just a slight disarrangement which can easily be corrected by glasses, but, in one form at least, is something which may turn out to be quite serious in terms of health.

The researchers tell us that they usually had better results in their vitamin E treatment if they gave other vitamins and also amino acids at the same time. Amino acids are forms of protein.

High-Protein Diet Prevents Myopia

This information does not surprise us. A British researcher, Dr. P. A. Gardiner, in *Food Field Reporter,* April 27, 1959, reported finding that myopic children who are given increased amounts of animal protein in their diet have decreased rates of deterioration in eyesight compared to children who do not receive the increased protein.

Dr. Gardiner used two groups of children for his research. All were nearsighted. In one, the control group, no effort was made to change the usual diet the children had been eating all their lives. The second group of children were given increased amounts of animal protein—we suppose, meat, eggs, fish and other protein foods.

Results were startling. In the 5-7 age group, the untreated children's visual deterioration was 4 times greater than that of the children getting the high protein diet. In the 8-9 year group, the deterioration in the

[623]

untreated group was 3 times greater. In children over 12, actual improvement in nearsightedness occurred in those cases taking the largest quantities of animal protein.

What does such a report mean to you, as you are planning your family's meals? It may mean that the child who goes off to school without breakfast may develop myopia and the child who eats a good breakfast may not. The difference between a breakfast of eggs and one of cereal may be important in preventing myopia. The child who eats a pickup lunch of potato chips and a sundae and the child who eats a well-planned lunch containing plenty of meat, eggs or fish may show clearly the difference, not just in general health, but also in susceptibility to myopia.

In this regard one should keep in mind that vitamin E is destroyed in the presence of rancid fats. Potato chips, salted nuts and many fried foods are dripping with rancid fats. If you fry foods in fats that are used over and over again, it is practically certain that these fats are rancid and are a serious threat to your family's health.

Vitamin E Not a Medicine

We were disappointed to note that the French researchers thought of vitamin E only as a medicine to be given to combat a condition and, even though they themselves said that myopia is caused by a deficiency in vitamin E, at no time did they suggest simply making vitamin E supplements a regular part of the child's diet! Instead they recommended giving a series of doses of the vitamin, then skipping a few weeks, then giving another series. Doesn't this seem to be very short-sighted?

[624]

Our own Food and Drug Administration has shown a similar shortsightedness in making their announcement about vitamin E in which they "warned of false claims for the product." Beware! said our Food and Drug Administration. "Any claim in the labeling of drugs or of foods offered for special dietary use by reason of vitamin E that there is need for dietary supplementation with vitamin E will be considered false." There is plenty of vitamin E in our diets, the report went on. Now, just when the Food and Drug Administration checked the individual diet of every known individual American, we do not know. But it seems that a great many French children are deficient in vitamin E, according to the article we have quoted above. And it does not seem unlikely that the same is true of many American children, considering the fact that every single survey done indicates that they have serious shortages in other vitamins and minerals, and considering the fact that all of the vitamin E has been removed from our best source—cereals and other seed foods.

Incidentally, the "warning" which the FDA issued appears in a press release in which they announced that vitamin E is now officially recognized as essential for human nutrition. It is a great victory for those of us who have been saying this for years. So, to confuse people and make it appear that vitamin E is actually not very important, the press notice contained the "warning" which was, of course, played up prominently by most newspapers.

How many of these foods richest in vitamin E does your child eat daily? Beans, beef liver, whole grain cereals (not refined or processed in any way), wheat germ, eggs, green peas, sweet potatoes, turnip greens, salad oils such as corn oil, cottonseed oil, peanut oil,

[625]

and all seed foods such as sunflower seeds, nuts and so forth. Do you think these foods play an appreciable part in the diet of the average American child? Don't you think their lack constitutes probably the most important cause of the great increase in myopia? The eating of enormous amounts of fried foods containing rancid fat must also be responsible for our national deficiency in vitamin E.

Make certain your children take vitamin E supplements along with the other food supplements they take. Make certain their diet is high in protein and vitamin E.

SECTION XXIX

CHAPTER 97

Can Osteoporosis Be Prevented?

Osteoporosis, as the name suggests, is porous bone, bone in which the spaces between deposits of mineral have become so large that the bone looks honeycombed. Such bone is, of course, soft and easily liable to fracture. The disease is especially common among older people.

An article in the *American Journal of Clinical Nutrition*, November-December, 1957, indicates that chronic lack of vitamin C may be related to this disease. Say the authors, Dr. H. Grusin and E. Samuel, "There is a wealth of experimental evidence to support the view that vitamin C is essential for the formation of osteoid [bone] tissue." This is rather surprising for we generally think of bone only in terms of minerals and vitamin D. And we generally think of bone as being something formed in childhood which does not change from then on. This is not the case, of course, for bone reacts to body conditions just as any other part of the

[627]

body does. In osteoporosis the bones are decalcified—that is, calcium has been lost from them. This is part of the reason why they are so weak and yield so easily to breakage.

The 16 patients described in this article were all African Bantus. Perhaps the most revealing aspect of the study is that 9 of these patients were suffering from acute scurvy when they entered the hospital. Scurvy is the disease of vitamin C deficiency. Two other patients had either some symptoms of scurvy or a past history of scurvy. So 69 per cent of the patients were or had been scorbutic.

The surprising thing about this is that both scurvy and osteoporosis are uncommon diseases at this hospital, yet they were frequently found together in the same patient. The main symptom of all patients was backache. X-rays of spines showed that much calcium had been lost, and fractured vertebrae in all cases.

Treatment with vitamin C did not bring the spines back to normal, with one exception. This patient was kept in the hospital for a year and was given a full hospital diet along with rest and massive doses of vitamin C. The other patients continued to eat their usual diet and returned home to hard physical labor (especially carrying heavy loads on their backs) much sooner than that.

The authors conclude that in such an African community there are many factors which might be responsible for osteoporosis. The diet contains little calcium and not too much in the way of animal protein. However, everyone in the community eats this same deficient diet and osteoporosis, as well as scurvy, are found very infrequently. When they do occur, they often occur in the same patient. Say Grusin and Samuel, "It is sug-

[628]

gested that these osteoporotic patients may have suffered from chronic scurvy or minor attacks of scurvy without being incapacitated and that their chronic vitamin-C deficient state eventually led to osteoporosis."

It was those words "chronic or minor attacks of scurvy . . . without being incapacitated" that caught our attention. We have found evidence that many people in America, especially older people, are suffering from these same conditions — minor attacks, or chronic scurvy, evidenced by loose teeth, bruise marks and swollen or inflamed or bleeding gums. In addition, lack of calcium is tragically obvious among our senior population. Could the osteoporosis not be related to these two important deficiencies?

As the doctors in Africa found out, it was not possible to cure the osteoporosis with even large doses (500 milligrams) of vitamin C. But a patient given a good all-round diet and rest, along with the vitamin C, showed improvement. We have in this article only a theory without the painstaking work that is necessary to establish a new principle in nutrition.

But it is enough, we think, to serve as a warning to those of us who are not getting enough vitamin C. Osteoporosis is a painful and often crippling disease. If you can prevent it by eating lots of fruit and vegetables, raw rather than cooked, and by taking additional vitamin C and calcium in natural food supplements (bone meal is the best source of natural calcium and other minerals), don't you think it's worth the effort?

CHAPTER 98

Chronic Phlebitis

"ALPHATOCOPHEROL (vitamin E) has been used successfully in the treatment of acute phlebitis. It seems to have very obvious advantages over other agents used in treating this condition."

The quote is from an address made before the Second World Congress of Obstetrics and Gynecology, Montreal, Canada, June 6, 1958. The speaker was Dr. Evan V. Shute of the Shute Institute, London, Ontario, Canada.

He went on to say, "For example it [vitamin E] decreases embolism [blood clots] to the merest minimum. It not only prevents extension of existing clots, as do the classical anticoagulants, but it quickly resolves what clot is present. It acts very rapidly, especially in relieving associated pain and tenderness. It has none of the side effects which dog the anticoagulants, since it never produces hemorrhage, for example. Moreover, it does not require frequent blood examinations, can be self-

[630]

administered far from any hospital or even medical care, and is as useful for clots in the vital organs as for clots in the peripheral vessels. It has an extraordinary ability to increase collateral circulation . . ."

In simple language, Dr. Shute is saying that for the greatest possible improvement in the health of the circulatory system, vitamin E is the thing. In diseases involving blood clots (of which phlebitis is one) it has been customary to give certain drugs which keep the blood from coagulating. This seems like a good idea except for one thing—when you are destroying those substances in the blood that make it clot, how are you going to know when to stop? Carrying the treatment too far will bring about a condition where the thickening power of the blood is seriously disturbed and then hemorrhages are likely to follow.

A blood clot is indeed a serious thing, especially if it occurs in a blood vessel leading to the brain or the heart. Permanent damage or death may result. But a hemorrhage into either of these organs can be just as serious. When you begin to tamper with the blood's ability to clot, you can see that you can get into serious trouble. Vitamin E does not work this way. It is a natural constituent of the body—not a drug. So, instead, it regulates those substances in the blood that cause clotting or hemorrhaging.

Dr. Shute says further that vitamin E "has an extraordinary ability to increase collateral circulation." What does this mean? When some part of the circulatory system is injured, an effort is made by the body to repair it. Let's say a blood vessel is clogged with a clot. Naturally that part of the body to which this blood vessel carries blood is going to suffer from loss of blood. So another blood vessel is brought into activity to detour around the obstruction. Vitamin E, says Dr.

Shute, has the ability to get this extra blood vessel into working order so that normal operations can proceed.

Patients Treated with Vitamin E Improve

Dr. Shute relates what happened to a group of 300 patients who were treated with vitamin E at the Shute Clinic. The first group consisted of 166 patients all of whom had chronic phlebitis, an inflammation of the veins which usually occurs in the legs and feet. It is more common among women and occurs frequently as an aftermath of childbirth. Dr. Shute gives the following as the causes of the disorder in 74 of his patients: pregnancy-30; abdominal operations-17; trauma, including fractures-15; general or local infections-5; intravenous injections-2; other operations-2; penicillin-1; hospital bed rest-1; food poisoning-1. (It is interesting to note that a total of 23 of these cases of phlebitis resulted from some kind of medical treatment.)

Most patients had suffered from one to five years. Some of them had had phlebitis for longer than 6 years. The main symptoms were swelling and "ache." In addition to the phlebitis, many of the patients had varicose veins, arteriosclerosis and ulcers on the legs. They were given at the clinic no other treatment but vitamins. Results were as follows: 35 cases had slight relief; 20 cases had moderate relief; 79 cases had good relief and 32 patients had excellent results or complete relief.

Some Histories of Phlebitis Patients

Here are some individual case histories. A man of 47 had suffered for 6 years. He was given 300 milligrams and later 400 milligrams of vitamin E daily. The trouble in one of his legs cleared 4 days after the dosage was raised to 400 milligrams. At his last visit he could walk half a mile each day and there was no tenderness in his leg. His feet swelled very slightly and ached slightly on rare occasions.

A woman of 51 had had aching legs for 4 years. She had high blood pressure (160/104) and hence the beginning dose of vitamin E was smaller—150 milligrams. (Dr. Shute has found that large doses of vitamin E may raise blood pressure in patients whose pressure is already too high.) Raising the dose gradually (225 milligrams within 2 months) he found great improvement including a lowered blood pressure—130/100. Nine months later she was entirely well except for rare swelling and slight tenderness, and her blood pressure was 130/80.

A 39-year-old patient complained of soreness and swelling in her right ankle for 3 years. She also suffered from cramps at night. She was greatly overweight. She was given 600 units of vitamin E daily, along with calcium and thyroid extract. She was also put on a reducing diet. Four months later she had lost 21 pounds, the swelling had disappeared and she was feeling well.

Here is how Dr. Shute explains phlebitis and the varicose veins that practically always accompany it. He says that deep phlebitis should be looked for whenever there are varicose veins, "however mild or early." He says, "we are surprised nowadays to find a patient who has varicosities and still no evidence of chronic phlebitis in the deep veins." By this he means the veins deep in the muscles of the legs rather than on the outside where they can be easily seen.

The veins deep inside the leg muscles are designed to carry about 80 per cent to 90 per cent of the return flow of blood from the feet. If something goes wrong so that one of these veins is plugged, the veins on the outside of the leg near the skin surface must take over.

In the effort to cope with this additional work, these veins dilate, twist and do their best to empty the blood from feet and legs. They enlarge and the valves which control the blood flow cease to function properly. The veins which join the deep set of vessels to the exterior ones become filled with blood and big varicose veins spray out over the ankles.

If a doctor injects or cuts or strips away these ugly veins on the outside of the leg, he is removing the only possible channel for the blood to flow through, since the deeper veins are already plugged. So the patient may end up far worse off than before the operation.

The Way Vitamin E Acts to Increase Circulation

What does vitamin E do, if it is used instead of an operation? It "produces collateral circulation about the obstructed deep veins by calling into play the great unused networks of veins lying in wait for emergency utilization. We have such venous reserves just as we have reserves of brain, lung and liver. Alphatocopherol mobilizes them. It does more. It has the unique power of enabling tissues to utilize oxygen better and hence the devitalized and congested leg tissues of the chronic phlebitic who is given alphatocopherol are receiving the equivalent of more oxygen," says Dr. Shute. It should be remembered, too, he adds, that taking vitamin E before you experience any of these painful symptoms is the best possible way of guarding against them.

A condition which frequently follows chronic phlebitis is called by Dr. Shute collagenosis, also cellulitis, or inflammation of cell structure. Of the 134 patients he treated for this condition, most of them had all but given up any search for treatment, since nothing that had been done for them seemed to help at all. These

[634]

were very severe cases, Dr. Shute says, which had been receiving drastic treatment before coming to him.

Here are some case histories. A man of 59 had had ulcers on his legs for 13 years. He was given 400 units of vitamin E daily along with 100,000 units of vitamin A. Seven months later he "felt like a young man" and had no further complaints. From that time on he was completely well, but continued on the vitamin E and vitamin A. Incidentally, this is an extremely large dose of vitamin A which we would not recommend as a permanent thing. Vitamin A accumulates in the body and can be dangerous if too much is taken.

A 46-year-old woman had had aching legs, cramps in her legs and varicose veins for several years. She was given 600 units of vitamin E as well as calcium and vitamin D for the cramps. "She returned a month later," says Dr. Shute, "unable to believe that she could be helped so much. She had been working day and night and yet her legs were not painful." Of course, she continued to take vitamin E.

A final history is that of an 84-year-old woman who had had enlarged veins in her legs for most of her adult life. Two months of treatment with 375 units of vitamin E left her completely well.

Forty-eight of the second group of patients could be said to have gotten fairly good results, we are told. Dr. Shute concluded his talk by recommending that physicians look for deep phlebitis in every case of varicose veins they see. He believes that phlebitis is usually the cause of varicose veins. High dosage of vitamin E is the secret to successful treatment of phlebitis, he says. He has used as high as 1000 units per day.

Always in speaking of high doses of vitamin E, Dr. Shute cautions against their use in patients with high blood pressure. An initial high dosage can raise the pressure sharply, causing serious trouble. So, if you have high blood pressure, it is best to begin taking vitamin E with small doses and increase them gradually.

We have used the terms milligrams and international units interchangeably throughout this chapter as they mean the same thing, in the case of this vitamin.

Exercise Important, Too

We have one other suggestion for the prevention of phlebitis and varicose veins, apart from taking vitamin E and, of course, making certain that your diet is well chosen. Doesn't it seem likely that some of our present-day difficulty with the blood vessels of our feet and legs comes from the fact that we just don't use them enough? We were made to be active all day long—and by active we don't mean driving a car or punching a TV tuning button.

We need to exercise, all of us, every day. Walking is one of the best and cheapest forms of exercise. Walk in the country if you can; walk barefoot if you can; walk before breakfast and before lunch and before dinner if you can. But regardless of how much you can walk, do plan your day's activities, no matter how much trouble it takes, to include at least one good long walk every day. You'll be amazed at how thoroughly the exercise will get the blood to flowing through in your feet and legs.

When you rest, put your feet up on something—a footstool if you're sitting, a pile of cushions or the arm of a chair if you're lying down.

SECTION XXXI

Polio

CHAPTER 99

Vitamin E and Post-Polio Disorders

THE PROBLEM OF CARING for recovering victims of polio becomes more important every year. A letter appearing in the *Canadian Medical Association Journal* (July 15, 1959), written by W. H. Jaques, M.D., Medical Director at Riverdale Isolation Hospital, Toronto, Ontario, Canada, suggests a very interesting therapeutic measure for chronic polio patients—vitamin E.

Dr. Jaques writes that polio victims with extensive residual paralysis often suffer from painful muscle cramps, tingling sensations and a feeling of coldness or numbing in the affected limbs. Because of previous success with the use of vitamin E for treating aged persons suffering with nocturnal muscle cramps, Dr. Jaques decided to try the vitamin on polio patients suffering from the above symptoms.

The results were most gratifying, as can be seen from the case histories Dr. Jaques includes in his letter. For example, a 28-year-old man who had been paralyzed completely in his extremities for 4 years, complained of painful cramps and ankle swelling. A month's treatment with vitamin E (1600 units per day) resulted in complete disappearance of cramps and a definite decrease in the swelling.

A 19-year-old female, with extensive paralysis and wasting of the left leg, suffered from cramps and a feeling of coldness in the left leg. Eight hundred units of vitamin E per day, for 4 weeks, was prescribed and complete recovery from cold and cramps followed.

An attack of polio resulted in complete paralysis of the right leg and part of the left in a 42-year-old female patient treated by Dr. Jaques. She, too, was troubled by crampy pains, tingling and numbness in the right leg. Conventional therapy was attempted, but to no avail. Three weeks of vitamin E therapy consisting of 800 units per day did the trick. Interestingly, it was found that when the vitamin E treatment was discontinued, the patient experienced a return of her symptoms within 10 days. A maintenance dose of 400 units of vitamin E per day was prescribed indefinitely.

Polio and Menstruation Difficulties

In some cases of polio involving women, the infection has the effect of disrupting the regular menstrual flow. The usual treatment consists of hormone injections. Dr. Jaques tells of two female patients who developed menstrual irregularity: one did not menstruate for 14 months, the other for 9 months. Hormone drugs proved useless. Vitamin E was tried, and after only one month of receiving a daily dosage of 400 units, complete regularity returned. The patients experienced no further difficulty even after the vitamin was discontinued. Three other women with irregularity after polio attacks, though not so pronounced, are mentioned as having equally good success with vitamin E.

Further Investigation Is Needed

We hope that the experience of Dr. Jaques will influence others who work with chronic polio patients, causing them to experiment with vitamin E therapy for the relief of the symptoms described. What is more important, we hope to see increased use of vitamin E among doctors treating similar disorders in patients who have not suffered them as an aftereffect of polio. The numbness, tingling and cramps in the extremities are common ailments of victims of poor circulation. If vitamin E will work in relieving such complaints among those whose limbs have been impaired by polio, why not with persons who are able to move about freely and do not have the phantom, and real, pains often associated with paralysis?

The usefulness of vitamin E in treating menstrual disorders has been established before, but the classic medical treatment for such conditions is still hormones, dangerous as they are. Again, if vitamin E can help in polio cases, where some physiological damage is likely to have caused interrupted menstruation, why not in cases where the extra hurdle of polio does not have to be met? Why not try vitamin E for hot flashes, painful or irregular menstruation, etc., before using drugs that are known to have severe side effects?

CHAPTER 100

Pulmonary Embolism: Is It Vitamin E Deficiency?

ON MAY 22 and 23 in Boston, a conclave of medical experts gathered to discuss a disease condition that is seldom recognized, though it is a major cause of death. Most times, it was stated, this condition is incorrectly diagnosed by most doctors as pneumonia, heart attack, or heart failure. Actually it is an embolism—a blood clot—that lodges in the lung, causing a pulmonary insufficiency and death.

If properly diagnosed, a pulmonary embolism will respond to medical treatment and almost invariably the patient's life can be saved. But Dr. Sasahara, chief of the cardio-pulmonary laboratory at the West Roxbury Veterans Administration Hospital, told the symposium that "our batting average [regarding diagnosis] is miserably low. We're only hitting about 30 per cent, which is terrible." The result, and the reason the Boston conference was called, is that these diagnostic failures are permitting thousands of people to die unnecessarily.

It seems to us, however, that the truly dismal failure is that these pulmonary embolisms are ever permitted to happen, when they should be so easy to prevent. This is a failure not only of the medical profession but of the giant food industries and of the public health agencies that are supposed to exercise supervision over the quality of our food supply. The true failure apparently lies in the fact that virtually the entire American public is starved for vitamin E and is not receiving it in its food supply.

Dr. Sasahara let the cat out of the bag when he explained the mechanism by which a pulmonary embolism forms. The condition, he said, is brought on by a blood clot which generally forms in a leg vein and moves through the blood stream up to the heart. It is able to pass through the relatively large valves of the heart but when it reaches the lung, it is trapped in one of the tiny blood vessels that carry blood to that vital organ. Blockage and failure of the blood supply results in suffocation combined with acute heart failure, leading to death.

So the real physiological villain is the formation of blood clots in the veins.

We know how such clots form. Because of our upright posture, it takes terrific pressure to return blood from our feet and legs to the heart. Any type of unusual abdominal pressure, such as may be caused by pregnancy or even constipation, or a job that requires standing for long periods of time without the compensation of vigorous exercise, can slow down the blood in the leg veins to a point that permits clot formation. That is one of the major reasons why we have long maintained that vitamin E—the most perfect and most natural anticoagulant we know—is a necessity in substantial quantities in everybody's diet.

[641]

In the *American Journal of Physiology* (Vol. 153, p. 127, 1948) **K. L. Zierler, D. Grob and J. L. Lilien-**thal described experiments in which vitamin E had a profound effect on the blood, especially its clotting qualities. They found a strong anticlotting effect both in laboratory experiments and in the veins and arteries of human beings. Dr. Evan Shute, the greatest living authority on vitamin E, is convinced that vitamin E not only inhibits the formation of blood clots, but also expands the blood vessels so that any clots that might exist can pass through them more freely without getting locked in and causing blockages. The *Canadian Medical Association Journal* (September 8, 1962) reported a study made at the Hospital of the University of Alberta of treatment by vitamin E of intermittent claudication. This condition is a blockage in the thigh arteries, a very difficult condition to treat once it has come into existence, but one in which vitamin E was reported to bring decided improvement to 8 out of 10 while no improvement at all was shown in a control group.

So we need have no doubt that this trouble with blood clots which leads to a killing pulmonary embolism would never occur if people only ate enough vitamin E in their daily diet. How much is enough? The absolute minimum has been estimated by such authorities as Horwitt and Shute at 50 to 60 milligrams per day of alphatocopherol alone. In the mixed tocopherols as which vitamin E generally occurs in food, one would have to ingest at least 100 milligrams a day in order to obtain 50 to 60 milligrams of the biologically active alphatocopherol.

But the sad fact is that most Americans consume a maximum of 6 to 12 milligrams of mixed tocopherols daily. Why? Because Americans do not eat such foods

[642]

as sunflower seeds and raw nuts, which contain substantial amounts of this vitamin. Of the kind of food the American public does eat, the only good source of vitamin E would be bread and wheat products, if the wheat that is used were not stripped of its germ. In the wheat germ there is a very high concentration of vitamin E, so high that wheat germ oil is one of the best sources for this vitamin. But the germ is ruthlessly stripped away from the wheat in the milling process, because its oil content might become rancid after a few months of storage. The flour that remains can be stored for years, and will do you just as little good and just as much harm after years of storage as it would if it were fresh.

This is a situation that seems to be fine with our public health authorities. When do you ever hear a voice raised in protest over the inadequacy of the vitamin E you can obtain from the average diet? Instead, they defend the food processing interests by trying to claim that minute quantities of vitamin E are all anybody needs.

Meanwhile, it turns out now that thousands and perhaps tens or hundreds of thousands of deaths, that have been diagnosed as heart failures, have really been caused by clots in the blood stream that might never have formed if the victims had been able to obtain enough vitamin E in their daily diets.

We, who follow the Prevention system, eat our sunflower seeds, take our wheat germ oil, and use unrefined corn or soy oil in our salads, may seem funny to some and faddists to others. But you can bet we're not going to die of pulmonary embolisms.

[643]

SECTION XXXIII

Scurvy

CHAPTER 101

Don't Wait for a Scurvy Diagnosis

NO ONE KNOWS, yet, the full impact of vitamin C in the diet. Since this vitamin is the very thing which holds our cells together, and since every bit of the body—the eyes, the liver, the heart, the hair, the fingernails, the skin, everything—is made up of cells, the value of vitamin C cannot be overestimated. When the cement of the cells is missing, tissues tend to give way. Skin breaks develop, capillaries and veins rupture under the stress of their normal job, stomach linings become weak enough to be attacked by gastric juices, and the result is ulcers. So it is true that, as we become more and more deficient in vitamin C, we quite literally fall apart.

How is this "falling apart" recognizable? Dr. Ian A. Kellock, M.D., described the condition in the *Medical Press* (July 12, 1961). He also told how a vitamin C deficiency can occur to the point of scurvy even in a country where fresh foods are available. Social

[644]

scurvy (scurvy is the technical name for extreme vitamin C deficiency) occurs chiefly in older males (usually
widowers) who live alone in a place where sleeping
quarters alone are provided. They have to fend for
themselves in old age, and they tend toward an amazing uniformity of diet which is usually inadequate.
They might eat corn flakes at every meal, or a steady
diet of bread and jam. Sometimes it's because these
men don't know how to cook anything else, or they
don't want to learn; sometimes they can't afford much
else and sometimes they are perfectly content to eat
only these simple and nutritionally barren foods. These
conditions may last for months, even years.

Iatrogenic Scurvy

There is another group subject to what the author
calls "Iatrogenic or Therapeutic Scurvy." These people
take special diets—often on medical advice—and stay
with them religiously. These diets often consist of milk
drinks, cereals, custards, soups, mashed potatoes, etc.,
and are almost completely lacking in vitamin C.

One should mention here that self-imposed diets
are often not well-rounded, and might be distressingly
short of vitamin C or some other vitamins. Any diet
should have ample amounts of all the vitamins and
minerals, plus enough protein, to keep the body functioning well.

The bare minimum of vitamin C is 30 milligrams
per day. That amount, it is thought, will keep one
from being confined to bed due to a C shortage. We
feel that this figure is grossly inadequate to the needs
of anyone who must live in the day-to-day civilization
we know. With every breath and with every bite of
food, we acquire noxious poisons which require vitamin C for their safe neutralization.

Perhaps it is because of the many unrecognized thieves of vitamin C today that the frank scurvy that was once considered to be a clinical curiosity now occurs with fair frequency. Dr. Kellock tells of 11 cases seen in the wards of two London hospitals within a period of 6 years. Another doctor described 75 cases of scurvy seen over a period of 15 years. As one expert put it, ". . . . to describe the condition as a rarity or a clinical curiosity in this country [England] is surely an overstatement." We are certain that the same statement applies in the United States as well.

The Way Scurvy Acts

What is scurvy like? Dr. Kellock gives the symptoms for us. It is painful, and the pain is characterized as a "rheumatic" feeling, usually an aching in the legs or in the back. Sometimes there is a stiffness of the legs. The patient often believes himself to be a lumbago victim. Aside from the pain, the scurvy patient feels weak and tired; his appetite is almost nonexistent. He may have a dry cough and get dizzy spells on the least exertion. His gums may be sore and may bleed. He might even spit blood.

That is the way the patient feels scurvy. The doctor must look for bruising—spontaneous bruising is one of the most common signs of scurvy in adults. Touching the skin lightly is often enough to cause this phenomenon in such persons, because the capillary walls which contain the blood are so very weak due to a lack of vitamin C. Hemorrhages of the mucous membranes around the nose and mouth and the eyes may also occur. Bronchitis is a fairly frequent manifestation of subclinical scurvy.

The outward manifestations are practically endless, as can be imagined when one reflects upon the place

[646]

of vitamin C in maintaining our physiology. There can be eruptions of the skin around hair follicles or an inflammation in the area, fever, jaundice, gray skin color, aggravation of acne conditions, low blood pressure and stoppage of circulation announced by the blue color of the skin. Anemia is often present.

A Case of Scurvy

An interesting example of the way improper diet can lead to scurvy is presented by Dr. Kellock. A widower, aged 64, was admitted to the hospital. Ten years prior to his admission he had been told he had a duodenal ulcer for which he was given a diet sheet. The sheet actually made provision for the addition of vegetables after the third week, but the patient hadn't noticed this, so for 10 years he firmly held to a diet consisting mainly of fish and eggs, with occasional porridge (much like our cream of wheat), bread, butter and jam. He ate no vegetables at all.

Two weeks before admission to the hospital he noticed purple bruises on his legs. He also complained of pain in his ankle.

The examining physician reported his general appearance to be pale and sallow. He had no teeth, but his gums were healthy, in spite of "blood spots" on the roof and floor of the mouth, and large red and purple swellings at the knee and ankle. X-rays showed generalized conditions compatible with bronchitis and shortness of breath.

The treatment consisted of nothing but vitamin C—1,000 milligrams each morning. The response was gratifying and all outward abnormalities soon disappeared. His legs were almost completely normal in less than 3 weeks and his blood count had greatly improved to well above the minimum. He was discharged with a maintenance dose of 150 milligrams of vitamin C plus added ferrous sulphate.

Interestingly enough, after 10 years on what he thought was a proper ulcer diet, x-rays showed that the patient's ulcer was still present. Of course, we know that with a diet that is short of vitamin C, it would be useless to hope for the healing of a break in the tissue, which is what an ulcer actually is. Several researchers have shown that high dosages of vitamin C serve as an excellent therapeutic measure in cases of ulcer.

One is amazed that the patient managed so long on the low vitamin C intake he was getting. Imagine his plight if a serious infection had attacked him. The need for vitamin C in such a case cannot be overemphasized. Dr. Kellock recommends, especially for the elderly, self-imposed or deliberate diets planned to contain adequate amounts of vitamin C.

We believe that everyone should keep a close eye on one's diet to assure proper vitamin C intake. While special situations faced by older people do present a hazard as to sufficient vitamin C foods in their diets, it must be admitted that most of us face the same possibility. Children whose parents allow them to indulge in sweets, in sodas, in pretzels and potato chips, at the expense of their appetites when nutritional foods are presented to them, have cause to be concerned over possible C deficiency. Mothers who rush through the busy day on a few cups of coffee and a bun or two, and fathers who snack on a soda and a hot dog for lunch, or maybe a candy bar in between, are excellent candidates for vitamin C shortage.

There is no sense to waiting for bruises, bleeding gums or swellings to appear before taking stock of one's vitamin C intake. Avoid any chance on missing out on sufficient vitamin C. You can never be sure you have enough, unless you actually run daily tests. Each day's needs are different. If your nerves are taut because the children have been particularly trying, if nothing has worked smoothly that day, if you are seething because of a disagreement, if the boss has been demanding too much of you, you are using extra vitamin C. If you are exposed to weather that is unusually hot, or unusually cold, if you've slept poorly, burned yourself on the stove, smoked even one cigarette, you are using extra vitamin C. If you've eaten foods with chemical additives, drunk liquor, been in a poorly ventilated room, breathed exhaust from a car or smelled cleaning fluid, you need extra vitamin C. If infection is in the air, vitamin C is needed to combat it. If you're having an operation—or a baby—you need more vitamin C to help your body to function properly.

You see, the day's need for vitamin C is utterly unpredictable and the body does not store this vitamin. How can the same amount that gets one through a peaceful day of vacation be enough on a day of crisis? How can a person who suffers from arthritis get along on the same amount as a high school pupil? He cannot, of course. So we say everybody should eat plenty of fresh fruits and vegetables with high vitamin C content, and a daily natural supplement of vitamin C as well. If there should be an excess, the body will quickly eliminate it, and no harm done. The important thing is to have what is needed when it is needed. Proper supplementation is the only way to do that.

Scurvy is not so rare as we thought, and we are sure that cases of "almost-scurvy" are really quite common. Don't let it happen to you.

CHAPTER 102

Poultices Made of Vitamin C

SORES WHICH WILL not heal are one of the most unpleasant and dangerous phenomena of ill health. Those of us who are apparently healthy often suffer from such sores. Bedfast individuals, as well as people in wheel chairs, are closely acquainted with the perils of bedsores—those stubborn, painful areas which arise chiefly because free movement is impossible for the patient. People who are afflicted with ulcers of any kind know well the prolonged, painful and disagreeable course such sores may take, with dressings that must be changed frequently, with unpleasant odors from the sores as well as from the drugs used to treat them.

How fine it would be if someone might discover a simple, quick and effective salve or poultice that would close such sores or wounds with healthy new tissue, thus giving the patient an opportunity to return to good health, and preventing any possibility of the open sore becoming more serious or malignant.

An English physician working with elderly bedridden patients in a London hospital has been experimenting with vitamin C applications. In the *Lancet*, February 11, 1961, Dr. A. J. Mester of the Geriatric Unit, St. Alfege's Hospital, London, writes of his experiments.

In cases of ulcers, says Dr. Mester, there is usually an impaired blood supply to the skin and tissue around the ulcer. There is also usually infection at these spots. So it seems reasonable to give such a patient large amounts of vitamin C by mouth to strengthen the tissues and to fight the infection. However, he goes on, "this rarely meets with much success." Perhaps as two other investigators have suggested, the work vitamin C does in regenerating healthy tissue is a purely local one. So why not apply the vitamin C directly to the ulcer, Dr. Mester asked himself.

Accordingly, he says, "since the beginning of this year I have used local ascorbic acid [vitamin C] in the treatment of pressure bedsores and chronic ulcers, particularly in bedfast geriatric patients who usually have arteriosclerosis and often some concurrent low-grade infection."

He treated indolent ulcers and pressure sores in the usual ways first, he says. He gave antibacterial drugs and drugs to dilate the patient's arteries. He relieved the pressure on the sores.

If all this effort was unsuccessful, he tried vitamin C. He irrigated the ulcer with "a sterile isotonic solution containing 15 milligrams of ascorbic acid at pH6, after which the wound was dressed with gauze soaked in 5 milliliters of the same solution. This procedure was repeated daily for a week."

Pharmacists and doctors will readily understand the terms used here. For the rest of us, suffice it to say that

[651]

"irrigating" a wound means simply to perfuse or wash it with the solution. The word isotonic means simply that the solution must be such that the character of the ascorbic acid is not destroyed. The phrase pH refers to the acidity of the mixture. Vitamin C is an acid and an effort was made here to reduce its acidity somewhat, probably so that its application would not be painful on an open sore.

How Ulcers React to Vitamin C

Here, in Dr. Mester's own words, are the results of his experiment. "Twenty-two patients have now completed this course of treatment; 3 have shown little improvement, but in the remaining 19 there has been a dramatic change with development of fresh granulations. Many of these elderly patients had had extremely indolent ulcers that had shown no improvement for months and even years. It is therefore unlikely that the sudden change with the formation of granulation tissue could have been part of the natural course of the lesion [sore].

"Once these fresh granulations had formed after 7 days of topical ascorbic acid treatment, the vitamin C was omitted and the wound left to heal spontaneously. In 17 patients healing has been complete, and 11 have been discharged from the hospital; the others, started more recently, are progressing satisfactorily." Dr. Mester believes that other physicians should make use of his experience in order to investigate more thoroughly the use of vitamin C locally at the sore point.

If you are already suffering from a sore that won't heal—an ulcer, a bedsore, a wound—can you use such a solution on it as Dr. Mester did? We see no reason why you should not. A poultice of vitamin C can easily be made at home. Vitamin C pills dipped in water and

[652]

rubbed on poison ivy, insect bites, skin disorders, burns, cuts and wounds of all kinds have been most successful in bringing about rapid healing and causing healthy new tissue to form. Members of our staff use it regularly for quick healing of such annoying everyday complaints.

However, we must remind you that vitamin C oxidizes rapidly, so solutions cannot be made and stored for future use, even in the refrigerator. That is, as soon as the water touches the vitamin pill, the vitamin is destroyed rapidly.

You know how long it takes for an apple or a peach to darken where you have sliced it with a knife? This means the vitamin C has been destroyed, almost as soon as the air hits it. This is how fast the vitamin C may disappear from the rose hip powder or the natural vitamin C tablet that you dip in water and apply to a sore spot.

So, if you use a natural vitamin C tablet for applying to the skin, work fast. And, if it is at all possible, keep a wet dressing saturated with the vitamin on the wound. We are speaking here of minor wounds—cuts, burns, insect bites, minor skin irritations. It has been our experience that vitamin C applied to such wounds goes to work immediately bringing healing to the injured tissues and, simultaneously, counteracting any infection that may be present.

CHAPTER 103

Vitiligo and a B-Vitamin

INQUIRIES HAVE come to us pleading for specific information concerning vitiligo, a painless skin disease which is characterized by the disappearance of natural color, or pigment, from patches on the skin. Even the fairest skins have some color, and when it goes, these patches of absolute white are very definitely visible and can be most embarrassing. In a darker skin the problem is emphasized.

Unfortunately, searches through medical literature led us only to descriptions of vitiligo, but no one seemed to know what to do about it. Now at last we have found something we can pass on. The article by Benjamin Sieve, M.D., at that time instructor in Medicine, Tufts Medical School, appeared in the *Virginia Medical Monthly* (January, 1945), and it gives a comprehensive history of the other treatments in use for the 15 years before that date as well as the then-current thinking on the subject. To the best of our knowledge,

[654]

very little has been accomplished in the treatment of vitiligo since then, so that Dr. Sieve's findings are still worth investigation and application.

Among some of the earlier treatments for vitiligo is that of H. W. Francis, M.D. He considered the cause to be an absence of free hydrochloric acid in the stomach because he had vitiligo and found an absence of the acid in himself. He took hydrochloric acid in 15 cubic centimeters doses at each meal for two years and noted that the vitiligo areas had completely disappeared. He used the same therapy on three other patients and reported similar results. Dr. Sieve suggests that the hydrochloric acid might help in the body's processing and absorption of necessary B vitamin factors in food.

In 1931 a paper described a Negro who suffered from vitiligo patches on his face, but was originally hospitalized for 16 weeks for treatment of a fracture. Though no specific remedy for the vitiligo was attempted, the patches regained their natural color during this time. It was assumed by the writers that the hospital diet was so far superior to that which the patient usually had, that the nutrients in it were partly responsible, along with the bedrest and absence of direct sunlight, for the return of proper skin color. The theory of nutrition and pigment was followed up by an article in the *Archives of Dermatology and Syphilology* (March, 1937) on the use of vitamin C to restore skin color. The following year a German medical journal carried another article on the same subject, again recommending vitamin C as a treatment, though we do not know the dosages used.

Para-amino-benzoic acid (Paba), a B vitamin, has been mentioned repeatedly in connection with the treatment of vitiligo. M. J. Costello, in the *Archives*

[655]

of Dermatology and Syphilology (February, 1943) told of success in treating vitiligo of the eyelids in a 2-year-old child with the daily administration of 100 milligrams of Paba. Two others who tried this treatment did not find it so effective. Dr. Sieve was still impressed with the potential of Paba, and decided to set up an experiment to observe its effect on 48 cases of vitiligo.

Successful Experiment

The group consisted of 25 females and 23 males, ranging in age from 10 to 70 years. The duration of the vitiligo condition had varied from 2 to 28 years. In most of the patients evidence of a poor diet from months to years and a history of gland imbalance was obtained. Fatigue, irritability and emotional instability were almost constant. Constipation, weight gain and various types of headaches were frequent. Arthritis was not uncommon. Physical examinations in general revealed varying types of deficiencies, of which many presented classic findings consistent with an underactive thyroid condition. Along with these came a preponderance of brittle nails, coarse and thickened skin and varying degrees of hypertension (high blood pressure).

An accurate history of each patient was obtained, including blood counts, smears, urine tests, blood sugar, basal metabolism, etc. The gland balance was established through the use of hormones. Then all patients were given a patent combination of B complex vitamins—more than the recommended daily dosage. In addition, Paba was administered in the form of 100-milligram tablets three or four times daily. This treatment continued for a period of ten months.

The rate of improvement in the skin using oral Paba was found to be slow. Some patients followed the de-

[656]

scribed regimen for 18 weeks with no results. The author instituted injections of the vitamin coupled with monoethanolamine (to help the vitamin remain in the blood longer) twice daily—evening and morning—and a 100-milligram tablet of Paba to be taken at noon and at bedtime. It was soon observed by the author and by the patients themselves that new pigmentation in the depigmented areas occurred. Within 4 to 8 weeks the milk white areas of vitiligo turned pinkish. In 6 to 16 weeks after therapy was started, small islands of brown pigment were usually noted within the areas of vitiligo. Soon streaks were thrown out from these islands and the streaks reached out to join other islands. Eventually the islands disappeared or the repigmentation became complete. The results of the therapy in all 48 patients were termed "striking" after 6 or 7 months.

One of Dr. Sieve's most impressive cases involved a young woman of 26 years who, when first seen, complained of irregular menstrual periods, lack of appetite, dry skin and brittle nails. She had vitiligo of the entire body, but especially both legs; slight graying of the hair was occurring. It had all begun 13 years previously after a bruising accident. Except for mild typhoid fever at 17, and a fairly common aversion to sunlight, her history gave no special clues as to the origin of the vitiligo. She ate practically no meat or fish.

Examination showed definite gland and vitamin imbalance. The entire torso had tiny areas of pigment loss and the legs from feet to knees had large areas in which the pigment was completely gone. A growth of white hair was noted through the areas of vitiligo, and the line of demarcation between the normal skin areas and those affected was clearly defined.

The treatment instituted by Dr. Sieve consisted of two Paba tablets of 100 milligrams each and two intra-

[657]

muscular injections of 144 milligrams per cubic centimeter of monoethanolamine para-amino-benzoic acid (Paba) given every day. An elixir of B complex (5 cubic centimeters) was taken 3 times daily. After 4 months the number of injections was reduced to one daily, until a total of 214 had been received.

Marked improvement in the vitiligo condition was noted within ten weeks after treatment was begun. Each successive examination showed additional improvement. After nine months of treatment the vitiligo throughout the body and torso was completely repigmented to such an extent that there was difficulty in distinguishing any of the areas. The hands and arms were almost entirely filled in, and the legs showed great improvement. Improvement continued through the next six months while the medication was taken spasmodically and there were no injections. At no time were any toxic manifestations from the medical treatment observed.

A Combination of Elements

Dr. Sieve asserts, time and again, the important part diet plays in vitiligo. He also believes that hormonal imbalance can cause the disease. Contributory factors can also be wounds, infections, pressure points and light rays. Dr. Sieve says that the problem of vitiligo is more complex than the simple lack of the B vitamin Paba. He insists that dietary deficiencies must be corrected, hormonal imbalances righted and local infections cleared up before a single specific vitamin can be expected to have any effect. He also emphasizes that the injections to supplement the tablets are essential, because the vitamin alone, taken orally, does not remain in the blood stream for a sufficient length of time to act effectively.

[658]

The B complex, as it appears in brewer's yeast, desiccated liver, wheat germ, and the organ meats, would seem to be essential in preventing the occurrence of vitiligo. This, of course, coupled with a diet complete in other essentials, will strengthen resistance to most diseases. For those who are plagued with vitiligo, we think Dr. Sieve's article on his experience with his treatment is a Godsend. At least it is something to be rid of this distressing problem—and apparently without danger of side effects. Talk to your doctor about it. Ask him if he can think of even one reason for ignoring the opportunity presented here. We feel sure he will want you to try Dr. Sieve's treatment. Incidentally, we cannot refer any inquiries to Dr. Sieve, as he died several years ago. His work, however, still lives.

CHAPTER 104

B Vitamins and a Healthy Skin

IT IS A SAYING in the medical profession that the dermatologist (skin specialist) is the most fortunate of physicians—his patients never die and they never get well. And there is a great deal of truth in this. Remarkably little is known about the causes of most skin diseases, and the treatments for them, for the most part, consist of remedies that are believed to help in some cases but always have such a high proportion of failures that they leave it an open question whether the successes were not due to the self-healing powers of the skin rather than whatever medication was used.

The problem very likely lies in the fact that the skin is in such an exposed position. For many years research scientists, following the normal pattern of medical investigation, have striven to identify various types of bacteria that might be held responsible for skin diseases and to find appropriate antibiotics to kill them. Boils, for example, are known to be an infection caused by the staphylococcus organism, and many efforts have been made to treat boils with antibiotics that would destroy this organism. Yet staph is in the air all around us and to completely cleanse an area of the skin of these bacteria still offers not even a possibility that they will not again be found on the skin in a few hours. In the course of time it has become obvious that the real problem is to determine how it is that a healthy skin can fight off these staph organisms without the slightest sign of distress or infection, while in others the same bacteria meet no resistance and are able to penetrate the skin and cause infections.

In other words, a long record of inability to cure skin ailments by direct treatment of infected areas has made the conclusion almost inescapable that the real problem is one of treating the whole man. The real problem of skin diseases, it would seem, is not so much the treatment of specific diseases by specific means as discovering and using the methods that will promote general health including healthy, disease-resistant skin.

Hopeful New Direction

That is precisely the direction that is being taken by at least one prominent dermatologist, Professor Katsu Takenouchi, M.D., professor of dermatology in the School of Medicine of Japan's Chiba University. In January, 1963, the *Journal of Chiba Medical Society* carried an exciting article by Professor Takenouchi titled "Thiamine Metabolism in the Field of Dermatology." Actually the title is a trifle too narrow in scope, for it was really three vitamins of the B complex, with which the dermatologist dealt.

And here is the first point his laboratory studies were able to establish:

"The presence of inflammation in the skin or the

regeneration of the hair in the anagenesis [regeneration] of hair cycle causes a large quantity of glycogen to appear in the prickle cells of the epidermis and the outer root sheath of the hair follicles. Its energy is directed to the repair of inflammation and the regeneration of the skin." And he then goes on to state that contrary to common belief, the glycogen in the skin does not release its energy without using air but actually has been proven to release it by oxidation.

B Vitamin Need

Such a discovery is of enormous importance as a demonstration that the skin requires and uses energy in precisely the same way as the internal organs. Glycogen is the storage form of blood sugar or glucose. A healthily functioning liver removes excess glucose from the blood and transforms it into glycogen which it then stores. Whenever the blood sugar level gets too low, the liver releases some glycogen to maintain a normal level. It is thus an enormously important chemical compound within the economy of the human body. And one of the most important single functions of various vitamins of the B complex is that they are indispensable to the metabolic processes by which glucose is converted into glycogen and glycogen is later released and transformed into energy.

Now let us recall Professor Takenouchi's statement that inflammations in the skin or the normal skin regenerative process cause a large quantity of glycogen to appear, and that the energy released by the glycogen is directed to these purposes. Such a function for glycogen means that the maintenance of a healthy skin and the ability of the skin to fight off infections are dependent on the body's having a store of glycogen and being able to use it as required.

[662]

Or, to express the same finding in another way, any protracted abnormality of the blood sugar level or any deficiency in even one of the B complex vitamins that are directly concerned with glycogen metabolism, can be expected to be revealed in poor skin health and inability of the skin to defend itself against infection.

Professor Takenouchi pursued this field of inquiry in the obvious manner. He compared the skins of healthy patients and dermatitis sufferers for their content of vitamin B. With regard to the healthy skin, he found that "Thiamine, riboflavin and pyridoxine have been demonstrated in the skin in relatively large amounts." But in those with various types of dermatoses (skin infections) it was found that 27 per cent were deficient or latently deficient in thiamine, 27 per cent equally deficient in riboflavin and 52 per cent deficient in pyridoxine. The small proportion of cases that showed no deficiency in these important B vitamins presumably had either elevated or depressed levels of blood sugar, both of which prevent the proper formation and use of glycogen.

Daily Replacement

The conclusion is clear. To maintain, and perhaps to gain, a healthy skin, it is absolutely necessary that the levels of the vitamins of the B complex be kept high in the system at all times. Professor Takenouchi points out that these water-soluble vitamins, even if not used, soon disappear from the skin and must constantly be replaced. He has also computed that about one per cent of the vitamin B we take into our systems is actually channeled to the skin. Thus, to maintain a level of one half a milligram in the skin it is necessary to consume 50 milligrams of thiamine. In fact, the one per cent figure for the vitamin B needs of the skin is

[663]

an excellent indication that there is not one of us who can get along without large amounts of the B complex vitamins eaten every single day. The best way to be sure of getting such amounts in proper balance is to take a good daily supplement of brewer's yeast or desiccated liver or both.

Specific Diseases

Professor Takenouchi has found the following diseases of the skin to be directly connected with B vitamin deficiencies: eczema, dermatitis, multiple erythema, keratosis, virus disease of the skin, skin tuberculosis, skin syphilis, baldness, and various types of discolorations of the skin.

For some reason Dr. Takenouchi made no investigation for a relationship between the most newly discovered and little known of the B vitamins, B_{12}, and skin health. Perhaps this was because vitamin B_{12} is utilized by the body in such microscopic amounts that it could not be determined in the skin at all. But we have previously reported an article by the German doctor H. Grabner in the *Munich Medical Weekly* (October 31, 1958) in which he described a case history of the cure of shingles with a combination of vitamin B_{12} and an antibiotic. There was a complete cure in two weeks' time and Dr. Grabner himself says that he does not know which of the two resulted in the cure.

From what we have learned of the Takenouchi investigation, there is every reason to suppose it was the vitamin, and not the antibiotic. An antibiotic can only kill bacteria, which are quickly replaced with fresh live ones in anything as exposed to the air as the skin. We can see no reason to believe that antibiotic therapy could give more than temporary relief in any skin

[664]

affliction. But a vitamin that makes it possible for the skin to produce more regenerative energy more efficiently—that's a different matter.

We'll stick to brewer's yeast, wheat germ and desiccated liver, thank you, and the meticulous avoidance of table sugar and sugar-containing foods. It seems to be the best technique anyone has yet found to keep skin healthy and beautiful.

SECTION XXXV

Tooth Decay

CHAPTER 105

Vitamin B₆ (Pyridoxine) and Tooth Decay

FLUORIDATIONISTS PUSH ON, trying to convince the country that there is no measure other than fluoridation that will halt the problem of tooth decay. However, with almost every publicity blurb, we see the same old song and dance that gets profluoridationists off the hook: "Of course fluoridation cannot eliminate all dental bills or all dental ills. Nor can it remove the necessity for such additional dental health practices as good diet, conscientious brushing and regular visits to the dentists."

Now you see, from all the other publicity we read, we got the impression that every child eating the usual quota of candy bars, drinking the regular number of sodas and licking the average number of ice cream cones could expect to see a big drop in dental decay. Apparently this is not the case. The child must eat a good diet to make fluoridation work. Cut the sodas, candy, ice cream; get calcium from milk or some milk substitute, eat vegetables and meats, and so on and on.

Then there is brushing. We thought that fluoridationists were promising healthy teeth to kids who brush or don't brush. Not so. You've got to brush them regularly if your teeth are to be free from decay in a fluoridated community.

Good Diet Works Without Fluoridation

Let's see now: good diet, careful brushing, regular dental consultation—it adds up to healthy teeth without fluorides, especially without fluorides. Why should we have trouble with our teeth if we eliminate decay-causing foods and eat foods which reinforce good, strong teeth? If we brush these strong teeth to eliminate food deposits, and if we visit the dentist to be sure no decay is beginning, there is nothing fluorides can do to make us safer.

There is no doubt that diet is of great value in preventing tooth decay. The value of the various nutrients that go to make up good diet has been established by scientists. We were interested to see the work that has been done on vitamin B_6 (pyridoxine) in relation to protection from dental caries. In the *New York State Dental Journal* (August-September, 1956) there appeared an article by L. P. Strean, Ph.D., D.D.S., Elizabeth W. Gilfillan, B.S., and Gladys A. Emerson, Ph.D., in which the suppressive effect of pyridoxine on dental caries of hamsters was noted.

Five male hamsters (the males usually develop 3 times as many caries as females) were placed on each of two dietary regimens average in their content of caries-causing foods. They each drank a 5 per cent sucrose solution in place of water. One of the groups had a supplement of 50 milligrams per 100 grams of

[667]

ration. The other had 20 times as much, or 1000 milligrams of pyridoxine per 100 grams of ration.

The study lasted 10 months to permit maximum development of caries. The average weights of both sets of animals were about the same throughout the test. A numerical scoring system, considering the 5 surfaces of each molar, was set up. A possible value of 240 was declared to mean that all tooth surfaces were destroyed. The better the state of the teeth, at the end of the experiment, the lower the number.

The results were astonishing even to the researchers, we are sure. The 5 hamsters which were fed the low B₆ rations showed an average of 26.1 per cent loss of tooth structure. Their total score was 313. The group which was given the large pyridoxine dosage in the ration showed an average tooth structure loss of 4.2 per cent. The total score for this group was 50.

Said the authors: "The 6-fold difference in the total score between the two groups appears to be more than coincidental. The fact that weights of the two groups were substantially the same would rule out any effect of inanition. The difference between the two groups would be that one received an intake of B₆ barely sufficient for maintenance while the other was supplied with an optimal amount (in fact, an excess) of this vitamin . . . The results observed in this preliminary study on a small group of hamsters are sufficiently encouraging to warrant further investigations. Mishett and Emerson have consistently observed dental abnormalities in monkeys and dogs deprived of vitamin B₆."

Why did the pyridoxine, or B₆, have this remarkable effect on the teeth of the hamsters? One guess was that the vitamin was able to maintain a climate of bacterial flora which is beneficial to the proper development and good health of the teeth. Dr. Lyon P. Strean decided to undertake further investigation of this possibility. His findings were published in the *New York State Dental Journal* (February, 1957).

The Theory Behind B_6 Activity

Dr. Strean theorized that some type of friendly bacteria, a lactobacilli, which would need B_6 as an essential nutrient, was multiplying rapidly with the extra B_6 dosage. Its growth worked to ease out and eliminate certain bacteria which are detrimental to the health of the teeth.

Dr. Strean found that, in pregnant women, notorious for their dental problems, a larger amount of cortisone is secreted from the adrenals. The cortisone interferes with the body's ability to use B_6. Therefore, pregnant women should make an especial effort to increase their B vitamin intake to offset this known interference.

In another study involving a large number of hospitalized children being treated for rheumatic fever, massive doses of cortisone were used. It was observed that these children developed rampant dental decay. It may be presumed, says Strean, that the stress of the crippling disease, plus the large amounts of cortisone administered, interfered with the availability of the pyridoxine to the tissues of the children.

Children who chew sugar cane, as it is used particularly in the Caribbean Islands, show resistance to dental caries, even though their hygienic practices are at a minimum. When Dr. Strean saw this he analyzed the sugar cane for its B_6 content, and found it to be very high in this nutrient. Also the molasses prepared from the sugar cane and eaten by these children is high in B_6.

Dr. Strean tells of a report by the Food and Drug

Administration (Public Health Report 71, May, 1956). There had been a series of cases of convulsions in infants that had been maintained on an infant milk formula which was found to be deficient in B$_6$. When the formula was changed to provide adequate quantities of this vitamin, complete recovery from the convulsions followed at once. The investigators concluded that the pyridoxine had effected a substantial and beneficial change in the intestinal flora. The action approximates the action of pyridoxine in the mouth.

An interesting observation on the values of pyridoxine was made in connection with a clinical trial involving the use of specially prepared pyridoxine lozenges (3 milligrams) for the control of dental caries in children. Some of the mothers decided to take the lozenges for the protection of their own teeth. Two of the mothers who had suffered from a form of mucous colitis, passing loose stool several times daily for 3 to 5 years without remission, reported that within 72 hours following the use of the lozenges the stool was well-formed. Relief was maintained for a period of one month, when the mothers were requested to stop taking the lozenge. Two days later the stool reverted to its previous consistency. When the lozenges were reinstituted, well-formed stools resulted.

How Pyridoxine Worked for the Children

The story of the mothers is interesting and informative, but one wonders about the effect of the lozenges upon the children's teeth for whom it was originated. Abram Cohen, D.D.S., and Carl Rubin, D.D.S., made that report in the *Bulletin of the Philadelphia Dental Society* (January, 1958). This is what they reported: "Of greater importance is the fact that the children receiving supplementary amounts of pyridoxine showed a lower DMF (Decayed, Missing, Filled—a measure used to evaluate teeth in oral examinations) rating when compared with the control group receiving placebo lozenges . . . This study suggests that pyridoxine supplementation may be an aid in the suppression of dental caries even in areas where the water is fluoridated . . ."

It is interesting to know that such an evaluation can be made about fluoridated areas. One wonders if, so long as the health authorities insisted on adding something to the water, pyridoxine wouldn't have made a better showing than fluorides. Also, the authors seemed to feel that if the children had been more consistent in the use of their supplementary lozenges, the results would have been even better.

A test, using similar lozenges, was done by Strean and others in a nonfluoridated area, and reported in the *New York State Dental Journal* (March, 1958). The study involved 28 children between the ages of 10 and 15 years. When the children who took pyridoxine lozenges for a period of one year were compared with a control group taking placebo lozenges, they showed a 40 per cent reduction in tooth decay over the control group.

Remember, the use of individual B vitamins is not wise. It is believed that serious imbalances occur in the body when the B complex is not taken as it occurs in nature. Therefore, we advocate the frequent inclusion in the diet of B-rich foods such as wheat germ and brewer's yeast, as well as the organ meats of all animals (desiccated liver tablets are an easy way to get these complete nutrients).

INDEX

Carbon, 24
Carbon dioxide, 160
Carbon monoxide, 27, 35, 80, 555-556
Carbuncles, 294
Carcinogenesis, 298, 316, 502-503, 509
Cardiovascular system, 365, 367, 381, 383
Caries. *See* Tooth decay
Carob, 169-170
Carotene, 13, 71, 121, 130-131, 132-133, 137, 145-146, 517
  see also Vitamin A
Carrots, 22-23, 71, 114, 133, 154, 210, 270, 349, 440, 500, 516
Cartilage, 268, 289-290, 417, 455-457, 481
Cashews, 177, 433
Catalase, 421
Catalyst, 63, 181
Cataracts, 267, 309, 310, 332, 359, 373, 547, 561, 601, 606, 607
Cauliflower, 177, 210, 218, 440,
Cavities. *See* Tooth decay
Celery, 22, 349
Celery cabbage, 114
Celiac disease, 145, 167, 168, 216
Cells, 60, 144, 146-147, 148, 173, 179, 181, 216, 235, 267, 275, 283, 291, 295, 301, 314, 355, 365, 367, 392, 400, 415, 416, 417, 419, 424, 463, 506, 509, 548, 566, 574, 644
Cerebral hemorrhage. *See* Stroke
Chairs, 482
Charcoal, 88
Chard, 114, 219, 272
Cheese, 114, 195, 210, 218, 237
Chemicals, 25-26, 27, 28, 33, 37, 85, 88, 132-133, 138, 149, 176, 408, 420, 579, 649
Cherries, 445, 452, 465
Chicken, 201, 205, 210, 218, 349, 432
Chickpea, 433
Childbirth, 437-439, 632
Children, 20, 38-39, 71, 75, 81, 106-107, 113, 122, 137, 221-222, 236, 250, 263, 268, 290, 297, 326, 327, 330-331, 332, 399, 401,

459, 513, 515, 602, 607, 610-611, 671
  vitamin requirements of, 113, 174, 195, 200, 205, 271, 339
Chili, 26
Chlorine, 24, 25, 87, 89
Chlorophyll, 310
Chocolate, 433, 574
Cholesterol, 46-47, 124-125, 156, 223, 230, 303, 305, 419, 422-423, 424-425, 427, 430, 559-562
Choline, 13, 34, 79, 157-159, 305, 502, 579-581
  foods rich in, 159
Choroid, 545
Chronic fluorosis, 321-325
Chronic phlebitis. *See* Phlebitis
Cigarettes. *See* Tobacco
Cilia, 515
Circulation. *See* Blood
Circulatory disorders, 352, 422
Cirrhosis, 66, 67, 388
Citrin, 442
Citrus fruits, 50, 292, 444-445, 465, 531
Civil defense, 361-362
Clams, 25, 83
Cleft palate, 105, 476
Coagulation. *See* Blood
Cocoa, 532, 574
Cocoa butter, 413
Coconut, 434
Coconut oil, 349, 413
Codfish, 433
Cod liver oil, 49, 50, 75, 113, 114, 115, 146, 154, 292, 331, 365
Coffee, 25, 48, 284, 310, 648
Coke, 106
  see also Soft drinks
Colds, 73-74, 78-79, 95, 112, 143, 145, 153, 267, 444, 509, 514, 516-517, 518-529, 566
Cold sweat, 585
Colitis, 24, 80, 194, 495, 532, 534, 670
Collagen, 294, 456, 544, 621
Collards, 177, 196, 272, 516
Colon, 317, 388
Compost, 43
Congenital defects, 57, 105, 298, 372, 391, 398, 471-478, 604, 606, 616, 617

[675]

[676]

[677]

freezing, 23, 140
fried, 624, 626
organic, 142
poisoning, 632
preparation, 21, 93, 105, 175, 205, 217-218, 269-271, 284, 451, 524, 529, 594
processing and refining, 19-20, 21, 23, 32, 82, 84-85, 93, 133, 149, 302, 347, 390, 417, 422, 425, 500, 621, 643
raw, 23, 24, 74, 102, 217, 269, 286, 451, 459, 493, 510, 629
storage of, 175, 269, 516
Fruits, 26, 102, 145, 157, 167, 170, 266, 275, 286, 301, 320, 347, 445, 451, 465, 498, 521, 533, 575, 577, 629
juice, 445
see also specific fruit
Fumigation, 87
Fungus, 566

Gall bladder, 388, 430, 495, 506, 575
Gallstones, 336
Gangrene, 372, 382, 485, 550-553, 571
Gas, 533
Gastric atony, 532
Gastric juices, 229, 239, 644
Gastritis, 501
Gastrointestinal ailments, 95, 113, 185, 216, 279-280, 317, 332, 388
Genitourinary system, 112, 128, 132, 144, 153
Germs, 112, 518, 523, 525, 528
Gingivitis, 94, 106, 307, 492
Girdles, 481
Glaucoma, 449-450
Glossitis, 216
Glossodynia, 492
Glucose, 84, 229, 307, 545, 662
Glycogen, 228, 662-663
Glycoprotein, 294
Goat, 432
Goiter, 112, 132, 153
Gout, 288, 456
Grains, 84, 168, 347, 368, 433, 553
Grand mal. *See* Epilepsy

Grapefruit, 157, 272, 349, 445, 452
Grapes, 445, 465
Gravy, 270
Green beans. *See* Beans, snap
Grippe, 516
"Growing pains," 268
Growth, 112, 137, 173, 250, 263, 398, 399, 415, 418, 424, 491
Guava, 272
Gums, 100-101, 106, 198, 267, 283, 307-308, 490, 510, 579, 629, 646, 648

Haddock, 349
Hair, 28, 77, 79, 122, 153, 156, 160, 209, 214, 408, 411, 559, 644, 657, 662
Halibut, 205, 433
Halibut liver oil, 54, 58, 114, 146, 154, 328
Hallucinations, 597, 610
Ham, 177, 201, 218
Hamburger, 26
Hands, 338
see also Fingernails
Hay fever, 264, 311-312
Hazelnuts, 196, 434
Headaches, 80, 199, 528, 532, 564, 585, 587, 607, 610, 656
Healing, 250, 277-278, 314, 316, 376, 400, 404, 510, 650, 652
Hearing. *See* Ears
Heart (food), 13, 20, 107, 157, 177, 196, 201
Heart (human), 36, 64, 84, 100, 101, 123, 156, 157, 173, 223, 229, 261, 305, 332, 343, 368, 409, 461, 555, 569, 640, 644
disorders, 15, 30, 66, 76, 123-124, 127, 158, 185-188, 242, 243, 253, 254, 261-262, 326, 345-346, 367, 370, 400, 404, 422, 439-440, 442, 554-558, 631
Heat pad, 479
Hemoglobin, 148, 223, 317
Hemolytic anemia, 392
Hemorrhage, 66, 82, 100, 229, 268, 279, 290, 293, 296, 297, 307, 313, 332, 343, 371, 372, 387, 399, 402,

[680]

Methylene blue, 366
Migraine, 66, ·192
Milk, 38, 44, 52, 115, 172, 177,
    193, 196, 210, 214, 237,
    310, 311, 322, 329, 333,
    339, 398, 409, 413, 432,
    476, 540, 566, 581, 645,
    666-667
Millet, 433
Milligrams, definition of, 13
Mineral oil, 26, 87, 113, 146, 346
Minerals, 22, 33, 63, 64, 72, 83,
    263, 412, 627
    see also specific mineral
Miscarriage, 182, 357, 362, 372,
    394, 397, 437, 443, 615-
    618
    see also Abortion
Molasses, 206, 214, 233, 440, 533,
    669
Mongolism, 54, 162-165
Moniliasis, 566
Mononucleosis, 306
Morning sickness, 191-192, 204
Mouth, 77, 78, 79, 81, 94, 112,
    129, 144, 194, 197, 243,
    288, 458, 490, 492, 497-
    498, 515, 576, 646, 647
Mucous colitis, 670
Mucous membrane, 112, 128, 144,
    153, 223, 297, 375, 491,
    492, 514, 574, 646
Multiple sclerosis, 235, 236, 247-
    248, 281, 286, 419
Muscles, 58, 81, 97, 99, 173, 185,
    203, 223, 229, 332, 336,
    343, 367, 373, 378, 387,
    409, 456, 481, 530, 532,
    582, 622, 633
Muscular atrophy, 344
Muscular dystrophy, 25, 55, 82,
    254, 258, 343, 344, 353,
    367, 373, 378, 393, 394
Mushrooms, 201, 210, 218
Mustard greens, 115, 196, 465,
    516, 578
Myelin, 419
Myopathy, 367
Myopia, 390, 601, 619-626

Narcotics, 87
Nausea, 69, 75, 191, 198, 223,
    317, 437, 467, 494, 530,
    532, 561, 565, 587
Navy beans. See Beans

Nearsightedness. See Myopia
Nectarines, 115
Neomycin, 567
Nephritis, 354, 371
Nerves, 253, 264, 358, 415, 419,
    424, 427, 567, 586, 611,
    649
Nervous breakdown, 199
Nervousness, 99, 101, 213, 493,
    585, 591, 593, 602-603,
    607, 610
Nervous system, 106-107, 112, 161,
    173, 179, 180-181, 249,
    332, 367, 394, 537, 568,
    611
Neurasthenia, 199, 548
Neuritis, 80, 208, 298, 344, 546,
    565, 567
Neuroblastoma, 249, 264
Neurological disorders, 419
Niacin, 13, 26, 45, 53, 65, 70, 79,
    93, 98, 104, 106, 197-201,
    322, 496, 546, 562, 591,
    611, 618
    see also Vitamin B₃;
    Nicotinic acid
Nicotine, 486, 509
Nicotinic acid, 46, 85, 103, 108,
    198, 502, 559-562
    see also Niacin; Vitamin B₃
Night blindness, 78, 112, 122, 132,
    145, 545, 546
Nitrates, 87, 132-133, 135-142
Nitrites, 87, 133, 135-142
Nitrogen, 18, 43, 133, 136, 138-
    139, 140-141
Nocturia, 412
Nose, 128, 194, 515, 646
Nosebleed, 435, 508, 582, 583-585
Numbness, 101, 199, 223, 532,
    597, 637
Nursing, 113, 146, 157, 174, 186,
    191, 195, 200, 236, 279,
    539
Nutrition, 33, 83-84, 179, 184,
    198, 202, 209
Nutritional therapy, 33, 34, 35
Nuts, 23, 368, 429, 613, 624, 626,
    643
    see also specific nut

Oat germ oil, 413
Oatmeal, 177, 349, 575
Oats, 210, 433

[681]

Phenobarbitol, 607
Phlebitis, 352-353, 402, 403, 405, 630-636
Phlebothrombosis, 387
Phocomelia, 471
Phosphatase, 26, 33, 88
Phosphorus, 43, 70, 75, 194, 243, 327, 328, 331, 333, 336-337, 341, 411, 418, 504, 611
Phosphorylase, 228-229
Photophobia, 194
Pie, 284, 320
Pigeon pea, 433
Pineapple, 272
Pink disease, 67
"Pins and needles," 569, 597
Pistachio, 434
Pituitary, 314
Placenta, 279, 398, 437, 438, 617
Plague, 294
Plants, 13, 136
Plastics, 503
Plastic surgery, 354
Plummer-Vinson disease, 492
Plums, 177, 445, 452, 465
Pneumonia, 26, 66, 112, 291, 292, 306, 458, 512, 640
Poisoning, 321, 449, 564, 568, 632
Poisons, 27, 36, 37, 86, 161, 307, 321, 460, 500, 579, 645
Poliomyelitis, 50, 72, 254, 258, 344, 444, 637-639
Polyneuritis, 236, 538
Polyunsaturated fats. See Unsaturated fatty acids; Fats
Pork, 177, 196, 201, 206, 211, 214, 219, 349, 432
sausage, 26, 177
Potash, 43
Potassium, 167, 533
Potatoes, 25, 206, 211, 219, 272, 349, 645
Prefrontal lobotomy. See Lobotomy
Pregnancy, 57, 65, 105, 107, 113, 146, 174, 186, 187, 191, 192, 195, 200, 204, 278-279, 298, 326-328, 335, 340, 357, 391-395, 396-401, 437-439, 443, 471-478, 540-541, 589, 615-618, 630, 641, 649, 669
Premature birth, 372, 379, 398

Preservatives, 135, 176
Prickly heat, 312
Primaquine, 305-306
Progesterone, 394, 589
Prolapsed disc, 257
Prostate, 144, 388, 411, 576
Protein, 12, 16, 17, 33, 34, 35, 60, 65, 72, 83, 88, 102, 138, 140, 145, 147, 160, 164, 168, 181, 204, 214, 220, 229, 250, 261, 263, 312, 377, 419, 464, 506, 534, 544, 545, 548, 626, 645
Prothrombin, 319, 435, 592
Prunes, 115, 452
Psoriasis, 389
Psychiatric illness. See Mental illness
Psychiatry, 590, 595
Psychological disturbances, 250
see also Mental illness
Psychosis, 596-597, 601, 612
Psychosomatic illness, 600, 605
Pteroylglutamic acid. See Folic acid
Pulmonary virus, 528
Pulse, 290
Pumpkin, 115, 133, 154
seed, 433
Purpura, 402
Pyorrhea, 267, 576, 578
Pyridoxine, 13, 53, 65, 79, 94, 202-205, 228-233, 305, 409, 427, 519, 537, 541, 546, 565, 567, 663, 666-671
Pyruvic acid, 565

Quinine, 548

Rabbit meat, 432
Radiation, 67, 377, 474
Radishes, 219, 273
Raisins, 157, 178, 532
Rape seeds, 433
Rashes, 263-264
Raspberries, 273
Raw food. See Food, raw
Reproductive system, 78, 82, 120, 236, 352, 355-356, 381, 409
Respiration, 365, 367, 368, 416, 515
Respiratory ailments, 95, 112, 144, 444, 556
Rest, 586, 609, 628, 632, 636, 655

[683]

Sodium nitrite, 135
  see also Nitrites
Soft drinks, 16, 40, 320, 459, 648, 666
Sores, 317, 508, 510, 650
Sorghum, 433
Soup, 175, 218, 270, 645
Soya lecithin, 54
Soybeans, 157, 161, 178, 211, 233, 427, 433
Soybean oil, 347, 349, 413, 418, 427, 434, 440, 643
Spastic paraplegia, 236
Sperm, 357, 398, 589
Spices, 503
Spinach, 21, 115-116, 159, 196, 216, 219, 273, 440, 517, 574
Spine, 289-290, 338, 481, 628
Spino-cerebellar disorders, 236, 479
Spleen, 156
Sprue, 145, 167, 168, 436, 532
Squash, 116, 517
  seed, 433
Staphylococcus, 566, 661
Starch, 16, 198, 199
Steak, *See* Beef
Steatorrhea, 379
  see also Diarrhea
Sterility, 25, 60, 82, 138, 147, 343, 358, 396-401, 402
Stiffness, 597, 646
Stillbirths, 107, 356, 372
Stomach, 126, 156, 157, 173, 194, 235, 238, 240, 243, 310-311, 316, 388, 420, 427, 531, 532, 597, 644
Stones, 541, 574
  see also Bladder; Kidney; Urinary tract
Strabismus, 601
Strawberries, 41, 211, 273, 578
Streptococcus, 458, 526
Streptomyces, 262
Streptomycin, 27, 528, 567
Stress, 311, 588
String beans. *See* Beans, snap
Stroke, 100, 371, 422, 446, 449, 464
Stuttering, 604
Sugar, 16, 19, 22, 32, 35, 40, 174, 184, 198, 199, 222, 228, 521, 532, 575, 665
Sulfa drugs, 27, 36, 85, 87, 89, 212, 216-217, 233, 276, 528

Sulfites, 87
Sunflower seeds, 395, 427, 428, 549, 557, 626, 643
  oil, 305, 413, 418, 431, 434
Sunlight, 76, 331, 333, 339, 469, 655
Suprarenal glands, 557
Surgery, 233, 268, 278, 295, 314-320, 435, 479, 480-481, 557, 565, 566, 568, 578, 608, 632, 649
Sweet potatoes, 22, 116, 133, 154, 206, 211, 272, 349, 517, 625
Swelling, 587, 632, 633, 638, 647, 648
Swiss chard. *See* Chard
Sword fish, 116, 201
Synovitis, 455
Syphilis, 664

Tangerines, 273
Tapioca, 532
Tartar, 575-576, 578
Tea, 102, 310, 532, 575
Teenagers, 16, 20, 104, 137, 205, 290
Teeth, 94, 100-101, 112, 122, 179, 233, 250, 267, 268, 276-277, 285, 297, 323, 325, 330, 332, 338, 415, 420, 508, 575-576, 579, 629
  see also Tooth decay
Temperature. *See* Fever
Tendons, 562
Teratogenicity, 471-478
Testicles, 343
Tetany. *See* Cramps
Thalidomide, 471, 477
Thiamin, 13, 16, 25, 26, 33, 46, 47, 55, 65, 66, 68, 70, 73, 79, 83-85, 108, 155, 172-192, 204, 317, 322, 373, 496, 519, 530, 532, 546, 610, 661, 663
  see also Vitamin B₁
Thrombin, 319, 436, 437
Thromboangiitis obliterans. *See* Buerger's disease
Thromboblastin, 435
Thrombophlebitis, 371, 387
Thrombosis, 343, 346, 370, 371, 382, 442
Thyroid, 64-65, 66, 137, 156, 310, 411, 580, 633, 656

[685]